# THE
# PRACTICE
## OF

# PRESENCE

# THE PRACTICE OF God's PRESENCE

ANDREW Murray

Whitaker House

## THE PRACTICE OF GOD'S PRESENCE

ISBN: 0-88368-590-6
Printed in the United States of America
Copyright © 1999 by Whitaker House

Whitaker House
30 Hunt Valley Circle
New Kensington, PA 15068

Library of Congress Cataloging-in-Publication Data

Murray, Andrew, 1828–1917.
     The practice of God's presence / by Andrew Murray.
          p.   cm.
     Includes bibliographical references.
     ISBN 0-88368-590-6 (trade paper : alk. paper)
     1. Spiritual life—Christianity.  I. Title.

     BV4501.2 .M7976  2000
     248.4—dc21                                        00-021013

1 2 3 4 5 6 7 8 9 10 11 12 13 / 09 08 07 06 05 04 03 02 01 00

# Contents

# About the Author

Andrew Murray (1828–1917) was an amazingly prolific Christian writer. He lived and ministered as both a pastor and author in the towns and villages of South Africa. Some of Murray's earliest writings were written to provide nurture and guidance to Christians, whether young or old in the faith; they were actually an extension of his pastoral work. Once books such as *Abide in Christ, Like Christ,* and *With Christ in the School of Prayer* were written, Murray became widely known, and new books from his pen were awaited with great eagerness throughout the world.

He wrote to give daily practical help to many of the people in his congregation who lived out in the farming communities and could only come into town for church services on rare occasions. As he wrote these books of instruction, Murray adopted the practice of placing many of his more devotional books into thirty-one separate readings to correspond with the days of the month.

At the age of seventy-eight, Murray resigned from the pastorate and devoted most of his time to his manuscripts. He continued to write profusely, moving from one book to the next with an intensity of purpose and a zeal that few men of God have ever equaled. He often said of himself, rather humorously, that he was like a hen about to hatch an egg; he was restless and unhappy until he got the burden of the message off his mind.

During these later years, after hearing of pocket-sized paperbacks, Andrew Murray immediately began to write books to be published in that fashion. He thought it was a splendid way to have the teachings of the Christian life at one's fingertips, where they could be carried around and read at any time of the day.

One source has said of Andrew Murray that his prolific style possesses the strength and eloquence that are born of deep earnestness and a sense of the solemnity of the issues of the Christian life. Nearly every page reveals an intensity of purpose and appeal that stirs men to the depths of their souls. Murray moves the emotions, searches the conscience, and reveals the sins and shortcomings of many of us with a love and hope born out of an intimate knowledge of the mercy and faithfulness of God.

Countless persons the world over have hailed Andrew Murray as their spiritual father and given credit for much of their Christian growth to the influence of his priceless devotional books.

# Book One

# The Power of the Blood of Jesus

# Preface

This book is a translation of a portion of a series of addresses by my late father, Rev. Andrew Murray, M.A., D.D., on "The Power of the Blood of Jesus."

The translator is Rev. William M. Douglas, B.A., who for many years was my father's close friend, having been associated with him in connection with the South African Keswick Convention Movement. During my father's lifetime, he permitted Mr. Douglas to translate his book, *The Prayer Life,* and he became the biographer of my father after his death.

I have read the manuscript and think the translation is excellent. He has reproduced the thoughts of my father exactly.

I feel sure that much blessing will result from the prayerful and thoughtful reading of these chapters.

Trusting you may learn to value and to live in the experience of the power of the precious blood of our Lord and Savior Jesus Christ,

I remain,
Yours in the Blessed Master's service,

M. E. MURRAY

## NOTE BY TRANSLATOR

It is necessary to remember that throughout these chapters, Dr. Murray refers only to "sacrificial blood." The blood in the Bible is always that.

It should be noted when reading chapter three that in the Dutch Bible that Dr. Murray used, the word *verzoening* is used for "propitiation." *Verzoening* means "reconciliation," and that is the word used in this translation.

chapter 1

# What the Scriptures Teach about the Blood

*Not without blood.*
—Hebrews 9:7

God has spoken to us in the Scriptures in many different portions and in various manners, but the voice is always the same. It is always the Word of the same God.

Hence, we see the importance of treating the Bible as a whole and receiving the witness it gives in its various portions concerning certain definite truths. In this way, we learn to recognize the place these truths actually occupy in revelation, or rather, in the heart of God. Also, in this way, we begin to discover what are the foundation truths of the Bible that, above others, demand attention. Standing so prominently as they do in each new departure in God's revelation, remaining unchanged when the dispensation changes, they carry a divine indication of their importance.

It is my objective, in the chapters that follow this introductory one, to show what the Scriptures teach us concerning the glorious power of the blood of Jesus and the wonderful blessings procured for us by it. I cannot lay a better foundation for my exposition, nor give a better proof of the superlative glory of that blood as the power of redemption, than by asking my readers to follow me through the Bible, and thus see the unique place that is given to the blood from the beginning to the end of God's revelation of Himself to man, as recorded in the Bible.

It will become clear that there is no single scriptural idea, from Genesis to Revelation, more constantly and more prominently kept in view, than that expressed by the words *the blood.*

Our inquiry, therefore, is what the Scriptures teach us about the blood:

- First, in the Old Testament
- Second, in the teaching of our Lord Jesus Himself
- Third, in what the apostles taught
- Fourth, in what John told us of it in Revelation
- Last, in the lessons we can learn from Scripture

## WHAT THE OLD TESTAMENT TEACHES

The scriptural record about the blood begins at the gates of Eden. Into the unrevealed mysteries of Eden I do not enter. But in connection with the sacrifice of Abel, all is plain. He brought *"the firstborn of his flock"* (Gen. 4:4) to the Lord as a sacrifice, and there, in connection with the first act of worship recorded in the Bible, blood was shed. We learn from Hebrews 11:4 that it was *"by faith"* Abel offered an acceptable sacrifice, and his name stands first in the record of those whom the Bible calls *believers*. He had this witness given to him *"that he pleased God"* (Heb. 11:5). His faith, and God's good pleasure in him, are closely connected with the sacrificial blood.

In the light of later revelation, this testimony, given at the very beginning of human history, is of deep significance. It shows that there can be no approach to God, no fellowship with Him by faith, no enjoyment of His favor, apart from the blood.

Scripture gives only a brief account of the following sixteen centuries. Then came the Flood, which was God's judgment on sin, by the destruction of the world of mankind. But God brought forth a new earth from that awful baptism of water.

Notice, however, that the new earth also had to be baptized with blood, and the first recorded act of Noah, after he had left the ark, was the offering of a burnt sacrifice to God. As with Abel, so with Noah at a new beginning, it was *"not without blood."*

Sin once again prevailed, and God laid an entirely new foundation for the establishment of His kingdom on earth.

By the divine call of Abraham, and the miraculous birth of Isaac, God undertook the formation of a people to serve Him.

But this purpose was not accomplished apart from the shedding of the blood. This is apparent in the most solemn hour of Abraham's life.

God had already entered into covenant relationship with Abraham, and his faith had already been severely tried, and had stood the test. It was reckoned, or counted to him, for righteousness (Rom. 4:9). Yet he had to learn that Isaac, the son of promise, who belonged wholly to God, could be truly surrendered to God only by death. Isaac had to die. For Abraham, as well as for Isaac, only by death could freedom from the self-life be obtained.

Abraham had to offer Isaac on the altar. (See Genesis 22:1–18.) This was not an arbitrary command of God. It was the revelation of a divine truth, that only through death is a life truly consecrated to God possible. But it was impossible for Isaac to die and rise again from the dead, for on account of sin, death would hold him fast. But the Scriptures tell us that Isaac's life was spared, and a ram was offered in his place (v. 13). Through the blood that then flowed on Mount Moriah, his life was spared. He and the people who sprang from him live before God *"not without blood."* By that blood, however, he was in a sense raised again from the dead. The great lesson of substitution is here clearly taught.

Four hundred years passed, and Isaac became, in Egypt, the people of Israel. Through her deliverance from Egyptian bondage, Israel was to be recognized as God's firstborn among the nations. Here, also, it was *"not without blood."* Neither the electing grace of God, nor His covenant with Abraham, nor the exercise of His omnipotence, which could so easily have destroyed their oppressors, could dispense with the necessity of the blood.

What the blood accomplished on Mount Moriah for one person, who was the father of the nation, now had to be experienced by that nation. By the sprinkling of the door frames of the Israelites with the blood of the Paschal lamb, and by the institution of the Passover as an enduring ordinance with the words, *"When I see the blood, I will pass over you"* (Exod. 12:13), the people were taught that life can be obtained only by the death of a substitute. Life was possible for them only through the blood of a life given in their place, and this life could be taken hold of by the sprinkling of that blood.

Fifty days later, this lesson was enforced in a striking manner. Israel had reached Sinai. God had given His law as the foundation of His covenant. That covenant now had to be established, but as it is expressly stated in Hebrews 9:7, *"not without blood."* The sacrificial blood had to be sprinkled, first on the altar; then on the book of the covenant, representing God's side of that covenant; then on the people, with the declaration, *"This is the blood of the covenant"* (Exod. 24:8).

In that blood, the covenant had its foundation and power. It is by the blood alone that God and man can be brought into covenant fellowship. That which had been foreshadowed at the gate of Eden, on Mount Ararat, on Moriah, and in Egypt, was now confirmed at the foot of Sinai in a most solemn manner. Without blood there could be no access by sinful man to a holy God.

There is, however, a significant difference between the manner of applying the blood in the former cases as compared with the latter. On Moriah the life was redeemed by the shedding of the blood. In Egypt it was sprinkled on the doorposts of the houses; but at Sinai, it was sprinkled on the persons themselves. The contact was closer, the application more powerful.

Immediately after the establishment of the covenant, the command was given, *"Let them make Me a sanctuary, that I may dwell among them"* (Exod. 25:8). They were to enjoy the full blessedness of having the God of the covenant abiding among them. Through His grace, they could find Him and serve Him in His house.

He Himself gave, with the minutest care, directions for the arrangement and service of that house. But you will notice that the blood is the center and reason of all this. Draw near to the vestibule of the earthly temple of the heavenly King, and the first thing visible is the altar of burnt offering, where the sprinkling of blood continues, without ceasing, from morning until evening. Enter the Holy Place, and the most conspicuous thing is the golden altar of incense, which also, together with the veil, is constantly sprinkled with the blood. Ask what lies beyond the Holy Place, and you will be told that it is the Most Holy Place where God dwells. If you ask how He dwells there and how He is approached, you will be told *"not without blood."* The golden throne, where His glory shines, is itself sprinkled with the blood, once every year when the high priest alone enters to bring in the blood and to worship God. The highest act in that worship is the sprinkling of the blood.

If you inquire further, you will be told that always, and for everything, the blood is the one necessary thing. At the consecration of the house or of the priests, at the birth of a child, in the deepest penitence on account of sin, in the highest festival—always and in everything—the way to fellowship with God is through the blood alone.

This continued for fifteen hundred years. At Sinai, in the desert, at Shiloh, in the temple on Mount Moriah, it continued—until our Lord came to make an end of all shadows by bringing in the substance and by establishing a fellowship with the Holy One, in spirit and truth.

## WHAT OUR LORD JESUS HIMSELF TAUGHT ABOUT THE BLOOD

With the coming of Christ, old things passed away, all things became new (2 Cor. 5:17). He came from the Father in heaven, and He told us in divine words the way to the Father.

It is sometimes said that the words *"not without blood"* belong to the Old Testament. But what did our Lord Jesus Christ say? Notice, first, that when John the Baptist announced His coming, he spoke of Him as filling a dual office: as *"the Lamb of God who takes away the sin of the world"* (John 1:29), and then as *"He who baptizes with the Holy Spirit"* (v. 33). The outpouring of the blood of the Lamb of God had to take place before the outpouring of the Spirit could be bestowed. Only when all that the Old Testament taught about the blood had been fulfilled could the dispensation of the Spirit begin.

The Lord Jesus Christ Himself plainly declared that His death on the cross was the purpose for which He came into the world, that it was the necessary condition of the redemption and life that He came to bring. He clearly stated that, in connection with His death, the shedding of His blood was necessary.

16

In the synagogue at Capernaum, He spoke of Himself as *"the bread of life"* (John 6:35, 48); of His flesh, that He would *"give [it] for the life of the world"* (v. 51). Four times over He said most emphatically, *"Unless you...drink [My] blood, you have no life in you. Whoever...drinks My blood has eternal life.... My blood is drink indeed. He who...drinks My blood abides in Me, and I in him"* (vv. 53–56). Our Lord thus declared the fundamental fact that He Himself, as the Son of the Father, who came to restore to us our lost life, could do this in no other way than by dying for us, by shedding His blood for us, and then making us partakers of its power.

Our Lord confirmed the teaching of the Old Testament offerings—that man can live only through the death of another, and thus obtain a life that through resurrection has become eternal.

But Christ Himself cannot make us partakers of the eternal life that He has procured for us, except by the shedding of His blood, and causing us to drink it. Marvelous fact! *"Not without blood"* can eternal life be ours.

Equally striking is our Lord's declaration of the same truth on the last night of His earthly life. Before He completed the great work of His life by giving it as *"a ransom for many"* (Matt. 20:28), He instituted the Holy Supper, saying, *"Drink from it, all of you. For this is My blood of the new covenant, which is shed for many for the remission of sins"* (Matt. 26:27–28). *"Without shedding of blood there is no remission [of sins]"* (Heb. 9:22). Without remission of sins, there is no life. But by the shedding of His blood, He has obtained a new life for us. By what He calls "the drinking of His blood," He shares His life with us. The blood shed in the Atonement, which frees us from the guilt of sin and from death—the punishment of sin—the blood, which by faith we drink, bestows on us His life.

## THE TEACHING OF THE APOSTLES UNDER THE INSPIRATION OF THE HOLY SPIRIT

After His resurrection and ascension, our Lord was not any longer known by the apostles *"according to the flesh"* (2 Cor.

17

5:16). All that was symbolic had passed away, and the deep spiritual truths expressed symbolically were unveiled.

But there is no veiling of the blood. It still occupies a prominent place.

Turn first to the epistle to the Hebrews, which was written purposely to show that the temple service had become unprofitable, and was intended by God to pass away, now that Christ had come.

Here, if anywhere, it might be expected that the Holy Spirit would emphasize the true spirituality of God's purpose, yet it is just here that the blood of Jesus is spoken of in a manner that imparts a new value to the phrase.

We read concerning our Lord that *"with His own blood He entered the Most Holy Place"* (Heb. 9:12). *"The blood of Christ… [will] cleanse your conscience"* (v. 14). *"Therefore, brethren, having boldness to enter the Holiest by the blood of Jesus"* (Heb. 10:19). *"You have come…to Jesus the Mediator of the new covenant, and to the blood of sprinkling"* (Heb. 12:22, 24). *"Jesus also, that He might sanctify the people with His own blood, suffered outside the gate"* (Heb. 13:12). *"God…brought up our Lord Jesus from the dead, that great Shepherd of the sheep, through the blood of the everlasting covenant"* (v. 20).

By such words the Holy Spirit teaches us that the blood is really the central power of our entire redemption. *"Not without blood"* is as valid in the New Testament as in the Old.

Nothing but the blood of Jesus, shed in His death for sin, can cover sin on God's side or remove it on ours.

We find the same teaching in the writings of the apostles. Paul wrote of *"being justified freely by his grace through the redemption that is in Christ Jesus…through faith in his blood"* (Rom. 3:24–25 KJV), and of *"having now been justified by His blood"* (Rom. 5:9).

To the Corinthians he declared that the *"cup of blessing which we bless, is…the communion of the blood of Christ"* (1 Cor. 10:16).

In the epistle to the Galatians, he used the word *cross* to convey the same meaning (see, for example, Galatians 6:14), while in Colossians he united the two words and spoke of *"the blood of His cross"* (Col. 1:20).

He reminded the Ephesians that *"we have redemption through His blood"* (Eph. 1:7), and that we *"have been brought near by the blood of Christ"* (Eph. 2:13).

Peter reminded his readers that they were *"elect...for obedience and sprinkling of the blood of Jesus Christ"* (1 Pet. 1:2), that they were redeemed by *"the precious blood of Christ"* (v. 19).

See how John assured his *"little children"* (1 John 2:1) that *"the blood of Jesus Christ His Son cleanses us from all sin"* (1 John 1:7). The Son is He *"who came...not only by water, but by water and blood"* (1 John 5:6).

All of these writers agreed together in mentioning the blood and in glorying in it as the power by which eternal redemption through Christ is fully accomplished and is then applied by the Holy Spirit.

But perhaps this is merely earthly language. What does heaven have to say? Let us examine the book of Revelation.

## WHAT THE BOOK OF REVELATION SAYS CONCERNING THE BLOOD

It is of the greatest importance to notice that, in the revelation that God has given in this book of the glory of His throne, and the blessedness of those who surround it, the blood still retains its remarkably prominent place.

On the throne John saw *"a Lamb as though it had been slain"* (Rev. 5:6). As the elders fell down before the Lamb, they sang a new song, saying, *"You are worthy...for You were slain, and have redeemed us to God by Your blood"* (v. 9).

Later on, when he saw the great company that no man could number, he was told in reply to his question as to who they were, "[They have] *washed their robes and made them white in the blood of the Lamb"* (Rev. 7:14).

Then again, when he heard the song of victory over the defeat of Satan, its words were, *"They overcame him by the blood of the Lamb"* (Rev. 12:11).

In the glory of heaven, as seen by John, there was no phrase by which the great purposes of God, the wondrous love of the Son of God, the power of His redemption, and the joy and thanksgiving of the redeemed could be gathered up and expressed besides this: *"The blood of the Lamb."*

## LESSONS TO LEARN FROM THE SCRIPTURES

From the beginning to the end of Scripture, from the closing of the gates of Eden to the opening of the gates of the heavenly Zion, there runs through Scripture a golden thread. It is the blood that unites the beginning and the end, that gloriously restores what sin had destroyed.

It is not difficult to see what lessons the Lord wishes us to learn from the fact that the blood occupies such a prominent place in Scripture.

### • THE ONLY MEANS OF DEALING WITH SIN

God has no other way of dealing with sin, or the sinner, except through the blood. For victory over sin and the deliverance of the sinner, God has no other means or thought than *"the blood of Christ"* (1 Cor. 10:16). Yes, it is indeed something that surpasses all understanding.

All the wonders of grace are focused here: the incarnation, by which He took upon Himself our flesh and blood; the love, which did not spare itself but surrendered itself to death; the righteousness, which could not forgive sin until the penalty was borne; the substitution, by which He, the Righteous One, atoned for us, the unrighteous; the atonement for sin; and the justification of the sinner. In this way, renewed fellowship with God was made possible, together with the cleansing and sanctification to equip us for the enjoyment of that fellowship; the true oneness in life with the Lord Jesus, as He gives us His blood to drink; the eternal joy of the hymn of praise, *"You…have redeemed us to God"* (Rev. 5:9). All these are but rays of the wondrous light that are reflected upon us from *"the precious blood of Christ"* (1 Pet. 1:19).

### • THE RIGHT VIEW OF THE BLOOD

The blood must have the same place in our hearts that it has with God. From the beginning of God's dealings with man, yes, from before the foundation of the world, the heart of God has rejoiced in that blood. Our hearts will never rest, nor find salvation, until we, too, learn to walk and glory in the power of that blood.

It is not only the penitent sinner, longing for pardon, who must thus value it. No! The redeemed will see that just as God in His temple sits upon a throne of grace, where the blood is ever in evidence, so there is nothing that draws our hearts nearer to God, filling them with God's love, joy, and glory, as living in a constant, spiritual view of that blood.

### • THE BLESSING AND POWER OF THE BLOOD

Let us take time and trouble to learn the full blessing and power of that blood. The blood of Jesus is the greatest mystery of eternity, the deepest mystery of divine wisdom. Let us not imagine that we can easily grasp its meaning. God thought four thousand years were necessary to prepare men for it, and we also must take time, if we are to gain a knowledge of the power of the blood.

Even taking time is of no avail unless there is also the effort of making a sacrifice. Sacrificial blood always meant the offering of a life. The Israelite could not obtain blood for the pardon of his sin, unless the life of something that belonged to him was offered in sacrifice. The Lord Jesus did not offer up His own life and shed His blood in order to spare us from the sacrifice of our lives. No, indeed! Rather, He did so to make the sacrifice of our lives possible and desirable.

The hidden value of His blood is the spirit of self-sacrifice, and where the blood really touches the heart, it works out in that heart a similar spirit of self-sacrifice. We learn to give up ourselves and our lives, in order to press into the full power of that new life that the blood has provided.

We give our time so that we may become acquainted with these things by God's Word. We separate ourselves from sin, worldly-mindedness, and self-will, so that the power of the blood may not be hindered, for it is just these things that the blood seeks to remove.

We surrender ourselves wholly to God in prayer and faith, so as not to think our own thoughts, and not to hold our own lives as a prize, but as possessing nothing except what He bestows. Then

He reveals to us the glorious and blessed life that has been prepared for us by the blood.

## • THE REVELATION OF THE POWER OF THE BLOOD

We can rely on the Lord Jesus to reveal to us the power of His blood. It is by this confident trust in Him that the blessing obtained by the blood becomes ours. We must never, in thought, separate the blood from the High Priest who shed it and who ever lives to apply it.

He who once gave His blood for us will surely, every moment, impart its effectiveness. Trust Him to do this. Trust Him to open your eyes and to give you a deeper spiritual insight. Trust Him to teach you to think about the blood as God thinks about it. Trust Him to impart to you, and to make effective in you, all that He enables you to see.

Above all, trust Him in the power of His eternal high priesthood to work out in you, unceasingly, the full merits of His blood, so that your whole life may be an uninterrupted abiding in the sanctuary of God's presence.

Believer, you who have come to the knowledge of the precious blood, listen to the invitation of your Lord. Come nearer. Let Him teach you; let Him bless you. Let Him cause His blood to become to you spirit, life, power, and truth.

Begin now, at once, to open your soul in faith, to receive the full, mighty, heavenly effects of the precious blood, in a more glorious manner than you have ever experienced. He Himself will work these things out in your life.

# chapter 2

# Redemption by Blood

*You were not redeemed with corruptible things,...but*
*with the precious blood of Christ, as of a lamb without*
*blemish and without spot.*
—1 Peter 1:18–19

T he shedding of His blood was the culmination of the sufferings of our Lord. The atonement offered by those sufferings was in that shed blood. It is therefore of great
importance that the believer should not rest satisfied with the
mere acceptance of the blessed truth that he is redeemed by that
blood, but should press on to a fuller knowledge of what is
meant by that statement and to learn what that blood is intended to do in a surrendered soul.

Its effects are manifold, for we read in Scripture of the following:

- Reconciliation through the blood
- Cleansing through the blood
- Sanctification through the blood
- Union with God through the blood
- Victory over Satan through the blood
- Life through the blood

These are separate blessings but are all included in one
phrase: "redemption by the blood." It is only where the believer
understands what these blessings are, and by what means they
may become his, that he can experience the full power of redemption.

Before considering these blessings in detail, let us first inquire, in a more general way, concerning the power of the blood
of Jesus:

- First, where does the power of that blood lie?
- Second, what has that power accomplished?
- Third, how can we experience its effects?

## WHERE DOES THE POWER OF THE BLOOD LIE?

What is it that gives such power to the blood of Jesus? How is it that, in the blood alone, there is power possessed by nothing else?

The answer to this question is found in Leviticus 17:11: *"For the life of the flesh is in the blood, and I have given it to you upon the altar to make atonement for your souls; for it is the blood that makes atonement for the soul."*

Because the soul, or life, is in the blood, and because the blood is offered to God on the altar, it has redemptive power.

### • THE LIFE IS IN THE BLOOD

The value of the blood corresponds to the value of the life that is in it. The life of a sheep or goat is of less value than the life of an ox, and so the blood of a sheep or a goat in an offering is of less value than the blood of an ox. (See Leviticus 4:13–14, 27–28.) The life of man is more valuable than that of many sheep or oxen.

Now, who can tell the value or the power of the blood of Jesus? In that blood dwelt the soul of the holy Son of God. The eternal life of the Godhead was carried in that blood. (See Acts 20:28.)

The power of that blood in its many effects is nothing less than the eternal power of God Himself. What a glorious thought for everyone who desires to experience the full power of the blood!

### • OFFERED TO GOD ON THE ALTAR

But the power of the blood lies above everything else in the fact that it is offered to God on the altar for redemption. When we think of blood as shed, we think of death; death follows when the blood or the soul is poured out. Death makes us think of sin, for death is the punishment of sin (Rom. 6:23). God gave Israel the blood on the altar as the atonement or covering for sin. This means that the sins of the transgressor were laid on the victim, and its death was reckoned as the death or punishment for the sins laid upon it.

The blood was thus life given up to death for the satisfaction of the law of God, and in obedience to His command. Sin was so entirely covered and atoned for, it was no longer reckoned as that of the transgressor. The transgressor was forgiven.

But all these sacrifices and offerings were only types and shadows, until the Lord Jesus came. His blood was the reality to which these types pointed.

His blood was in itself of infinite value, because it carried His soul or life. But the atoning virtue of His blood was infinite also, because of the manner in which it was shed. In holy obedience to the Father's will, He subjected Himself to the penalty of the broken law by pouring out His soul unto death. By that death, not only was the penalty borne, but the law was satisfied and the Father was glorified. His blood atoned for sin and thus made it powerless. It has a marvelous power for removing sin and opening heaven for the sinner, whom it cleanses and sanctifies and makes fit for heaven.

It is because of the wonderful Person whose blood was shed, and because of the wonderful way in which it was shed, fulfilling the law of God while satisfying its just demands, that the blood of Jesus has such wonderful power. It is the blood of atonement, and hence it has the power to redeem, accomplishing everything for and in the sinner that is necessary for salvation.

## WHAT HAS THAT POWER ACCOMPLISHED?

As we see something of the wonders that this power has accomplished, we will be encouraged to believe that it can do the same for us. Our best plan is to note how the Scriptures glory in the great things that have taken place through the power of the blood of Jesus.

### • THE BLOOD OPENED THE GRAVE

We read in Hebrews 13:20, *"The God of peace...brought up our Lord Jesus from the dead, that great Shepherd of the sheep, through the blood of the everlasting covenant."* It was through the virtue of the blood that God raised up Jesus from the dead. God's almighty power was not exerted to raise Jesus from the dead, apart from the blood.

He came to earth as Surety and Bearer of the sin of mankind. It was through the shedding of His blood alone that He had the right, as man, to rise again and to obtain eternal life through resurrection. His blood had satisfied the law and righteousness of God. By so doing, He had overcome the power of sin and brought it to nothing. In the same way, death was defeated; its sting, sin, had been removed; and the Devil, who had the power of death, was also defeated, having now lost all right over Him and us. His blood has destroyed the power of death, the Devil, and hell; the blood of Jesus has opened the grave.

He who truly believes this perceives the close connection that exists between the blood and the almighty power of God. It is only through the blood that God exerts His almightiness in dealing with sinful men. Where the blood is, there the resurrection power of God gives entrance into eternal life. The blood has made a complete end of all the power of death and hell. Its effects surpass all human thought.

## • THE BLOOD OF JESUS OPENED HEAVEN

We read in Hebrews 9:12 that Christ *"by his own blood... entered in once into the holy place, having obtained eternal redemption for us"* (KJV). We know that in the Old Testament tabernacle, God's manifested presence was inside the veil. No power of man could remove that veil. The high priest alone could enter there, but only with blood, or the loss of his own life. That was a picture of the power of sin in the flesh, which separates us from God. The eternal righteousness of God guarded the entrance to the Most Holy Place, so that no flesh might approach Him.

But now our Lord appears, not in an earthly temple, but in the true temple. As High Priest and Representative of His people, He asks for Himself, and for sinful children of Adam, an entrance into the presence of the Holy One. *"That where I am, there* [they] *may be also"* (John 14:3) is His request. He asks that heaven may be opened for each one, even for the greatest sinner, who believes in Him. His request is granted. But how is

26

this? It is through the blood. He entered through His own blood. The blood of Jesus has opened heaven.

So it is always through the blood that the throne of grace remains settled in heaven. Nearest to *"God the Judge of all"* (Heb. 12:23), and to *"Jesus the Mediator"* (v. 24), the Holy Spirit gives a prominent place to *"the blood of sprinkling"* (v. 24).

It is the constant "speaking" of that blood that keeps heaven open for sinners and sends streams of blessing down on earth. It is through that blood that Jesus, as Mediator, carries on His mediatorial work without ceasing. The throne of grace ever owes its existence to the power of that blood.

Oh, the wonderful power of the blood of Christ! Just as it has broken open the gates of the grave and of hell to let Jesus out, and us with Him, so it has opened the gates of heaven for Him, and us with Him, to enter. The blood has an almighty power over the kingdom of darkness and hell beneath, and over the kingdom of heaven and its glory above.

## • ALL-POWERFUL IN THE HUMAN HEART

Since the blood avails so powerfully with God and over Satan, does it not avail even more powerfully with man, for whose sake it was actually shed? We may be sure of it.

The wonderful power of the blood is especially manifested on behalf of sinners on earth. Our text is just one of many Scripture passages where this is emphasized. *"You were...redeemed ...from your aimless conduct...with the precious blood of Christ"* (1 Pet. 1:18–19).

The word *"redeemed"* has a depth of meaning. It particularly indicates deliverance from slavery by emancipation or purchase. The sinner is enslaved under the hostile power of Satan, the curse of the law, and sin. Now it is proclaimed, "You are redeemed through the blood," which had paid the debt of guilt and destroyed the power of Satan, the curse, and sin.

Where this proclamation is heard and received, redemption begins in a true deliverance from a vain manner of life, from a life of sin. The word *redemption* includes everything God does for a sinner from the pardon of sin, in which it begins (Eph. 1:14; 4:30), to the full deliverance of the body by resurrection (Rom. 8:23–24).

Those to whom Peter wrote were *"elect...for...sprinkling of the blood of Jesus Christ"* (1 Pet. 1:2). The proclamation about the precious blood had touched their hearts and brought them to repentance, awakening faith in them, and filling their souls with life and joy. Each believer was an illustration of the wonderful power of the blood.

Further on, when Peter exhorted them to holiness, his plea was still the precious blood. He wanted them to focus on it.

For the Jew in his self-righteousness and hatred of Christ, for the heathen in his godlessness, there was only one means of deliverance from the power of sin. It is still the one power that brings about daily deliverance for sinners. How could it be otherwise? The blood that availed so powerfully in heaven and over hell, is all-powerful in a sinner's heart, too. It is impossible for us to think too highly of, or to expect too much from, the power of Jesus' blood.

## HOW DOES THIS POWER WORK?

Our third question is, In what conditions, under what circumstances, can the power of the blood secure, unhindered in us, the mighty results it is intended to produce?

### • THROUGH FAITH

The first answer, just as it is everywhere in the kingdom of God, is that it is through faith. But faith is largely dependent on knowledge. If knowledge of what the blood can accomplish is imperfect, then faith expects little, and the more powerful effects of the blood are impossible. Many Christians think that if now, through faith in the blood, they have received the assurance of the pardon of their sins, then they have a sufficient knowledge of its effects.

They have no idea that the words of God, like God Himself, are inexhaustible, that they have a wealth of meaning and blessing that surpasses all understanding.

They do not remember that when the Holy Spirit speaks of cleansing through the blood, such words are only imperfect human expressions of the effects and experiences by which the blood, in an unspeakably glorious manner, will reveal its heavenly life-giving power to the soul. Feeble ideas of its power prevent the deeper and more perfect manifestations of its effects.

As we seek to find out what the Scriptures teach about the blood, we will see that faith in the blood, even as we now understand it, can produce in us greater results than we have yet known; and in the future, a ceaseless blessing may be ours.

Our faith may be strengthened by noticing what the blood has already accomplished. Heaven and hell bear witness to this. Faith will grow by exercising confidence in the fathomless fullness of the promises of God. Let us heartily expect that as we enter more deeply into the fountain of Christ's blood, its cleansing, quickening, life-giving power will be revealed more blessedly.

When we bathe, we enter into the most intimate relationship with the water, giving ourselves up to its cleansing effects. The blood of Jesus is described as *"a fountain...opened...for sin and for uncleanness"* (Zech. 13:1). By the power of the Holy Spirit, it streams through the heavenly temple. By faith, I place myself in closest contact with this heavenly stream; I yield myself to it; I let it cover me and go through me. I bathe in the fountain. It cannot withhold its cleansing and strengthening power. I must in simple faith turn away from what is seen, to plunge into the spiritual fountain that represents the Savior's blood, with the assurance that it will manifest its blessed power in me.

So let us with childlike, persevering, expectant faith open our souls to an ever increasing experience of the wonderful power of the blood.

## • THE SPIRIT AND THE BLOOD

But there is still another reply to the question as to what else is necessary so that the blood may manifest its power. Scripture connects the blood most closely with the Spirit. It is only where the Spirit works that the power of the blood will be manifested.

We read in First John that *"there are three that bear witness on earth: the Spirit, the water, and the blood; and these three agree as one"* (1 John 5:8). The water refers to baptism unto repentance and the laying aside of sin. The blood refers to redemption in Christ. The Spirit is He who supplies power to the water and the blood. So also the Spirit and the blood are associated in Hebrews 9:14, where we read, *"How much more shall the blood of Christ, who through the eternal Spirit offered Himself without spot to God, cleanse your conscience."* It was by the eternal Spirit in our Lord that His blood had its value and power. It is always through the Spirit that the blood possesses its living power in heaven and in the hearts of men.

The blood and the Spirit always bear testimony together. Where the blood is honored in faith or preaching, there the Spirit works; and where He works, He always leads souls to the blood. The Holy Spirit could not be given until the blood was shed. The living bond between the Spirit and the blood cannot be broken.

It should be seriously noticed that, if the full power of the blood is to be manifested in our souls, we must place ourselves under the teaching of the Holy Spirit.

We must firmly believe that He is in us, carrying on His work in our hearts. We must live as those who know that the Spirit of God really dwells within, as a seed of life, and He will bring to perfection the hidden, powerful effects of the blood. We must allow Him to lead us.

Through the Spirit, the blood will cleanse us, sanctify us, and unite us to God. When Peter wanted to urge believers to listen to God's voice with His call to holiness, *"Be holy, for I am holy"* (1 Pet. 1:16), he reminded them that they had been redeemed by the precious blood of Christ.

## • KNOWLEDGE

His readers had to know that they had been redeemed and what that redemption signified, but above all, they had to know that it was not *"with corruptible things, like silver or gold"* (v. 18), things in which there was no power of life, *"but with the precious blood of Christ"* (v. 19). To have a correct perception of what the preciousness of that blood was (as the power of a perfect redemption), would be to them the power of a new and holy life.

Beloved Christians, this statement also applies to us. We must know that we are redeemed by *"the precious blood."* We must know about redemption and the blood before we can experience its power.

As we more fully understand what redemption is, and what the power and preciousness of the blood are, by which redemption has been obtained, we will more fully experience its value.

## • NEED AND DESIRE

Let us take ourselves to the school of the Holy Spirit to be led into a deeper knowledge of redemption through the precious blood. Two things are needed for this: first, a deeper sense of need; and second, a desire to understand the blood better. The blood has been shed to take away sin. The power of the blood is to nullify the power of sin.

We are, unfortunately, too easily satisfied with the first beginnings of deliverance from sin. Oh, that what remains of sin in us might become unbearable to us! May we no longer be contented with the fact that we, as redeemed ones, sin against God's will in so many things.

May the desire for holiness become stronger in us. Should not the thought that the blood has more power than we know of, and can do for us greater things than we have yet experienced, cause our hearts to go out in strong desire? If there were more desire for deliverance from sin, for holiness and intimate friendship with a holy God, it would be the first thing that is necessary for being led further into the knowledge of what the blood can do.

## • EXPECTATION

The second thing will follow. Desire must become expectation.

As we inquire from the Word, in faith, what the blood has accomplished, it must be a settled matter with us that the blood can manifest its full power also in us. No sense of unworthiness, ignorance, or helplessness must cause us to doubt. The blood works in the surrendered soul with a ceaseless power of life.

Surrender yourself to God the Holy Spirit.

Fix the eyes of your heart on the blood.

Open your whole inner being to its power.

Take shelter under the ever continuing sprinkling of the blood. The blood on which the throne of grace in heaven is founded can make your heart the temple and throne of God.

Ask the Lamb of God Himself to make the blood effective in you.

You will surely experience that there is nothing to compare with the wonder-working power of the blood of Jesus.

chapter 3

# Reconciliation through the Blood

*Being justified freely by his grace through the redemption that is in Christ Jesus: whom God hath set forth to be a propitiation [reconciliation] through faith in his blood.*
—Romans 3:24–25 KJV

As we have seen, several distinct blessings have been procured for us by the power of the blood of Jesus, which are all included in the one word *redemption*. Among these blessings, reconciliation takes the first place. *"God hath set forth [Jesus] to be a [reconciliation] through faith in his blood."* In our Lord's work of redemption, reconciliation naturally comes first. It stands first also among the things that must be done by the sinner who desires to have a share in redemption. Through it, a participation in the other blessings of redemption is made possible.

Also of great importance is that the believer, who has already received reconciliation, should obtain a deeper and more spiritual idea of its meaning and blessedness. If the power of the blood in redemption is rooted in reconciliation, then a fuller knowledge of reconciliation is the surest way to obtain a fuller experience of the power of the blood. The heart that is surrendered to the teaching of the Holy Spirit will surely learn what reconciliation means. May our hearts be opened wide to receive it.

To understand what reconciliation by the blood means, let us consider the following:

- First, sin that has made reconciliation necessary
- Second, God's holiness that foreordained reconciliation
- Third, the blood of Jesus that obtained it
- Last, the pardon that results from it

33

## SIN MADE RECONCILIATION NECESSARY

In all the work of Christ, and above all in reconciliation, God's objective is the removal and destruction of sin. Knowledge of sin is necessary for the knowledge of reconciliation.

We need to understand what there is in sin that needs reconciliation, and how reconciliation renders sin powerless. Then faith has something to take hold of, and the experience of that blessing is made possible.

Sin has had a twofold effect. It has had an effect on God, as well as on man. We generally emphasize its effect on man. But the effect it has exercised on God is more terrible and serious. Because of this effect on God, sin has its power over us. God, as Lord of all, could not overlook sin. It is His unalterable law that sin must bring forth sorrow and death. When man fell into sin, he, by that law of God, was brought under the power of sin. Thus, redemption must begin with the law of God, for if sin is made powerless against God, and the law of God gives sin no authority over us, then its power over us is destroyed. The knowledge that sin is speechless before God assures us that it no longer has authority over us.

What, then, was the effect of sin upon God? In His divine nature, He ever remains unchanged and unchangeable, but in His relationship and conduct toward man, an entire change has taken place. Sin is disobedience, a contempt of the authority of God; it seeks to rob God of His honor as God and Lord. Sin is determined opposition to a holy God. It not only can, but it must, awaken His wrath.

While it was God's desire to continue in love and friendship with man, sin has compelled Him to become an opponent. Although the love of God toward man remains unchanged, sin made it impossible for Him to allow man to have fellowship with Himself. It has compelled Him to pour out upon man His wrath and curse and punishment, instead of His love. The change that sin has caused in God's relationship to man is enormous.

Man is guilty before God. Guilt is debt. We know what debt is. It is something that one person can demand from another, a claim that must be met and settled.

When sin is committed, its aftereffects may not be noticed, but its guilt remains. The sinner is guilty. God cannot disregard His own demand that sin must be punished; and His glory, which has been dishonored, must be upheld. As long as the debt is not discharged, or the guilt expiated, it is, in the nature of the case, impossible for a holy God to allow the sinner to come into His presence.

We often think that the great question for us is how we can be delivered from the indwelling power of sin, but that is a question of less importance than how we can be delivered from the guilt that is heaped up before God. Can the guilt of sin be removed? Can the effect of sin upon God, in awakening His wrath, be removed? Can sin be blotted out before God? If these things can be done, the power of sin will be broken in us also. The guilt of sin can be removed only through reconciliation.

The word translated as "reconciliation" means actually "to cover." Even heathen people had an idea of this. But in Israel, God revealed a reconciliation that could so truly cover and remove the guilt of sin that the original relationship between God and man can be entirely restored. This is what true reconciliation must do. It must so remove the guilt of sin, which is the effect of sin on God, that man can draw near to God in the blessed assurance that there is no longer the least guilt resting on him to keep him away from God.

## RECONCILIATION FOREORDAINED BY THE HOLINESS OF GOD

If we are to understand reconciliation correctly, we must also consider the holiness of God that foreordained it. God's holiness is His infinite, glorious perfection, which leads Him always to desire what is good in others as well as in Himself. He bestows and works out what is good in others, and He hates and condemns all that is opposed to what is good.

In His holiness, both the love and wrath of God are united: His love bestows itself, and according to the divine law of righteousness, His wrath casts out and consumes what is evil. It is as the Holy One that God ordained reconciliation in Israel and took up His abode on the mercy seat. It is as the Holy One that He, in expectation of New Testament times, so often called Himself *"your Redeemer, the Holy One of Israel."* (See, for example, Isaiah 41:14.) It is as the Holy One that God worked out His plan of reconciliation in Christ.

The wonder of this plan is that both the holy love and the holy wrath of God find satisfaction in it. Apparently they were in irreconcilable strife with one another. The holy love was unwilling to let man go. Notwithstanding all his sin, it could not give him up. He had to be redeemed. The holy wrath, likewise, could not surrender its demands. The law had been despised; God had been dishonored. God's rights had to be upheld. There could be no thought of releasing the sinner as long as the law was not satisfied. The terrible effect of sin on God had to be counteracted; the guilt of sin had to be removed; otherwise the sinner could not be delivered. The only possible solution was reconciliation.

We have seen that reconciliation means covering. It means that something else has taken the place where sin was established, so that sin can no longer be seen by God.

But because God is the Holy One, and *"His eyes [are] like a flame of fire"* (Rev. 1:14), that which covered sin must be something of such a nature that it really counteracted the evil that sin had done, and also that it blotted out sin before God, so that it was really destroyed and was not now to be seen.

Reconciliation for sin can take place only by satisfaction. Satisfaction is reconciliation. And as satisfaction is through a substitute, sin can be punished, and the sinner can be saved. God's holiness also would be glorified and its demands would be met. The demand of God's love would be satisfied in the redemption of the sinner, and the demand of His righteousness would be satisfied in the maintenance of the glory of God and of His law.

We know how this was set forth in the Old Testament laws of the offerings. A clean animal took the place of a guilty man. His sin was laid, by confession, on the head of the animal, which bore the punishment by surrendering its life unto death. Then the blood, representing a clean life that now through the bearing of punishment is free from guilt, can be brought into God's presence; the blood or life of the animal has borne the punishment in place of the sinner. That blood made reconciliation and covered the sinner and his sin, because it had taken his place and atoned for his sin.

There was reconciliation in the blood. But that was not a reality. The blood of cattle or of goats could never take away sin; it was only a shadow, a picture, of the real reconciliation.

Blood of a totally different character was necessary for an effective covering of guilt. According to the plan of the holy God, nothing less than the blood of God's own Son could bring about reconciliation. Righteousness demanded it; Love offered it. *"Being justified freely by his grace through the redemption that is in Christ Jesus: whom God hath set forth to be a propitiation* [reconciliation] *through faith in his blood."*

## RECONCILIATION OBTAINED BY THE BLOOD OF JESUS

Our third point of consideration is that reconciliation must be the satisfaction of the demands of God's holy law. The Lord Jesus accomplished this. By a willing and perfect obedience, He fulfilled the law under which He had placed Himself. In the same spirit of complete surrender to the will of the Father, He bore the curse that the law had pronounced against sin. He rendered, in fullest measure of obedience or punishment, all that the law of God could ever ask or desire. The law was perfectly satisfied by Him. But how can His fulfilling of the demands of the law be reconciliation for the sins of others? Because, both in creation and in the holy covenant of grace that the Father had made with Him, He was recognized as the Head of the human race.

Because of this, He was able, by becoming flesh, to become the Second Adam. When He, the Word, became flesh, He placed Himself in a real fellowship with our flesh that was under the power of sin, and He assumed the responsibility for everything that sin had done in the flesh against God. His perfection and obedience were not merely those of one man among others, but those of Him who had placed Himself in fellowship with all other men, and who had taken their sin upon Himself.

As Head of mankind through creation, as their Representative in the covenant, He became their Surety. As a perfect satisfaction of the demands of the law was accomplished by the shedding of His blood, this was the reconciliation, the covering of our sin.

Above all, we must never forget that He was God. This bestowed a divine power on Him, to unite Himself with His creatures and to take them up into Himself. It bestowed on His sufferings a virtue of infinite holiness and power. It made the merit of His blood-shedding more than sufficient to deal with all the guilt of human sin. It made His blood such a real reconciliation, such a perfect covering of sin, that the holiness of God no longer beholds it. Sin has been, in truth, blotted out. The blood of Jesus, God's Son, has procured a real, perfect, and eternal reconciliation.

What does this mean?

I have spoken of the awful effect of sin on God, of the terrible change that took place in heaven through sin. Instead of favor, friendship, blessing, and the life of God from heaven, man had nothing to look for except wrath, curse, death, and perdition. He could think of God only with fear and terror, without hope, and without love. Sin never ceased to call for vengeance; guilt had to be dealt with in full.

But see! The blood of Jesus, God's Son, has been shed. Atonement for sin has been made. Peace is restored. A change has taken place again, as real and widespread as that which sin had brought about. For those who receive the reconciliation, sin has been brought to nothing. The wrath of God turns around and hides itself in the depth of divine love.

The righteousness of God no longer terrifies man. It meets him as a friend, with an offer of complete justification. God's countenance beams with pleasure and approval as the penitent sinner draws near to Him, and He invites him to intimate fellowship. He opens for him a treasure of blessing. There is nothing now that can separate him from God (Rom. 8:38–39).

The reconciliation through the blood of Jesus has covered his sins; they no longer appear in God's sight. God no longer attributes sin to him. Reconciliation has brought out a perfect and eternal redemption.

Oh, who can tell the worth of this precious blood?

It is no wonder that mention will forever be made of that blood in the song of the redeemed, and through all eternity. As long as heaven lasts, the praise of the blood will resound: *"You were slain, and have redeemed us to God by Your blood"* (Rev. 5:9).

But here is the wonder, that the redeemed on earth do not more heartily join in that song, and that they are not abounding in praise for the reconciliation that the power of the blood has accomplished.

## PARDON FOLLOWS RECONCILIATION

That the blood has made reconciliation for sin and covered it, and that as a result of this, such a wonderful change has taken place in the heavenly realms—all this will avail us nothing, unless we obtain a personal share in it.

It is in the pardon of sin that this takes place. God has offered a perfect acquittal from all our sin and guilt. Because reconciliation has been made for sin, we can now be reconciled to Him. *"God was in Christ reconciling the world to Himself, not imputing their trespasses to them"* (2 Cor. 5:19). Following this word of reconciliation is the invitation, *"Be reconciled to God"* (v. 20). Whoever receives reconciliation for sin is reconciled to God. He knows that all his sins are forgiven.

The Scriptures use many illustrations to emphasize the fullness of forgiveness and to convince the fearful heart of the sinner that the blood has really taken his sin away. *"I have blotted out, like a thick cloud, your transgressions, and like a cloud, your sins"* (Isa. 44:22). *"You have cast all my sins behind Your back"* (Isa. 38:17). *"You will cast all our sins into the depths of the sea"* (Micah 7:19). *"The iniquity of Israel shall be sought, but there shall be none; and the sins of Judah, but they shall not be found; for I will pardon those whom I preserve"* (Jer. 50:20).

This is what the New Testament calls justification. It is thus named in Romans 3:23–26:

*For all have sinned...being justified freely* [for nothing] *by His grace through the redemption that is in Christ Jesus, whom God set forth as a propitiation by His blood, through faith, to demonstrate His righteousness...that He might be just and the justifier of the one who has faith in Jesus.*

So perfect is the reconciliation, and so really has sin been covered and blotted out, that he who believes in Christ is looked upon, and treated by God, as entirely righteous. The acquittal that he has received from God is so complete that there is nothing, absolutely nothing, to prevent him from approaching God with the utmost freedom.

For the enjoyment of this blessedness, nothing is necessary except faith in the blood. The blood alone has done everything.

The penitent sinner who turns from his sin to God, needs only faith in that blood. That is, he needs only faith in the power of the blood, that it has truly atoned for sin, and that it really has atoned for him. Through that faith, he knows that he is fully reconciled to God, and that there is now not the least thing to hinder God's pouring out on him the fullness of His love and blessing.

If he looks toward heaven, which formerly was covered with clouds, black with God's wrath, and a coming awful judgment, those clouds are no longer to be seen; everything is bright in the glad light of God's face and God's love. Faith in the blood manifests in his heart the same wonder-working power that it exercised in heaven. Through faith in the blood, he becomes partaker of all the blessings that the blood has obtained for him from God.

Fellow believers, pray earnestly that the Holy Spirit may reveal to you the glory of this reconciliation and the pardon of your sins, made yours through the blood of Jesus. Pray for enlightened hearts to see how completely the accusing and condemning power of your sin has been removed, and how God in the fullness of His love and good pleasure has turned toward you. Open your hearts to the Holy Spirit so that He may reveal in you the glorious effects that the blood has had in heaven. God has set forth Jesus Christ Himself as a reconciliation through faith in His blood. He is the reconciliation for our sins. Rely on Him as having already covered your sin before God. Set Him between yourselves and your sins, and you will experience how complete the redemption is that He has accomplished, and how powerful the reconciliation is through faith in His blood.

Then, through the living Christ, the powerful effects that the blood has brought about in heaven will increasingly be manifested in your hearts, and you will know what it means to walk, by the Spirit's grace, in the full light and enjoyment of forgiveness.

And you who have not yet obtained forgiveness of your sins, does this word not come to you as an urgent call to faith in His blood? Will you never allow yourself to be moved by what God has done for you as a sinner? *"In this is love, not that we loved God, but that He loved us and sent His Son to be the propitiation for our sins"* (1 John 4:10).

The precious blood divine has been shed; reconciliation is complete; and the message comes to you, *"Be reconciled to God"* (2 Cor. 5:20).

If you repent of your sins, and if you desire to be delivered from sin's power and bondage, exercise faith in the blood. Open your heart to the influence of the word that God has sent to be spoken to you. Open your heart to the message, so that the blood can deliver you—yes, even you—this moment. Only believe it. Say, "This blood is also for me." If you come as a guilty, lost sinner, longing for pardon, you may rest assured that the blood, which has already made a perfect reconciliation, immediately covers your sin and restores you to the favor and love of God.

So I urge you, exercise faith in the blood. This moment bow down before God and tell Him that you do believe in the power of the blood for your own soul. Having said that, stand by it; cling to it. Through faith in His blood, Jesus Christ will be the reconciliation for your sins also.

chapter 4

# Cleansing through the Blood

*If we walk in the light as He is in the light, we have fellowship
with one another, and the blood of Jesus Christ His Son
cleanses us from all sin.*
—1 John 1:7

We have seen that the most important effect of the blood is reconciliation for sin. But this first effect of the blood is not the only one. The more the soul, through faith, yields itself to the Spirit of God to understand and enjoy the full power of reconciliation, the more power the blood exerts in the imparting of the other blessings that, in Scripture, are attributed to it.

One of the first results of reconciliation is cleansing from sin. Let us see what God's Word has to say about this. Cleansing is often spoken about among us as if it were no more than the pardon of sins, or the cleansing from guilt. This, however, is not so. Scripture does not speak of being cleansed from guilt. Cleansing from sin means deliverance from the pollution, not from the guilt, of sin. The guilt of sin concerns our relationship to God, and our responsibility to make good our misdoings (or to bear the punishment of them). The pollution of sin, on the other hand, is the sense of defilement and impurity that sin brings to our inner beings, and cleansing has to do with this.

It is of the greatest importance, for every believer who desires to enjoy the full salvation that God has provided for him, to understand correctly what the Scriptures teach about this cleansing. Let us consider the following:

- First, what does the word *cleansing* mean in the Old Testament?

- Second, what is the blessing indicated by this word in the New Testament?
- Third, how may we experience the full enjoyment of this blessing?

## CLEANSING IN THE OLD TESTAMENT

In the service of God as ordained by the hand of Moses for Israel, there were two ceremonies to be observed by God's people in preparation for approach to Him. These were the offerings or sacrifices and the cleansings or purifications. Both were to be observed but in different manners. Both were intended to remind man how sinful he was, and how unfit to draw near to a holy God. Both were to typify the redemption by which the Lord Jesus Christ would restore to man fellowship with God. As a rule, only the offerings are regarded as typical of redemption through Christ. The epistle to the Hebrews, however, emphatically mentions the cleansings as symbols *"for the time then present, in which were offered...sacrifices...and divers washings"* (Heb. 9:9–10 KJV).

If we can imagine the life of an Israelite, we will understand that the consciousness of sin and the need for redemption were awakened no less by the cleansings than the offerings. We must also learn from them what the power of the blood of Jesus actually is.

We may take one of the more important cases of cleansing as an illustration. If anyone was in a hut or house where a dead body lay, or if he had even touched a dead body or bones, he was unclean for seven days. Death, as the punishment for sin, made everyone who came into association with it unclean. Cleansing was accomplished by using the ashes of a young heifer that had been burned, as described in Numbers 19. (Compare Hebrews 9:13–14.) These ashes, mixed with water, were sprinkled by means of a bunch of hyssop on the one who was unclean; he then had to bathe himself in water, after which he was once more ceremonially clean.

The words *unclean, cleansing,* and *clean* were also used in reference to the healing of leprosy, a disease that might be described as a living death. Here, he who was to be cleansed had to bathe in water, having been first sprinkled with water, in which the blood of a bird, sacrificially offered, had been mixed. Seven days later, he was again sprinkled with sacrificial blood. (See Leviticus 13 and 14.)

An attentive contemplation of the laws of cleansing will teach us that the difference between the cleansings and the offerings was twofold. First, the offering had definite reference to the transgression for which reconciliation had to be made. Cleansing had more to do with conditions that were not sinful in themselves, but were the result of sin, and therefore had to be acknowledged by God's holy people as defiled. Second, in the case of the offering, nothing was done to the offerer himself. He saw the blood sprinkled on the altar or carried into the Holy Place; he had to believe that this procured reconciliation before God. But nothing was done to himself. In cleansing, on the other hand, what happened to the person was the chief thing. Defilement was something that, either through internal disease or outward touch, had come upon the man; so the washing or sprinkling with water had to take place on himself as ordained by God.

Cleansing was something that he could feel and experience. It brought about a change not only in his relationship to God, but also in his own condition. In the offering, something was done for him; by cleansing, something was done in him. The offering had respect to his guilt; the cleansing, to the pollution of sin.

The same meaning of the words *clean* and *cleansing* is found elsewhere in the Old Testament. David prayed in Psalm 51, *"**Cleanse** me from my sin....Purge me with hyssop, and I shall be **clean**"* (vv. 2, 7, emphasis added). The word used by David here is that which is used most frequently for the cleansing of anyone who had touched a dead body. Hyssop was also used in such cases. David prayed for more than pardon. He confessed that he had been *"brought forth in iniquity"* (v. 5), that his nature was sinful. He prayed that he might be made pure within. *"**Cleanse** me from my sin"* was his prayer. He used the same word later on in the same psalm when he prayed, *"Create in me a **clean** heart, O God"* (v. 10, emphasis added). Cleansing is more than pardon.

In the same manner, this word was used by Ezekiel and refers to an inner condition that must be changed. This is evident from Ezekiel 24:13, where, speaking of uncleanness being melted out, God said, *"Because I have cleansed you, and you were not cleansed."* Later on in Ezekiel 36:25, speaking of the new covenant, He said, *"Then I will sprinkle clean water on you, and you shall be clean; I will cleanse you from all your filthiness and from all your idols."*

Malachi used the same word, connecting it with fire: *"He will sit as a refiner and a purifier of silver; He will purify* [cleanse] *the sons of Levi"* (Mal. 3:3).

Cleansing by water, by blood, and by fire are all typical of the cleansing that would take place under the new covenant—an inner cleansing and deliverance from the stain of sin.

## CLEANSING AS BLESSING IN THE NEW TESTAMENT

Mention is often made in the New Testament of a clean or pure heart. Our Lord said, *"Blessed are the pure in heart"* (Matt. 5:8).

Paul spoke of *"love from a pure heart"* (1 Tim. 1:5). He also spoke of *"a pure conscience"* (1 Tim. 3:9).

Peter exhorted his readers to *"love one another fervently with a pure heart"* (1 Pet. 1:22). The word *cleansing* is also implied in this same verse: *"You have purified your souls."*

We read of those who are described as God's people, that God purified (cleansed) their hearts through faith (Acts 15:9).

The purpose of the Lord Jesus concerning those who were His was to *"purify* [cleanse] *for Himself His own special people"* (Titus 2:14).

Regarding ourselves, we read, *"Let us cleanse ourselves from all filthiness of the flesh and spirit"* (2 Cor. 7:1).

All these places teach us that cleansing is an inward work in the heart and that it is subsequent to pardon.

We are told in 1 John 1:7 that *"the blood of Jesus Christ His Son cleanses us from all sin."* This word *cleanses* does not refer to the grace of pardon received at conversion, but to the effect of grace in God's children who walk in the light. We read, *"If we walk in the light as He is in the light, we have fellowship with one another, and the blood of Jesus Christ His Son cleanses us from all sin.*" That it refers to something more than pardon appears from what follows in verse 9: "*He is faithful and just to forgive us our sins and to cleanse us from all unrighteousness.*" Cleansing is something that comes after pardon and is the result of it, by the inward and experiential reception of the power of the blood of Jesus in the heart of the believer.

This takes place according to the Word, first in the purifying of the conscience. "*How much more shall the blood of Christ...cleanse your conscience from dead works to serve the living God?*" (Heb. 9:14). The mention already made of the ashes of a heifer sprinkling the unclean typifies a personal experience of the precious blood of Christ. Conscience is not only a judge to give sentence on our actions; it is also the inward voice that bears witness to our relationship to God, and to God's relationship to us. When it is cleansed by the blood, then it bears witness that we are well-pleasing to God.

It is written in Hebrews 10:2, "*The worshipers, once purified, would have had no more consciousness of sins.*" We receive through the Spirit an inward experience that the blood has so fully delivered us from the guilt and power of sin that we, in our regenerated nature, have escaped entirely from its dominion (Rom. 6:14). Sin still dwells in our flesh, with its temptations, but it has no power to rule. The conscience is cleansed; there is no need for the least shadow of separation between God and us; we look up to Him in the full power of redemption. The conscience cleansed by the blood bears witness to nothing less than a complete redemption, the fullness of God's good pleasure.

And if the conscience is cleansed, so also is the heart, of which the conscience is the center. We read of having a heart cleansed from an evil conscience (Heb. 10:22). Not only must the conscience be cleansed, but the heart also must be cleansed, including the understanding and the will, with all our thoughts and desires. Through the blood, by the shedding of which Christ delivered Himself up to death, and by virtue of which He entered again into heaven, the death and resurrection of Christ are ceaselessly effective. By this power of His death and resurrection, sinful lusts and inclinations are slain.

*"The blood of Jesus Christ His Son cleanses us from all sin"*—from original, as well as actual, sin. The blood exercises its spiritual, heavenly power in the soul. The believer in whose life the blood is fully effective knows that his old nature is hindered from manifesting its power. Through the blood, its lusts and desires are subdued and slain, and everything is cleansed so that the Spirit can bring forth His glorious fruit. In case of the least stumbling, the soul finds immediate cleansing and restoration. Even unconscious sins are rendered powerless.

We have noted a difference between the guilt and the pollution of sin. This is of importance for a clear understanding of the matter, but in actual life, we must ever remember that they are not thus divided. Through the blood, God deals with sin as a whole. Every true operation of the blood manifests its power simultaneously over the guilt and the pollution of sin. Reconciliation and cleansing always go together, and the blood is ceaselessly operative.

Many seem to think that the blood is there, so that if we have sinned again, we can turn again to it to be cleansed. But this is not so. Just as a fountain flows always, and always purifies what is placed in it or under its stream, so it is with this fountain, opened *"for sin and for uncleanness"* (Zech. 13:1). The eternal power of life of the eternal Spirit works through the blood. Through Him the heart can abide always under the flow and cleansing of the blood.

In the Old Testament, cleansing was necessary for each sin. In the New Testament, cleansing depends on Him who ever lives to intercede (Heb. 7:25). When faith sees and desires and lays hold of this fact, the heart can abide every moment under the protecting and cleansing power of the blood.

## EXPERIENCING THE FULL ENJOYMENT OF THIS BLESSING

Everyone who through faith obtains a share in the atoning merit of the blood of Christ also has a share in its cleansing power. But the experience of its power to cleanse is, for several reasons, sadly imperfect. It is therefore of great importance to understand what the conditions are for the full enjoyment of this glorious blessing.

First of all, knowledge is necessary. Many think that pardon of sin is all that we receive through the blood. They ask for and so obtain nothing more.

It is a blessed thing to begin to see that the Holy Spirit of God has a special purpose in making use of different words in Scripture concerning the effects of the blood. Then we begin to inquire about their special meaning. Let everyone who truly longs to know what the Lord desires to teach us by this one word *cleansing,* attentively compare all the places in Scripture where the word is used, where cleansing is spoken of. He will soon feel that there is more promised to the believer than the removal of guilt. He will begin to understand that cleansing through washing can take away stain, and although he cannot fully explain in what way this takes place, he will, however, be convinced that he may expect a blessed inward operation of the cleansing away of the effects of sin by the blood. Knowledge of this fact is the first condition of experiencing it.

Second, there must be desire. It is to be feared that our Christianity is only too pleased to postpone to a future life the experience of the beatitude that our Lord intended for our earthly lives: *"Blessed are the pure in heart, for they shall see God"* (Matt. 5:8).

It is not sufficiently recognized that purity of heart is a characteristic of every child of God, that it is the necessary condition of fellowship with Him, of the enjoyment of His salvation. There is too little inner longing to be truly in all things, at all times, well-pleasing to the Lord. Sin and the stain of sin trouble us too little.

God's Word comes to us with the promise of blessing that ought to awaken all our desires. Believe that the blood of Jesus cleanses from all sin. If you learn how to yield yourself correctly to its operation, it can do great things in you. Should you not every hour desire to experience its glorious cleansing effectiveness; to be preserved, in spite of your depraved nature, from the many stains for which your conscience is constantly accusing you? May your desires be awakened to long for this blessing. Put God to the test to work out in you what He as the Faithful One has promised—cleansing *"from all unrighteousness"* (1 John 1:9).

The third condition is a willingness to separate yourself from everything that is unclean. Through sin, everything in our natures and in the world is defiled. Cleansing cannot take place where there is not an entire separation from, and giving up of, everything unclean. *"Do not touch what is unclean"* (2 Cor. 6:17) is God's command to His chosen ones. I must recognize that all the things surrounding me are unclean.

My friends, my possessions, my spirit must all be surrendered so that I may be cleansed in each relationship by the precious blood, and so that all the activities of my spirit, soul, and being may experience a thorough cleansing.

He who will keep back anything, however small, cannot obtain the full blessing. He who is willing to pay the full price so as to have his whole being baptized by the blood is on the way to understand fully this word: *"The blood of Jesus...cleanses us from all sin."*

The last condition is exercising faith in the power of the blood. It is not as if we, through our faith, give the blood its effectiveness. No, the blood always retains its power and effectiveness, but our unbelief closes our hearts and hinders its operation. Faith is simply the removal of that hindrance, the setting open of our hearts, for the divine power by which the living Lord will bestow His blood.

Yes, let us believe that there is cleansing through the blood.

You have perhaps seen a spring in the midst of a patch of grass. From the much traveled road that runs by that patch, dust is constantly falling over the grass that grows by the side of the road. But where the water from the spring falls in a refreshing and cleansing spray, there is no sign of dust, and everything is green and fresh. Similarly, the precious blood of Christ carries on its blessed work without ceasing in the soul of the believer who by faith takes hold of it. For him who by faith commits himself to the Lord and believes that this can and will take place, it will be given to him.

The heavenly, spiritual effect of the blood can be really experienced every moment. Its power is such that I can always abide in the fountain, always dwell in the wounds of my Lord.

Believer, come, I entreat you; put to the test how the blood of Jesus can cleanse your heart from all sin.

You know with what joy a weary traveler would bathe in a fresh stream, plunging into the water to experience its cooling, cleansing, strengthening effect. Lift up your eyes and see by faith how ceaselessly a stream flows from heaven above to earth beneath. It is the blessed Spirit's influence, through whom the power of the blood of Jesus flows earthward over souls, to heal and to purify them. Oh, place yourself in this stream; simply believe that the words *"the blood of Jesus...cleanses us from all sin"* have a divine meaning—deeper, wider, than you have ever imagined. Believe that it is the Lord Jesus Himself who will cleanse you in His blood and fulfill His promise in power in you. And consider the cleansing from sin by His blood as a blessing, in the daily enjoyment of which you can confidently abide.

chapter 5

# Sanctification through the Blood

*Therefore Jesus also, that He might sanctify the people with His own blood, suffered outside the gate.*
—Hebrews 13:12

To a superficial observer, it might seem that there is little difference between cleansing and sanctification, that the two words mean about the same thing. But the difference is great and important. As I indicated in the previous chapter, cleansing has to do chiefly with the old life and the stain of sin that must be removed. It is only a preparatory work. Sanctification, on the other hand, concerns the new life and the characteristic of it that must be imparted to it by God. Sanctification, which means "union with God," is the fullness of blessing purchased for us by the blood.

The distinction between these two things is clearly marked in Scripture. Paul reminded us that *"Christ also loved the church and gave Himself for her, that He might sanctify and cleanse her"* (Eph. 5:25–26). Having first cleansed it, He then sanctifies it. Writing to Timothy, Paul said, *"Therefore if anyone cleanses himself…he will be a vessel for honor, sanctified and useful for the Master"* (2 Tim. 2:21). Sanctification is a blessing that follows, and surpasses, cleansing.

Sanctification is also strikingly illustrated by the ordinances connected with the consecration of the priests compared with that of the Levites. In the case of the latter, who took a lower position than the priests in the service of the sanctuary, no mention is made of sanctification, but the term *cleanse* is used four times in Numbers 8. In the consecration of the priests, on the other hand, the word *sanctify is* often used, for the priests stood in a closer relationship to God than the Levites. (See Exodus 29 KJV; Leviticus 8 KJV.)

51

At the same time, this record emphasizes the close connection between sanctification and the sacrificial blood. In the case of the consecration of the Levites, reconciliation for sin was made, and they were sprinkled with the water of purification for cleansing, but they were not sprinkled with blood. But in the consecration of the priests, blood had to be sprinkled upon them. They were sanctified by a more personal and intimate application of the blood.

All this was a foreshadowing of the sanctification through the blood of Jesus, and this is what we now seek to understand, so that we may obtain a share in it. Let us then consider:

- First, what sanctification is
- Second, that it was the great purpose of the sufferings of Christ
- Last, that it can be obtained through the blood

## WHAT SANCTIFICATION IS

To understand what the sanctification of the redeemed is, we must first learn what the holiness of God is. He alone is the Holy One. Holiness in the creature must be received from Him.

God's holiness is often spoken of as though it consisted in His hatred of, and hostility to, sin; but this gives no explanation of what holiness actually is. It is a merely negative statement— that God's holiness cannot bear sin.

Holiness is the attribute of God that causes Him always to will and do what is supremely good. Because of His holiness, He desires what is supremely good in His creatures and bestows it upon them.

God is called *"the Holy One"* (2 Kings 19:22, for example) in Scripture, not only because He punishes sin, but also because He is the Redeemer of His people. It is His holiness, which ever wills what is good for all, that moved Him to redeem sinners. Both the wrath of God that punishes sin and love of God that redeems the sinner spring from the same source—His holiness. Holiness is the perfection of God's nature.

Holiness in man is a disposition in entire agreement with that of God, which chooses in all things to will as God wills, as it is written: *"As He who called you is holy, you also be holy in all your conduct"* (1 Pet. 1:15). Holiness in us is nothing else than oneness with God. The sanctification of God's people is brought about by the communication to them of the holiness of God. There is no way of obtaining sanctification, except by the holy God bestowing what He alone possesses. He alone is the Holy One. He is the Lord who sanctifies.

By the different meanings that Scripture attaches to the words *sanctification* and *to sanctify,* a certain relationship with God, into which we are brought, is pointed out.

The first and simplest meaning of the word *sanctification* is separation. That which is taken out of its surroundings, by God's command, and is set aside or separated as His own possession and for His service—that thing is holy. This does not mean separation from sin only, but from all that is in the world, even from what may be permissible. (See 1 Corinthians 6:12.) Thus God sanctified the seventh day. The other days were not unclean, for God saw all that He had made and *"indeed it was very good"* (Gen. 1:31). But that day alone was holy because God had taken possession of it by His own special act. In the same way, God had separated Israel from other nations, and in Israel had separated the priests, to be holy unto Him. This separation unto sanctification is always God's own work, and so the electing grace of God is often closely connected with sanctification. *"And you shall be holy to Me, for I...have separated you from the peoples, that you should be Mine"* (Lev. 20:26). *"The man whom the LORD chooses is the holy one"* (Num. 16:7). *"You are a holy people to the LORD your God; the LORD your God has chosen you"* (Deut. 7:6). God cannot take part with other lords. He must be the sole possessor and ruler of those to whom He reveals and imparts His holiness.

But this separation is not all that is included in the word *sanctification.* It is only the indispensable condition of what must follow. When separated, man stands before God in no respect differing from an inanimate object that has been sanctified to the service of God. If the separation is to be of value, something more must take place. Man must surrender himself willingly and heartily to this separation. Sanctification includes personal consecration to the Lord to be His.

Sanctification can become ours only when it sends down its roots into and takes up its abode in the depths of our personal lives, in our wills, and in our love. God sanctifies no man against his will; therefore, the personal, hearty surrender to God is an indispensable part of sanctification.

It is for this reason that the Scriptures not only speak of God sanctifying us, but they say often that we must sanctify ourselves.

But even by consecration, true sanctification is not yet complete. Separation and consecration are together only the preparation for the glorious work that God will do as He imparts His own holiness to the soul. Partaking of the divine nature is the blessing that is promised to believers in sanctification. *"That we may be partakers of His holiness"* (Heb. 12:10)—this is the glorious aim of God's work in those whom He separates for Himself. But this impartation of His holiness is not a gift of something that is apart from God Himself. No! It is in personal fellowship with Him, and partaking of His divine life, that sanctification can be obtained.

As the Holy One, God dwelt among the people of Israel to sanctify His people (Exod. 29:45–46). As the Holy One, He dwells in us. It is the presence of God alone that can sanctify. But so surely is this our portion that Scripture does not shrink from speaking of God's dwelling in our hearts in such power that we may be *"filled with all the fullness of God"* (Eph. 3:19). True sanctification is fellowship with God and His dwelling in us. So it was necessary that God in Christ should take up His abode in the flesh, and that the Holy Spirit should come to dwell in us. This is what sanctification means.

## SANCTIFICATION AS THE PURPOSE FOR WHICH CHRIST SUFFERED

Christ suffered for the purpose of sanctification. This is plainly stated in Hebrews 13:12: *"Jesus also, that He might sanctify the people with His own blood, suffered."* In the wisdom of God, a participation in His holiness is the highest destiny of man. Therefore, this was the central purpose of the coming of our Lord Jesus to earth and, above all, of His sufferings and death. It was *"that He might sanctify the people"* and that they *"should be holy and without blame"* (Eph. 1:4).

How the sufferings of Christ attained this end, and became our sanctification, is made plain to us by the words that He spoke to His Father when He was about to allow Himself to be bound as a sacrifice. *"For their sakes I sanctify Myself, that they also may be sanctified by the truth"* (John 17:19). Because His sufferings and death were a sanctification of Himself, they can become sanctification for us.

What does this mean? Jesus was *"the Holy One of God"* (Mark 1:24; Luke 4:34). He was *"Him whom the Father sanctified and sent into the world"* (John 10:36)—and did He have to sanctify Himself? He had to do so; it was indispensable.

The sanctification that He possessed was not beyond the reach of temptation. In His temptation, He had to maintain it and show how perfectly His will was surrendered to the holiness of God. We have seen that true holiness in man is the perfect oneness of His will with that of God. Throughout our Lord's life, from the temptation in the wilderness onward, He had subjected His will to the will of His Father, and had consecrated Himself as a sacrifice to God. But it was chiefly in Gethsemane that He did this. There was the hour and the power of darkness; the temptation to put away the terrible cup of wrath from His lips and to do His own will came with almost irresistible power, but He rejected the temptation. He offered up Himself and His will to the will and holiness of God. He sanctified Himself by a perfect oneness of will with that of God.

This sanctification of Himself has become the power by which we also may be sanctified through the truth. This is in perfect accord with what we learn from the epistle to the Hebrews where, in reference to the words used by Christ, we read, *"I have come to do Your will, O God"* (Heb. 10:9), and then it is added, *"By that will we have been sanctified through the offering of the body of Jesus Christ once for all"* (v. 10). Because the offering of His body was His surrender of Himself to do the will of God, we become sanctified by that will. He sanctified Himself there for us so that we might be sanctified through the truth. The perfect obedience in which He surrendered Himself, so that God's holy will might be accomplished in Him, was not only the meritorious cause of our salvation, but is at the same time the power by which sin was forever conquered, and by which the same disposition, and the same sanctification, may be created in our hearts.

Elsewhere in the book of Hebrews, the true relationship of our Lord to His own people is even more clearly characterized as having sanctification for its chief end. After we read of how fitting it was that our Lord suffered as He did, we find, *"For both He who sanctifies and those who are being sanctified are all of one"* (Heb. 2:11). The unity between the Lord Jesus and His people consists in the fact that they both receive their life from one Father, and both have a share in one and the same sanctification. Jesus is the Sanctifier; they become the sanctified. Sanctification is the bond that unites them. *"Therefore Jesus also, that He might sanctify the people with His own blood, suffered."*

If we are truly willing to understand and experience what sanctification by the blood means, then it is of the utmost importance for us to first lay hold of these facts: that sanctification is the characteristic and purpose of the entire sufferings of our Lord, and that regarding those sufferings, the blood was the fruit and means of blessing. His sanctification of Himself has the characteristic of those sufferings, and therein lay its value and power. Our sanctification is the purpose of those sufferings, and only to attain that purpose do they work out the perfect blessing. The more this becomes clear to us, the more we will press forward into the true meaning and blessing of His sufferings.

It was as the Holy One that God foreordained redemption. It was His will to glorify His holiness in victory over sin by the sanctification of mankind after His own image. It was with the same purpose that our Lord Jesus endured and accomplished His sufferings; we must be consecrated to God. And if the Holy Spirit, the holy God as Spirit, comes into us to reveal in us the redemption that is in Jesus, this also continues to be the main purpose with Him. As the Holy Spirit, He is the spirit of holiness.

Reconciliation, pardon, and cleansing from sin all have an unspeakable value; they all, however, point onward to sanctification. It is God's will that each one who has been marked by the precious blood should know that it is a divine mark, characterizing his entire separation to God; that this blood calls him to an undivided consecration to a life wholly for God; and that this blood is the promise and the power of a participation in God's holiness, through which God Himself will make His abiding place in him and be his God.

Oh, that we might understand and believe that *"Jesus also, that He might sanctify the people with His own blood, suffered."*

## HOW TO OBTAIN SANCTIFICATION BY THE BLOOD

How can this sanctification be obtained? An answer to this question, in general, is that everyone who is a partaker of the virtue of the blood is also a partaker of sanctification and is in God's sight a sanctified person.

To the extent that he lives in close and abiding contact with the blood, he continues to experience, increasingly, its sanctifying effects, even though he still understands little of how those effects are produced. Let no one think that he must first understand how to take hold of or explain everything before he may, by faith, pray that the blood might manifest its sanctifying power in him. No, it was in connection with cleansing—the washing of the disciples' feet—that the Lord Jesus said, *"What I am doing you do not understand now, but you will know after this"* (John 13:7). It is the Lord Jesus Himself who sanctifies His people *"with His own blood."* He who heartily gives himself up to believing worship of and intimacy with the Lamb, who has bought us with His blood, will experience through that blood a sanctification beyond what he can imagine. The Lord Jesus will do this for him.

But the believer ought to grow in knowledge also; only in this way can he enter into the full blessing that is prepared for him. We not only have the right, but it is our duty to inquire earnestly what is the essential connection between the blessed effect of the blood and our sanctification, and in what way the Lord Jesus will work out in us, by His blood, those things that we have ascertained to be the chief qualities of sanctification.

We have seen that the beginning of all sanctification is separation to God, as His entire possession, to be at His disposal.

This is just what the blood proclaims: that the power of sin is broken; that we are loosed from its bonds; that we are no longer its bondservants, but belong to Him who purchased our freedom with His blood. *"You are not your own...you were bought at a price"* (1 Cor. 6:19–20). This is the language in which the blood tells us that we are God's possession. Because He desires to have us entirely for Himself, He has chosen us, bought us, and set upon us the distinguishing mark of the blood, as those who are separated from everything around them, to live only for His service.

This idea of separation is clearly expressed in the words we so often repeat, *"Jesus also, that He might sanctify the people with His own blood, suffered outside the gate. Therefore let us go forth to Him, outside the camp, bearing His reproach"* (Heb. 13:12–13). Going forth from all that is of this world was the characteristic of Him who was holy, undefiled, separate from sinners; and it must also be the characteristic of all His followers.

Believer, the Lord Jesus has sanctified you through His own blood, and He desires to make you experience, through that blood, the full power of this sanctification. Endeavor to gain a clear impression of what has taken place in you through the sprinkling of that blood. The holy God desires to have you entirely for Himself. No one, nothing, may any longer have the least right over you, nor have you any right over yourself. God has separated you unto Himself, and so that you might feel this, He set His mark upon you. This mark is the most wonderful thing that is to be found on earth or in heaven—the blood of Jesus. The blood in which the life of the eternal Son of God is found, the blood that on the throne of grace is ever before God's face, the blood that assures you of full redemption from the power of sin—that blood is sprinkled upon you as a sign that you belong to God.

Believer, I urge you, let every thought about the blood awaken in you the glorious confession, "By His own blood, the Lord Jesus has sanctified me. He has taken complete possession of me for God, and I belong entirely to God."

We have seen that sanctification is more than separation. That is only the beginning. We have also seen that personal consecration, and hearty and willing surrender to live only for and in God's holy will, are part of sanctification.

In what way can the blood of Christ work out this surrender in us and sanctify us in that surrender? The answer is not difficult. It is not enough to believe in the power of the blood to redeem us and to free us from sin, but we must, above all, notice the source of this power.

We know that it has this power because of the willingness with which the Lord Jesus surrendered Himself. In the shedding of His blood, He sanctified Himself, offered Himself entirely to God and His holiness. It is because of this that the blood is so holy and possesses such sanctifying power. In the blood we have an impressive representation of the utter self-surrender of Christ. The blood ever speaks of the consecration of Jesus to the Father as the opening of the way to, and supplying the power for, victory over sin. The closer we come into contact with the blood, and the more we live under the deep impression of having been sprinkled by the blood, we will hear more clearly the voice of the blood declaring, "Entire surrender to God is the way to full redemption from sin."

The voice of the blood will not speak simply to teach us or to awaken thought; the blood speaks with a divine and life-giving power. What it commands, it also bestows. It works out in us the same disposition that was in our Lord Jesus. By His own blood Jesus sanctifies us, so that we, holding nothing back, might surrender ourselves with all our hearts to the holy will of God.

But consecration itself, even along with and following separation, is still only a preparation. Entire sanctification takes place when God takes possession of and fills with His glory the temple that is consecrated to *Him*. *"There I will meet with the children of Israel, and the tabernacle shall be sanctified by My glory"* (Exod. 29:43). Actual, complete sanctification consists in God's impartation of His own holiness—of Himself.

Here also the blood speaks; it tells us that heaven is opened, that the powers of the heavenly life have come down to earth, that every hindrance has been removed. God can make His abode with man.

Immediate nearness and fellowship with God are made possible by the blood of Jesus. The believer who surrenders himself unreservedly to the blood obtains the full assurance that God will bestow Himself wholly and will reveal His holiness in him.

How glorious are the results of such a sanctification! Through the Holy Spirit, the soul's intimacy is in the living experience of God's abiding nearness, accompanied by the awakening of the tenderest carefulness against sin, guarded by caution and the fear of God.

But to live in watchfulness against sin does not satisfy the soul. The temple must not only be cleansed, but it must be filled with God's glory. All the virtues of divine holiness, as manifested in the Lord Jesus, are to be sought and found in fellowship with God. Sanctification means union with God, fellowship in His will, sharing His life, conformity to His image.

Christians, *"Jesus also, that He might sanctify the people with His own blood, suffered outside the gate. Therefore let us go forth to Him, outside the camp, bearing His reproach"* (Heb. 13:12–13). Yes, it is He who sanctifies His people. *"Let us go forth to Him."* Let us trust Him to make known to us the power of the blood. Let us yield ourselves wholly to its blessed power. This blood, through which He sanctified Himself, has entered heaven to open it for us. It can make our hearts also a throne of God, so that the grace and glory of God may dwell in us. Yes, *"let us go forth to Him, outside the camp."* He who is willing to lose and say farewell to everything, in order that Jesus may sanctify him, will not fail to obtain the blessing. He who is willing at any cost to experience the full power of the precious blood can confidently know that he will be sanctified by Jesus Himself, through that blood.

*"May the God of peace Himself sanctify you completely"* (1 Thess. 5:23). Amen.

chapter 6

# Cleansed by the Blood to Serve the Living God

*Now in Christ Jesus you who once were far off have been brought near by the blood of Christ.*
—Ephesians 2:13

*How much more shall the blood of Christ...cleanse your conscience...to serve the living God?*
—Hebrews 9:14

A fter our study of sanctification through the blood, we will now consider what is the intimate relationship with God into which we are introduced by sanctification.

Sanctification and intimacy are closely related facts in Scripture. Apart from sanctification there can be no such relationship. How could one who is unholy have fellowship with a holy God? On the other hand, without this relationship there can be no growth in holiness; it is always and only in fellowship with the Holy One that holiness can be found.

The intimate connection between sanctification and relationship appears plainly in the story of the revolt of Nadab and Abihu. God made this the occasion of a clear statement concerning the distinctive nature of the priesthood in Israel. He said, *"I will be sanctified in them that come nigh me"* (Lev. 10:3 KJV). Then again in the conspiracy of Korah against Moses and Aaron, Moses speaking for God said, *"Tomorrow morning the LORD will show who is His and who is holy, and will cause him to come near to Him. That one whom He chooses He will cause to come near to Him"* (Num. 16:5).

We have already seen that God's election and separation unto Himself of His own are closely bound up with sanctification. It is evident here, also, that the glory and blessing secured by this election to holiness is nothing else than intimacy with God. This is indeed the highest, the one perfect blessing for man, who was created for God and to enjoy His love. The psalmist sang, *"Blessed is the man You choose, and cause to approach You, that he may dwell in Your courts"* (Ps. 65:4). In the nature of the case, consecration to God and nearness to Him are the same thing.

The sprinkling of the blood, which sanctifies man unto God and takes possession of him for God, bestows at the same time the right of intimacy.

It was thus with the priests in Israel. In the record of their consecration we read, *"Then [Moses] brought Aaron's sons. And Moses put some of the blood on the tips of their right ears, on the thumbs of their right hands"* (Lev. 8:24). Those who belong to God may, and indeed must, live in nearness to Him; they belong to Him. This is illustrated in the case of our Lord, our great High Priest, who *"with His own blood...entered the Most Holy Place once for all"* (Heb. 9:12).

It is the same with every believer, according to the Word: *"Therefore, brethren, having boldness to enter the Holiest by the blood of Jesus...let us draw near...having our hearts sprinkled from an evil conscience"* (Heb. 10:19, 22). The word *enter,* as used in this verse, is the word used of the approach of the priest to God. In the same way, in the book of Revelation, our right to draw near as priests is declared to be by the power of the blood. We were *"washed...from our sins in His own blood"*—the blood of Him who *"has made us kings and priests to His God and Father, to Him be glory and dominion forever and ever"* (Rev. 1:5–6). *"These are the ones who...washed their robes and made them white in the blood of the Lamb. Therefore they are before the throne of God, and serve Him day and night in His temple"* (Rev. 7:14–15).

One of the most glorious blessings made possible for us by the power of the blood is that of drawing near the throne into the very presence of God. So that we may understand what this blessing means, let us consider what is contained in it. It includes:

• First, the right to dwell in the presence of God

- Second, the duty of offering spiritual sacrifices to God
- Third, the power to procure blessing for others

## THE RIGHT TO DWELL IN THE PRESENCE OF GOD

Although this privilege belonged exclusively to the priests in Israel, we know that *they* had free access to the dwelling place of God. They had to abide there continually. As members of the household of God, they ate the showbread and partook of the sacrifices. A true Israelite thought there was no higher privilege than this. It was thus expressed by the psalmist, *"Blessed* [happy] *is the man You choose, and cause to approach You, that he may dwell in Your courts. We shall be satisfied with the goodness of Your house, of Your holy temple"* (Ps. 65:4).

It was because of the manifested presence of God there that believers, in those old days, longed for the house of God with such strong desire. The cry was, *"When shall I come and appear before God?"* (Ps. 42:2). They understood something of the spiritual meaning of the privilege of drawing near to God. It represented to them the enjoyment of His love, His fellowship, His protection, and His blessing. They could exclaim, *"Oh, how great is Your goodness, which You have laid up for those who fear You....You shall hide them in the secret place of Your presence"* (Ps. 31:19–20).

The precious blood of Christ has opened the way for the believer into God's presence, and intimacy with Him is a deep, spiritual reality. He who knows the full power of the blood is brought so near that he can always live in the immediate presence of God and in the enjoyment of the unspeakable blessings attached to it. There, the child of God has the assurance of God's love; he experiences and enjoys it. God Himself imparts it. He lives daily in the friendship and fellowship of God. As God's child he makes known to the Father, with perfect freedom, his thoughts and wishes. In this intimacy with God, he possesses all that he needs; he lacks no *"good thing"* (Ps. 84:11). His soul is kept in perfect rest and peace, because God is with him (Isa. 26:3). He receives all necessary direction and teaching. God's eye is ever upon him, guiding him. In intimacy with God, he is able to hear the softest whispers of the Holy Spirit. He learns to understand the slightest sign of his Father's will and to follow it. His strength continually increases, for God is his strength, and God is ever with him.

Fellowship with God has a wonderful influence on his life and character. The presence of God fills him with humility, fear, and a holy circumspection. He lives as in the presence of a king. Fellowship with God produces God-like inclinations in him. Beholding the image of God, he is changed into the same image (2 Cor. 3:18). Dwelling with the Holy One makes him holy. He can say, *"It is good for me to draw near to God"* (Ps. 73:28).

Oh, you who are the children of the new covenant, do you not have a thousand times more reasons to speak in the same way, now that the veil has been torn asunder and the way opened for living always in God's holy presence? May this high privilege awaken our desires. Intimacy with God, fellowship with God, dwelling with God and He with us—may it become impossible for us to be satisfied with anything less. This is the true Christian life.

But relationship with God is not only so blessed because of the salvation enjoyed in it, but also on account of the service that may be rendered because of that intimacy. Let us therefore consider the spiritual sacrifices that we may offer to God.

## THE DUTY OF OFFERING SPIRITUAL SACRIFICES TO GOD

Our duty to bring spiritual sacrifices to God is a further privilege. The enjoyment of the priests in drawing near to God in His dwelling place was subordinated entirely to something higher. They were there as servants of the Holy Place, to bring to God, in His house, that which belonged to Him. Only as they found joy in drawing near to God could that service become truly blessed.

The service consisted in the bringing in of the blood of sprinkling; the preparation of the incense to fill the house with its fragrance; and, further, the ordering of everything that pertained, according to God's word, to the arrangement of His house.

Their duty was to so guard and serve and provide for the dwelling place of the Most High, that it would be worthy of Him and of His glory, and that His good pleasure in it might be fulfilled.

If the blood of Jesus brings us near, it is also, chiefly, so that we will live before God as His servants and bring to Him the spiritual sacrifices that are well-pleasing in His sight.

The priests brought the blood into the Holy Place before God. In our relationship with God, there is no offering that we can bring more pleasing to Him than a believing honoring of the blood of the Lamb. Every act of humble trust or of hearty thanksgiving, in which we direct the attention of the Father to the blood and speak its praises, is acceptable to Him. Our whole abiding there, and our intimacy, from hour to hour must be a glorifying of the blood before God.

The priests brought the incense into the Holy Place so as to fill God's house with fragrance. The prayers of God's people are the delightful incense with which He desires to be surrounded in His habitation. The value of prayer does not consist merely in its being the means of obtaining things we need. No! It has a higher aim than that. It is a ministry of God in which He delights.

The life of a believer who truly enjoys drawing near to God through the blood is a life of unceasing prayer. In a deep sense of dependence, for each moment, for each step, grace is sought and expected. In the blessed conviction of God's nearness and unchanging goodness, the soul pours itself out in the confident assurance of faith that every promise will be fulfilled. In the midst of the joy that the light of God's face bestows, thanksgiving and adoration arise along with prayer.

These are the spiritual offerings—the offerings of the lips of the priests of God—continually presented to Him. They have been sanctified and brought near by the blood so that they might ever live and walk in His presence.

But there is still something more. It was the duty of the priests to attend to everything for cleansing or provision that was necessary in the ministry of the house. What is the ministry now, under the new covenant? Thanks be to God, there are no outward or exclusive arrangements for divine worship. No! The Father has so ordered that whatever anyone does who is walking in His presence, just because of this fact, presents a spiritual offering to God. Everything the believer does, if only he does it as in God's presence and as a service to God, it is a priestly sacrifice, well-pleasing to God. *"Therefore, whether you eat or drink, or whatever you do, do all to the glory of God"* (1 Cor. 10:31). *"Whatever you do in word or deed, do all in the name of the Lord Jesus, giving thanks to God the Father through Him"* (Col. 3:17). In this way, all our actions become thank-offerings to God.

How little Christians recognize the glory of a life of complete consecration, to be spent always in intimacy with God!

Cleansed, sanctified, and brought near by the power of the blood, my earthly calling, my whole life, even my eating and drinking are a spiritual service. My work, my business, my money, my house, and everything with which I have dealings becomes sanctified by the presence of God, because I walk in His presence. The poorest earthly work is a priestly service when it is performed by a priest of God's temple.

But even this does not exhaust the glory of the blessing of intimacy. The highest blessing of the priesthood is that the priest appears as the representative of others before God.

## THE POWER TO PROCURE BLESSING FOR OTHERS

This is what gives full glory to nearness to God.

In Israel the priests were the mediators between God and the people. They carried into the presence of God the sins and needs of the people; they obtained from God the power to declare the pardon of sin and the right of blessing the people.

This privilege now belongs to all believers, as the priestly family of the new covenant. When God permitted His redeemed ones to approach Him through the blood, it was so that He might bless them in order that they might become a blessing to others. Priestly mediation; a priestly heart that can have the needed sympathy with those who are weak; a priestly power to obtain the blessing of God in the temple and convey it to others—in these things, intimacy, the drawing near to God through the blood, manifests its highest power and glory.

We can exercise our priestly dignity in a twofold manner: first, by intercession, and second, as instruments.

- ## BY INTERCESSION

The ministry of intercession is one of the highest privileges of the child of God. It does not mean that in this ministry we, having ascertained that there is a need in the world or in some particular person, pour out our wishes in prayer to God, asking for the necessary supply. That is good, so far as it goes, and brings a blessing with it. But the ministry of intercession is something more wonderful than that and finds its power in *"the prayer of faith"* (James 5:15). This *"prayer of faith"* is a different thing than the outpouring of our wishes to God, and leaving them with Him.

In the true *"prayer of faith,"* the intercessor must spend time with God to take hold of the promises of His Word, and he must permit himself to be taught by the Holy Spirit whether the promises can be applied to this particular case. He takes upon himself, as a burden, the sin and need that are the subject of prayer. He then lays hold of the promise concerning it, as though it were for himself. He remains in the presence of God, until God by His Spirit awakens the faith that in this matter the prayer has been heard. In this way parents sometimes pray for their children, ministers for their congregations, laborers in God's vineyard for the souls committed to them, until they know that their prayer is heard. It is the blood that, by its power of bringing us near to God, bestows such wonderful liberty to pray until the answer is obtained.

Oh, if we understood more perfectly what it really means to dwell in the presence of God, we would manifest more power in the exercise of our holy priesthood!

- ## AS INSTRUMENTS

A further manifestation of our priestly mediation is that we not only obtain some blessing for others by intercession, but we become the instruments by whom it is ministered. Every believer is called and feels himself compelled by love to labor on behalf of others. He knows that God has blessed him so that he might be a blessing to others, yet the complaint is generally that believers have no power for this work of bringing blessing to others. They are not, they say, in a condition to exercise an influence over others by their words. This is no surprise, if they will not dwell in the sanctuary. We read that *"the LORD separated the tribe of Levi...to stand before the LORD to minister to Him and to bless in His name"* (Deut. 10:8). The priestly power of blessing depends on the priestlike life in the presence of God. He who experiences there the power of the blood to preserve him, the helpless one, will have courage to believe that the blood can really deliver others. The holy life-giving power of the blood will create in him the same disposition as that in which Jesus shed it—the sacrifice of himself to redeem others.

In intimacy with God, our love will be set on fire by the love of God; our belief that God will surely make use of us will be strengthened; the Spirit of Jesus will take possession of us to enable us to labor in humility, in wisdom, and in power; and our weakness and poverty will become the vessels in which God's power can work. From our words and examples, blessing will flow because we dwell with Him who is pure blessing, and He will not permit anyone to be near Him without also being filled with His blessing.

Beloved, is not the life prepared for us a glorious and a blessed one: the enjoyment of the blessedness of being near to God; the carrying out of the ministry of His house; the imparting of His blessing to others?

Let no one think that the full blessing is not for him, that such a life is too high for him. In the power of Jesus' blood, we have the assurance that this drawing near is also for us, if only we wholly yield ourselves to it.

For those who truly desire this blessing, I give the following advice. Remember that this, and nothing less, is designed for you. All of us who are God's children have been brought near by the blood. All of us can desire the full experience of it. Let us only hold fast to this: "The life of intimacy with God is for me." The Father does not wish that one of His children should be far off. We cannot please our God as we ought if we live without this blessing. We are priests; grace to live as priests is prepared for us; free entrance into the sanctuary as our abiding place is for us. We can be assured of this: as His children, we have been given God's indwelling holy presence as our right. Let us lay hold of this.

Seek to make the full power of the blood your own possession in all its blessed effects. It is in the power of the blood that relationship is possible. Let your heart be filled with faith in the power of the blood of reconciliation. Sin has been so entirely atoned for and blotted out that its power to keep you away from God has been completely, and forever, taken away. Live in the joyful knowledge that sin is powerless to separate you one moment from God. Believe that by the blood you have been fully justified, and thus you have a righteous claim to a place in the sanctuary. Let the blood also cleanse you. From the fellowship that follows, you can expect the inner deliverance from the defilement of sin that still dwells in you. Say with the Scriptures, *"How much more shall the blood of Christ...cleanse your conscience...to serve the living God?"* Let the blood sanctify you, separate you for God in undivided consecration, to be filled by Him. Let the pardoning, cleansing, sanctifying power of the blood have free course in you. You will discover how this brings you, as it were, automatically near to God and protects you.

Do not fear to expect that Jesus Himself will reveal in you the power of the blood to bring you near to God. The blood was shed to unite us to God. The blood has accomplished its work, and will perfect it in you. The blood has unspeakable virtue and glory in Gods sight.

The mercy seat sprinkled with blood is the chosen place of God's abode and is His throne of grace. He draws near with joy and good pleasure to the heart that surrenders itself entirely to the effectiveness of the blood.

The blood has irresistible power. Through the blood Jesus was raised up from the grave and carried into heaven. Be assured that the blood is able to preserve you every day in God's presence by its divine life-giving power.

As precious and all powerful as the blood is, so sure and certain is your abiding with God, if only your trust is steadfast.

*"Washed...and made...white in the blood of the Lamb. Therefore they are before the throne of God, and serve Him day and night in His temple"* (Rev. 7:14–15). This word about the eternal glory also has a bearing upon our lives on earth. The fuller our faith and experience of the power of the blood, the closer the intimacy; the surer our abiding near the throne, the wider the entrance to the unbroken ministry of God in His

sanctuary; and here on earth, the greater the power to serve the living God, the richer the priestly blessing that you will spread around you. O Lord, may this word have its full power over us now, here, and hereafter!

# chapter 7

# Dwelling in "The Holiest"
# through the Blood

*Therefore, brethren, having boldness to enter the Holiest by the blood of Jesus, by a new and living way which He consecrated for us, through the veil, that is, His flesh, and having a High Priest over the house of God, let us draw near with a true heart in full assurance of faith, having our hearts sprinkled from an evil conscience and our bodies washed with pure water.*
—Hebrews 10:19–22

I n the words of this Scripture passage, we have a summary of the chief contents of this epistle, and of the good news about God's grace, as the Holy Spirit caused it to be presented to the Hebrews and also to us.

Through sin, man was driven out of Eden, away from the presence and fellowship of God. God in His mercy sought from the beginning to restore the broken fellowship.

To this end, He gave to Israel, through the shadowy types of the tabernacle, the expectation of a time to come, when the wall of partition would be removed, so that His people might dwell in His presence. *"When shall I come and appear before God?"* (Ps. 42:2) was the longing sigh of the believers of the old covenant.

It is also the sigh of many of God's children under the new covenant who do not understand that the way into the Holiest has really been opened, and that every child of God may and ought to have his real dwelling place there.

Oh, my brothers and sisters, who long to experience the full power of the redemption that Jesus has accomplished, come with me to hear what our God says to us about the opened Holy Place, and the freedom with which we can enter through the blood.

The passage at the beginning of this chapter shows us in a first series of four words what God has prepared for us, as the sure ground on which our fellowship with Him may rest. Then, in a second series of four words that follow, we learn how we may be prepared to enter into that fellowship and to live in it.

Read the text with attention, and you will see that the words *"let us draw near"* are the center of it all. Let us consider the following:

- First, what God has prepared for us
- Second, how God prepares us for what He has prepared for us
- Finally, *"let us draw near"*

> *Therefore, brethren, having boldness to enter the Holiest by the blood of Jesus, by a new and living way which He consecrated for us, through the veil, that is, His flesh, and having a High Priest over the house of God, let us draw near with a true heart in full assurance of faith, having our hearts sprinkled from an evil conscience and our bodies washed with pure water.*

## WHAT GOD HAS PREPARED FOR US

### • THE HOLIEST

*"Having boldness to enter the Holiest...let us draw near."*

To bring us into the Holiest is the end of the redemptive work of Jesus, and he who does not know what the Holiest is cannot enjoy the full benefit of redemption.

What is this Holiest? It is just the place where God dwells: the Holiest, the dwelling place of the Most High. This does not refer only to heaven, but to the holiest spiritual place of God's presence.

Under the old covenant there was a material sanctuary (Heb. 8:2; 9:1), the dwelling place of God, in which the priests dwelt in God's presence and served Him. Under the new covenant there is the true spiritual tabernacle, not confined to any place; this is the Holiest, where God reveals Himself (John 4:23–25).

What a glorious privilege it is to enter into the Holiest and dwell there, to walk all day long in the presence of God. What a rich blessing is poured out there. In the Holiest, the favor and fellowship of God are enjoyed, the life and blessing of God are experienced, the power and joy of God are found. Life is spent in the Holiest in priestly purity and consecration; there the incense of sweet savor is burned and sacrifices acceptable to God are offered. It is a holy life of prayer and blessedness.

Under the old covenant everything was material; the sanctuary was also material. Under the new covenant everything is spiritual; the true sanctuary owes its existence to the power of the Holy Spirit. Through the Holy Spirit, a real life in the Holiest is possible, and the knowledge that God walks there can be as certain as in the case of the priests of old. The Spirit makes real in our experience the work that Jesus has accomplished.

Believer in Jesus Christ, do you have liberty to enter into and abide in the Holiest? As one who has been redeemed, it is a fitting thing for you to make your home there, and not elsewhere, for Christ cannot elsewhere reveal the full power of His redemption. But there, He can bless you richly. Understand it, then, and let the purpose of God and of our Lord Jesus be yours also. May it be the one desire of our hearts to enter into the Holiest, to live in the Holiest, to minister in the Holiest. We can confidently expect the Holy Spirit to give us a right idea of the glory of entering into a dwelling in the Holiest.

### • LIBERTY THROUGH THE BLOOD

Admission to the Holiest, like the Holiest itself, belongs to God. God Himself thought of it and prepared it; we have the liberty, the freedom, the right to enter by the blood of Jesus. The blood of Jesus exercises such a wonderful power that through it a son of perdition may obtain full freedom to enter into the divine sanctuary, the Holiest. *"You who once were far off have been brought near by the blood of Christ"* (Eph. 2:13).

And how does the blood exercise this wonderful power? Scripture says, *"The life...is in the blood"* (Lev. 17:11). The power of the blood is in the worth of the life. In the blood of Jesus, the power of the divine life dwelt and worked; in Him the blood already has almighty and unceasing power.

But that power could not be exercised for reconciliation until it was first shed. By bearing the punishment of sin unto death, the Lord Jesus conquered the power of sin and brought it to nothing. *"The strength of sin is the law"* (1 Cor. 15:56). By perfectly fulfilling the law when He shed His blood under its curse, His blood has made sin entirely powerless. So the blood has its wonderful power, not only because the life of God's Son was in it, but because it was given as an atonement for sin. This is the reason Scripture speaks so highly about the blood. Through the blood of the everlasting covenant, God has brought our Lord Jesus from the dead (Heb. 13:20).

Through His own blood He has entered into the Holiest (Heb. 9:12). The power of the blood has entirely destroyed the power of sin, death, the grave, and hell, so that our Surety could go out from hell. The power of the blood has opened heaven so that our Surety could freely enter its blessedness.

And now, we also have liberty to enter through the blood. Sin took away our liberty of approach to God; the blood perfectly restores this liberty to us. He who will take time to meditate on the power of that blood, taking hold of it believingly for himself, will obtain a wonderful view of the liberty and directness with which we can now have intimacy with God.

Oh, the divine, wonderful power of the blood! Through the blood, we enter into the Holiest. The blood pleads for us and in us with an eternal, ceaseless effect. It removes sin from God's sight and from our consciences. Every moment we have free, full entrance, and we can have intimacy with God through the blood.

Oh, that the Holy Spirit might reveal to us the full power of the blood! Under His teaching, we enjoy a full entrance to intimate fellowship with the Father. Our life is in the Holiest through the blood.

### • "A New and Living Way"

*"Therefore, brethren, having boldness to enter the Holiest by the blood of Jesus, by a new and living way which He consecrated for us, through the veil, that is, His flesh."* The blood bestows our right of entrance. The way, as a living and life-giving one, bestows the power. That He has consecrated this way by His flesh does not mean that this is merely a different way of saying, *"Through His blood"* (Eph. 1:7; Col. 1:14). By no means.

74

Jesus has shed His blood for us; in this particular action we cannot follow Him. But the way by which He walked when He shed His blood, the tearing of the veil of His flesh—in that way we must follow Him. What He did by opening that way is a living power that draws and carries us as we enter the Holiest. The lesson we have to learn here is this: the way into the Holiest is through the torn veil of the flesh.

It was so with Jesus. The veil that separated God and us was the flesh. Sin has its power in the flesh, and only through the taking away of sin may the veil be removed. When Jesus came in the flesh, He could tear the veil only by dying. Therefore, in order to bring to nothing the power of the flesh and sin, He offered up the flesh and delivered it to death. This is what gave worth and power to the shedding of His blood.

And this now remains the law for each one who desires to enter the Holiest through His blood: it must be through the torn veil of the flesh. The blood demands, the blood accomplishes the tearing of the flesh. Where the blood of Jesus works powerfully, there always follows the putting to death of the flesh. He who desires to spare the flesh cannot enter into the Holiest. The flesh must be sacrificed, given over to death. To the extent that the believer perceives the sinfulness of his flesh, and puts to death all that is in the flesh, he will better understand the power of the blood. The believer does not do this in his own strength; he comes by a living way that Jesus has consecrated. The life-giving power of Jesus works in this way. The Christian is crucified and dead with Jesus: *"Those who are Christ's have crucified the flesh"* (Gal. 5:24). It is in fellowship with Christ that we enter through the veil.

Oh, glorious way, the *"new and living way,"* full of life-giving power, that Christ has *"consecrated for us"*! By this way, we have the liberty to enter into the Holiest by the blood of Jesus. May the Lord God lead us along this way, through the torn veil, through the death of the flesh, to the full life of the Spirit. Then we will find our dwelling place within the veil, in the Holiest with God. Each sacrifice of the flesh leads us, through the blood, further into the Holiest.[*]

---

[*] Author's Note: Compare further, with care, 1 Peter 3:18, *"Christ...*[was] *put to death in the flesh"*; 1 Peter 4:1, *"Christ suffered for us in the flesh"*; and Romans 8:3, *"God...condemned sin in the flesh."*

### • THE GREAT PRIEST

*"Having a High Priest over the house of God, let us draw near."*

Praised be God, we have not only the work, but also the living person of Christ, as we enter the Holiest; not only the blood and the living way, but Jesus Himself, as *"High Priest over the house of God."*

The priests who went into the earthly sanctuary could do so only because of their relationship to the high priest; none but the sons of Aaron were priests. We have an entrance into the Holiest because of our relationship to the Lord Jesus. He said to the Father, *"Here am I and the children whom the LORD has given me!"* (Isa. 8:18).

He is the great Priest. The epistle to the Hebrews has shown us that He is the true Melchizedek, the eternal Son, who has an eternal and changeless priesthood, and as Priest is seated on the throne. He lives there to pray always; *"therefore He is also able to save to the uttermost those who come to God through Him"* (Heb. 7:25), a great and all-powerful Priest.

*"A High Priest over the house of God,"* He is appointed over the entire ministry of the Holiest, of the house of God. All the people of God are under His care. If we desire to enter the Holiest, He is there to receive us, and to present us to the Father. He Himself will complete in us the sprinkling of the blood. Through the blood He has entered; through the blood He also brings us in. He will teach us all the duties of the Holiest and of our responsibilities there. He makes acceptable our prayers, our offerings, and the duties of our ministry, however weak they are. Moreover, He bestows on us heavenly light and heavenly power for our work and our lives in the Holiest. It is He who imparts the life, and the Spirit of the Holiest. Just as His blood procured an entrance, His sacrifice of His flesh is the *"living way."* As we enter, it is He by whom we are kept abiding there, and are able always to walk in a way that is well-pleasing to God. As the sympathetic High Priest, He knows how to stoop to each one, even the weakest. Yes, this is what makes intimacy with God in the Holiest so attractive: we find Jesus there, as a *"High Priest over the house of God."*

And just when it seems to us as if the Holiest is too high or too holy for us, and that we cannot understand what the power of the blood is, and how we are to walk in the *"new and living way,"* then we may look up to the living Savior Himself to teach us and to bring us Himself into the Holiest. He is the *"Priest over the house of God."* You have only to cling to Him, and you will be in the Holiest.

*"Let us draw near,"* seeing that we have the Holiest where God waits for us, the blood that gives us liberty, the living way that carries us, and the High Priest to help us. *"Let us draw near."* Yes, *"let us draw near."* Let nothing hold us back from making use of these wonderful blessings that God has designed for us. It is into the Holiest that we are to enter; our right has been obtained for us by the blood of Jesus; by His own footsteps He has consecrated the way. He lives in His eternal priesthood to receive us in the Holiest, to sanctify, to preserve, to bless us. Oh, let us no longer hesitate or turn back. Let us sacrifice all for this one thing; in view of what God has prepared for us, *"let us draw near"* by the hand of Jesus to appear before our Father and to find our life in the light of His countenance.

And do we desire to know how we can now be prepared to enter? Our text gives us a glorious answer to this question.

## How We Are Prepared

### • Draw Near with a True Heart

*"With a true heart"*—this is the second series of four words, which tells us how we are prepared. This is the first of the four demands made on the believer who wishes to *"draw near."* It is coupled with the second demand, *"in full assurance of faith,"* and it is chiefly in its union with the second demand that we correctly understand what *"a true heart"* means.

The preaching of the Gospel always begins with repentance and faith. Man cannot receive God's grace by faith if, at the same time, sin is not forsaken. In the progress of the life of faith, this law is always binding. The *"full assurance of faith"* cannot be reached without *"a true heart,"* a heart that is wholly honest with God, that is surrendered entirely to Him.

The Holiest cannot be entered without *"a true heart,"* a heart that is truly desirous of seeking what it claims to seek.

*"Let us draw near with a true heart"*—a heart that truly desires to forsake everything to dwell in the Holiest, and forsaking everything, to possess God; a heart that truly abandons everything in order to yield itself to the authority and power of the blood; a heart that truly chooses the *"new and living way"* in order to go through the veil with Christ by the tearing of the flesh; a heart that truly and entirely gives itself to the indwelling and lordship of Jesus.

*"Let us draw near with a true heart."* Without a true heart there is no entrance into the Holiest.

But who has a true heart? The new heart that God has given is *"a true heart."* Recognize this. By the power of the Spirit of God who dwells in that new heart, place yourself, by an exercise of your will, on the side of God against the sin that is still in your flesh. Say to the Lord Jesus, the High Priest, that you submit and cast down before Him every sin and all of your self-life, forsaking all to follow Him.

And regarding the hidden depths of sin in your flesh, of which you are not yet conscious, and the malice of your heart— for them provision is also made. *"Search me, O God, and know my heart"* (Ps. 139:23). Subject yourself continually to the heart-searching light of the Spirit. He will uncover what is hidden from you. He who does this has *"a true heart"* to enter into the Holiest.

Let us not be afraid to say to God that we *"draw near with a true heart."* Let us be assured that God will not judge us according to the perfection of what we do, but according to the honesty with which we yield ourselves to lay aside every known sin, and with which we accept conviction by the Holy Spirit of all our hidden sin. A heart that does this honestly is, in God's sight, *"a true heart."* And with *"a true heart"* the Holiest is approached through the blood. Praised be God! Through His Spirit, we have *"a true heart."*

## • IN FULL ASSURANCE OF FAITH

We know what place faith occupies in God's dealings with man. *"Without faith it is impossible to please Him"* (Heb. 11:6).

Here at the entrance into the Holiest, all depends on the *"full assurance of faith."*

There must be a *"full assurance of faith"* that there is a Holy Place where we can dwell and walk with God; that the power of the precious blood has conquered sin so perfectly that nothing can prevent our undisturbed fellowship with God; that the way that Jesus has sanctified through His flesh is a living way, which carries those who tread on it with eternal living power; that the great *"High Priest over the house of God"* can *"save to the uttermost those who come to God through Him"* (Heb. 7:25); and that He by His Spirit works in us everything that is necessary for life in the Holiest. These things we must believe and hold fast in the *"full assurance of faith."*

But how can I get there? How can my faith grow to this full assurance? By fellowship with *"Jesus, the author and finisher of our faith"* (Heb. 12:2). As the great *"Priest over the house of God,"* He enables us to take hold of faith. By considering Him, His wonderful love, His perfect work, His precious and all-powerful blood, faith is sustained and strengthened. God has given Him to awaken faith. By keeping our eyes fixed on Him, faith and the *"full assurance of faith"* become ours.

In handling the Word of God, remember that *"faith comes by hearing, and hearing by the word of God"* (Rom. 10:16). Faith comes by the Word and grows by the Word, but not the Word as letter, but as the voice of Jesus. Only *"the words that I speak to you are spirit, and they are life"* (John 6:63); only in Him are the promises of God *"Yes, and...Amen"* (2 Cor. 1:20). Take time to meditate on the Word and treasure it in your heart, but always with a heart set on Jesus Himself. It is faith in Jesus that saves. The Word that is taken to Jesus in prayer and talked over with Him is the Word that is effective.

Remember that *"whoever has, to him more will be given"* (Matt. 13:12). Make use of the faith that you have; exercise it; declare it; and let your believing trust in God become the chief occupation of your life. God wishes to have children who believe Him; He desires nothing so much as faith. Get accustomed to say with each prayer, "Lord I believe that I will obtain this." As you read each promise in Scripture, say, "Lord, I believe You will fulfill this in me." The whole day through, make it your holy habit in everything—yes, in everything—to exercise trust in God's guidance and God's blessing.

To enter into the Holiest, *"full assurance of faith"* is necessary. *"Let us draw near...in full assurance of faith."* Redemption through the blood is so perfect and powerful; the love and grace of Jesus so overflowing; the blessedness of dwelling in the Holiest is so surely for us and within our reach—*"let us draw near ...in full assurance of faith."*

### • WITH OUR HEARTS CLEANSED

*"Let us draw near...having our hearts sprinkled* [cleansed] *from an evil conscience."*

The heart is the center of human life, and the conscience is the center of the heart. By his conscience, a person realizes his relationship to God; and an evil conscience tells him that all is not right between God and himself—not merely that he commits sin, but that he is sinful and alienated from God. A good or clear conscience bears witness that he is well-pleasing to God (Heb. 11:5). It bears witness not only that his sins are forgiven but also that his heart is sincere before God. He who desires to enter the Holiest must have his heart cleansed from an evil conscience. The words are translated *"our hearts sprinkled from an evil conscience."* It is the sprinkling of the blood that avails. The blood of Christ will purify your conscience to serve the living God.

We have already seen that entrance to the Holiest is by the blood, by which Jesus went to the Father. But that is not enough. There is a twofold sprinkling: the priests who drew near to God were not only reconciled through the sprinkling of blood before God on the altar, but their very persons had to be sprinkled with the blood. The blood of Jesus must be brought by the Holy Spirit into direct contact with our hearts so that our hearts become cleansed from an evil conscience. The blood removes all self-condemnation. It cleanses the conscience. Conscience then witnesses that the removal of guilt has been so perfectly completed that there is no longer the least separation between God and us. Conscience bears witness that we are well-pleasing to God; that our hearts are cleansed; that we through the sprinkling of the blood are in true living fellowship with God. Yes, the blood of Jesus Christ cleanses from all sin, not only from the guilt but also from the stain of sin.

Through the power of the blood, our fallen nature is prevented from exercising its power. Just as a fountain by its gentle spray cleanses the grass that otherwise would be covered with dust and keeps it fresh and green, so the blood works with a ceaseless effect to keep the soul clean. A heart that lives under the full power of the blood is a clean heart, cleansed from a guilty conscience, prepared to *"draw near"* with perfect freedom. The whole heart, the whole inner being, is cleansed by a divine operation.

*"Let us draw near...having our hearts sprinkled from an evil conscience."* Let us *"in full assurance of faith"* believe that our hearts are cleansed. Let us honor the blood greatly, by confessing before God that it cleanses us. The High Priest will, by His Holy Spirit, make us understand the full meaning and power of having the heart cleansed by the blood, having the entrance to the Holy Place prepared through the blood, and having our hearts prepared by the blood for entrance. Having the heart cleansed, how glorious, then, it is to enter into and to abide in the Holiest!

### • WITH THE BODY WASHED

*"Let us draw near...having...our bodies washed with pure water."*

We belong to two worlds, the seen and the unseen. We have an inner, hidden life that brings us into touch with God, and an outer, bodily life by which we are in relationship with mankind. If this Scripture refers to the body, it refers to the entire life in the body, with all its activities.

The heart must be sprinkled with blood; the body must be washed with pure water. When the priests were consecrated, they were washed with water as well as sprinkled with blood (Exod. 29:4, 20–21). And if they went into the Holy Place, there was not only the altar with its blood, but also the laver with its water. Christ, likewise, came *"by water and blood"* (1 John 5:6). He had His baptism with water and later with blood (Luke 12:50).

For us there is also a twofold cleansing with water and blood. Baptism with water is for repentance, for laying aside of sin. *"Be baptized, and wash away your sins"* (Acts 22:16). While the blood cleanses the heart, the inner man, baptism is the yielding of the body, with all its visible life, to separation from sin.

So *"let us draw near...having our hearts sprinkled from an evil conscience and our bodies washed with pure water."* The power of the blood to cleanse inwardly cannot be experienced unless we also cleanse ourselves from all filthiness of the flesh. The divine work of cleansing by the sprinkling of blood and the human work of cleansing by laying aside sin are inseparable.

We must be clean to enter into the Holiest. Just as you would never dream of entering into the presence of a king unwashed, so you cannot imagine that you could come into the presence of God, in the Holy Place, if you are not cleansed from every sin. In the blood of Christ that cleanses from all sin, God has bestowed on you the power to cleanse yourself. Your desire to live with God in the Holiest must always be united with the most careful laying aside of even the least sin. The unclean may not enter the Holiest.

Praised be God, He desires to have us there. As His priests, we must minister to Him there. He desires our purity so that we may enjoy the blessing of the Holiest—that is, His holy fellowship. And He has taken care that, through the blood and by the Spirit, we may be clean.

*"Let us draw near...having our hearts sprinkled from an evil conscience and our bodies washed with pure water."*

## "LET US DRAW NEAR"

The Holiest is open even for those in our congregations who have not yet truly turned to the Lord. For them the sanctuary has been opened. The precious blood, the living way, and the High Priest are for them. With great confidence we dare to invite even them. *"Let us draw near."* Oh, do not despise it, my friends still far from God; oh, despise no longer God's wonderful grace. Draw near to the Father who has so earnestly sent this invitation to you, who at the cost of the blood of His Son has opened a way for you into the Holiest, who waits in love to receive you again into His dwelling place as His child. Oh! I beseech you, *"let us* [all] *draw near."* Jesus Christ, the *"High Priest over the house of God,"* is a perfect Savior.

*"Let us draw near."* The invitation comes especially to all believers. Do not be satisfied to stand outside the sanctuary. It is not sufficient to cherish the hope that your sins are forgiven. *"Let us draw near";* let us enter within the veil; let us in spirit press on to real nearness to our God. *"Let us draw near"* and live nearer to God, wholly taking up our abode in His holy presence. *"Let us draw near";* our place is the innermost sanctuary.

*"Let us draw near with a true heart in full assurance of faith."* He who gives himself sincerely and entirely to God will through the Holy Spirit experience the *"full assurance of faith"* to take for himself, freely and gladly, all that the Word has promised. Our weakness of faith arises from duplicity of heart. *"Let us draw near with a true heart in full assurance"* that the blessing is ours. The blood has so perfectly atoned for and conquered sin that nothing can hold the believer back from free admission to God.

*"Let us draw near...having our hearts sprinkled from an evil conscience and our bodies washed with pure water."* Let us receive into our hearts faith in the perfect power of the blood, and let us lay aside everything that is not in accord with the purity of the Holy Place. Then we will begin to feel ourselves daily more at home in the Holiest. In Christ, who is our Life, we are also there. Then we will learn to carry on all our work in the Holiest. All that we do is a spiritual sacrifice well-pleasing to God in Jesus Christ. Dear brothers and sisters, *"let us draw near"* as God waits for us in the Holiest.

*"Let us draw near."* This call has special reference to prayer. Not as though we, as priests, are not always in the Holiest, but there are moments of closer fellowship when the soul turns itself entirely to God to be engaged with Him alone. Unfortunately, our prayer is too often a calling out to God from a distance, with little power in it. Let us with each prayer see that we are really in the Holiest. Let us with hearts perfectly sprinkled from an evil conscience, in silent faith, take hold of the full effect of the blood, by which sin, as a separation between God and us, is entirely removed. Let us take time until we know, "I am in the Holiest through the blood," and then pray. Then we

can lay our desires and wishes before our Father in the assurance that they are acceptable incense. Then prayer is a true drawing near to God, an exercise of inner fellowship with Him; then we have courage and power to carry on our work of priestly intercession and to pray blessings on others. He who dwells in the Holy Place through the power of the blood is truly one of God's saints, and the power of God's holy and blessed presence goes out from him upon those who are around him.

Brothers and sisters, *"let us draw near."* Let us pray for ourselves, for one another, for everyone. Let the Holiest so become our fixed abode that we may carry with us everywhere the presence of our God. Let this be the fountain of life for us that grows *"from strength to strength"* (Ps. 84:7), *"from glory to glory"* (2 Cor. 3:18), always dwelling in the Holiest by the blood. Amen.

chapter 8

# Life in the Blood

*Jesus said to them, "Most assuredly, I say to you, unless you eat the
flesh of the Son of Man and drink His blood, you have no life in
you. Whoever eats My flesh and drinks My blood has eternal life,
and I will raise him up at the last day. For My flesh is food indeed,
and My blood is drink indeed. He who eats My flesh and drinks
My blood abides in Me, and I in him."*
—John 6:53–56

*The cup of blessing which we bless, is it not the
communion of the blood of Christ?*
—1 Corinthians 10:16

The drinking of the blood of the Lord Jesus is the subject
brought before us in these words. Just as water has a twofold effect, so is it also with this holy blood.

When water is used for washing, it cleanses; but if we drink
it, we are refreshed and revived. He who desires to know the full
power of the blood of Jesus must be taught by Him what the
blessing of drinking the blood is. Everyone knows the difference
between washing and drinking. Necessary and pleasant as it is
to use water for cleansing, it is much more necessary and reviv-
ing to drink it. Without its cleansing, it is not possible to live as
we ought; but without drinking, we cannot live at all. It is only
by drinking that we enjoy the full benefit of its power to sustain
life.

Without drinking the blood of the Son of God—that is,
without taking hold of it heartily—eternal life cannot be obtained.

To many there is something unpleasant in the phrase
"drinking the blood of the Son of Man," but it was still more
disagreeable to the Jews, for the use of blood was forbidden by

the Law of Moses under severe penalties. When Jesus spoke of drinking His blood, it naturally annoyed them, but it was also an unspeakable offense to their religious feelings. Our Lord, we may be sure, would not have used the phrase had He been able in some other way to make plain to them and to us the deepest and most glorious truths concerning salvation by the blood.

In seeking to become partakers of the salvation here spoken of as "drinking the blood of our Lord," let us endeavor to understand the following:

- First, what the blessing is that is described as "drinking the blood"
- Second, how this blessing is worked out in us
- Last, what our attitude should be toward it

## THE BLESSING OF "DRINKING THE BLOOD"

We saw just now that drinking expresses a much more intimate connection with water than washing, and hence produces a more powerful effect. There is a blessing in the fellowship with the blood of Jesus that goes much further than cleansing or sanctification; rather, we are enabled to see how far-reaching is the influence of the blessing indicated by this phrase.

Not only must the blood do something for us, by placing us in a new relationship to God; but it must do something in us, entirely renewing us within. The Lord Jesus drew our attention to this with these words: *"Unless you eat the flesh of the Son of Man and drink His blood, you have no life in you."* Our Lord distinguished between two kinds of life. The Jews there in His presence had a natural life of body and soul. Many among them were devout, well-intentioned men, but He said they had no life in them unless they ate His flesh and drank His blood. They needed another life—a new, heavenly life that He possessed and that He could impart. All creaturely life must obtain nourishment outside of itself. The natural life was naturally nourished by bread and water. The heavenly life must be nourished by heavenly food and drink by Jesus Himself. *"Unless you eat the flesh of the Son of Man and drink His blood, you have no life in you."* Nothing less must become ours than His life—the life that He, as Son of Man, lived on earth.

Our Lord emphasized this still more strongly when He again explained what the nature of that life is: *"Whoever eats My flesh and drinks My blood has eternal life, and I will raise him up at the last day."* Eternal life is the life of God. Our Lord came to earth to reveal this eternal life in the flesh and then to communicate it to us who are in the flesh. In Him we see the eternal life dwelling in its divine power, in a body of flesh, which was taken up into heaven. He told us that those who eat His flesh and drink His blood, who partake of His body as their sustenance, will experience also in their own bodies the power of eternal life. *"I will raise him up at the last day."* The marvel of the eternal life in Christ is that it was eternal life in a human body. We must be partakers of that body, not less than in the activities of His Spirit; then our bodies, also possessing that life, will one day be raised from the dead.

Our Lord said, *"My flesh is food indeed, and My blood is drink indeed."* The word translated *"indeed"* here is the same as the one He used when He spoke His parable of the true vine: *"I am the true* [the indeed] *vine"* (John 15:1), thus indicating the difference between what was only a symbol and what is actual truth. Earthly food is not real food, for it imparts no real life. The one true food is the body and blood of the Lord Jesus Christ, which imparts and sustains life, and does so in no shadowy or merely symbolical manner. No, this Scripture indicates that, in a full and real sense, the flesh and blood of the Lord Jesus are the food by which eternal life is nourished and sustained in us: *"My flesh is food indeed, and My blood is drink indeed."*

In order to point out the reality and power of this food, our Lord added, *"He who eats My flesh and drinks My blood abides in Me, and I in him."* Nourishment by His flesh and blood brings about the most perfect union with Him. This is the reason that His flesh and blood have such power of eternal life. Our Lord declared here that those who believe in Him are to experience not only certain influences from Him in their hearts, but are to be brought into the closest and most abiding union with Him. *"He who...drinks My blood abides in Me, and I in him."*

This, then, is the blessing of drinking the blood of the Son of man: becoming one with Him, becoming a partaker of the divine nature in Him. How real this union is may be seen from the words that follow: *"As...I live because of the Father, so he who feeds on Me will live because of Me"* (John 6:57). Nothing except the union that exists between our Lord and the Father can serve as a symbol of our union with Him. Just as in the indivisible, divine nature, the two Persons are truly One, so man becomes one with Jesus. The union is just as real as the one in the divine nature, only with this difference—that as human nature cannot exist apart from the body, this union also includes the body.

Our Lord prepared for Himself a body into which He took up a human body. This body became, by the body and blood of Jesus, a sharer in eternal life, in the life of our Lord Himself. Those who desire to receive the fullness of this blessing must be careful to enjoy all that the Scripture offers them in the holy mysterious expression, "to drink the blood of Christ."

## HOW THIS BLESSING IS WORKED OUT IN US

We will now try to understand what the "drinking of the blood of Jesus" really is.

The first idea that here presents itself is that "drinking" indicates the deep, true grasping in our spirits, by faith, of all we understand concerning the power of the blood.

We speak sometimes of "drinking in" the words of a speaker when we heartily give ourselves up to listen to and receive them. Likewise, when the heart of anyone is filled with a sense of the preciousness and power of the blood, when he with real joy is lost in the contemplation of it, when he with wholehearted faith takes it for himself and seeks to be convinced in his inner being of the life-giving power of that blood, then it may be rightly said that he "drinks the blood of Jesus." Everything that his faith enables him to see of redemption, of cleansing, of sanctification by the blood, he absorbs into the depths of his soul.

There is a deep truth in this representation, and it gives us a very glorious demonstration of the way in which the full blessing by the blood may be obtained. And yet it is certain that our Lord intended something more than this by so repeatedly making use of the expression about eating His flesh and drinking His blood. What this further truth is becomes clear by His institution of the Lord's Supper. For, although our Savior did not actually deal with that Supper when He taught in Capernaum, He spoke on the subject of which later the Supper was made the visible confirmation.

In the Reformed churches, there are two aspects of viewing the Holy Supper. According to one view, which is that of the reformer Huldreich Zwingli (1484–1531), the bread and wine in the Supper are merely tokens, or representations of a spiritual truth to teach us that, as sure as bread and wine nourish and revive us when they are eaten or drunk, so surely—and even more surely—the body and blood recognized and taken hold of by faith nourish and quicken the soul.

According to the other view, which bears the name of Calvin, there is something more than this in the eating of the Supper. He taught that in a hidden and incomprehensible way, but no less truly, we, through the Holy Spirit, become so nourished by the body and blood of Jesus in heaven that even our bodies, through the power of His body, become partakers in the power of eternal life. Hence He connected the resurrection of the body with the eating of Christ's body in the Supper. He wrote,

> The bodily presence which the Sacrament demands is such, and exercises such a power here (in the Supper) that it becomes not only the undoubted assurance in our spirit of eternal life, but also assures the immortality of the flesh. If anyone asks me how this can be, I am not ashamed to acknowledge that it is a mystery too high for my spirit to comprehend, or my words to express. I feel it more than I can understand it.
>
> It may seem incredible indeed that the flesh of Christ should reach us from such immense distance so as to become our food. But we must remember how far the power of the Holy Spirit transcends all our senses. Let faith then embrace what the understanding cannot grasp, namely: the sacred communication of His flesh and blood by which Christ transfuses His life into us, just as if it penetrated our bones and marrow.

The communion of the flesh and blood of Christ is necessary for all who desire to inherit eternal life. The apostle Paul said, *"The church...is His body"* (Eph. 1:22–23); *"[Christ] is the head*

*...from whom the whole body, joined and knit together...causes growth of the body"* (Eph. 4:15–16). Our bodies are *"members of Christ"* (1 Cor. 6:15). We see that all this cannot take place if He is not attached to us in body and spirit. The apostle again made use of a glorious expression, *"We are members of His body, of His flesh and of His bones"* (Eph. 5:30). Then he cried out, *"This is a great mystery"* (v. 32). It would therefore be foolish not to recognize the communion of believers in the body and blood of the Lord, a communion that the apostle esteemed so great that he wondered at it rather than explained it.

There is something more in the Supper than simply the believer taking hold of the redemptive work of Christ. This is made clear in the Heidelberg Catechism in Question 76: "What is it, then, to eat the crucified body of Christ and to drink His shed blood?" The answer is,

> It is not only to embrace with a believing heart all the sufferings and death of Christ, and thereby to receive pardon of sin and eternal life; but also, besides that, to become more and more united to His sacred body by the Holy Spirit who dwells at once both in Christ and in us, so that we, though Christ is in heaven and we on earth, are, notwithstanding, flesh of His flesh, and bone of His bones; and we live and are governed forever by one Spirit.

The thoughts that are expressed in this teaching are in entire agreement with Scripture.

In the creation of man, the remarkable thing that distinguished him from the spirits that God had previously created, and that made man the crowning work of God's wisdom and power, was that he revealed the life of the spirit and the glory of God in a body formed out of dust. Through the body, lust and sin came into the world. Full redemption is designed to deliver the body and to make it God's abode. Redemption will be perfect and God's purpose accomplished only then. This was the purpose for which the Lord Jesus came in the flesh, and in Him dwelt *"all the fullness of the Godhead bodily"* (Col. 2:9). For this He *"bore our sins in His own body on the tree"* (1 Pet. 2:24); and by His death and resurrection, He delivered the body, as well as the spirit, from the power of sin and death.

As the firstfruits of this redemption, we are now one body, as well as one Spirit, with Him. We are of His body, of His flesh, and of His bones. Because of this, in the observance of the Holy Supper, the Lord comes to the body also and takes possession of it. He does not work by His Spirit only on our spirits, so that our bodies will one day share in redemption at the resurrection but do not share in it now. Rather, the body that is here on earth is the temple of the Spirit; and the sanctification of soul and spirit will progress the more gloriously, to the extent that the undivided personality, including the body, which exercises such an opposing influence, has a share in it.

Thus we are in the Supper so intentionally fed by "the real natural body, and the real blood of Christ"*—not following the teaching of Luther that the body of Christ is so in the bread that even an unbeliever eats the holy body of Christ, but "real" in such a way that faith, in a secret way, by the Spirit, truly receives the power of the holy body and blood from heaven as the food by which soul and body become partakers of eternal life.

All that has now been said about the Supper must have its full application to the drinking of the blood of Jesus. It is a deep spiritual mystery in which the most intimate, the most perfect union with Christ, is brought about. It takes place where the soul, through the Holy Spirit, fully takes hold of the communion of the blood of Christ and becomes a true partaker of the disposition that He revealed in the shedding of His blood. The blood is the soul, the life of the body; where the believer as one body with Christ desires to abide perfectly in Him, there through the Spirit, in a superhuman powerful way, the blood will support and strengthen the heavenly life. The life that was poured out in the blood becomes his life. The life of the old "I" dies to make room for the life of Christ in him. By perceiving how this drinking is the highest participation in the heavenly life of the Lord, faith has one of its highest and most glorious offices.

---

* The words within quotation marks, "the real natural body, and the real blood of Christ," are quoted by Dr. Murray from the Articles of the Confession of Faith of the Reformed churches of Holland. Dr. Murray did not include the words immediately following, which declare that "the manner of our partaking of the same is not by the mouth, but by the Spirit, through faith." Dr. Murray remained true to the Reformed faith. His own view is expressed in his earlier quotation from the Heidelberg Catechism.

## OUR ATTITUDE TOWARD THIS DRINKING

Beloved, you have already seen that we have here one of the deepest mysteries of the life of God in us. It is fitting that we draw near with very deep reverence while we ask the Lord Jesus to teach us and bestow upon us what He means by this drinking of His blood.

Only he who longs for full union with Jesus will truly learn what it is to drink the blood of Jesus. *"He who...drinks My blood abides in Me, and I in him."* He who is satisfied with just the forgiveness of his sins; he who does not thirst to drink abundantly of the love of Jesus; he who does not desire to experience redemption for soul and body, in its full power, so as to have truly in himself the same disposition that was in Jesus—he will have only a small share in this drinking of the blood. On the other hand, he who sets before him as his chief objective that which is also the objective of Jesus—*"Abide in Me, and I in you"* (John 15:4)—and who desires the power of eternal life to operate in his body, he will not allow himself to be frightened by the impression that these words are too high or too mysterious. He longs to become heavenly minded because he belongs to heaven and is going there; therefore, he desires to obtain his food and drink from heaven. Without thirst, there is no drinking. The longing for Jesus and perfect fellowship with Him is the thirst that is the best preparation for being made to drink the blood.

It is by the Holy Spirit that the thirsty soul will be made to drink of the heavenly refreshment of this life-giving drink. We have already seen that this drinking is a heavenly mystery. In heaven where *"God the Judge of all"* (Heb. 12:23) is, and where *"Jesus the Mediator of the new covenant"* (v. 24) is, there is also *"the blood of sprinkling"* (v. 24). When the Holy Spirit teaches us—taking us, as it were, by the hand—He bestows more than our merely human understanding can grasp. All the thoughts that we can entertain about the blood or the life of Jesus, about our share in that blood as members of His body, and about the impartation to us of the living power of that blood, are only feeble rays of the glorious reality that He, the Holy Spirit, will bring into being in us through our union with Jesus.

Where, in our human bodies, do we find that the blood is actually received and, as it were, drunk in? Is it not through the veins, the bloodstream that is continually renewed from the heart? Each part of a healthy body ceaselessly and abundantly drinks in the blood. In the same way, the Spirit of life in Christ Jesus, who unites us to Him, will make this drinking of the blood the natural action of the inner life. When the Jews complained that what the Lord had spoken concerning eating His flesh and drinking His blood was *"a hard saying"* (John 6:60), He said, *"It is the Spirit who gives life; the flesh profits nothing"* (v. 63). It is the Holy Spirit who makes this divine mystery life and power in us—a true living experience, in which we abide in Jesus and He in us.

There must be on our part a quiet, strong, settled expectancy of faith that this blessing will be bestowed on us. We must believe that everything the precious blood can do or bestow is really for us.

Let us believe that the Savior Himself will cause us, through the Holy Spirit, to drink His blood unto life. Let us believe, and very heartily and continuously take hold of, those effects of the blood that we understand better: namely, its reconciling, cleansing, sanctifying effects.

We may then, with the greatest certainty and joy, say to the Lord, "O Lord, Your blood is my life-drink. You who have washed and cleansed me by that blood, You will teach me every day to *'eat the flesh of the Son of Man and drink His blood,'* so that I may abide in You and You in me." He will surely do this.

chapter 9

# Victory through the Blood

*And they overcame him by the blood of the Lamb and
by the word of their testimony, and they did not love
their lives to the death.*
—Revelation 12:11

For thousands of years there had been a mighty conflict for the possession of mankind, between the old Serpent, who led man astray, and "the seed of the woman." Often it seemed as though the kingdom of God had come in power; then at other times the might of evil obtained such supremacy that the battle appeared to be hopeless.

It was the same in the life of our Lord Jesus. By His coming and His wonderful words and works, the most glorious expectations of a speedy redemption were awakened. How terrible was the disappointment that the death of Jesus brought to all who had believed in Him! It seemed, indeed, as if the powers of darkness had conquered and had established their kingdom forever.

But, behold! Jesus is risen from the dead; an apparent victory proved to be the terrible downfall of the prince of darkness. By bringing about the death of the Lord of life, Satan permitted Him, who alone was able to break open the gates of death, to enter his kingdom. *"Through death He...destroy*[ed] *him who had the power of death, that is, the devil"* (Heb. 2:14). In that holy moment when our Lord shed His blood in death, and it seemed as if Satan were victorious, the Adversary was robbed of the authority he had possessed until then.

Our text verse gives a very grand representation of these memorable events. The best commentators, notwithstanding differences in details of exposition, are united in thinking that we have here a vision of the casting out of Satan from heaven as a result of the ascension of Christ.

We read in Revelation 12:

*She bore a male Child who...was caught up to God and His throne....And war broke out in heaven: Michael and his angels fought with the dragon; and the dragon and his angels fought, but they did not prevail, nor was a place found for them in heaven any longer. So the great dragon was cast out, that serpent of old, called the Devil and Satan, who deceives the whole world; he was cast to the earth, and his angels were cast out with him.* (Rev. 12:5, 7–9)

Then follows the song from which our text verse is taken:

*Now salvation, and strength, and the kingdom of our God, and the power of His Christ have come, for the accuser of our brethren, who accused them before our God day and night, has been cast down. And they overcame him by the blood of the Lamb and by the word of their testimony, and they did not love their lives to the death. Therefore rejoice, O heavens, and you who dwell in them!* (Rev. 12:10–12)

The point that deserves our special attention is that, while the conquest of Satan and his being cast out of heaven are first represented as the results of the ascension of Jesus and the war in heaven that followed, yet in the song of triumph that was heard in heaven, victory is ascribed chiefly to the blood of the Lamb. The blood was the power by which the victory was gained.

Throughout the book of Revelation, we see the Lamb on the throne. It is as the slain Lamb that He has gained that position: the victory over Satan and all his authority is by the blood of the Lamb.

I have spoken about the blood in its manifold effects. Now it is fitting that we seek to understand how victory is always ascribed to the blood of the Lamb. We shall consider the following:

• First, victory as gained once for all
• Second, victory as being always carried on
• Third, victory as one in which we have a share

## THE VICTORY THAT WAS GAINED ONCE FOR ALL

In the exalted representation given in our text, we see what a high position was once occupied by Satan, the great Enemy of the human race. He had entrance into heaven and appeared there as *"the accuser of our brethren"* (Rev. 12:10) and as the opponent of whatever was done in the interests of God's people.

We know how this is taught in the Old Testament. In the book of Job, we see Satan coming with the sons of God to present himself before the Lord and to obtain permission from Him to tempt His servant Job. (See Job 2.) We also read that Zechariah saw *"Joshua the high priest standing before the Angel of the LORD, and Satan standing at his right hand to oppose him* [or, *"be his adversary,"* RV]*"* (Zech. 3:1). Then there is the statement of our Lord, recorded in Luke 10:18, *"I saw Satan fall like lightning from heaven."* Later on, in His agony of soul, as He felt beforehand His approaching sufferings, He said, *"Now is the judgment of this world; now the ruler of this world will be cast out"* (John 12:31).

It may, at first thought, seem strange that the Scriptures represent Satan as being in heaven. But to understand this correctly, it is necessary to remember that heaven is not a small, circumscribed dwelling place where God and Satan had a relationship as neighbors. No, heaven is a limitless sphere, with many different divisions, filled with innumerable hosts of angels who carry out God's will in nature. Among them, Satan also still held a place. Then remember, he is not represented in Scripture to be the black, grisly figure in outward appearance as he is generally pictured, but as *"an angel of light"* (2 Cor. 11:14). He was a prince with many thousands of servants.

When he had brought about the fall of man, and had also transferred the world to himself and became its prince, he had real authority over all that was in it. Man had been destined to be king of this world, for God has said, *"Have authority"* (Luke 19:17). When Satan had conquered man, he took his entire kingdom under his authority, and this authority was recognized by God. God, in His holy will, had ordained that if man listened to Satan, he would suffer the consequences and become subject to his tyranny. God never in this matter used His power or exercised force, but always took the way of law and right; and so Satan retained his authority until it was taken from him in a lawful manner.

This is the reason he could appear before God in heaven, as Accuser of the brethren and in opposition to them, for the four thousand years of the old covenant. He had obtained authority over all flesh, and only after he was conquered in flesh, as the sphere of his authority, could he be cast out forever, as Accuser, from the court of heaven.

So the Son of God also had to come in the flesh in order to fight and conquer Satan on his own ground.

Also for this reason our Lord, at the commencement of His public life and after His anointing, being thus openly recognized as the Son of God, *"was led up by the Spirit into the wilderness to be tempted by the devil"* (Matt. 4:1). Victory over Satan could be gained only after He had personally endured and resisted his temptations.

But even this victory was not sufficient. Christ came in order that *"through death He might destroy him who had the power of death, that is, the devil"* (Heb. 2:14). The Devil had that power of death because of the law of God. That law had installed him as jailer of its prisoners. Scripture says, *"The sting of death is sin, and the strength of sin is the law"* (1 Cor. 15:56). Victory over and the casting out of Satan could not take place until the righteous demands of the law were perfectly fulfilled. The sinner had to be delivered from the power of the law before he could be delivered from the authority of Satan.

It was through His death and the shedding of His blood that the Lord Jesus fulfilled the law's demands. Ceaselessly, the law had been declaring that *"the wages of sin is death"* (Rom. 6:23) and *"the soul who sins shall die"* (Ezek. 18:4). By the ministry of the temple, by the sacrifices with the shedding of blood and sprinkling of blood, the law had foretold, through types, that reconciliation and redemption could take place only by the shedding of blood. As our Surety, the Son of God was born under the law. He obeyed it perfectly. He resisted the temptations of Satan to withdraw Himself from under its authority. He willingly gave Himself up to bear the punishment of sin. He gave no ear to the temptation of Satan to refuse the cup of suffering.

When He shed His blood, He had devoted His whole life, to its very end, to the fulfilling of the law. When the law had been thus perfectly fulfilled, the authority of sin and Satan was brought to an end. Therefore, death could not hold Him. *"Through the blood of the everlasting covenant"* (Heb. 13:20), God brought Him *"up...from the dead"* (v. 20). So also He entered heaven *"with His own blood"* (Heb. 9:12) to make His reconciliation effective for us.

The text verse gives us a striking description of the glorious result of the appearing of our Lord in heaven. We read concerning the woman:

> *She bore a male Child who...was caught up to God and His throne....And war broke out in heaven: Michael and his angels fought with the dragon; and the dragon and his angels fought, but they did not prevail, nor was a place found for them in heaven any longer. So the great dragon was cast out, that serpent of old, called the Devil and Satan, who deceives the whole world; he was cast to the earth, and his angels were cast out with him.* (Rev. 12:5, 7–9)

Then follows the song of victory in which the words of our text occur: *"They overcame him by the blood of the Lamb."*

In the book of Daniel we read of a previous conflict between this Michael, who stood on the side of God's people Israel, and the opposing world powers. But only now can Satan be cast out, because of the blood of the Lamb. Reconciliation for sin and the fulfillment of the law have taken all his authority from him. The blood, as we have already seen, that had done such wonderful things in heaven with God in blotting out sin and bringing it to nothing, had a similar power over Satan. He now no longer has any right to accuse. *"Now salvation, and strength, and the kingdom of our God, and the power of His Christ have come, for the accuser of our brethren...has been cast down. And they overcame him by the blood of the Lamb"* (Rev. 12:10–11).

## VICTORY AS BEING ALWAYS CARRIED ON

There is a progressive victory that follows this first victory. Satan having been cast down to earth, the heavenly victory must now be carried out here. This is indicated in the words of the song of victory, *"They overcame him by the blood of the Lamb."* This was primarily spoken concerning *"the brethren"* mentioned, but it also refers to the victory of the angels. The victory in heaven and on earth progresses simultaneously, resting on the same ground. We know from the passage in Daniel already mentioned (Dan. 10:12–13) what fellowship exists between heaven and earth in carrying on the work of God. As soon as Daniel prayed, the angel became active, and the three weeks' conflict in the heavenlies was three weeks of prayer and fasting on earth. The conflict here on earth is the result of a conflict in the invisible region of the heavenlies. Michael and his angels, as well as the brethren on earth, gained the victory *"by the blood of the Lamb."*

In the twelfth chapter of Revelation, we are clearly taught how the conflict was moved from heaven to earth. *"Woe to the inhabitants of the earth,"* exclaimed the voice in heaven, *"'...for the devil has come down to you, having great wrath, because he knows that he has a short time.' Now when the dragon saw that he had been cast to the earth, he persecuted the woman who gave birth to the male Child"* (Rev. 12:12–13). The woman signifies nothing else than the church of God, out of which Jesus was born. When the Devil could not harm Him any more, he persecuted His church. The disciples of our Lord and the church in the first three centuries experienced this. In the bloody persecutions in which hundreds of thousands of Christians perished as martyrs, Satan did his utmost to lead the church into apostasy or to root it out altogether. But in its full sense, the statement that *"they overcame him by the blood of the Lamb and by the word of their testimony, and they did not love their lives to the death"* applies to the martyrs.

After the centuries of persecution, there came to the church centuries of rest and worldly prosperity. Satan had tried force in vain. By the favor of the world, he might have better success. In the church conformed to the world, everything became darker and darker, until in the Middle Ages the Roman apostasy reached its climax. Nevertheless, during all these ages, there were not a few who in the midst of surrounding misery fought the *"fight of faith"* (1 Tim. 6:12), and by the piety of their lives and witness for the Lord, the statement was often established: *"They overcame him by the blood of the Lamb and by the word of their testimony, and they did not love their lives to the death."*

This was no less the secret power by which, through the blessed Reformation, the mighty authority that Satan had gained in the church was broken down. *"They overcame him by the blood of the Lamb."* It was the discovery, experience, and preaching of the glorious truth that we are *"justified freely by His grace through the redemption that is in Christ Jesus, whom God set forth as a propitiation by His blood, through faith"* (Rom. 3:24–25), that gave to the Reformers such wonderful power and such a glorious victory.

Since the days of the Reformation, it is still apparent that to the extent that the blood of the Lamb is gloried in, the church is constantly inspired by a new life to obtain the victory over deadness or error. Yes, even in the midst of the wildest heathen, where the throne of Satan has been undisturbed for thousands of years, this is still the weapon by which its power must be destroyed. The preaching of "the blood of the cross" as the reconciliation for the sin of the world and the ground of God's free, forgiving love is the power by which the most darkened heart is opened and softened, and, from being a dwelling place of Satan, is changed into a temple of the Most High.

What avails for the church is available for each Christian. In *"the blood of the Lamb,"* he always has victory. When the soul is convinced of the power that the blood has with God in heaven to bring about a perfect reconciliation by the blotting out of sin; to rob the Devil of his authority over us completely and forever; to work out in our hearts a full assurance of the favor of God; and to destroy the power of sin—this is when the soul lives in the power of the blood and the temptations of Satan cease to ensnare.

Where the holy blood of the Lamb of God is sprinkled, there God dwells, and Satan is put to flight. In heaven, on earth, and in our hearts, that word as the announcement of a progressive victory is valid: *"They overcame him by the blood of the Lamb."*

## OUR SHARE IN THIS VICTORY

We also have a share in this victory if we are reckoned among those who have been cleansed *"by the blood of the Lamb."* To have the full enjoyment of this, we must pay attention to the following facts.

### • NO VICTORY WITHOUT CONFLICT

We must recognize that we dwell in an enemy's territory. What was revealed to the apostle in his heavenly vision must hold good in our daily lives. Satan has been cast down to the earth; he has great wrath because he has only *"a short time"* (Rev. 12:12). He cannot now reach the glorified Jesus, but seeks to reach Him by attacking His people. We must live always under the holy consciousness that we are watched, every moment, by an enemy of unimaginable cunning and power who is unwearied in his endeavor to bring us entirely, or even partially—however little it may be—under his authority. He is literally *"the ruler of this world"* (John 12:31). All that is in the world is ready to serve him, and he knows how to make use of it in his attempts to lead the church to be unfaithful to her Lord, and to inspire her with his spirit, the spirit of the world.

He makes use not only of temptations to what is commonly thought to be sin, but he knows how to gain an entrance into our earthly activities and businesses—our daily bread and necessary money, our politics, our commercial associations, our literature and science, our knowledge, and all things—so that he may make all that is lawful in itself into a tool to forward his devilish deceptions.

The believer who desires to share in the victory over Satan *"by the blood of the Lamb"* must be a fighter. He must make the effort to understand the character of his enemy. He must allow himself to be taught by the Spirit through the Word what the secret cunning of Satan is, which is called in Scripture *"the depths of Satan"* (Rev. 2:24), by which he so often blinds and deceives men. He must know that this battle is not *"against flesh and blood, but against principalities, against powers, against the rulers of the darkness of this age, against spiritual hosts of wickedness in the heavenly places"* (Eph. 6:12). He must devote himself, in every way, and at all costs, to carry on the battle until death. Only then will he be able to join in the song of victory, *"They overcame him by the blood of the Lamb and by the word of their testimony, and they did not love their lives to the death."*

### • VICTORY THROUGH FAITH

*"And this is the victory that has overcome the world; our faith. Who is he who overcomes the world, but he who believes that Jesus is the Son of God?"* (1 John 5:4–5). *"Be of good cheer,"* said our Lord Jesus, *"I have overcome the world"* (John 16:33). Satan is an already conquered enemy. He has nothing, absolutely nothing by right, to say to one who belongs to the Lord Jesus. By not believing, or by letting go my hold of, the fact that I have a participation in the victory of Jesus, I may again give Satan an authority over me that he does not otherwise possess. But when I know, by a living faith, that I am one with the Lord Jesus, that the Lord Himself lives in me, and that He maintains and carries on in me the victory that He gained, then Satan has no power over me. Victory *"by the blood of the Lamb"* is the power of my life.

Only this faith can inspire courage and joy in the conflict. By thinking of the terrible power of the Enemy, of his never-sleeping watchfulness, of the way in which he has taken possession of everything on earth by which to tempt us, it might well be said—as some Christians think—that the battle is too severe, that it is not possible to live always under such tension, that life would be impossible. This is perfectly true, if we in our weakness had to meet the Enemy or gain the victory by our own might. But that is not what we are called upon to do. Jesus is the Victor; we need only to have our souls filled with the heavenly vision of Satan being cast out of heaven by Jesus, filled with faith in the blood by which Jesus Himself conquered, and filled with faith that He Himself is with us to maintain the power and victory of His blood. Then we also *"are more than conquerors through Him who loved us"* (Rom. 8:37).

### • VICTORY IN FELLOWSHIP WITH THE BLOOD OF THE LAMB

Faith is not merely a thought of which I lay hold, a conviction that possesses me. Rather, it is a life. Faith brings the soul into direct contact with God and the unseen things of heaven, but above all, with the blood of Jesus. It is not possible to believe in victory over Satan by the blood without being myself brought entirely under its power.

Belief in the power of the blood awakens in me a desire for an experience of its power in myself; each experience of its power makes belief in victory more glorious.

Seek to enter more deeply into the perfect reconciliation with God that is yours. Live, constantly, exercising faith in the assurance that *"the blood...cleanses us from all sin"* (1 John 1:7); yield yourself to be sanctified and brought near to God through the blood; let it be your life-giving nourishment and power. You will thus have an unbroken experience of victory over Satan and his temptations. He who walks with God as a consecrated priest will rule as a conquering king of Satan.

Believers, our Lord Jesus by His blood has made us not only priests but also kings unto God, not only so that we may draw near to God in priestly purity and ministry, but also that in kingly power we may rule for God. A kingly spirit must inspire us, a kingly courage to rule over our enemies. The blood of the Lamb must increasingly be a token and seal, not only of reconciliation for all guilt, but also of victory over all the power of sin.

The resurrection and ascension of Jesus and the casting out of Satan were the results of the shedding of His blood. In you also, the sprinkling of the blood will open the way for the full enjoyment of resurrection with Jesus, and of being seated with Him in the heavenly places. (See Ephesians 1:20.)

I once more, therefore, urge you to open your entire being to the incoming of the power of the blood of Jesus. Your life will become a continual observance of the resurrection and ascension of our Lord and a continual victory over all the powers of hell. Your heart, too, will constantly unite with the song of heaven, *"Now salvation, and strength, and the kingdom of our God, and the power of His Christ have come, for the accuser of our brethren, who accused them before our God day and night, has been cast down. And they overcame him by the blood of the Lamb"* (Rev. 12:10–11).

# chapter 10

# Heavenly Joy through the Blood

*After these things I looked, and behold, a great multitude which no*
*one could number,...standing before the throne and before the*
*Lamb,...and crying out with a loud voice, saying, "Salvation*
*belongs to our God who sits on the throne, and to the*
*Lamb!"... "These are the ones who come out of the*
*great tribulation, and washed their robes and made them*
*white in the blood of the Lamb."*
*—Revelation 7:9–10, 14*

These words occur in the well-known vision of the great multitude in heavenly glory, *"which no one could number."* In his spirit, the apostle saw them standing before the throne of God and of the Lamb, clothed with long white robes, and with palm branches in their hands; and they sang with a loud voice, *"Salvation belongs to our God who sits on the throne, and to the Lamb!"* All the angels answered this song by falling down on their faces before the throne to worship God and to offer eternal praise and glory to Him.

Then one of the elders, pointing out the great multitude and the clothing that distinguished them, asked John the question, *"Who are these arrayed in white robes, and where did they come from?"* (Rev. 7:13). John replied, *"Sir, you know"* (v. 14). Then the elder said, *"These are the ones who come out of the great tribulation, and washed their robes and made them white in the blood of the Lamb. Therefore they are before the throne of God, and serve Him day and night in His temple"* (vv. 14–15).

This explanation, given by one of the elders who stood around the throne, concerning the state of the redeemed in their heavenly glory, is of great value. It reveals to us the fact that not only in this world of sin and strife is the blood of Jesus the one hope of the sinner, but also in heaven, when every enemy has been subdued, the precious blood of Christ will be recognized forever as the ground of our salvation. And we learn that the blood must exercise its power with God in heaven, not only as long as sin has still to be dealt with here beneath. But throughout eternity, to the praise and glory of the blood, each one of the redeemed will bear the sign of how the blood has availed for him and that he owes his salvation entirely to it.

If we have a clear insight into this, we will understand better what a true and vital connection there is between the *"sprinkling of the blood"* (1 Pet. 1:2) and the joys of heaven, and that a true intimate connection with the blood on earth will enable the believer while still on earth to share the joy and glory of heaven.

Joy in heaven through the blood is possible because it is the blood that does the following:

- First, it bestows the right to a place in heaven
- Second, it makes us fit for the pleasures of heaven
- Last, it provides subject matter for the song of heaven

## THE BLOOD BESTOWS THE RIGHT TO A PLACE IN HEAVEN

It is clear that this is the leading thought in the text verse. In the question, *"Who are these arrayed in white robes, and where did they come from?"* (Rev. 7:13), the elder desires to awaken attention and inquiry as to who these favored persons really are who stand before the throne and before the Lamb with palm branches in their hands. And, as he himself gives the reply, we expect that he will surely mention what might be thought to be the most remarkable thing in their appearance. He replies to the question *"Where did they come from?"* by saying that they *"come out of the great tribulation."* To the question *"Who are these?"* he replies that they have *"washed their robes and made them white in the blood of the Lamb."*

This is the one thing to which, as their distinguishing mark, he draws attention. This alone gives them the right to the place that they occupy in glory. This becomes evident if we notice the words that immediately follow: *"Therefore they are before the throne of God, and serve Him day and night in His temple. And He who sits on the throne will dwell among them"* (Rev. 7:15). It is because of the blood that they are before the throne. They owe it to the blood of the Lamb that they occupy that place so high in glory. The blood gives the right to heaven.

Right to heaven! Can such a thing be spoken of in connection with a condemned sinner? Would it not be better to glory only in the mercy of God, who by free grace admits a sinner to heaven, than to speak of a right to heaven? No! It would not be better, for then we would not understand the value of the blood or why it had to be shed. We would also entertain false ideas about both our sin and God's grace, and remain unfit for the full enjoyment of the glorious redemption that the Savior has accomplished for us.

I have already spoken of the casting out of Satan from heaven, and have shown from this incident that a holy God always acts according to law. Just as the Devil was not cast out except according to law, so the sinner cannot be admitted in any other way. The prophet said, *"Zion shall be redeemed with justice, and her penitents with righteousness"* (Isa. 1:27). Paul told us that *"grace...reign*[s] *through righteousness"* (Rom. 5:21). This was the purpose for which God sent His Son into the world. Instead of being afraid that speaking of having a right to enter heaven might belittle grace, it will be seen that the highest glory of grace consists in bestowing that right.

This insight is sometimes missing from the church, where it might be most expected. Recently I asked a man, who spoke of the hope he had of going to heaven when he died, on what ground he based his hope. He was not by any means a careless man, nor did he trust his own righteousness, yet he replied, "Well, I think that I do my best to seek the Lord, and to do His will." When I told him that this was no ground on which to stand before the judgment seat of a holy God, he appealed to the mercy of God. When I told him again that he needed more than mercy, it was something new for him to hear that it was only the righteousness of God that could grant him entrance into heaven. It is to be feared that there are many who listen to the preaching of "justification by faith," but who have no idea that they cannot have a share in eternal blessedness except by being declared legally righteous.

Entirely different was the testimony of a certain lad who did not have the full use of his intellectual abilities, but whose heart the Spirit of God had enlightened to understand the meaning of the crucifixion of Jesus. When on his deathbed, he was asked about his hope, and he indicated that there was a great book that contained a page on which his many sins had been written. Then with the finger of his right hand, he pointed to the palm of his left hand, indicating the print of the nail there. Taking, as it were, something from the pierced hand—he was thinking of the blood that marked it—he showed how all that was written on that page was now blotted out. The blood of the Lamb was the ground of his hope.

The blood of the Lamb gives the believing sinner a right to heaven. *"Behold! The Lamb of God who takes away the sin of the world!"* (John 1:29). By shedding His blood, He really bore the punishment of sin. He gave Himself up to death in our place. He gave His life as *"a ransom for many"* (Matt. 20:28). The punishment has been borne, and our Lord's blood has really been shed as a ransom and appears before the throne of God in heaven. Thus, the righteousness of God declares that the sinner's Surety has fulfilled all the requirements of the law, regarding both punishment and obedience, and God pronounces the sinner who believes in Christ to be righteous. Faith is just the recognition that Christ has really done everything for me, that God's declaration of righteousness is only His declaration that, according to the law, I have a claim to salvation. God's grace bestows on me the right to heaven. The blood of the Lamb is the evidence of this right. If I have been cleansed by that blood, I can meet death with full confidence: I have a right to heaven.

You desire and hope to get to heaven. Listen, then, to the answer given to the question, "Who are they who will find a place before the throne of God?" They have *"washed their robes and made them white in the blood of the Lamb."* That washing takes place, not in heaven and not at death, but here during our life on earth. Do not deceive yourself with a hope of heaven if you have not been cleansed, really cleansed, by that precious blood. Do not dare to meet death without knowing that Jesus Himself has cleansed you by His blood.

## THE BLOOD BESTOWS THE FITNESS FOR HEAVEN

It is of little use for men to have a right to anything unless they are equipped to enjoy it. However costly the gift, it is of little use if the inner disposition necessary to enjoy it is lacking. To bestow the right to heaven on those who are not at the same time prepared for it would give them no pleasure, but would be in conflict with the perfection of all God's works.

The power of the blood of Jesus not only sets open the door of heaven for the sinner, but it also operates on him in such a divine way that, as he enters heaven, it will appear that the blessedness of heaven and he have been really fitted for each other.

What constitutes the blessedness of heaven, and what the disposition is that is fitted for it, we are told by words connected with our text:

> *Therefore they are before the throne of God, and serve Him day and night in His temple. And He who sits on the throne will dwell among them. They shall neither hunger anymore nor thirst anymore; the sun shall not strike them, nor any heat; for the Lamb who is in the midst of the throne will shepherd them and lead them to living fountains of waters. And God will wipe away every tear from their eyes.*
>
> (Rev. 7:15–17)

Nearness to and fellowship with God and the Lamb constitute the blessedness of heaven. To be before the throne of God, to see His face, to serve Him *"day and night in His temple,"* to be overshadowed by Him who sits upon the throne, to be fed and led by the Lamb—all these expressions point out how little the blessedness of heaven depends on anything else than on God and the Lamb. To see them, to have intimacy with them, to be acknowledged, loved, and cared for by them—that is blessedness.

What preparation is needed for having such relationship with God and the Lamb? It consists of two things: inner agreement in mind and will, and delight in His nearness and fellowship. Both are purchased by the blood.

## • INNER AGREEMENT IN MIND AND WILL

There can be no thought of fitness for heaven apart from oneness with God's will. How could two dwell together unless they agree (Amos 3:3)? And because God is the Holy One, the sinner must be cleansed from his sin and sanctified; otherwise he remains utterly unfit for what constitutes the happiness of heaven. *"Without* [holiness] *no one will see the Lord"* (Heb. 12:14). Man's entire nature must be renewed, so that he may think, desire, will, and do what pleases God, not as a matter of mere obedience in keeping a commandment, but from natural pleasure and because he cannot do or will otherwise. Holiness must become his nature.

Isn't this just what we have seen that the blood of the Lamb does? *"The blood of Jesus Christ His Son cleanses us from all sin"* (1 John 1:7). Where reconciliation and pardon are applied by the Holy Spirit and are retained by a living faith, there the blood operates with a divine power, killing sinful lusts and desires. The blood exercises constantly a wonderful cleansing power. In the blood, the power of the death of Jesus operates; we died with Him to sin. Through a believing relationship with the blood, the power of the death of Jesus presses into the innermost parts of our hidden lives. The blood breaks the power of sin and cleanses us from all sin.

The blood also sanctifies. We have seen that cleansing is only one part of salvation—the taking away of sin. The blood does more than this; it takes possession of us for God and inwardly bestows the very same disposition that was in Jesus when He shed His blood. In shedding that blood, He sanctified Himself for us, so that we also would be sanctified by the truth. As we delight and lose ourselves in that holy blood, the power of entire surrender to God's will and glory, the power to sacrifice everything and to abide in God's love that inspired the Lord Jesus, is at work in us.

The blood sanctifies us for the emptying and surrender of ourselves, so that God may take possession of us and fill us with Himself. This is true holiness: to be possessed by and filled with God. This is worked out by the blood of the Lamb, and so we are prepared here on earth to meet God in heaven with unspeakable joy.

### • DELIGHT IN HIS NEARNESS AND FELLOWSHIP

In addition to having one will with God, fitness for heaven also consists of the desire and capacity for enjoying fellowship with God. In this, the blood bestows, here on earth, the true preparation for heaven. We have seen how the blood brings us near to God, leading to a priestlike approach. Yes, we have liberty, by the blood, to enter into the Holiest of God's presence, and to make our dwelling place there. We have seen that God attaches to the blood such incomprehensible value that, where the blood is sprinkled, there is His throne of grace. When a heart places itself under the full operation of the blood, there God dwells, and there His salvation is experienced. The blood makes possible the practice of fellowship with God, and also with the Lamb, the Lord Jesus Himself. Have we forgotten His word, *"He who eats My flesh and drinks My blood abides in Me, and I in him"* (John 6:56)? The full blessing of the power of the blood, in its highest effect, is full abiding union with Jesus. It is only our unbelief that separates the work from the person, and the blood from the Lord Jesus. It is He Himself who cleanses by His blood, who brings us near, and who causes us to drink. It is only through the blood that we are fitted for full fellowship with Jesus in heaven, just as with the Father.

You who are redeemed, here you can see what is needed to mold you for heaven, to make you, even here, heavenly minded. See that the blood, which always has a place at the throne of grace above, always manifests its power in your hearts. Then your lives will become an unbroken fellowship with God and the Lamb—the foretaste of life in eternal glory. Let the thought enter deeply into your souls: here on earth, the blood already bestows in the heart the blessedness of heaven. The precious blood makes life on earth and life in heaven one.

## THE BLOOD PROVIDES SUBJECT MATTER FOR THE SONG OF HEAVEN

What I have said so far has been taken from what the elder stated about the redeemed. But how far is this their experience and testimony? Have we anything out of their own mouths concerning this? Yes, they themselves bear witness. In the song contained in our text, they were heard to cry with loud voice, *"Salvation belongs to our God who sits on the throne, and to the Lamb!"* It is as the slain Lamb that the Lord Jesus is in the midst of the throne, as a Lamb whose blood had been shed. As such, He is the object of the worship of the redeemed.

This appears still more clearly in the *"new song"* that they sing, *"You are worthy to take the scroll, and to open its seals; for You were slain, and have redeemed us to God by Your blood out of every tribe and tongue and people and nation, and have made us kings and priests to our God"* (Rev. 5:9–10).

Or in words somewhat different, used by the apostle in the beginning of the book, where he, under the impression of all that he had seen and heard in heaven concerning the place that the Lamb occupied, at the first mention of the name of the Lord Jesus, cried out, *"To Him who loved us and washed us from our sins in His own blood, and has made us kings and priests to His God and Father, to Him be glory and dominion forever and ever. Amen"* (Rev. 1:5–6).

Without ceasing, the blood of the Lamb continues to be the power to awaken the saved to their song of joy and thanksgiving. This is because, in the death of the Cross, the sacrifice took place in which He gave Himself for them and won them for Himself. Because the blood is the eternal seal of what He did and of the love that moved Him to do it, it remains also the inexhaustible, overflowing fountain of heavenly bliss.

So that we may better understand this, notice the expression, *"Him who loved us and washed us from our sins in His own blood."* In all our consideration about the blood of Jesus, we have had until now no occasion intentionally to stop there. And of all the glorious things that the blood means, this is one of the most glorious: His blood is the sign, the measure, yes, the impartation of His love. Each application of His blood, each time that He causes the soul to experience its power, is a fresh outflowing of His wonderful love. The full experience of the power of the blood in eternity will be nothing else than the full revelation of how He gave Himself up for us, and how He gives Himself to us in a love as eternal, unending, and incomprehensible as God Himself.

*"Him who loved us and washed us from our sins in His own blood."* This love is indeed incomprehensible. What has that love not moved Him to do? He gave Himself for us (Gal. 1:3–4; 2:20); He became sin for us (2 Cor. 5:21); He was made a curse for us (Gal. 3:13). Who would dare to use such language; who could ever have dared to think such a thing if God had not revealed it to us by His Spirit? Who would dare to say that He really gave Himself up for us, not because it was laid upon Him to do so, but by the impulse of a love that really longed for us, so that we might forever be identified with Him?

Because it is such a divine wonder, we feel it so little. But blessed be the Lord, there is a time coming when we will feel it, when under the ceaseless and immediate love-sharing of the heavenly life, we will be filled and satisfied with that love. Yes, praised be the Lord! Even here on earth there is hope that through a better knowledge of and a more perfect trust in the blood, the Spirit will more powerfully pour out *"the love of God...in our hearts"* (Rom. 5:5). There is nothing to prevent our hearts from being filled with the love of the Lamb and our mouths from being filled with His praise here on earth by faith, as is done in heaven by sight. Each experience of the power of the blood will become increasingly an experience of the love of Jesus.

It has been said that it is not desirable to lay too much emphasis on the word *blood,* that it sounds coarse, and that the thought expressed by it can be conveyed in a way more in accordance with our modern ways of speaking or thinking. I must acknowledge that I do not share this view. I receive this word as coming, not just from John, but from the Lord Himself. I am deeply convinced that the word chosen by the Spirit of God, and by Him made living and filled with the power of the eternal life from which the song containing it comes to us, carries in itself a power of blessing beyond our understanding. Changing the expression into our way of thinking has all the imperfection of a human translation. He who desires to know and experience *"what the Spirit says to the churches"* (Rev. 2:7) will accept the word by faith, as having come from heaven, as the word in which the joy and power of eternal life is enfolded in a most distinct manner. Those expressions, *"Your blood"* (Rev. 5:9) and *"the blood of the Lamb"* (Rev. 7:14; 12:11), will make the Holiest, the place of God's glory, resound eternally with the joyful notes of the *"new song"* (Rev. 5:9).

Heavenly joy through the blood of the Lamb will be the portion of all, here on earth, who with undivided heart yield to its power; and of all above, in heaven, who have become worthy to take a place among the multitude around the throne.

My comrades in redemption, we have learned what those in heaven say and how they sing about the blood. Let us pray earnestly that these tidings may have the effect on us that our Lord intended. We have seen that to live a real heavenly life, it is necessary to abide in the full power of the blood. The blood bestows the right to enter heaven.

As the blood of reconciliation, it works out in the soul the full, living consciousness that belongs to those who are at home in heaven. It brings us truly into the Holiest, near to God. It makes us fit for heaven.

As the cleansing blood, it delivers us from the lust and power of sin, and preserves us in the fellowship of the light and life of the holy God. The blood inspires the song of praise in heaven. As the blood of the Lamb *"who loved* [us] *and gave Himself for* [us]*"* (Gal. 2:20), it speaks not only of what He has done for us, but chiefly of Him who has done all. In the blood, we have the most perfect impartation of Himself. He who by faith gives himself up to fully experience what the blood is able do will soon find an entrance into a life of happy singing, of praise and love, that only heaven itself can surpass.

My comrades in redemption, this life is for you and me. May the blood be all our glory, not only at the cross with its awesome wonders, but also at the throne. Let us plunge deep, and ever deeper, into the living fountain of blood of the Lamb. Let us open our hearts wide, and ever wider, for its operation. Let us firmly, and ever more firmly, believe in the ceaseless cleansing by which the great eternal Priest Himself will apply that blood to us. Let us pray with burning desire, and ever more desire, that nothing—yes, nothing—may be in our hearts that does not experience the power of the blood. Let us unite joyfully, and ever more joyfully, in the song of the great multitude, who know of nothing so glorious as this: *"You...have redeemed us to God by Your blood"* (Rev. 5:9).

May our lives on earth become what they ought to be: one ceaseless song to *"Him who loved us and washed us from our sins in His own blood, and has made us kings and priests to His God and Father, to Him be glory and dominion forever and ever. Amen"* (Rev. 1:5–6).

# Book Two

# Humility

# Preface

There are three great motives that urge us to humility: it suits one as a creature, as a sinner, and as a believer. The first motive we see in the heavenly hosts, in unfallen man, and in Jesus as the Son of Man. The second motive appeals to us in our fallen state and points out the only way through which we can return to our right place as men and women. In the third motive, we have the mystery of grace, which teaches us that, as we lose ourselves in the overwhelming greatness of redeeming love, humility becomes to us the consummation of everlasting blessedness and adoration.

In our ordinary Christian teaching, the second aspect of man as sinner has been too exclusively put in the foreground. Some have even gone to the extreme of saying that we must keep sinning if we are indeed to remain humble. Others have thought that the strength of self-condemnation is the secret of humility. And the Christian life has suffered loss, because believers have not been distinctly guided to see that nothing is more natural and beautiful and blessed than to be nothing, so that God may be all. It has not been made clear that it is not sin that humbles us most, but grace. It is the soul, led through its sinfulness to be occupied with God in His wonderful glory as God, as Creator and Redeemer, that will truly take the lowest place before Him.

In these meditations I have, for more than one reason, almost exclusively directed attention to the humility that is suitable to us as men and women. It is not only because the connection between humility and sin is already abundantly set forth in all our Christian teaching, but because I believe that for the fullness of the Christian life, it is indispensable that prominence be given to the other aspect. If Jesus is indeed to be our example in His humility, we need to understand the principles in which it was rooted. We need to find the common ground on which we stand with Him, and in which our likeness to Him is to be attained. If we are indeed to be humble, not only before God but toward men—if humility is to be our joy—we must see that it is not just viewed as the mark of shame because of sin. It must also be understood apart from all sin as a covering with the very beauty and blessedness of heaven and of Jesus.

We will see that, just as Jesus found His glory in taking the form of a servant, so also He said to us, *"He who is greatest among you shall be your servant"* (Matt. 23:11). He simply taught us the blessed truth that there is nothing so divine and heavenly as being the servant and helper of all. The faithful servant who recognizes his position finds a real pleasure in supplying the wishes of the master or his guests. When we see that humility is something infinitely deeper than contrition, and accept it as our participation in the life of Jesus, we will begin to learn that it is our true nobility. We will begin to understand that being servants of all is the highest fulfillment of our destiny, as men and women created in the image of God.

When I look back on my own religious experience, or on the church of Christ in the world, I stand amazed at the thought of how seldom humility is sought after as the distinguishing feature of the discipleship of Jesus. In preaching and living, in the daily activities of the home and social life, in the more special fellowship with Christians, in the direction and performance of work for Christ—there is much proof that humility is not considered the cardinal virtue. It is not considered the only root from which the graces can grow, and the one indispensable condition of true fellowship with Jesus. The accusation that those who claim to be seeking the higher holiness have not always done so with increased humility is a call to all earnest Christians to prove that meekness and lowliness of heart are the chief marks by which they follow the meek and humble Lamb of God.

ANDREW MURRAY

chapter 1

# Humility: The Glory of the Creature

*The twenty-four elders...cast their crowns before the throne,*
*saying: "You are worthy, O Lord, to receive glory and honor and*
*power; for You created all things, and by Your will they*
*exist and were created."*
—Revelation 4:10–11

When God created the universe, it was with the one objective of showing in it the glory of His love, His wisdom, and His power, and of making man the partaker of His perfection and blessedness. God wished to reveal Himself in and through created beings by communicating to them as much of His own goodness and glory as they were capable of receiving. But this did not mean that man was given something that he could possess in itself, or a certain life or goodness that he could control and use whenever he wanted. By no means.

As God is the ever living, ever present, ever acting One—who upholds all things by the word of His power (Heb. 1:3), and in whom all things exist (Col. 1:17)—the relationship of man to God could only be one of unceasing, absolute, universal dependence. As truly as God by His power once created, so truly by that same power must God, every moment, maintain. Man needs only to look back to the origin of existence, and he will acknowledge that he owes everything to God. Man's chief care, his highest virtue, and his only happiness, now and throughout eternity, is to present himself as an empty vessel in which God can dwell and manifest His power and goodness.

The life God bestows is imparted not once and for all, but each moment continuously, by the unceasing operation of His mighty power. Humility, the place of entire dependence on God, is, from the very nature of things, the first duty and the highest virtue of man. It is the root of every virtue.

And so pride, or the loss of this humility, is the root of every sin and evil. When the now fallen angels began to look upon themselves with self-satisfaction, they were led to disobedience and were cast down from the light of heaven into outer darkness. When the Serpent breathed the poison of his pride—the desire to be *"like God, knowing good and evil"* (Gen. 3:5)—into the hearts of our first parents, they, too, fell from their high estate into all the wretchedness in which man is now sunk. In all heaven and earth, pride and self-exaltation are the gate and the curse of hell. (See Note A on page 172.)

Hence, it follows that nothing can redeem us but the restoration of our lost humility, the original and only true relationship of man to God. Jesus came to bring humility back to earth, to make us partakers of it, and by it to save us. In heaven, He humbled Himself to become man. The humility we see in Him, He possessed in heaven; it brought Him, and He brought it, from there. Here on earth *"He humbled Himself and became obedient to the point of death"* (Phil. 2:8). His humility gave His death its value, and so became our redemption. And now the salvation He imparts is nothing less than a communication of His own life and death, His own disposition and spirit. His own humility has become the ground and root of His relationship to God and His redeeming work. Jesus Christ took the place and fulfilled the destiny of man by His life of perfect humility. His humility is our salvation. His salvation is our humility.

And so the lives of the saved ones, of the saints, must bear this stamp of deliverance from sin and full restoration to their original state. Their whole relationship to both God and man must be marked by an all-pervading humility. Without this, there can be no true abiding in God's presence or experience of His favor and the power of His Spirit. Without this, there can be no abiding faith or love or joy or strength. Humility is the only soil in which the graces take root; the lack of humility is the sufficient explanation of every defect and failure. Humility is not so much a grace or virtue along with others; it is the root of all, because it alone assumes the right attitude before God and allows Him as God to do all.

God gave us a sense of reason. Because of this, the truer our insight into the real nature or the absolute need of a command, the fuller and more ready our obedience to it will be. The call to humility has been too little regarded in the church because its true nature and importance have been too little understood. It is not something that we bring to God or that He bestows. It is simply the sense of entire nothingness, which comes when we see how truly God is all, and in which we make way for God to be all. Man must realize that this is the true nobility. He must consent to be—with his will, his mind, and his desires—the form and the vessel in which the life and glory of God are to work and manifest themselves. Then he will see that humility is simply acknowledging the truth of his position as man and yielding to God His place.

In the lives of earnest Christians, of those who pursue and profess holiness, humility ought to be the chief mark of their uprightness. It is often said that it is not so. One reason may be that in the teaching and example of the church, humility has never had the place of supreme importance that rightfully belongs to it. This results from the neglect of this truth: that although sin is a powerful motive to humility, there is a motive of still wider and mightier influence—that which makes the angels, that which made Jesus, that which makes the holiest of saints in heaven, so humble. That is, that the first and chief mark of the relationship of man with God, the secret of his blessedness, is the humility and nothingness that leaves God free to be all.

I am sure there are many Christians who will confess that their experience has been very much like my own in this—that we had known the Lord for a long time without realizing that meekness and lowliness of heart should be the distinguishing feature of the disciple, as it was of the Master. Such humility is not a thing that will come on its own. It must be made the object of special desire, prayer, faith, and practice. As we study the Word, we will see what very distinct and often repeated instructions Jesus gave His disciples on this point, and how slow they were in understanding Him.

From the beginning, let us admit that there is nothing so natural to man, nothing so insidious and hidden from our sight, nothing so difficult and dangerous, as pride. Let us feel that nothing but a very determined and persevering waiting on God and Christ will disclose how lacking we are in the grace of humility, and how weak we are to obtain what we seek. Let us study the character of Christ until our souls are filled with the love and admiration of His humility. And let us believe that, when we are broken down under a sense of our pride, and realize our inability to cast it out, Jesus Christ Himself will give us this grace as a part of His wondrous life within us.

# chapter 2

# Humility: The Secret of Redemption

*Let this mind be in you which was also in Christ Jesus, who...made Himself of no reputation, taking the form of a bondservant....He humbled Himself and became obedient to the point of death, even the death of the cross. Therefore God also has highly exalted Him.*
—Philippians 2:5–9

No tree can grow except on the root from which it sprang. Throughout its existence, it can only live with the life that was in the seed that gave it being. This truth, in its application to the First Adam and the Second Adam, can greatly help us to understand both the need and the nature of the redemption that is in Jesus.

## MAN's NEED FOR REDEMPTION

First, let us understand the need for redemption. When the old Serpent—who had been cast out from heaven for his pride, whose whole nature as the Devil was pride—spoke his words of temptation into the ear of Eve, his words carried with them the very poison of hell. And when she listened, and yielded her desire and her will to the prospect of being like God—knowing good and evil—the poison entered into her soul and blood and life. It destroyed forever the blessed humility and dependence on God that would have been our everlasting happiness. Instead of this, her life, and the life of the human race that sprang from her, became corrupted to its very root with that most terrible of all sins and all curses—the poison of Satan's own pride.

All the wretchedness in this world has its origin in what this cursed, hellish pride—either our own, or that of others—has brought us. All wars and bloodshed among the nations, all selfishness and suffering, all ambitions and jealousies, all broken hearts and embittered lives, with all the daily unhappiness, are a result of this same wicked pride.

It is pride that made redemption necessary. It is from our pride we need, above everything, to be redeemed. And our insight into the need for redemption will largely depend on our knowledge of the terrible nature of the power that has entered our beings.

The power that Satan brought from hell and cast into man's life is working daily—hourly—with mighty power throughout the world. Men suffer from it; they fear and fight and flee it. But they still do not know where it comes from or from whom it gets its terrible power.

Pride has its root and strength in a terrible spiritual power, outside of us as well as within us. We must confess it, deplore it, and be aware of its satanic origin. This may lead us to despair of ever conquering it or casting it out. But it will also lead us all the sooner to that supernatural power in which alone our deliverance is to be found—the redemption of the Lamb of God. The hopeless struggle against the workings of self and pride within us may, indeed, become still more hopeless as we think of the power of darkness behind it all. But eventually, we will better realize and accept the power and life outside of ourselves—the humility of heaven, as brought down by the Lamb of God to cast out Satan and his pride.

Just as we need to look at the First Adam and his fall in order to know the power of the sin within us, we need to know well the Second Adam and His power in order to give us an inner life of humility as real and abiding and overmastering as that of pride has been. We have our life from and in Christ as truly, and even more truly, than from and in Adam. We are to walk *"rooted...in Him,"* (Col. 2:7), *"holding fast to the Head, from whom all the body...grows with the increase that is from God"* (v. 19).

The life of God, which in the Incarnation entered human nature, is the root in which we are to stand and grow. The same almighty power that worked there, and from then on to the Resurrection, works daily in us. Our one need is to study and know and trust the life that has been revealed in Christ as the life that is now ours. It waits for our consent to gain possession and mastery of our entire beings.

In this context, it is of inconceivable importance that we should have a correct understanding of who Christ is. We should properly comprehend what really constitutes Him, the Christ, and especially what may be counted as His chief characteristic—the root and essence of all His character as our Redeemer. There can be only one answer: it is His humility. What is the incarnation but His heavenly humility, His emptying Himself and becoming man? What is His life on earth but humility, His taking the form of a servant? And what is His atonement but humility? *"He humbled Himself and became obedient to the point of death."* And what is His ascension and His glory, but humility exalted to the throne and crowned with glory? *"He humbled Himself....Therefore God also has highly exalted Him."*

In heaven where He was with the Father, in His birth, in His life, in His death, and in His sitting on the throne, it is all humility; it is nothing but humility. Christ is the humility of God embodied in human nature. He is eternal love humbling itself, clothing itself in the garb of meekness and gentleness, to win and serve and save us. As the love and condescension of God makes Him the benefactor and helper and servant of all, so Jesus is and always will be the incarnate humility. Even in the midst of the throne, He is the meek and lowly Lamb of God.

## THE NATURE OF REDEMPTION THROUGH CHRIST

If humility is the root of the tree, its nature must be seen in every branch, leaf, and fruit. If humility is the first, the all-inclusive grace of the life of Jesus, the secret of His atonement, then the health and strength of our spiritual lives will entirely depend upon our putting this grace first, too. We must make humility the chief thing we admire in Him, the chief thing we ask of Him, the one thing for which we sacrifice all else. (See Note B on page 172.)

Is it any wonder that the Christian life is so often feeble and fruitless, when the very root of the Christ-life is neglected, is unknown? Is it any wonder that the joy of salvation is so little felt, when the one thing in which Christ found it and brings it is

125

so little sought? We must seek a humility that rests in nothing less than the end and death of self; that gives up all the honor of men as Jesus did, to seek the honor that comes from God alone; that absolutely makes and considers itself nothing so that God may be all, so that the Lord alone may be exalted. Until we seek humility in Christ as our chief joy, and welcome it at any price, there is very little hope of a religion that will conquer the world.

How much of the spirit of the meek and lowly Lamb of God do we see around us, in those who are called by His name? Think about all the lack of love; the indifference to the needs, feelings, and weaknesses of others; the sharp and hasty judgments and utterances so often excused by our cries of being upright and honest; the manifestations of temper and irritation; the bitterness and estrangement—all of these have their root in pride. Pride seeks only itself.

Devilish pride creeps in almost everywhere. What would happen if believers were to become permanently guided by the humility of Jesus? Oh, for the humility of Jesus in myself and everyone around me! We must honestly focus our hearts on our own lack of the humility revealed in Christ's life. Only then will we begin to feel what Christ and His salvation truly are.

Dear believer, study the humility of Jesus. This is the secret, the hidden root of your redemption. Sink down into it more deeply day by day. Believe with your whole heart that Christ, whom God has given us, will work in us, making us what the Father wants us to be.

# chapter 3

# Humility in the Life of Jesus

*I am among you as the One who serves.*
—Luke 22:27

In the gospel of John, the inner life of our Lord becomes open to us. Jesus spoke frequently of His relationship to the Father, of the motives by which He was guided, and of His consciousness of the power and spirit in which He acted. Though the word *humble* is not written, there is no other place in Scripture where His humility is so clearly revealed.

We have already said that this grace is, in truth, nothing but man's simple consent to let God be all, to surrender himself to God's working alone. In Jesus we will see how both as the Son of God in heaven, and as man on earth, He took the place of entire subordination. He gave God the honor and the glory that are due to Him. And what He taught so often was made true of Himself: *"He who humbles himself will be exalted"* (Luke 18:14). *"He humbled Himself....Therefore God also has highly exalted Him"* (Phil. 2:8–9).

Read the words from John's gospel, in which our Lord spoke of His relationship to the Father, and see how unceasingly He used the words *not* and *nothing* of Himself. The *"not I"* (Gal. 2:20 KJV), in which Paul expressed his relationship to Christ, is the very spirit of what Christ said of His relationship to the Father.

*The Son can do nothing of Himself* (John 5:19).

*I can of Myself do nothing....My judgment is righteous, because I do not seek My own will* (v. 30).

*I do not receive honor from men* (v. 41).

*For I have come down from heaven, not to do My own will (John 6:38).*

*My doctrine is not Mine (John 7:16).*

*I have not come of Myself (v. 28).*

*I do nothing of Myself (John 8:28).*

*Nor have I come of Myself, but He sent Me (v. 42).*

*I do not seek My own glory (v. 50).*

*The words that I speak to you I do not speak on My own authority (John 14:10).*

*The word which you hear is not Mine (v. 24).*

These words open to us the deepest roots of Christ's life and work. They tell us how the almighty God was able to work His mighty redemptive work through Him. They show how important Christ considered the state of heart that suited Him as the Son of the Father. They teach us the essential nature and life of the redemption that Christ accomplished and now communicates.

Christ was nothing, so that God might be all. He resigned Himself with His will and His powers entirely for the Father to work in Him. Of His own power, His own will, and His own glory, of His whole mission with all His works and His teaching, He said, "It is not I; I am nothing; I have given Myself to the Father to work. I am nothing; the Father is all."

Christ found this life of entire self-renunciation, of absolute submission and dependence upon the Father's will, to be one of perfect peace and joy. He lost nothing by giving everything to God. The Father honored His trust and did everything for Him, and then exalted Him to His own right hand in glory. And because Christ had thus humbled Himself before God, and God was ever before Him, He found it possible to humble Himself before men, too. He was able to be the servant of all. His humility was simply the surrender of Himself to God, to allow the Father to do in Him what He pleased, no matter what men around might say of Him or do to Him.

In this state of mind, in this spirit and disposition, the redemption of Christ has its virtue and effectiveness. We are made partakers of Christ so that God might bring us to this disposition. This is the true self-denial to which our Savior calls us: the acknowledgment that self has nothing good in it except as an empty vessel that God must fill, and also that its claim to be or do anything may not for a moment be allowed. It is in this, above and before everything, that the conformity to Jesus consists. It is the being and doing nothing by ourselves so that God may be all.

Here we have the root and nature of true humility. It is because this is not understood or sought after that our humility is so superficial and so feeble. We must learn of Jesus how He is meek and lowly of heart (Matt. 11:29). He teaches us where true humility takes its rise and finds its strength—in the knowledge that it is God *"who works all in all"* (1 Cor. 12:6), that our place is to yield to Him in perfect resignation and dependence, in full consent to be and to do nothing of ourselves. This is the life Christ came to reveal and to impart—a life in God that comes through death to sin and self.

Feelings that this life is too high for us and beyond our reach must, even more, urge us to seek it in Him. It is the indwelling Christ who will live this life in us, meek and lowly. If we long for this, let us, above everything, seek the holy secret of the knowledge of God's nature as He every moment works all in all. The secret—of which all nature and every person and, above all, every child of God, is to be the witness—is that he is nothing but a vessel, a channel, through which the living God can manifest the riches of His wisdom, power, and goodness. The root of all virtue and grace—of all faith and acceptable worship—is that we know that we have nothing but what we receive, and we bow in deepest humility to wait upon God for it.

Because this humility was not only a temporary sentiment—awakened and brought into exercise whenever He thought of God—but the very spirit of His whole life, Jesus was just as humble in His fellowship with men as with the Father. He considered Himself to be the servant of God for the men whom God made and loved. As a natural consequence, He considered Himself to be the servant of men, so that through Him the Father might do His work of love. He never for a moment thought of seeking His honor, or asserting His power to vindicate

Himself. His whole spirit was that of a life yielded to God so that God might work in it. It is not until Christians study the humility of Jesus as the very essence of His redemption, and as the very blessedness of the life of the Son of God, that the void that should be filled with humility becomes a burden. It is not until they study His humility as the only true relationship to the Father, and therefore as that which Jesus must give us if we are to have any part with Him, that the terrible lack of actual, heavenly, manifested humility will become a sorrow. Our ordinary religion should be set aside to secure this, the first and the chief of the marks of Christ within us.

Brother or sister, are you clothed with humility? Look closely at your daily life. Ask Jesus. Ask your friends. Ask the world. And begin to praise God that there is opened up to you in Jesus a heavenly humility that you have hardly known, and through which a heavenly blessedness (which you possibly have never yet tasted) can come into you.

chapter 4

# Humility in the Teaching of Jesus

*Learn from Me, for I am gentle and lowly in heart.*
—Matthew 11:29

*And whoever desires to be first among you, let him be your slave;
just as the Son of Man did not come to be served, but to serve.*
—Matthew 20:27–28

We have seen humility in the life of Christ as He laid open His heart to us. Now let us read His teaching. There we will see how He spoke of it, and how far He expects men, and especially His disciples, to be as humble as He was. Let us carefully study the passages, which I can do little more than quote, to receive the full impression of how often and how earnestly He taught it. It may help us to realize what He asks of us.

## WHAT JESUS TAUGHT ABOUT HUMILITY

### • THE BLESSINGS OF HEAVEN AND EARTH

Look at the commencement of His ministry. In the Beatitudes with which the Sermon on the Mount opens, He said, *"Blessed are the poor in spirit, for theirs is the kingdom of heaven....Blessed are the meek, for they shall inherit the earth"* (Matt. 5:3, 5). The very first words of His proclamation of the kingdom of heaven reveal the open gate through which alone we enter. To the poor, who have nothing in themselves, the kingdom comes. For the meek, who seek nothing in themselves, theirs will be the earth. The blessings of heaven and earth are for the lowly. For the heavenly and the earthly life, humility is the secret of blessing.

### • PERFECT REST FOR THE SOUL

*"Learn from Me, for I am gentle and lowly in heart, and you will find rest for your souls"* (Matt. 11:29). Jesus offered Himself as Teacher. He told us of the spirit that we find in Him as Teacher—a spirit that we can learn and receive from Him. Meekness and lowliness are the things He offers us; in these we will find perfect rest of soul. Humility is to be our salvation.

### • GREATNESS IN THE KINGDOM

The disciples had been disputing who would be the greatest in the kingdom and had agreed to ask the Master (Matt. 18:1). He set a child in their midst and said, *"Therefore whoever humbles himself as this little child is the greatest in the kingdom of heaven"* (v. 4). The question is indeed a far-reaching one. What will be the chief distinction in the heavenly kingdom? No one but Jesus would have given this answer. The chief glory of heaven, the true heavenly mindedness, the chief of the graces is humility. *"He who is least among you all will be great"* (Luke 9:48).

### • THE STANDARD OF GLORY

The sons of Zebedee had asked Jesus if they might sit on His right and left, the highest places in the kingdom. Jesus said it was not His to give, but the Father's, who would give it to those for whom it was prepared. They must not look or ask for it. Their thought must be of the cup and the baptism of humiliation. And then He added, *"And whoever desires to be first among you, let him be your slave; just as the Son of Man did not come to be served, but to serve."* Humility, as it is the mark of Christ the heavenly, will be the one standard of glory in heaven. The lowliest is the nearest to God. The prime position in the church is promised to the humblest.

### • THE ONLY WAY TO HONOR

Speaking to the multitude and the disciples about the Pharisees and their love of the chief seats, Christ said once again, *"He who is greatest among you shall be your servant"* (Matt. 23:11). Humiliation is the only ladder to honor in God's kingdom.

### • THE SELF-ABASED ARE EXALTED

On another occasion, in the house of a Pharisee, He spoke the parable of the guest who would be invited to come up higher (Luke 14:1–11), and He added, *"For whoever exalts himself will be humbled, and he who humbles himself will be exalted"* (v. 11). The demand is inalterable; there is no other way. Self-abasement alone will be exalted.

### • WORSHIP IN HUMILITY

After the parable of the Pharisee and the publican, Christ spoke again, *"Everyone who exalts himself will be humbled, and he who humbles himself will be exalted"* (Luke 18:14). In the temple and presence and worship of God, everything is worthless that is not pervaded by deep, true humility toward God and men.

### • THE ESSENTIAL ELEMENT OF DISCIPLESHIP

After washing the disciples' feet, Jesus said, *"If I then, your Lord and Teacher, have washed your feet, you also ought to wash one another's feet"* (John 13:14). The authority of command, example, and every thought, either of obedience or conformity, makes humility the first and most essential element of discipleship.

### • THE PATH IN WHICH JESUS WALKED

At the Last Supper table, the disciples still disputed who should be greatest, and Jesus said, *"He who is greatest among you, let him be as the younger, and he who governs as he who serves"* (Luke 22:26). The path in which Jesus walked and that He opened up for us, the power and spirit in which He brought about salvation, and to which He saves us, is the humility that always makes me the servant of all.

## BECOMING A SERVANT OF ALL

How little this is preached. How little it is practiced. How little the lack of it is felt or confessed. I do not say, How few reach some recognizable measure of likeness to Jesus in His humility. But rather, How few ever think of making it a distinct object of continual desire or prayer. How little the world has seen it. How little it has been seen even in the inner circle of the church.

*"Whoever desires to be first among you, let him be your slave."* God wants us to believe that Jesus meant this! We all know what the character of a faithful servant or slave implies: devotion to the master's interests, thoughtful study and care to please him, delight in his prosperity and honor and happiness. There have been servants on earth in whom these dispositions have been seen, and to whom the name of servant has never been anything but a glory.

To many of us it has been a new joy in the Christian life to know that we may yield ourselves as servants, as slaves to God, and to find that His service is our highest liberty—the liberty from sin and self. We need now to learn another lesson—that Jesus calls us to be servants of one another, and that, as we accept it heartily, this service will also be a most blessed one. It will be a new and fuller liberty from sin and self. At first it may appear hard; this is only because of the pride that still considers itself to be something.

If we learn that to be nothing before God is the glory of man, the spirit of Jesus, and the joy of heaven, we will welcome with our whole hearts the discipline we may have in serving even those who try to trouble us. When our own hearts are set upon this, the true sanctification, we will study each word of Jesus concerning humility with new zeal, and no place will be too low for us. No stooping will be too deep, and no service too lowly or too long continued, if we may only fellowship with Him who said, *"I am among you as the One who serves"* (Luke 22:27).

Brothers and sisters, here is the path to the higher life: down, lower down! This was what Jesus always said to the disciples who were thinking of being great in the kingdom, and of sitting on His right hand and His left. Do not seek or ask for exaltation; that is God's work. See to it that you abase and humble yourselves, and take no place before God or man but that of servant. That is your work. Let that also be your one purpose and prayer. *"God is faithful"* (1 Cor. 1:9). Just as water always seeks and fills the lowest place, so the moment God finds men abased and empty, His glory and power flow in to exalt and to bless. He who humbles himself (this must be our one care) will be exalted (this is God's care). By His mighty power and in His great love, He will do it.

People sometimes speak as if humility and meekness will rob us of what is noble and bold and manlike. Oh, that everyone would believe that this is the nobility of the kingdom of heaven! If they would only understand that this is the royal spirit that the King of heaven displayed, that this is God-like, to humble oneself, to become the servant of all! This is the path to the joy and the glory of Christ's presence ever in us, His power ever resting on us.

Jesus, the meek and lowly One, calls us to learn from Him the path to God. Let us study the words we have been reading, until our hearts are filled with the thought, "My one need is humility." And let us believe that what He shows, He gives; what He is, He imparts. As the meek and lowly One, He will come in and dwell in the longing heart.

135

chapter 5

# Humility in the Disciples of Jesus

*Let...he who governs* [be] *as he who serves.*
—Luke 22:26

W e have studied humility in the person and teaching of
Jesus. Let us now look for it in the circle of His chosen
companions, the twelve apostles. If we find a lack of it
in them, then the contrast between Christ and men will be
brought out more clearly, and it will help us to appreciate the
mighty change that Pentecost worked in them. It will prove how
real our participation can be in the perfect triumph of Christ's
humility over the pride that Satan had breathed into man.

In the Scriptures quoted from the teaching of Jesus, we
have already seen what the occasions were on which the disciples had proved how entirely lacking they were in the grace of
humility. Once, they had been disputing about which of them
should be the greatest. Another time, the sons of Zebedee, with
their mother, had asked for the first places—the seats on the
right hand and the left. And, later on, at the table of the Last
Supper, there was again a contention over who should be accounted the greatest.

Not that there were not moments when they indeed humbled themselves before their Lord. So it was with Peter when he
cried out, *"Depart from me, for I am a sinful man, O Lord!"*
(Luke 5:8). The disciples also fell down and worshipped Him
who had stilled the storm (Matt. 14:22–33). But such occasional
expressions of humility only bring into stronger contrast the habitual state of their minds. This state was shown in the natural
and spontaneous revelation, cited at other times, of the place
and the power of self. As we study the meaning of all this, we
will learn several important lessons.

## RECOGNIZING OUR UNDERLYING PRIDE

First, we learn how much there may be of earnest and active Christianity while humility is still sadly lacking. We see this in the disciples. They had a fervent attachment to Jesus. They had forsaken all for Him. The Father had revealed to them that He was the Christ of God. They believed in Him; they loved Him; they obeyed His commandments. They had forsaken all to follow Him. When others went back, they clung to Him. They were ready to die with Him. But deeper than all this, there was the dark power of pride—the existence and the hideousness of which they were hardly conscious—that had to be slain and cast out before they could be the witnesses of the power of Jesus to save.

It is still the same today. We may find ministers, evangelists, workers, missionaries, and teachers in whom the gifts of the Spirit are visible and abundant, yet they lack the grace of humility. There are those who are the channels of blessing to multitudes, but of whom—when the testing time comes, or when closer fellowship gives fuller knowledge—it is only too painfully obvious that the abiding characteristic of the grace of humility is scarcely to be seen. All this tends to confirm the lesson that humility is one of the chief and highest graces. It is one of the most difficult to attain, and one to which our first and greatest efforts ought to be directed. It is a grace that only comes in power, when the fullness of the Spirit makes us partakers of the indwelling Christ, and when He lives within us.

## PUTTING OFF PERSONAL EFFORT

Second, we learn how weak all external teaching and all personal effort is in the conquering of pride or in the obtaining of a meek and lowly heart. For three years the disciples had been in the training school of Jesus. He had told them that the chief lesson He wished to teach them was, *"Learn from Me, for I am gentle and lowly in heart"* (Matt. 11:29).

Time after time He had spoken to them, to the Pharisees, to the multitudes, about humility as the only path to the glory of God. He had not only lived before them as the Lamb of God in

137

His divine humility, He had more than once unfolded to them the innermost secret of His life: *"The Son of Man did not come to be served, but to serve"* (Mark 10:45); *"I am among you as the One who serves"* (Luke 22:27).

He had washed their feet and told them they were to follow His example. And yet they had learned little. At the Last Supper, there was still the contention as to who should be greatest. Undoubtedly, they had often tried to learn His lessons and firmly resolved not to grieve Him again—but all in vain. The much-needed lesson is that no outward instruction, not even of Christ Himself—no argument, however convincing; no sense of the beauty of humility, however deep; no personal resolve or effort, however sincere and earnest—can cast out the devil of pride. When Satan casts out Satan, it is only to enter again in a mightier, though more hidden, power. Nothing can avail but that the new nature, in its divine humility, will be revealed in power to take the place of the old. It will become as truly our nature as the old ever was.

## TAKING HOLD OF THE INDWELLING CHRIST

Third, we see that only by the indwelling of Christ in His divine humility do we become truly humble. We have our pride from another, from Adam; we must have our humility from Another, too. Pride is ours, and it rules in us with such terrible power, because it is our self, our very nature. Humility must be ours in the same way; it must be our very self, our very nature. As natural and easy as it has been to be proud, it must be—it will be—to be humble. The promise is, *"Where,"* even in the heart, *"sin abounded, grace abounded much more"* (Rom. 5:20). All Christ's teaching to His disciples, and all their futile efforts, were the necessary preparation for His entering into them in divine power—to give and be in them what He had taught them to desire.

In His death, Christ destroyed the power of the Devil; He put away sin, and He brought about an everlasting redemption. In His resurrection, He received from the Father an entirely new life. It was a life in the power of God, capable of being communicated to men and entering, renewing, and filling their lives with His divine power. In His ascension, He received the Spirit of the Father, through whom He might do what He could not do while on earth. Then He was able to make Himself one with those He loved, and actually live their lives for them, so that they could live before the Father in a humility like His, because it was He Himself who lived and breathed in them. And on the Day of Pentecost, He came and took possession. The work of preparation and conviction, the awakening of desire and hope that His teaching had caused, were perfected by the mighty change that Pentecost brought about. And the lives and the epistles of James and Peter and John bear witness that all was changed, and that the spirit of the meek and suffering Jesus indeed had possession of them.

What will we say to these things? I am sure there is more than one class among my readers. There may be some who have never yet thought very much of the matter, and cannot at once realize its immense importance as a life question for the church and all its members. There are others who have felt condemned for their shortcomings and have put forth very earnest efforts, only to fail and be discouraged. Others, again, may be able to give joyful testimony of spiritual blessing and power, and yet there has never been the necessary conviction of what those around them still see as lacking. And still others may be able to witness that in regard to this grace, too, the Lord has given deliverance and victory, while He has taught them how much they still need and may expect out of the fullness of Jesus.

To whichever class we may belong, I urge the pressing need for each of us to seek a still deeper conviction of the unique place that humility holds in becoming like Christ. We must understand the utter impossibility of the church or the believer in being what Christ would have them be, as long as His humility is not recognized as His chief glory, His first command, and our highest blessedness. Let us deeply consider how far the disciples were advanced while this grace was still so terribly lacking. Let us pray to God that other gifts may not so satisfy us that we never grasp the fact that the absence of this grace is the secret reason why the power of God cannot do its mighty work. It is only where we, like the Son, truly know and show that we can do nothing of ourselves, that God will do all. When the truth of an indwelling Christ takes the place it claims in the experience of believers, the church will put on her beautiful garments, and humility will be seen in her teachers and members as the beauty of holiness.

# chapter 6

# Humility in Daily Life

*He who does not love his brother whom he has seen, how
can he love God whom he has not seen?*
—1 John 4:20

What a solemn thought, that our love for God will be measured by our everyday fellowship with men and the love it displays. How solemn that our love for God will be found to be a delusion, unless its truth is proved in standing the test of daily life with our fellowmen. It is even so with our humility. It is easy to think we humble ourselves before God. Yet humility toward men will be the only sufficient proof that our humility before God is real. It will be the only proof that humility has taken up its abode in us and become our very nature—that we actually, like Christ, have made ourselves *"of no reputation"* (Phil. 2:7). When in the presence of God lowliness of heart has become, not a posture we assume for a time when we think of Him or pray to Him, but the very spirit of our lives, it will manifest itself in all our behavior toward our fellowmen.

This lesson is one of deep importance. The only humility that is really ours is not that which we try to show before God in prayer, but that which we carry with us, and carry out, in our ordinary conduct. The insignificances of daily life are the tests of eternity because they prove what spirit really possesses us. It is in our most unguarded moments that we really show and see what we are. To know the humble man, to know how the humble man behaves, you must follow him in the common course of daily life.

Is this not what Jesus taught? He taught His lessons of humility when the disciples disputed who should be greatest, when He saw how the Pharisees loved the chief place at feasts and the chief seats in the synagogues, and when He had given the disciples the example of washing their feet. Humility before God is nothing if not proved in humility before men.

It is even so in the teaching of Paul. To the Romans he wrote, *"In honor giving preference to one another"* (Rom. 12:10), and *"Do not set your mind on high things, but associate with the humble. Do not be wise in your own opinion"* (v. 16). To the Corinthians: *"Love,"* and there is no love without humility as its root, *"does not parade itself, is not puffed up;...does not seek its own, is not provoked"* (1 Cor. 13:4–5). To the Galatians: *"Through love serve one another"* (Gal. 5:13), and *"Let us not become conceited, provoking one another, envying one another"* (v. 26). To the Ephesians, immediately after the three wonderful chapters on the heavenly life: *"Therefore...walk...with all lowliness and gentleness, with longsuffering, bearing with one another in love"* (Eph. 4:1–2), and *"Giving thanks always,... submitting to one another in the fear of God"* (Eph. 5:20–21). To the Philippians: *"Let nothing be done through selfish ambition or conceit, but in lowliness of mind let each esteem others better than himself"* (Phil. 2:3); *"Let this mind be in you which was also in Christ Jesus, who...made Himself of no reputation, taking the form of a bondservant, and...humbled Himself"* (vv. 5–8). And to the Colossians: *"Put on tender mercies, kindness, humility, meekness, longsuffering; bearing with one another, and forgiving one another,...even as Christ forgave you"* (Col. 3:12–13).

It is in our relationships to one another, in our treatment of one another, that the true lowliness of mind and the humility of heart are to be seen. Our humility before God has no value unless it prepares us to reveal the humility of Jesus to our fellowmen. Let us now study humility in daily life in the light of these words.

The humble man seeks at all times to act on the rule, "Prefer one another in honor; serve one another; esteem others as better than oneself; submit yourself one to another." It is often asked, How can we count others better than ourselves, when we see that they are far below us in wisdom and in holiness, in natural gifts, or in grace received? The question proves at once how little we understand about real lowliness of mind. True humility comes when, in the light of God, we have seen ourselves to be nothing, have consented to part with and cast away self—to let God be all. The soul that has done this and can say, "I have lost myself in finding You," no longer compares itself with others. It has forever given up every thought of self in God's presence. It meets its fellowman as one who is nothing, and seeks nothing for itself. It is a soul that serves God and, for His sake, serves all. A faithful servant may be wiser than the master, and yet retain the true spirit and posture of the servant.

The humble man looks upon every child of God—even the feeblest and unworthiest—and honors him and prefers him in honor as the son of a King. The spirit of Him who washed the disciples' feet makes it a joy to us to be indeed the least, to be servants one of another.

The humble man feels no jealousy or envy. He can praise God when others are preferred and blessed before him. He can bear to hear others praised and himself forgotten, because in God's presence he has learned to say with Paul, *"I am nothing"* (2 Cor. 12:11). He has received the spirit of Jesus, who did not please Himself and did not seek His own honor, as the spirit of his life.

Amid what are considered the temptations to impatience and touchiness, to hard thoughts and sharp words—which come from the failings and sins of fellow Christians—the humble man carries the often repeated injunction in his heart, and shows it in his life: *"Bearing with one another, and forgiving one another,...even as Christ forgave you"* (Col. 3:13). He has learned that in putting on the Lord Jesus, he has put on the heart of compassion, kindness, humility, meekness, and long-suffering (v. 12). Jesus has taken the place of self, and it is not an impossibility to forgive as Jesus forgave. His humility does not consist merely in thoughts or words of self-depreciation, but in a heart of humility. It is a heart encompassed by compassion and kindness, meekness and long-suffering—the sweet and lowly gentleness recognized as the mark of the Lamb of God.

In striving after the higher experiences of the Christian life, the believer is often in danger of aiming at and rejoicing in what one might call the more human virtues. Such virtues are boldness, joy, contempt of the world, zeal, self-sacrifice—even the old Stoics taught and practiced these. Meanwhile, the deeper, gentler, more divine, and more heavenly graces are scarcely thought of or valued. These virtues are those that Jesus first taught upon earth—because He brought them from heaven—those that are more distinctly connected with His Cross and the death of self: poverty of spirit, meekness, humility, lowliness. Therefore, let us put on a heart of compassion, kindness, humility, meekness, long-suffering. Let us prove our Christlikeness, not only in our zeal for saving the lost, but in our conduct with all our fellowmen, bearing with and forgiving one another, even as the Lord forgave us (Col. 3:12–13).

Fellow Christians, let us study the biblical portrait of the humble man. And let us ask our fellow believers, and ask the world, whether they recognize in us the likeness to the original. Let us be content with nothing less than taking each of these Scripture verses as the promise of what God will work in us. Let us take them as the revelation in words of what the Spirit of Jesus will give as a birth within us. And let each failure and shortcoming simply urge us to turn humbly and meekly to the meek and lowly Lamb of God. Have full assurance that where He is enthroned in the heart, His humility and gentleness will be one of the streams of living water that flow from within us.[*]

Once again I repeat what I have said before. I feel deeply that we have very little idea of what the church suffers from the lack of this divine humility—the nothingness that makes room for God to prove His power. It has not been long since a Christian of a humble, loving spirit—acquainted with many mission stations of various societies—expressed his deep sorrow that in some cases the spirit of love and patience was sadly lacking. Men and women, brought close together with others of uncongenial minds, find it hard to bear and to love and to *"keep the unity of the Spirit in the bond of peace"* (Eph. 4:3). And those who should have been fellow-helpers of each other's joy become a hindrance and a weariness. And all for one reason—the lack of the humility that considers itself nothing, that rejoices in becoming and

---

[*] "I knew Jesus, and He was very precious to my soul: but I found something in me that would not keep sweet and patient and kind. I did what I could to keep it down, but it was there. I besought Jesus to do something for me, and when I gave Him my will, He came to my heart, and took out all that would not be sweet, all that would not be kind, all that would not be patient, and then He shut the door."—George Foxe

being counted the least, and that only seeks, like Jesus, to be the servant, the helper, and the comforter of others, even the lowest and unworthiest.

And what is the reason that men who have joyfully given themselves up for Christ find it so hard to give themselves up for their fellowmen? Is the church not to blame? It has so little taught its members that the humility of Christ is the first of the virtues, the best of all the graces and powers of the Spirit. The church has so little proved that a Christlike humility is what it, like Christ, places and preaches first, as what is needed and possible, too. But let us not be discouraged. Let the discovery of the lack of this grace stir us to larger expectation from God. Let us look on every brother or sister who irritates or troubles us as God's means of grace. Let us look on him or her as God's instrument for our purification, for our exercise of the humility that Jesus, our Life, breathes within us. And let us have such faith in the all of God and the nothing of self, so that we may, in God's power, seek only to serve one another in love.

# chapter 7

# Humility and Holiness

*Who say, "Keep to yourself, do not come near me,*
*for I am holier than you!"*
—Isaiah 65:5

W e speak of the Holiness Movement in our times, and praise God for it. We hear a great deal about seekers after holiness, about those who profess holiness, about holiness teaching and holiness meetings. The blessed truths of holiness in Christ, and holiness by faith, are being emphasized as never before. The great test of whether the holiness we claim to seek or to attain is truth and life will be whether it produces an increasing humility in us. In man, humility is the one thing needed to allow God's holiness to dwell in him and shine through him. In Jesus, the Holy One of God who makes us holy, a divine humility was the secret of His life, His death, and His exaltation. The one infallible test of our holiness will be the humility before God and men that marks us. Humility is the bloom and the beauty of holiness.

The chief mark of counterfeit holiness is its lack of humility. Every seeker after holiness needs to be on his guard, so that, unconsciously, what was begun in the Spirit is not perfected in the flesh (Gal. 3:3), and pride does not creep in where its presence is least expected. *"Two men went up to the temple to pray, one a Pharisee and the other a tax collector ["publican," KJV]"* (Luke 18:10). There is no place or position so sacred that the proud man, the "Pharisee," cannot enter. Pride can lift its head in the very temple of God, and make His worship the scene of its self-exaltation.

Since the time Christ so exposed his pride, the Pharisee has put on the garb of the publican. The confessor of deep sinfulness, equally with the one who claims the highest holiness, must be on the watch. Just when we are most anxious to have our hearts be the temple of God, we will find the two men coming up to pray. And the publican will find that his danger is not from the Pharisee beside him, who despises him, but from the Pharisee within, who commends and exalts. In God's temple, when we think we are in the Holiest of All, in the presence of His holiness, let us beware of pride. *"Now there was a day when the sons of God came to present themselves before the LORD, and Satan also came among them"* (Job 1:6).

*"God, I thank You that I am not like other men...or even as this tax collector"* (Luke 18:11). Self finds its cause of complacency in what is just cause for thanksgiving, in the very thanksgiving that we render to God, and in the very confession that God has done it all. Yes, even in the temple, when the language of penitence and trust in God's mercy alone is heard, the Pharisee may take up the note of praise, and in thanking God be congratulating himself. Pride can clothe itself in the garments of praise or of penitence.

Even though the words *"I am not like other men"* are openly rejected and condemned, their spirit may too often be found in our feelings and language toward our fellow worshippers and fellowmen. If you want to know if this is really so, just listen to the way in which churches and Christians often speak of one another. How little of the meekness and gentleness of Jesus is to be seen. It is so little remembered that deep humility must be the keynote of what the servants of Jesus say of themselves or each other. Is there not many a church or congregation, many a mission or convention, many a society or committee, even many a mission away in heathendom, where the harmony has been disturbed and the work of God hindered? Is it not because men who are considered Christians have proved in touchiness and haste and impatience, in self-defense and self-assertion, in sharp judgments and unkind words, that they did not each esteem others better than themselves? Is it not because their holiness has in it so little of the meekness of the saints?*

---

* "Me is a most exacting personage, requiring the best seat and the highest place for itself, and feeling grievously wounded if its claim is not recognized. Most of the quarrels among Christian workers arise from the clamoring of this gigantic Me. How few of us understand the true secret of taking our seats in the lowest rooms."—Hannah Whitall Smith

In their spiritual history, people may have had times of great humbling and brokenness, but what a different thing this is from being clothed with humility, and from having a humble spirit. How different this is from having that lowliness of mind in which each counts himself the servant of others, and so shows forth the very mind that was also in Jesus Christ.

*"Do not come near me, for I am holier than you!"* What a parody on holiness! Jesus the Holy One is the humble One. The holiest will always be the humblest. There is none holy but God (1 Sam. 2:2). We have as much of holiness as we have of God. And according to what we have of God will be our real humility, because humility is nothing but the disappearance of self in the vision that God is all. The holiest will be the humblest. Alas! Though the bare-faced boasting Jew of the days of Isaiah is not often to be found—even our manners have taught us not to speak in this way—how often his spirit is still seen, whether in the treatment of fellow believers or of the men and women of the world. In the spirit in which opinions are given, work is undertaken, and faults are exposed, how often the voice is still that of the Pharisee, though the garb is that of the publican: *"God, I thank You that I am not like other men"* (Luke 18:11).

Is there, then, any humility to be found, such that men will indeed still consider themselves *"less than the least of all the saints"* (Eph. 3:8), the servants of all? There is. *"Love does not parade itself, is not puffed up;...does not seek its own"* (1 Cor. 13:4–5). The power of a perfect love forgets itself and finds its blessedness in blessing others—in bearing with and honoring them, however feeble they may be. The power of this love is given where the spirit of love is poured out in the heart (Rom. 5:5), where the divine nature comes to a full birth, and where Christ, the *"meek and lowly"* (Matt. 11:29 KJV) Lamb of God, is truly formed within. Where this love enters, God enters. And where God has entered in His power and reveals Himself as all, man becomes nothing. And where man becomes nothing before God, he cannot be anything but humble toward his fellowmen. The presence of God becomes not a thing of times and seasons, but the covering under which the soul always dwells. Its deep humility before God becomes the holy place of His presence from which all its words and works proceed.

May God teach us that our thoughts and words and feelings concerning our fellowmen are His test of our humility toward Him. May He teach us that our humility before Him is the only power that can enable us to be always humble with our fellowmen. Our humility must be the life of Christ, the Lamb of God, within us.

Let all teachers of holiness, whether in the pulpit or on the platform, and all seekers after holiness, whether in the prayer closet or in the congregation, take warning. There is no pride so dangerous, none so subtle and insidious, as the pride of holiness. It is not that a man ever says, or even thinks, *"Do not come near me, for I am holier than you!"* No, indeed, the thought would be regarded with abhorrence. But there grows up, all unconsciously, a hidden habit of soul that feels complacency in its attainments. It cannot help seeing how far it is in advance of others. It can be recognized, not always in any special self-assertion or self-laudation, but simply in the absence of the deep self-abasement that is the mark of the soul that has seen the glory of God (Job 42:5–6; Isa. 6:5). It reveals itself, not only in words or thoughts, but in a tone—a way of speaking to others—in which those who have the gift of spiritual discernment cannot help but recognize the power of self. Even the world with its keen eyes notices it. The world points to it as a proof that the claim of a heavenly life does not bear any especially heavenly fruits.

Oh, brothers and sisters, let us beware! Unless we make the increase of humility our study, we may find that we have been delighting in beautiful thoughts and feelings, in solemn acts of consecration and faith, while the only sure mark of the presence of God—the disappearance of self—was missing the entire time. Come and let us flee to Jesus, and hide ourselves in Him until we are clothed with His humility. That alone is our holiness.

# chapter 8

# Humility and Sin

*Sinners, of whom I am chief.*
—1 Timothy 1:15

H umility is often identified with penitence and contrition. As a consequence, there appears to be no way of fostering humility except by keeping the soul occupied with its sin. We have learned, I think, that humility is something else and something more. We have seen in the teaching of our Lord Jesus and in the Epistles how often the virtue is earnestly taught without any reference to sin. In the very nature of things—in the whole relationship of man to the Creator—in the life of Jesus as He lived it and imparts it to us, humility is the very essence of holiness and of blessedness. It is the displacement of self by the enthronement of God. Where God is all, self is nothing.

Though it is this aspect of the truth I have felt it especially necessary to emphasize, I hardly need to say what new depth and intensity man's sin and God's grace give to the humility of believers. We have only to look at a man like the apostle Paul to see how, through his life as a ransomed and holy man, the deep consciousness of having been a sinner lives inextinguishably.

We all know the passages in which Paul referred to his life as a persecutor and blasphemer. *"I am the least of the apostles, who am not worthy to be called an apostle, because I persecuted the church of God....I labored more abundantly than they all, yet not I, but the grace of God which was with me"* (1 Cor. 15:9–10). *"To me, who am less than the least of all the saints, this grace was given, that I should preach among the Gentiles"* (Eph. 3:8). *"I was formerly a blasphemer, a persecutor, and an insolent man; but I obtained mercy because I did it ignorantly in unbelief....Christ Jesus came into the world to save sinners, of whom I am chief"* (1 Tim. 1:13, 15).

God's grace had saved Paul; God remembered his sins no more; but never, never could he forget how terribly he had sinned. The more he rejoiced in God's salvation, and the more his experience of God's grace filled him with unspeakable joy, the clearer was his consciousness that he was a saved sinner. And he was more aware that salvation had no meaning or sweetness except as the sense of his being a sinner made it precious and real to him. Never for a moment could he forget that it was a sinner whom God had taken up in His arms and crowned with His love.

The Scriptures just quoted are sometimes referred to as Paul's confession of daily sinning. One has only to read them carefully in their context to see how little this is the case. They have a far deeper meaning. They refer to what lasts throughout eternity, and what will give its deep undertone of amazement and adoration to the humility with which the ransomed bow before the throne, as those who have been washed from their sins by the blood of the Lamb. Never, even in glory, can they be anything other than ransomed sinners. Never for a moment in this life can God's child live in the full light of His love without understanding that the sin out of which he has been saved is his one only right and title to all that grace has promised to do.

The humility with which he first came as a sinner acquires a new meaning when he learns how it suits him as a man. And then ever again, the humility in which he was born as a man has its deepest, richest tones of adoration in the memory of what it is to be a monument of God's wondrous, redeeming love.

The true significance of what these expressions of Paul teach us comes out all the more strongly when we notice the remarkable fact that, through his whole Christian course, we never find anything like a confession of sin. Not even in the Epistles, where he expounded on the most intensely personal admissions, did he confess his sins. Nowhere is there any mention of shortcoming or defect, nowhere any suggestion to his readers that he has failed in duty, or sinned against the law of perfect love.

On the contrary, there are many passages in which he vindicated himself in language that means nothing if it does not appeal to a faultless life before God and men. *"You are witnesses, and*

*God also, how devoutly and justly and blamelessly we behaved ourselves among you who believe"* (1 Thess. 2:10). *"Our boasting is this: the testimony of our conscience that we conducted ourselves in the world in simplicity and godly sincerity,...and more abundantly toward you"* (2 Cor. 1:12). This is not an ideal or an aspiration. It is an appeal to what his actual life had been. However we may account for this absence of confession of sin, anyone will admit that it must point to a life in the power of the Holy Spirit, such as is seldom realized or expected in our time.

The point that I wish to emphasize is this: the very fact of the absence of such confession of sinning only gives more force to the truth that the secret of deeper humility is not to be found in daily sinning. Rather, it is to be found in the habitual, never-for-a-moment-to-be-forgotten position, which the more abundant grace will keep more distinctly alive. Our true place—the only place of blessing, our one abiding position before God—must be that of those whose highest joy is to confess that they are sinners saved by grace.

Coupled with Paul's deep remembrance of having sinned so terribly in the past, before grace and the consciousness of being kept from present sinning had met him, was the abiding remembrance of the dark, hidden power of sin ever ready to come in, and only kept out by the presence and power of the indwelling Christ. *"In me (that is, in my flesh) nothing good dwells"* (Rom. 7:18). These words describe the flesh as it is to the end. *"The law of the Spirit of life in Christ Jesus has made me free from the law of sin and death"* (Rom. 8:2). This glorious deliverance is neither the annihilation nor the sanctification of the flesh, but a continuous victory given by the Spirit as He puts to death *"the deeds of the body"* (v. 13).

As health expels disease, and light swallows up darkness, and as life conquers death, so the indwelling of Christ through the Spirit is the health and light and life of the soul. But with this, the conviction of our helplessness and danger always tempers our faith in this momentary and unbroken action of the Holy Spirit, giving us a chastened sense of dependence and making faith and joy the handmaids of humility. This humility lives only by the grace of God.

The three passages quoted above all show that it was the wonderful grace bestowed upon Paul, and for which he felt the need every moment, that humbled him so deeply. The grace of God that was with him enabled him to labor more abundantly than the others. The very nature and glory of grace for the sinner is the grace to preach to the heathen *"the unsearchable riches of Christ"* (Eph. 3:8). It is also the grace that was exceedingly abundant, with the faith and love that are in Christ Jesus (1 Tim. 1:14). It was this grace that kept Paul's consciousness of having once sinned, and being liable to sin, so intensely alive. *"Where sin abounded, grace abounded much more"* (Rom. 5:20). This reveals how the very essence of grace is to deal with and take away sin, and how it must always be so. The more abundant the experience of grace, the more intense the consciousness of being a sinner. It is not sin, but God's grace showing a man and constantly reminding him what a sinner he was, that will keep him truly humble. It is not sin, but grace, that will make me indeed know myself as a sinner, and make the sinner's place of deepest humility the place I never leave.

I fear that there are many who have sought to humble themselves by strong expressions of self-condemnation and self-denunciation, and yet have to confess with sorrow that a humble spirit, accompanied by kindness, compassion, meekness, and patience, is still as far off as ever. Being occupied with self, even amid the deepest self-abhorrence, can never free us from self. It is the revelation of God, not only by the law condemning sin, but by His grace delivering us from it, that will make us humble. The law may break the heart with fear. But it is only grace that works the sweet humility that becomes a joy to the soul as its second nature. It was the revelation of God in His holiness, drawing near to make Himself known in His grace, that made Abraham and Jacob, Job and Isaiah, bow so low. There will be no room for self in the soul that waits for, trusts, worships, and is filled with the presence of God the Creator as the all of man in his nothingness, and God the Redeemer as the all of the sinner in his sinfulness. Only in this way can the promise be fulfilled: *"The haughtiness of men shall be brought low; the LORD alone will be exalted in that day"* (Isa. 2:17).

It is the sinner dwelling in the full light of God's holy, redeeming love—in the experience of that full indwelling of divine love, which comes through Christ and the Holy Spirit—who cannot be anything but humble. Not to be occupied with your sin, but to be occupied with God, brings deliverance from self.

chapter 9

# Humility and Faith

*How can you believe, who receive honor from one another, and*
*do not seek the honor that comes from the only God?*
—John 5:44

I
n an address I heard recently, the speaker said that the
blessings of the higher Christian life were often like the ob-
jects exposed in a shop window—one could see them clearly
and yet could not reach them. If told to stretch out his hand and
take, a man would answer, "I cannot; there is a thick pane of
glass between me and them." Likewise, Christians may clearly
see the blessed promises of perfect peace and rest, of overflowing
love and joy, of abiding communion and fruitfulness, yet feel
that there is something hindering the true possession. And what
might that be? Nothing but pride.

The promises made to faith are so free and sure, the invita-
tions and encouragements are so strong, and the mighty power
of God on which they may depend is so near and free, that only
something that hinders faith can hinder the blessing from being
ours. In our text verse, Jesus discloses to us that it is indeed
pride that makes faith impossible. *"How can you believe, who*
*receive honor from one another?"* As we see how pride and faith
are irreconcilably at variance in their very natures, we will learn
that faith and humility are one at their roots. We will learn that
we can never have more of true faith than we have of true humility. We will see that we may indeed have strong intellectual
conviction and assurance of the truth while pride is kept in the
heart, but that these make a living faith—which has power with
God—an impossibility.

We need only to think for a moment what faith is. Is it not
the confession of nothingness and helplessness, the surrender

and the waiting to let God work? Is it not in itself the most humbling thing there can be—the acceptance of our place as dependents, who can claim or get or do nothing but what grace bestows? Humility is simply the disposition that prepares the soul for living on trust. And even the most secret breathing of pride—in self-seeking, self-will, self-confidence, or self-exaltation—only serves to strengthen the self that cannot enter into the kingdom or possess the things of the kingdom, because it refuses to allow God to be what He is and must be—the all in all.

Faith is the sense organ by which we perceive and understand the heavenly world and its blessings. Faith seeks the glory that comes from God—that only comes where God is all. As long as we take glory from one another, as long as we seek and love and jealously guard the glory of this life—the honor and reputation that come from men—we do not seek and cannot receive the glory that comes from God. Pride renders faith impossible. Salvation comes through a Cross and a crucified Christ. Salvation is the fellowship with the crucified Christ in the Spirit of His Cross. Salvation is union with, delight and participation in, the humility of Jesus. Is it any wonder that our faith is so feeble when pride still reigns so much, and we have hardly learned to long or pray for humility as the most necessary and blessed part of salvation?

Humility and faith are more nearly allied in Scripture than many people realize. See it in the life of Christ. There are two cases in which He spoke of a great faith. In the first instance, the centurion said, *"I am not worthy that You should come under my roof"* (Matt. 8:8). At this humility, Jesus marveled and replied, *"I have not found such great faith, not even in Israel!"* (v. 10). In the second case, the mother humbly spoke, *"Yes, Lord, yet even the little dogs eat the crumbs"* (Matt. 15:27). And the Lord answered her, *"O woman, great is your faith!"* (v. 28). It is the humility that brings a soul to be nothing before God that also removes every hindrance to faith. Humility makes the soul fear that it would dishonor Him by not trusting Him wholly.

Dear readers, do we not have here the cause of failure in the pursuit of holiness? Is it not this that made our consecration and our faith so superficial and so short-lived? We had no idea to what an extent pride and self were still secretly working within us. We were not aware of how God alone, by His incoming and His mighty power, could cast them out. We did not understand how nothing but the new and divine nature, entirely taking the place of the old self, could make us really humble. We did not know that absolute, unceasing, universal humility must be the root disposition of every prayer and every approach to God, as well as of every dealing with our fellowman. We did not realize that we might as well attempt to see without eyes, or live without breath, as believe or draw near to God or rest in His love without an all-pervading humility and lowliness of heart.

Have we not been making a mistake in taking so much trouble to believe, while all the time there was the old self in its pride seeking to take hold of God's blessing and riches? No wonder we could not believe. Let us change our course. Let us seek first of all to humble ourselves *under the mighty hand of God, that He may exalt* [us]" (1 Pet. 5:6). The Cross, the death, and the grave, into which Jesus humbled Himself, were His path to the glory of God. And they are our path. Let our one desire and our fervent prayer be to be humbled with Him and like Him. Let us gladly accept whatever can humble us before God or men— this alone is the path to the glory of God.

You perhaps feel inclined to ask a question. I have spoken of some who have blessed experiences, or are the means of bringing blessing to others, and yet are lacking in humility. You ask whether these do not prove that they have true, strong faith, even though they all too clearly seek the honor that comes from men.

More than one answer can be given. But the principal answer in our present context is this: they indeed have a measure of faith, in proportion to which, and with the special gifts bestowed upon them, is the blessing they bring to others. But in that very blessing, the work of their faith is hindered through the lack of humility. The blessing is often superficial or transitory just because they are not the nothing that opens the way for God to be all. A deeper humility would, without a doubt, bring a deeper and fuller blessing. The Holy Spirit not only working in them as a Spirit of power, but dwelling in them in the fullness of His grace—especially that of humility—would communicate Himself to them for a life of power, holiness, and steadfastness now seen all too little.

*"How can you believe, who receive honor from one another?"* Brothers and sisters! Nothing can cure you of the desire to receive honor from men, or of the sensitivity and pain and anger that come when it is not given, except giving yourself to seek only the glory that comes from God. Let the glory of the all-glorious God be everything to you. You will be freed from the glory of men and of self, and be content and glad to be nothing. Out of this nothingness you will grow *"strong in faith, giving glory to God"* (Rom. 4:20 KJV). You will find that the deeper you sink in humility before Him, the nearer He is to fulfill every desire of your faith.

# chapter 10

# Humility and Death to Self

*He humbled Himself and became obedient to the point of death.*
*—Philippians 2:8*

Humility is the path to death, because in death it gives the highest proof of its perfection. Humility is the blossom of which death to self is the perfect fruit. Jesus humbled Himself unto death and opened the path in which we, too, must walk. As there was no way for Him to prove His surrender to God to the very uttermost, or to give up and rise out of His human nature to the glory of the Father, except through death, so it is with us. Humility must lead us to die to self. We must prove how wholly we have given ourselves up to it and to God. Only in this way are we freed from fallen nature and can we find the path that leads to life in God, to the full birth of the new nature of which humility is the breath and the joy.

I have spoken of what Jesus did for His disciples when He communicated His resurrection life to them. In the descent of the Holy Spirit, He, the glorified and enthroned meekness, actually came from heaven Himself to dwell in them. He won the power to do this through death; in its innermost nature, the life He imparts is a life out of death. It is a life that has been surrendered to death and has been won through death. He who came to dwell in them was Himself One who had been dead and now lives forevermore. His life, His person, His presence bears the marks of death, of being a life begotten out of death.

This life in His disciples bears the death-marks, too. Only as the Spirit of the death of the dying One dwells and works in the soul can the power of His life be known. The first and chief of the marks of the dying of the Lord Jesus—the death-marks that show the true follower of Jesus—is humility. For these two reasons, only humility leads to perfect death. Only death perfects humility. Humility and death are in their very nature one. Humility is the bud; in death the fruit is ripened to perfection.

## HUMILITY LEADS TO PERFECT DEATH

Humility means the giving up of self and becoming perfect nothingness before God. Jesus *"humbled Himself and became obedient to the point of death"* (Phil. 2:8). In death He gave the highest, the perfect proof of having given up His will to the will of God. In death He gave up His self, with its natural reluctance to drink the cup. He gave up the life He had in union with our human nature. He died to self and the sin that tempted Him, and, as man, He entered into the perfect life of God. If it had not been for His boundless humility, counting Himself as nothing except as a servant to do and suffer the will of God, He would never have died.

This gives us the answer to the question so often asked, and of which the meaning is so seldom clearly understood: How can I die to self? The death to self is not your work; it is God's work. In Christ you are dead to sin. The life that is in you has gone through the process of death and resurrection. You may be sure you are indeed dead to sin. But the full manifestation of the power of this death in your disposition and conduct depends on the measure in which the Holy Spirit imparts the power of the death of Christ. And it is here that the teaching is needed. If you want to enter into full fellowship with Christ in His death, and know the full deliverance from self, humble yourself. This is your one duty.

Place yourself before God in your utter helplessness. Consent heartily to the fact of your weakness to slay or make yourself alive. Sink down into your own nothingness, in the spirit of meek and patient and trustful surrender to God. Accept every humiliation, look upon every person who tries your patience or irritates you, as a means of grace to humble you. Use every opportunity of humbling yourself before your fellowmen as a help to remain humble before God. It is by the mighty strengthening of His Holy Spirit that God reveals Christ fully in you. In this manner, Christ, in His form of a servant, is truly formed in you and dwells in your heart. God will accept such humbling of yourself as the proof that your whole heart desires it. He will accept it as your very best prayer for it, and as your preparation for His mighty work of grace. It is the path of humility that leads to perfect death, the full and perfect experience that we are dead in Christ.

## DEATH LEADS TO PERFECT HUMILITY

Only this death leads to perfect humility. Oh, beware of the mistake so many make, who would like to be humble, but are afraid to be too humble. They have so many qualifications and limitations, so many reasonings and questionings, as to what true humility is to be and to do, that they never unreservedly yield themselves to it. Beware of this. Humble yourself to the point of death. It is in the death of self that humility is perfected. You can be sure that at the root of all real experience of more grace, of all true advance in consecration, of all actually increasing conformity to the likeness of Jesus, there must be a deadness to self that proves itself to God and men in our dispositions and habits.

It is sadly possible to speak of the death-life and the Spirit-walk, while even the tenderest love sees how much there is of self. The death to self has no surer death-mark than a humility that makes itself *"of no reputation"* (Phil. 2:7), that empties out self and takes the form of a servant. It is possible to speak much and honestly of fellowship with a *"despised and rejected"* Jesus (Isa. 53:3), and of bearing His Cross, while the meek, lowly, kind, and gentle humility of the Lamb of God is not seen—is scarcely sought. The Lamb of God means two things—meekness and death. Let us seek to receive Him in both forms. In Him they are inseparable; they must be in us also.

What a hopeless task if we had to do the work! Nature can never overcome nature, not even with the help of grace. Self can never cast out self, even in the regenerate man. Praise God! The work has been done, finished and perfected forever. The death of Jesus, once and forever, is our death to self. And the ascension of Jesus, His entering once and forever into the Holiest, has given us the Holy Spirit to communicate to us in power, and makes the power of the death-life our very own. As the soul, in the pursuit and practice of humility, follows in the steps of Jesus, its consciousness of the need of something more is awakened. Its desire and hope is quickened; its faith is strengthened; and it learns to look up and claim and receive that true fullness of the Spirit of Jesus. That fullness can daily maintain His death to self and sin in its full power, and make humility the all-pervading spirit of our lives. (See Note C on page 172.)

*"Do you not know that as many of us as were baptized into Christ Jesus were baptized into His death?"* (Rom. 6:3). *"Likewise you also, reckon yourselves to be dead indeed to sin, but alive to God in Christ Jesus our Lord....Present yourselves to God as being alive from the dead"* (vv. 11, 13). The whole self-consciousness of the Christian is to be characterized by the Spirit that animated the death of Christ. He has to ever present himself to God as one who has died in Christ, and in Christ is alive from the dead, *"always carrying about in* [his] *body the dying of the Lord Jesus"* (2 Cor. 4:10). His life ever bears the twofold mark: its roots striking in true humility deep into the grave of Jesus, the death to sin and self, and its head lifted up in resurrection power to the heaven where Jesus is.

Believer, claim in faith the death and the life of Jesus as yours. Enter, in His grave, into the rest from self and its work—the rest of God. With Christ, who committed His spirit into the Father's hands (Luke 23:46), humble yourself and descend each day into that perfect, helpless dependence on God. God will raise you up and exalt you.

Every morning, sink in deep, deep nothingness into the grave of Jesus. Every day, the life of Jesus will be manifested in you. Let a willing, loving, restful, happy humility be the sign that you have indeed claimed your birthright—the baptism into the death of Christ. *"By one offering He has perfected forever those who are being sanctified"* (Heb. 10:14). The souls that enter into His humiliation will find in Him the power to see and consider self dead, and, as those who have learned and received of Him, will walk with all lowliness and meekness, supporting one another in love. The death-life is seen in a meekness and humility like that of Christ.

# chapter 11

# Humility and Happiness

*Therefore most gladly I will rather boast in my infirmities, that the power of Christ may rest upon me. Therefore I take pleasure in infirmities....For when I am weak, then I am strong.*
—2 Corinthians 12:9–10

In case Paul should exalt himself, by reason of the exceeding greatness of the revelations he had received from God, he was sent a thorn in the flesh to keep him humble. Paul's first desire was to have it removed, and three times he asked the Lord that it might depart. The answer came that the trial was a blessing; that, in the weakness and humiliation it brought, the grace and strength of the Lord could be better manifested. Paul at once entered into a new stage in his relationship to the trial. Instead of simply enduring it, he most gladly gloried in it. Instead of asking for deliverance, he took pleasure in it. He had learned that the place of humiliation is the place of blessing, of power, and of joy.

Virtually every Christian passes through these two stages in his pursuit of humility. In the first stage, he fears and flees and seeks deliverance from all that can humble him. He has not yet learned to seek humility at any cost. He has accepted the command to be humble and seeks to obey it, though only to find out how utterly he fails. He prays for humility, at times very earnestly. But in his secret heart, he prays more—if not in word, then in wish—to be kept from the very things that will make him humble. He is not yet so in love with humility as the beauty of the Lamb of God, and the joy of heaven, that he would sell all to procure it. In his pursuit of it, and his prayer for it, there is still somewhat of a sense of burden and of bondage. To humble himself has not yet become the spontaneous expression of a life and a nature that are essentially humble. It has not yet become his joy and only pleasure. He cannot yet say, "Most gladly do I glory in weakness; I take pleasure in whatever humbles me."

But can we hope to reach the stage in which this will be the case? Undoubtedly. And what will it be that brings us there? That which brought Paul there—a new revelation of the Lord Jesus. Nothing but the presence of God can reveal and expel self. A clearer insight was given to Paul into the deep truth that the presence of Jesus will banish every desire to seek anything in ourselves and will make us delight in every humiliation that prepares us for His fuller manifestation. Our humiliations lead us, in the experience of the presence and power of Jesus, to choose humility as our highest blessing. Let us try to learn the lessons the story of Paul teaches us.

We may have advanced believers, eminent teachers, and men of heavenly experiences, who have not yet fully learned the lesson of perfect humility, gladly glorying in weakness. We see this in Paul. The danger of exalting himself was coming very near. He did not yet know perfectly what it was to be nothing; to die, so that Christ alone might live in him; to take pleasure in all that brought him low. It appears as if this were the highest lesson that he had to learn—full conformity to his Lord in that self-emptying where he gloried in weakness so that God might be all.

The highest lesson a believer has to learn is humility. Oh, that every Christian who seeks to advance in holiness may remember this well! There may be intense consecration and fervent zeal and heavenly experience, and yet, if it is not prevented by very special dealings of the Lord, there may be an unconscious self-exaltation with it all. Let us learn the lesson—the highest holiness is the deepest humility. Let us remember that it does not come by itself, but only as it is made a matter of special dealing on the part of our faithful Lord and His faithful servant.

Let us look at our lives in the light of this experience and see whether we gladly glory in weakness, whether we take pleasure, as Paul did, in trials, in necessities, and in distresses. Yes, let us ask whether we have learned to regard a reproof, just or unjust, a reproach from friend or enemy, trouble or difficulty into which others bring us, as, above all, an opportunity of proving how Jesus is all to us. It is an opportunity to prove how our own pleasure or honor are nothing, and how humiliation is truly what we take pleasure in. It is indeed blessed—it is the deep happiness of heaven—to be so free from self that whatever is said about us or done to us is lost and swallowed up in the thought that Jesus is all.

Let us trust Him who took charge of Paul to take charge of us, too. Paul needed special discipline and special instruction to learn what was more precious than even the unutterable things he had heard in heaven—what it is to glory in weakness and lowliness. We need it, too—oh, so much. He who cared for Paul will care for us, too. He watches over us with a jealous, loving care, lest we exalt ourselves. When we are exalting ourselves, He seeks to disclose to us the evil, and to deliver us from it. In trial and weakness and trouble, He seeks to bring us low, until we learn that His grace is all, and to take pleasure in the very thing that brings us and keeps us low. His strength made perfect in our weakness, His presence filling and satisfying our emptiness, becomes the secret of a humility that need never fail. This humility can, in full sight of what God works in and through us, always say, as Paul did, *"In nothing was I behind the most eminent apostles, though I am nothing"* (2 Cor. 12:11). His humiliations had led him to true humility, with its wonderful gladness and glorying and pleasure in all that humbles.

*"Most gladly I will rather boast in my infirmities, that the power of Christ may rest upon me. Therefore I take pleasure in infirmities."* The humble man has learned the secret of abiding gladness. The weaker he feels, the lower he sinks, and the greater his humiliations appear, the more the power and the presence of Christ are his portion. Then, as he says, *"I am nothing"* (2 Cor. 12:11), the Word of his Lord brings ever deeper joy: *"My grace is sufficient for you"* (v. 9).

I feel as if I must once again sum up everything in these two lessons: the danger of pride is greater and nearer than we think, and the grace for humility is also.

## THE DANGER OF PRIDE

The danger of pride is greater and nearer than we think, especially at the time of our richest experiences. The preacher of spiritual truth with an admiring congregation hanging on his words, the gifted speaker on a holiness platform expounding the secrets of the heavenly life, the Christian giving testimony to a blessed experience, the evangelist moving on in triumph and made a blessing to rejoicing multitudes—no man knows the hidden, the unconscious danger to which these are exposed. Paul was in danger without knowing it. What Jesus did for him is written for our admonition, so that we may know our danger and know our only safety. Let it be said no more that one who teaches or professes holiness is full of self, or that he does not practice what he preaches, or that his blessing has not made him humbler or gentler. Jesus, in whom we trust, can make us humble.

## THE GRACE FOR HUMILITY

Yes, the grace for humility is greater and nearer, too, than we think. The humility of Jesus is our salvation. Jesus Himself is our humility. Our humility is His care and His work. His grace is sufficient for us (2 Cor. 12:9) to meet the temptation of pride, too. His strength will be perfected in our weakness (v. 9). Let us choose to be weak, to be low, to be nothing. Let humility be joy and gladness to us.

Let us gladly glory and take pleasure in weakness—in all that can humble us and keep us low. The power of Christ will rest upon us. Christ humbled Himself; therefore God exalted Him (Phil. 2:8–9). Christ will humble us and keep us humble. Let us heartily consent; let us trustfully and joyfully accept all that humbles. The power of Christ will rest upon us. We will find that the deepest humility is the secret of the truest happiness, of a joy that nothing can destroy.

chapter 12

# Humility and Exaltation

*He who humbles himself will be exalted.*
*—Luke 14:11*

*Humble yourselves in the sight of the Lord, and He will lift you up.*
*—James 4:10*

*Therefore humble yourselves under the mighty hand of God,*
*that He may exalt you in due time.*
*—1 Peter 5:6*

J ust yesterday I was asked the question, How am I to conquer this pride? The answer was simple. Two things are
needed. Do what God says is your work; humble yourself.
Trust Him to do what He says is His work; He will exalt you.

The command is clear: humble yourself. This does not mean
that it is your work to conquer and cast out the pride of your
nature and to form within yourself the lowliness of the holy Jesus. No, this is God's work, the very essence of the exaltation in
which He lifts you up into the real likeness of the beloved Son.
What the command does mean is this: take every opportunity of
humbling yourself before God and man. Humble yourself and
stand persistently, not withstanding all failure and falling, under this unchanging command. Do this with faith in the grace
that is already working in you and in the assurance that more
grace will be available for the victory that is coming. Look to the
light that conscience flashes on the pride of the heart and its
workings.

Accept with gratitude everything that God allows from
within or without, from friend or enemy, in nature or in grace,
to remind you of your need of humbling, and to help you to it.
Believe humility to indeed be the highest virtue, your very first
duty before God, and the one perpetual safeguard of the soul.

Set your heart upon it as the source of all blessing. The promise is divine and sure: *"He who humbles himself will be exalted."* See that you do the one thing God asks: humble yourself. God will see that He does the one thing He has promised. He will give more grace; He will exalt you in due time.

All God's dealings with man are characterized by two stages. There is the time of preparation, when command and promise—with the mingled experience of effort and inability, of failure and partial success, with the holy expectancy of something better that these awaken—train and discipline men for a higher stage. Then comes the time of fulfillment, when faith inherits the promise and enjoys what it had so often struggled for in vain. This law holds good in every part of the Christian life and in the pursuit of every separate virtue. This is because it is grounded in the very nature of things.

In all that concerns our redemption, God must take the initiative. When that has been done, man's turn comes. In the effort toward obedience and attainment, he must learn to know his weakness. In self-despair, he must learn to die to himself, and so be voluntarily and intelligently equipped to receive the promise from God. The Father will complete what man had accepted at the beginning in ignorance. So God, who had been the beginning before man rightly knew Him or fully understood what His purpose was, is longed for and welcomed as the end—as the all in all.

It is the same in the pursuit of humility. To every Christian the command comes from the throne of God Himself: humble yourself. The earnest attempt to listen and obey will be rewarded—yes, rewarded—with the painful discovery of two things. The one is the depth of pride—unwillingness to consider oneself and to be considered nothing, to submit absolutely to God—that existed, that one never knew. The other is what utter weakness there is in all our efforts, and also in all our prayers for God's help, to destroy the hideous monster. Blessed is the man who now learns to put his hope in God and to persevere, notwithstanding all the power of pride within him, in acts of humility before God and men.

We know the law of human nature: acts produce habits, habits breed dispositions, dispositions form the will, and the rightly-formed will is character. It is not any different in the work of grace. As acts, persistently repeated, beget habits and dispositions, and these strengthen the will, He who works *"both to will and to do"* (Phil. 2:13) comes with His mighty power and Spirit. The humbling of the proud heart, with which the penitent saint casts himself so often before God, is rewarded with the "more grace" of the humble heart, in which the Spirit of Jesus has conquered and brought the new nature to its maturity. In this heart, He, the meek and lowly One, now dwells forever.

*"Humble yourselves in the sight of the Lord, and He will lift you up";* He will exalt you. And of what does this exaltation consist? The highest glory of man is in being only a vessel, to receive and enjoy and show forth the glory of God. Man can do this only as he is willing to be nothing in himself so that God may be all. Water always fills the lowest places first. The lower, the emptier a man lies before God, the speedier and the fuller the inflow of the divine glory will be.

The exaltation God promises is not, cannot be, any external thing apart from Himself. All that He has to give or can give is only more of Himself, to take more complete possession. The exaltation is not, like an earthly prize, something arbitrary, in no necessary connection with the conduct to be rewarded. No, but it is in its very nature the effect and result of the humbling of ourselves. It is nothing but the gift of a divine indwelling humility—a conformity to and possession of the humility of the Lamb of God—which equips us for fully receiving the indwelling of God.

*"He who humbles himself will be exalted."* Jesus Himself is the proof of the truth of these words. He is the pledge of the certainty of their fulfillment to us. Let us take His yoke upon us and learn from Him, for He is meek and lowly of heart (Matt. 11:29). If we are willing to stoop to Him, as He has stooped to us, He will yet stoop to each one of us again, and we will find ourselves equally yoked with Him. As we enter deeper into the fellowship of His humility, and either humble ourselves or bear the humbling of men, we can count on the Spirit of His exaltation, *"the Spirit of glory and of God"* (1 Pet. 4:14), to rest upon us. The presence and the power of the glorified Christ will come to those who are of a humble spirit.

When God can again have His rightful place in us, He will lift us up. Make His glory your main concern in humbling yourself. He will make your glory His concern in perfecting your humility, and breathing into you, as your abiding life, the very Spirit of His Son. As the all-pervading life of God possesses you, there will be nothing so natural and nothing so sweet as to be nothing, with not a thought or wish for self, because all is occupied with Him who fills all. *"Most gladly I will rather boast in my infirmities, that the power of Christ may rest upon me"* (2 Cor. 12:9).

Fellow believers, do we not have here the reason why our consecration and our faith have availed so little in the pursuit of holiness? It was by self and its strength that the work was done under the name of faith. It was for self and its happiness that God was called in. It was, unconsciously, but still truly, in self and its holiness that the soul rejoiced. We never knew that humility—absolute, abiding, Christlike humility, pervading and marking our entire lives with God and man—was the most essential element of the life of the holiness we sought.

It is only in the possession of God that I lose myself. In the height and breadth and glory of the sunshine, the littleness of a particle of dust is seen playing in the sunlight. In the same way, humility is our being, in God's presence, nothing but specks dwelling in the sunlight of His love.

> How great is God! how small am I!
> Lost, swallowed up in Love's immensity!
> God only there, not I.

May God teach us to believe that to be humble, to be nothing in His presence, is the highest attainment and the fullest blessing of the Christian life. He speaks to us: *"I dwell in the high and holy place, with him who has a contrite and humble spirit"* (Isa. 57:15). May this be our destiny!

> Oh, to be emptier, lowlier,
> Mean, unnoticed, and unknown,
> And to God a vessel holier,
> Filled with Christ, and Christ alone!

## FINAL WORDS

Until the spirit of the heart is renewed, until it is emptied of all earthly desires and stands in a habitual hunger and thirst after God—which is the true spirit of prayer—all our prayer will be too much like lessons given to scholars. We will mostly say them only because we dare not neglect them. But do not be discouraged. Take the following advice, and then you may go to church without any danger of mere lip service or hypocrisy, even though there is a hymn or a prayer whose language is higher than that of your heart. Do this, go to the church as the tax collector went to the temple. Stand inwardly in the spirit of your mind in the form that he outwardly expressed when he cast down his eyes and could only say, *"God, be merciful to me a sinner"* (Luke 18:13). Stand unchangeably, at least in your desire, in this form or state of heart. It will sanctify every petition that comes out of your mouth. When anything is read or sung or prayed that is more exalted than your heart is, make this an occasion of further sinking down in the spirit of the tax collector. You will then be helped and highly blessed by the prayers and praises that seem only to belong to a heart better than yours.

This, my friend, is a secret of secrets. It will help you to reap where you have not sown, and it will be a continual source of grace in your soul. For everything that inwardly stirs in you, or outwardly happens to you, becomes a real good to you if it finds or excites in you this humble state of mind. For nothing is in vain, or without profit, to the humble soul. It stands always in a state of divine growth; everything that falls upon it is like a dew of heaven to it. Shut yourself up, therefore, in this form of humility. All good is enclosed in it; it is a water of heaven that turns the fire of the fallen soul into the meekness of the divine life and creates the oil out of which the love of God and man gets its flame. Always be enclosed in it—let it be as a garment with which you are always covered. Breathe nothing but in and from its spirit. See nothing but with its eyes. Hear nothing but with its ears. And then, whether you are in the church or out of the church, hearing the praises of God or receiving wrongs from men and the world, all will be edification, and everything will help your growth in the life of God move forward.

# Notes

## • NOTE A

All this is to make it known that pride can degrade the highest angels into devils, and humility can raise fallen flesh and blood to the thrones of angels. Thus, this is the great end of God's raising a new creation out of a fallen kingdom of angels. For this reason, it stands in its state of war between the fire and pride of fallen angels, and the humility of the Lamb of God. It is here that the last trumpet may sound the great truth throughout the depths of eternity: that evil can have no beginning but from pride, and no end but from humility.

The truth is this: pride must die in you, or nothing of heaven can live in you. Under the banner of the truth, give yourself up to the meek and humble spirit of the holy Jesus. Humility must sow the seed, or there can be no reaping in heaven. Do not look at pride as only an unbecoming temper, or at humility as only a decent virtue. The one is death, and the other is life; the one is all hell, the other is all heaven.

As much as you have of pride within you, so you have of the fallen angel alive in you. As much as you have of true humility, so you have of the Lamb of God within you. If you could see what every stirring of pride does to your soul, you would beg of everything you meet to tear the viper from you, though it may mean the loss of a hand or an eye. If you could see what a sweet, divine, transforming power there is in humility, how it expels the poison of your nature and makes room for the Spirit of God to live in you, you would rather wish to be the footstool of all the world than lack the smallest degree of it.

## • NOTE B

"We need to know two things: first, that our salvation consists wholly in being saved from ourselves, or that which we are by nature; and second, that in the whole nature of things, nothing could be this salvation or savior to us but such a humility of God as is beyond all expression. Hence, the first unalterable condition given by the Savior to fallen man is this: Unless a man denies himself, he cannot be My disciple (Matt. 16:24). Self is the whole evil of fallen nature; self-denial is our capacity of being saved. Humility is our savior. Self is the root, the branches, the tree, of all the evil of our fallen state. All the evils of fallen angels and men have their birth in the pride of self. On the other hand, all the virtues of the heavenly life are the virtues of humility. It is humility alone that bridges the impassable gulf between heaven and hell. What is then, or in what lies, the great struggle for eternal life? It lies entirely in the battle between pride and humility. Pride and humility are the two master powers—the two kingdoms at war for the eternal possession of man.

"There never was, and never will be, but one humility, and that is the one humility of Christ. Pride and self have the all of man, until man has his all from Christ. Therefore, he only fights the good fight that is fought so that the self-idolatrous nature he has from Adam may be brought to death by the supernatural humility of Christ brought to life in him."—William Law

## • NOTE C

"To die to self or to come from under its power is not, cannot be, done by any active resistance we can make to it by the powers of nature. The one true way of dying to self is the way of patience, meekness, humility, and resignation to God. This is the truth and perfection of dying to self. For if I ask you what the Lamb of God means, must you not tell me that it means the perfection of patience, meekness, humility, and resignation to God? Must you not therefore say that a desire and faith in these virtues is an application to Christ, is a giving up of yourself to Him and the perfection of faith in Him? And then, because this inclination of your heart to sink down in patience, meekness, humility, and resignation to God is truly giving up all that you are and all that you have from fallen Adam, it is leaving all you have to follow Christ. It is your highest act of faith in Him. Christ is nowhere but in these virtues. When they are there, He is in His own kingdom. Let this be the Christ you follow.

"The Spirit of divine love can have no birth in any fallen creature until it wills and chooses to be dead to all self, in a patient, humble resignation to the power and mercy of God.

"I seek all my salvation through the merits and mediation of the meek, humble, patient, suffering Lamb of God. He alone has the power to bring forth the blessed birth of these heavenly virtues in my soul. There is no possibility of salvation but in and by the birth of the meek, humble, patient, resigned Lamb of God in our souls. When the Lamb of God has brought forth a real birth of His own meekness, humility, and full resignation to God in our souls, then it is the birthday of the Spirit of love in our souls. Whenever we attain this, our souls will feast with such a peace and joy in God that the remembrance of everything that we called peace or joy before will be blotted out.

"This way to God is infallible. This infallibility is grounded in the twofold character of our Savior: first, as He is the Lamb of God, a principle of all meekness and humility in the soul; and second, as He is the Light of heaven, and blesses eternal nature, and turns it into a kingdom of heaven. When we are willing to get rest for our souls in meek, humble resignation to God, then He, as the light of God and heaven, joyfully breaks in upon us. He turns our darkness into light and begins the kingdom of God and of love within us that will never have an end."—William Law

# A Prayer for Humility

Here I will give you an infallible touchstone that will tie everything to the truth. It is this: retire from the world and all conversation, only for one month. Neither write, nor read, nor debate anything with yourself. Stop all the former workings of your heart and mind. And, with all the strength of your heart, stand for the entire month, as continually as you can, in the following form of prayer to God. Offer it frequently on your knees. But whether sitting, walking, or standing, be always inwardly longing and earnestly praying this one prayer to God:

"Lord, I pray that of Your great goodness You would make known to me, and take from my heart, every kind and form and degree of pride, whether it be from evil spirits, or my own corrupt nature; and that You would awaken in me the deepest depth and truth of the humility that can make me capable of Your light and Holy Spirit."

Reject every thought, except that of waiting and praying in this matter from the bottom of your heart, with the kind of truth and earnestness that is used by people in torment who wish to pray and be delivered from it. If you can and will give yourself up in truth and sincerity to this spirit of prayer, I will venture to affirm that, if you had twice as many evil spirits in you as Mary Magdalene had, they will all be cast out of you, and you will be forced with her to weep tears of love at the feet of the holy Jesus.

# Book Three

# Absolute Surrender

# chapter 1

# Absolute Surrender

*Now Ben-Hadad the king of Syria gathered all his forces together;
thirty-two kings were with him, with horses and chariots. And he
went up and besieged Samaria, and made war against it. Then he
sent messengers into the city to Ahab king of Israel, and said to
him, "Thus says Ben-Hadad: 'Your silver and your gold are mine;
your loveliest wives and children are mine.'" And the king
of Israel answered and said, "My lord, O king, just as you say, I
and all that I have are yours."*
—1 Kings 20:1–4

Ahab gave what was asked of him by Ben-hadad—absolute
surrender. I want to use these words, *"My lord, O king,
just as you say, I and all that I have are yours,"* as the
words of absolute surrender with which every child of God ought
to yield himself to his Father. We have heard it before, but we
need to hear it very definitely—the condition of God's blessing is
absolute surrender of everything into His hands. Praise God! If
our hearts are willing for this, there is no end to what God will
do for us, and to the blessing God will bestow.

*Absolute surrender*—let me tell you where I got those words.
I used them myself often, and you have heard them numerous
times. But once, in Scotland, I was part of a group of people
talking about the condition of Christ's church, and what the
great need of the church and of believers is. There was in our
group a godly Christian worker who was involved in training
other workers for Christ, and I asked him what he would say
was the great need of the church—the message that ought to be
preached. He answered very quietly and simply and determinedly, "Absolute surrender to God is the one thing."

The words struck me as never before. And that man began
to tell how, in the Christian workers whom he trained, he found

that if they were sound on that point, they were willing to be taught and helped, and they always improved. Conversely, others who were not sound there very often went back and left the work. The condition for obtaining God's full blessing is *absolute surrender* to Him.

And now, I desire by God's grace to give to you this message—that your God in heaven answers the prayers that you have offered for blessing on yourselves and for blessing on those around you by this one demand: *Are you willing to surrender yourselves absolutely into His hands?* What is our answer to be? God knows there are hundreds of hearts who have said it, and there are hundreds more who long to say it but hardly dare to do so. And there are hearts who have said it, yet who have miserably failed, and who feel themselves condemned because they did not find the secret of the power to live that life. May God have a word for all!

Let me say, first of all, that God expects it from us.

## GOD EXPECTS YOUR SURRENDER

Yes, absolute surrender has its foundation in the very nature of God. God cannot do otherwise. Who is God? He is the Fountain of life, the only Source of existence and power and goodness. Throughout the universe there is nothing good but what God works. God has created the sun, the moon, the stars, the flowers, the trees, and the grass. Are they not all absolutely surrendered to God? Do they not allow God to work in them just what He pleases? When God clothes the lily with its beauty, is it not yielded up, surrendered, given over to God as He works in it its beauty? (See Matthew 6:28–29.) And God's redeemed children—can you think that God can do His work if there is only half or a part of them surrendered? God cannot do it. God is life, love, blessing, power, and infinite beauty, and God delights in communicating Himself to every child who is prepared to receive Him. But this lack of absolute surrender is just the thing that hinders God. And now He comes, and as God, He claims it.

You know in daily life what absolute surrender is. You know that everything has to be given up to its special, definite purpose and service. I have a pen in my pocket, and that pen is absolutely surrendered to the one work of writing. That pen must be absolutely surrendered to my hand if I am to write properly with it. If another person holds it partly, I cannot write properly. This coat I am wearing is absolutely given up to me to cover my body. This building is entirely given up to religious services. And now, do you expect that in your immortal being, in the divine nature that you have received by regeneration, God can work His work, every day and every hour, unless you are entirely given up to Him? God cannot. The temple of Solomon was absolutely surrendered to God when it was dedicated to Him. And every one of us is a temple of God, in which God will dwell and work mightily on one condition—absolute surrender to Him. God claims it, God is worthy of it, and without it God cannot work His blessed work in us.

God not only claims it, but God will work it Himself.

## GOD ACCOMPLISHES YOUR SURRENDER

I am sure there are many hearts that say, "Ah, but that absolute surrender implies so much!" Someone says, "Oh, I have passed through so much trial and suffering, and there is so much of the self-life still remaining. I dare not face entirely giving it up because I know it will cause so much trouble and agony."

Alas! How unfortunate that God's children have such thoughts of Him, such cruel thoughts. I come with a message to those who are fearful and anxious. God does not ask you to give the perfect surrender in your strength, or by the power of your will; God is willing to work it in you. Do we not read, *"It is God who works in you both to will and to do for His good pleasure"* (Phil. 2:13)? And that is what we should seek—to go on our faces before God, until our hearts learn to believe that the everlasting God Himself will come in to drive out what is wrong. He will conquer what is evil and work what is well-pleasing in His blessed sight. God Himself will work it in you.

Look at the men in the Old Testament, like Abraham. Do you think it was by accident that God found that man, the father of the faithful and the friend of God? Do you think it was Abraham himself, apart from God, who had such faith and such

181

obedience and such devotion? You know it is not so. God raised him up and prepared him as an instrument for His glory.

Did God not say to Pharaoh, *"For this purpose I have raised you up, that I may show My power in you"* (Exod. 9:16)? And if God said that of him, will God not say it far more of every child of His?

Oh, I want to encourage you, and I want you to cast away every fear. Come with that feeble desire. If there is the fear that says, "Oh, my desire is not strong enough. I am not willing to accept everything that may come, and I do not feel bold enough to say I can conquer everything," then I implore you, learn to know and trust your God now. Say to Him, "My God, I am willing that You should make me willing." If there is anything holding you back, or any sacrifice you are afraid of making, come to God now and prove how gracious your God is. Do not be afraid that He will command from you what He will not bestow.

God comes and offers to work this absolute surrender in you. All these searchings and hungerings and longings that are in your heart, I tell you, they are the drawings of the divine magnet, Christ Jesus. He lived a life of absolute surrender. He has possession of you; He is living in your heart by His Holy Spirit. You have hindered Him terribly, but He desires to help you to get a hold of Him entirely. And He comes and draws you now by His message and words. Will you not come and trust God to work in you that absolute surrender to Himself? Yes, blessed be God! He can do it, and He will do it.

God not only claims it and works it, but God accepts it when we bring it to Him.

## GOD ACCEPTS YOUR SURRENDER

God works it in the secret places of our hearts; God urges us by the hidden power of His Holy Spirit to come and speak it out, and we have to bring and yield to Him that absolute surrender. But remember, when you come and bring God that absolute surrender, it may, as far as your feelings or your consciousness goes, be a thing of great imperfection. You may doubt and hesitate and say, "Is it absolute?"

But remember, there was once a man to whom Christ had said, *"If you can believe, all things are possible to him who believes"* (Mark 9:23). And his heart was afraid, and he cried out, *"Lord, I believe; help my unbelief!"* (v. 24).

That was a faith that triumphed over Satan, and the evil spirit was cast out. And if you come and say, "Lord, I yield myself in absolute surrender to my God," even though you do so with a trembling heart and with the consciousness, "I do not feel the power; I do not feel the determination; I do not feel the assurance," it will succeed. Do not be afraid, but come just as you are. Even in the midst of your trembling, the power of the Holy Spirit will work.

Have you not yet learned the lesson that the Holy Spirit works with mighty power, while on the human side everything appears feeble? Look at the Lord Jesus Christ in Gethsemane. We read that He, *"through the eternal Spirit"* (Heb. 9:14), offered Himself as a sacrifice unto God. The almighty Spirit of God was enabling Him to do it. And yet, what agony and fear and exceeding sorrow came over Him, and how He prayed! Externally, you can see no sign of the mighty power of the Spirit, but the Spirit of God was there. And even so, while you are feeble and fighting and trembling, with faith in the hidden work of God's Spirit do not fear, but yield yourself.

And when you do yield yourself in absolute surrender, let it be with the faith that God does now accept it. This is the great point, and this is what we so often miss—that believers should be thus occupied with God in this matter of surrender. Be occupied with God. We need to get help, every one of us, so that in our daily lives God will be clearer to us, God will have the right place, and be all in all. And if we are to have this through life, let us begin now and look away from ourselves and look up to God. Let each one believe, "I, a poor worm on earth and a trembling child of God, full of failure, sin, and fear, bow here, and no one knows what passes through my heart." Simply say, "Oh God, I accept Your terms. I have pleaded for blessing on myself and others. I have accepted Your terms of absolute surrender." While your heart says this in deep silence, remember there is a God present who takes note of it and writes it down in His book. There is a God present who at that very moment takes possession of you. You may not feel it, you may not realize it, but God takes possession if you will trust Him.

God not only claims it and works it and accepts it when I bring it, but God also maintains it.

## GOD MAINTAINS YOUR SURRENDER

This is the great difficulty with many. People say, "I have often been stirred at a meeting or at a convention, and I have consecrated myself to God. But it has passed away. I know it may last for a week or for a month, but it fades away. After a time it is all gone."

But listen! It is because you do not believe what I am now going to tell you and remind you of. When God has begun the work of absolute surrender in you, and when God has accepted your surrender, then God holds Himself bound to care for it and to keep it. Will you believe that?

In this matter of surrender, there are two participants: God and you—God the everlasting and omnipotent Jehovah, and you a worm (Job 25:6). Worm, will you be afraid to trust yourself to this mighty God now? God is willing. Do you not believe that He can keep you continually, day by day, and moment by moment?

> Moment by moment I'm kept in His love;
> Moment by moment I've life from above.

If God allows the sun to shine on you moment by moment, without intermission, will God not let His life shine on you every moment? And why have you not experienced it? Because you have not trusted God for it, and you do not surrender yourself absolutely to God in that trust.

A life of absolute surrender has its difficulties. I do not deny that. Yes, it has something far more than difficulties; it is a life that is absolutely impossible by man's own power. But by the grace of God, by the power of God, by the power of the Holy Spirit dwelling in us, it is a life to which we are destined, and a life that is possible for us. Praise God! Let us believe that God will maintain it.

Some of you have read the words of George Müller, who, on his ninetieth birthday, told of all God's goodness to him. What did he say he believed to be the secret of his happiness and of all the blessing that God had given him? He said he believed there were two reasons. The one was that he had been enabled by grace to maintain a good conscience before God day by day. The other was that he was a lover of God's Word. Ah, yes, a good conscience is complete obedience to God day by day, and fellowship with God every day in His Word and prayer—that is a life of absolute surrender.

Such a life has two sides. On one side, there is absolute surrender to work what God wants you to do; on the other side, you must let God work what *He* wants to do.

First, what does it mean to do what God wants you to do?

Give yourselves up absolutely to the will of God. You know something of that will; not enough, far from all. But say absolutely to the Lord God, "By Your grace I desire to do Your will in everything, every moment of every day." Say, "Lord God, not a word upon my tongue but for Your glory. Not a movement of my temper but for Your glory. Not a feeling of love or hate in my heart but for Your glory, and according to Your blessed will."

Someone says, "Do you think that is possible?"

I ask, What has God promised you, and what can God do to fill a vessel absolutely surrendered to Him? Oh, God wants to bless you in a way beyond what you expect. From the beginning, no ear has heard, no eye has seen, what God has prepared for those who love Him (1 Cor. 2:9). God has prepared unheard-of things, blessings much more wonderful than you can imagine, more mighty than you can picture. They are divine blessings. Oh, say now, "I give myself absolutely to God, to His will, to do only what God wants."

It is God who will enable you to carry out the surrender.

And, on the other side, come and say, "I give myself absolutely to God, to let Him work in me *to will and to do for His good pleasure*' (Phil. 2:13), as He has promised to do."

Yes, the living God wants to work in His children in a way that we cannot understand, but that God's Word has revealed. He wants to work in us every moment of the day. God is willing to maintain our lives. Only let our absolute surrender be one of simple, childlike, and unbounded trust.

## GOD BLESSES WHEN YOU SURRENDER

This absolute surrender to God brings wonderful blessings.

What Ahab said to his enemy, King Ben-hadad, will we not say to our God and loving Father? *"My lord, O king, just as you say, I and all that I have are yours."* If we do say it, God's blessing will come upon us. God wants us to be separate from the world. We are called to come out from the world that hates God. Come out for God and say, "Lord, anything for You." If you say this with prayer and speak this into God's ear, He will accept it, and He will teach you what it means.

I say again, God will bless you. You have been praying for blessing. But do remember, there must be absolute surrender. Why is tea poured into a cup? Because it is empty, and given up to the tea. But put ink or vinegar or wine into it, and will anyone pour tea into the cup? Likewise, can God fill you, can God bless you if you are not absolutely surrendered to Him? He cannot. Let us believe that God has wonderful blessings for us if we will only stand up for God and say, though it may be with trembling wills, yet with believing hearts, "O God, I accept Your demands. I and all that I have are Yours. Absolute surrender is what my soul yields to You by divine grace."

You may not have such strong, clear feelings of surrender as you would like to have, but humble yourself in His sight, and acknowledge that you have grieved the Holy Spirit by your self-will, self-confidence, and self-effort. Bow humbly before Him, confessing your self-reliance, and ask Him to break your heart and to bring you into the dust before Him. Then, as you bow before Him, just accept God's teaching that in your flesh *"nothing good dwells"* (Rom. 7:18), and that nothing will help you except another life that must come in. You must deny self once and for all. Denying self must every moment be the power of your life, and then Christ will come in and take possession of you.

When was Peter delivered? When was the change accomplished? The change began with Peter weeping, and the Holy Spirit came down and filled his heart.

God the Father loves to give us the power of the Spirit. We have the Spirit of God dwelling within us. We come to God confessing this, and praising God for it, and yet confessing how we have grieved the Spirit. And then we bow our knees to the Father to ask that He would strengthen us with all might by the Spirit in the inner man, and that He would fill us with His mighty power. (See Ephesians 3:14–19.) And as the Spirit reveals Christ to us, Christ comes to live in our hearts forever, and the self-life is cast out.

Let us bow before God in humility, and in that humility confess before Him the state of the whole church. No words can tell the sad state of the church of Christ on earth. I wish I had words to speak what I sometimes feel about it. Just think of the Christians around you. I do not speak of nominal Christians, or of professing Christians, but I speak of hundreds and thousands of honest, earnest Christians who are not living a life in the power of God or to His glory. So little power, so little devotion or consecration to God, so little perception of the truth that a Christian is a man utterly surrendered to God's will! Oh, we need to confess the sins of God's people around us and to humble ourselves.

We are members of that sickly body. The sickliness of the body will hinder us and break us down unless we come to God. We must, in confession, separate ourselves from partnership with worldliness, with coldness toward each other. We must give ourselves up to be entirely and wholly for God.

How much Christian work is being done in the spirit of the flesh and in the power of self! How much work goes on, day by day, in which human energy—our wills and our thoughts about the work—is continually manifested, and in which there is little waiting upon God and upon the power of the Holy Spirit! Let us make a confession. But as we confess the state of the church, and the feebleness and sinfulness of work for God among us, let us come back to ourselves. Who is there who truly longs to be delivered from the power of the self-life, who truly acknowledges that it is the power of self and the flesh, and who is willing to cast all at the feet of Christ? There is deliverance.

I heard of one who had been an earnest Christian, and who spoke about the "cruel" thought of separation and death. But you do not think that, do you? What are we to think of separation and death? We are to think that this death is the path to glory for Christ. Christ, *"for the joy that was set before Him[,] endured the cross"* (Heb. 12:2). The Cross was the birthplace of His everlasting glory. Do you love Christ? Do you long to be in Christ, and yet not *like* Him? Let death be to you the most desirable thing on earth—death to self, and fellowship with Christ. Separation—do you think it a hard thing to be called to be entirely free from the world, and by that separation to be united to God and His love, by separation to become prepared for living and walking with God every day? Surely one ought to say, "Anything to bring me to separation, to death, for a life of full fellowship with God and Christ."

Come and cast this self-life and flesh-life at the feet of Jesus. Then trust Him. Do not worry yourselves with trying to understand everything about it, but come in the living faith that Christ will come into you with the power of His death and the power of His life. Then the Holy Spirit will bring the whole Christ—Christ crucified and risen and living in glory—into your hearts.

# chapter 2

# The Spirit of Love

*The fruit of the Spirit is love.*
—Galatians 5:22

I want to look at the life filled with the Holy Spirit more from the practical side. I want to show how this life will reveal itself in our daily walk and conduct.

Under the Old Testament, the Holy Spirit often came upon men as a divine Spirit of revelation to reveal the mysteries of God, or for power to do the work of God. But He did not dwell in them then. Now, many people want just the Old Testament gift of power for work, but they know very little of the New Testament gift of the indwelling Spirit, animating and renewing the whole life. When God gives the Holy Spirit, His great purpose is the formation of a holy character. It is a gift of a holy mind and spiritual disposition, and what we need, above everything else, is to say, "I must have the Holy Spirit sanctifying my whole inner life if I am really to live for God's glory."

You might say that when Christ promised the Spirit to the disciples, He did so in order that they might have power to be witnesses. True, but then they received the Holy Spirit in such heavenly power and reality that He took possession of their whole beings at once and equipped them as holy men for doing the work with power as they had to do it. Christ spoke of power to the disciples, but it was the Spirit filling their whole beings that worked the power.

I wish now to dwell upon the passage found in Galatians 5:22: *"The fruit of the Spirit is love."*

We read that *"love is the fulfillment of the law"* (Rom. 13:10), and my desire is to tell of love as a fruit of the Spirit with a twofold purpose. One is that this word may be a searchlight in our hearts, and give us a test by which to try all our thoughts about the Holy Spirit and all our experience of the holy life. Let us try ourselves by this word. Has this been our daily habit, to seek to be filled with the Holy Spirit as the Spirit of love? *"The fruit of the Spirit is love."* Has it been our experience that the more we have of the Holy Spirit, the more loving we become? In claiming the Holy Spirit, we should make this the first object of our expectation. The Holy Spirit comes as a Spirit of love.

Oh, if this were true in the church of Christ, how different her state would be! May God help us to get hold of this simple, heavenly truth, that the fruit of the Spirit is a love that appears in the life. Just as the Holy Spirit gets real possession of the life, the heart will be filled with real, divine, universal love.

One of the great reasons why God cannot bless His church is the lack of love. When the body is divided, there cannot be strength. In the time of their great religious wars, when Holland stood out so nobly against Spain, one of their mottoes was, "Unity gives strength." Only when God's people stand as one body, one before God in the fellowship of love, one toward another in deep affection, one before the world in a love that the world can see—only then will they have power to secure the blessing that they ask of God.

Remember that if a vessel that ought to be whole is cracked into many pieces, it cannot be filled. You can take one part of the vessel and dip a little water into that, but if you want the vessel full, the vessel must be whole. This is literally true of Christ's church. And if there is one thing we must pray for still, it is this: "Lord, melt us together into one by the power of the Holy Spirit. Let the Holy Spirit, who at Pentecost made them all of one heart and one soul, do His blessed work among us." Praise God, we can love each other in a divine love, for *"the fruit of the Spirit is love."* Give yourselves up to love, and the Holy Spirit will come; receive the Spirit, and He will teach you to love more.

## GOD IS LOVE

Now, why is it that the fruit of the Spirit is love? Because *"God is love"* (1 John 4:8).

And what does this mean?

It is the very nature and being of God to delight in communicating Himself. God has no selfishness; God keeps nothing to Himself. God's nature is to be always giving. You see it in the sun and the moon and the stars, in every flower, in every bird in the air, in every fish in the sea. God communicates life to His creatures. And the angels around His throne, the seraphim and cherubim who are flames of fire—where does their glory come from? It comes from God because He is love, and He imparts to them part of His brightness and His blessedness. And we, His redeemed children—God delights to pour His love into us. Why? Because, as I said, God keeps nothing for Himself. From eternity God had His only begotten Son, and the Father gave Him all things, and nothing that God had was kept back. *"God is love"* (1 John 4:8).

One of the old church fathers said that we cannot better understand the Trinity than as a revelation of divine love—the Father, the loving One, the Fountain of love; the Son, the beloved One, the Reservior of love, in whom the love was poured out; and the Spirit, the living love that united both and then overflowed into this world. The Spirit of Pentecost, the Spirit of the Father, the Spirit of the Son is love. And when the Holy Spirit comes to us and to other men and women, will He be less a Spirit of love than He is in God? It cannot be; He cannot change His nature. The Spirit of God is love, and *"the fruit of the Spirit is love."*

## MANKIND NEEDS LOVE

Love was the one great need of mankind, the thing that Christ's redemption came to accomplish: to restore love to this world.

When man sinned, why did he sin? Selfishness triumphed; he sought self instead of God. And just look! Adam at once began to accuse the woman of having led him astray. Love of God had gone; love of man was lost. Also consider that, of Adam's first two children, the one became a murderer of his brother.

Does this not teach us that sin had robbed the world of love? Oh, what a proof the history of the world has been of love having been lost! There may have been beautiful examples of love even among the heathen, but only as a little remnant of what was lost. One of the worst things sin did for man was to make him selfish, for selfishness cannot love.

The Lord Jesus Christ came down from heaven as the Son of God's love. *"God so loved the world that He gave His only begotten Son"* (John 3:16). God's Son came to show what love is, and He lived a life of love here on earth in fellowship with His disciples, in compassion over the poor and miserable, in love even for His enemies. He died the death of love. When He went back to heaven, whom did He send down? The Spirit of love, to come and banish selfishness and envy and pride, and to bring the love of God into the hearts of men. *"The fruit of the Spirit is love."*

And what was the preparation for the promise of the Holy Spirit? Before Christ promised the Holy Spirit, He gave a new commandment, and about that new commandment He said wonderful things. One thing was, *"As I have loved you,...love one another"* (John 13:34). To them His dying love was to be the only law of their conduct and fellowship with each other. What a message to those fishermen, to those men full of pride and selfishness! "Learn to love each other," said Christ, "as I have loved you." And by the grace of God they did it. When Pentecost came, they *"were of one heart and one soul"* (Acts 4:32). Christ did it for them.

And now He calls us to live and to walk in love. He demands that, though a man hate you, still you must love him (Matt. 5:44). True love cannot be conquered by anything in heaven or on earth. The more hatred there is, the more love triumphs through it all and shows its true nature. This is the love that Christ commanded His disciples to exercise.

What more did He say? *"By this all will know that you are My disciples, if you have love for one another"* (John 13:35).

You all know what it is to wear a badge. And Christ said to His disciples, in effect, "I give you a badge, and that badge is love. That is to be your mark. It is the only thing in heaven or on earth by which men can know Me."

Do we not begin to fear that love has fled from the earth? That if we were to ask the world, "Have you seen us wear the badge of love?" the world would say, "No, what we have heard of the church of Christ is that there is not a place where there is no quarreling and separation"? Let us ask God with one heart that we may wear the badge of Jesus' love. God is able to give it.

## LOVE CONQUERS SELFISHNESS

*"The fruit of the Spirit is love."* Why? Because nothing but love can expel and conquer our selfishness.

Self is the great curse, whether in its relation to God, to our fellowmen in general, or to fellow Christians. It causes us to think of ourselves and to seek our own way. Self is our greatest curse. But, praise God, Christ came to redeem us from self. We sometimes talk about deliverance from the self-life—and thank God for every word that can be said about it to help us. But I am afraid some people think deliverance from the self-life means that now they are no longer going to have any trouble in serving God. They forget that deliverance from self-life means to be a vessel overflowing with love to everybody all day long.

And here you have the reason why many people pray for the power of the Holy Spirit. They get something, but oh, so little, because they prayed for power for work, and power for blessing, but they have not prayed for power for full deliverance from self. This means not only the righteous self in fellowship with God, but also the unloving self in fellowship with men. And there is deliverance. *"The fruit of the Spirit is love."* I bring you the glorious promise of Christ that He is able to fill our hearts with love.

A great many of us try hard at times to love. We try to force ourselves to love, and I do not say this is wrong; it is better than nothing. But the end of it is always very sad. "I fail continually," many must confess. And what is the reason? The reason is simply this: they have never learned to believe and accept the truth that the Holy Spirit can pour God's love into their heart. The blessed Scripture has often been limited—*"The love of God has been poured out in our hearts"* (Rom. 5:5). It has often been understood only in the sense that the love of God has been poured out *to me*. Oh, what a limitation! That is only the beginning. The love of God is always the love of God in its entirety, in its fullness as an indwelling power. It is a love of God for me that leaps back to Him in love, and overflows to my fellowmen in love—God's love for me, and my love for God, and my love for my fellowmen. The three are one; you cannot separate them.

Believe that the love of God can be poured out in your heart and mind so that you can love throughout the day.

"Oh," you say, "how little I have understood that!"

Why is a lamb always gentle? Because that is its nature. Does it cost the lamb any trouble to be gentle? No. Why not? It is so beautiful and gentle. Must a lamb study to be gentle? No. Why does it come so easily? It is its nature. And a wolf—why does it cost a wolf no trouble to be cruel, and to put its fangs into the poor lamb or sheep? Because that is its nature. It does not have to summon up its courage; the wolf's nature is there.

And how can I learn to love? I cannot learn to love until the Spirit of God fills my heart with God's love, and I begin to long for God's love in a very different sense from which I have sought it so selfishly—as a comfort, a joy, a happiness, and a pleasure to myself. I will not learn it until I realize that *"God is love"* (1 John 4:8), and I claim and receive it as an indwelling power for self-sacrifice. I will not love until I begin to see that my glory, my blessedness, is to be like God and like Christ, in giving up everything in myself for my fellowmen. May God teach us this! Oh, the divine blessedness of the love with which the Holy Spirit can fill our hearts! *"The fruit of the Spirit is love."*

## LOVE IS GOD'S GIFT

Why do we need God to give us love? My answer is, Without His love we cannot live the daily life of love.

How often, when we speak about the consecrated life, we have to speak about *temperament,* and people have sometimes said, "You make too much of temperament."

I do not think we can make too much of it. Think for a moment of a clock and of what its hands mean. The hands tell me what is within the clock, and if I see that the hands stand still, or that the hands point wrong, or that the clock is slow or fast, I say that something inside the clock is not working properly. A person's temperament is just like the revelation that the clock's face gives of what is within. Temperament is proof of whether the love of Christ is filling the heart or not. There are many people who find it easier in church, in prayer meeting, or in work for the Lord—diligent, earnest work—to be holy and happy than in their daily lives with their families. How many find it easier to be holy and happy outside the home than in it! Where is the love of God? In Christ. God has prepared for us a wonderful redemption in Christ, and He longs to make something supernatural of us. Have we learned to long for it, ask for it, and expect it in its fullness?

Then there is the tongue! We sometimes speak of the tongue when we talk of the better life and the restful life, but just think what liberty many Christians give to their tongues. They say, "I have a right to say what I please."

When they speak about each other, when they speak about their neighbors, when they speak about other Christians, how often there are sharp remarks! May God keep me from saying anything that would be unloving. May God shut my mouth if I am not speaking in tender love. What I am saying is a fact. How often sharp criticism, harsh judgment, hasty opinion, unloving words, secret contempt and condemnation of each other are found among Christians who are banded together in work! Oh, just as a mother's love covers her children, delights in them, and has the tenderest compassion with their foibles or failures, so there ought to be in the heart of every believer a motherly love toward every brother and sister in Christ. Have you aimed at that? Have you sought it? Have you ever pleaded for it? Jesus Christ said, *"As I have loved you,...love one another"* (John 13:34). And He did not put that among the other commandments, but He said, in effect, "This is a new commandment, the one commandment: Love one another as I have loved you."

It is in our daily lives and conduct that *"the fruit of the Spirit is love."* From this source come all the graces and virtues in which love is manifested—joy, peace, long-suffering, gentleness, goodness, no sharpness or hardness in your tone, no unkindness or selfishness, meekness before God and man. You see that all these are the gentler virtues. I have often thought as I read those words in Colossians, *"Therefore, as the elect of God, holy and beloved, put on tender mercies, kindness, humility, meekness, longsuffering"* (Col. 3:12), that if we had written this, we would have put in the foreground the strong virtues, such as zeal, courage, and diligence. But we need to see how the gentler, the tenderest virtues are especially connected with dependence on the Holy Spirit. These are indeed heavenly graces. They never were found in the heathen world. Christ was needed to come from heaven to teach us. Your blessedness is long-suffering, meekness, kindness; your glory is humility before God. The fruit of the Spirit that He brought from heaven out of the heart of the crucified Christ, and that He gives in our hearts, is, first and foremost, love.

You know what John said: *"No one has seen God at any time. If we love one another, God abides in us"* (1 John 4:12). That is, I cannot see God, but as a compensation I can see my brother, and if I love him, God dwells in me. Is that really true—that I cannot see God, but I must love my brother, and God will dwell in me? Loving my brother is the way to real fellowship with God. You know what John further said in that most solemn test: *"If someone says, 'I love God,' and hates his brother, he is a liar; for he who does not love his brother whom he has seen, how can he love God whom he has not seen?"* (v. 20).

You might know of someone who is most unlovable. He upsets you every time you meet him. His disposition is the very opposite to yours. You are a careful businessman, and you have to associate with him in your business. He is untidy, unbusinesslike. You say, "I cannot love him." Oh, friend, you have not learned the lesson that Christ wanted to teach above everything. Let a man be what he will; you are to love him. Love is to be the fruit of the Spirit all day long and every day. Yes, listen! If you don't love that unlovable man whom you have seen, how can you love God whom you have not seen? You can deceive yourself with beautiful thoughts about loving God. You must prove your love for God by your love for your brother; this is the one standard by which God will judge your love for Him. If the love of God is in your heart, you will love your brother. *"The fruit of the Spirit is love."*

And what is the reason why God's Holy Spirit cannot come in power? Is it not possible?

You remember the comparison I used in speaking of the vessel. I can put a little water into a small vessel, but if a vessel is to be full, it must be unbroken. And the children of God, wherever they come together, to whatever church or congregation they belong, must love each other intensely, or the Spirit of God cannot do His work. We talk about grieving the Spirit of God by worldliness and ritualism and formality and error and indifference. But I tell you, the one thing above everything that grieves God's Spirit is this lack of love. Let every heart search itself and ask that God may search it.

## OUR LOVE SHOWS GOD'S POWER

Why are we taught that *"the fruit of the Spirit is love"*? Because the Spirit of God has come to make our daily lives an exhibition of divine power and a revelation of what God can do for His children.

In Acts, we read that the disciples were *"of one heart and one soul"* (Acts 4:32). During the three years they had walked with Christ, they never had been in that spirit. All Christ's teaching could not make them *"of one heart and one soul."* But the Holy Spirit came from heaven and poured out the love of God in their hearts, and they were *"of one heart and one soul."* The same Holy Spirit that brought the love of heaven into their hearts must fill us, too. Nothing less will do. Even as Christ did, one might preach love for three years with the tongue of an angel (see 1 Corinthians 13:1), but that would not teach any man to love unless the power of the Holy Spirit came upon him to bring the love of heaven into his heart.

Think of the church at large. What divisions! Think of the different bodies. Take the question of holiness, take the question of the cleansing blood, take the question of the baptism of the Spirit—what differences are caused among believers by such questions! That there are differences of opinion does not trouble me. We do not all have the same temperament and mind. But how often hate, bitterness, contempt, separation, and unlovingness are caused by the holiest truths of God's Word! Our doctrines, our creeds, have been more important than love. We often think we are valiant for the truth, and we forget God's command to speak *"the truth in love"* (Eph. 4:15). And it was so in the time of the Reformation between the Lutheran and

197

Calvinistic churches. What bitterness there was in regard to Communion, which was meant to be the bond of union among all believers! And so, through the ages, the very dearest truths of God have become mountains that have separated us.

If we want to pray in power, if we want to expect the Holy Spirit to come down in power, and if we indeed want God to pour out His Spirit, we must enter into a covenant with God that we will love one another with a heavenly love.

Are you ready for this? Only this is true love that is large enough to take in all God's children, the most unloving and unlovable and unworthy and unbearable and trying. If my vow— absolute surrender to God—is sincere, then it must mean absolute surrender to the divine love to fill me. I must be a servant of love to love every child of God around me. *"The fruit of the Spirit is love."*

Oh, God did something wonderful when He gave Christ, at His right hand, the gift of the Holy Spirit, who was to come down out of the heart of the Father and His everlasting love. And how we have degraded the Holy Spirit into a mere power by which we have to do our work! God forgive us! Oh, that the Holy Spirit might be held in honor as a power to fill us with the very life and nature of God and of Christ!

## CHRISTIAN WORK REQUIRES LOVE

*"The fruit of the Spirit is love."* Why is it so? And the answer comes: This is the only power in which Christians really can do their work.

Yes, it is love that we need. We need not only love that is to bind us to each other, but we also need a divine love in our work for the lost around us. Oh, do we not often undertake a great deal of work from a natural spirit of compassion for our fellowmen? Do we not often undertake Christian work because our minister or friend calls us to it? And do we not often perform Christian work with a certain zeal but without having had a baptism of love?

People often ask, "What is the baptism of fire?"

I have answered more than once, "I know no fire like the fire of God, the fire of everlasting love that consumed the sacrifice on

Calvary." The baptism of love is what the church needs, and to get this we must begin at once to get down on our faces before God in confession, and plead, "Lord, let love from heaven flow down into my heart. I am giving up my life to pray and live as one who has given himself up for the everlasting love to dwell in and fill him."

Ah, yes, if the love of God were in our hearts, what a difference it would make! There are hundreds of believers who say, "I work for Christ, and I feel I could work much harder, but I do not have the gift. I do not know how or where to begin. I do not know what I can do."

Brother, sister, ask God to baptize you with the Spirit of love, and love will find its way. Love is a fire that will burn through every difficulty. You may be a shy, hesitating person who cannot speak well, but love can burn through everything. God fills us with love! We need it for our work.

Perhaps you have read many touching stories of love expressed, and you have said, "How beautiful!" I heard one not long ago. A lady had been asked to speak at a rescue home where there were a number of poor women. As she arrived there and passed by the window with the matron, she saw a wretched woman sitting outside and asked, "Who is that?"

The matron answered, "She has been into the house thirty or forty times, and she has always gone away again. Nothing can be done with her, she is so low and hard."

But the lady said, "She must come in."

The matron then said, "We have been waiting for you, and the company is assembled, and you have only an hour for the address."

The lady replied, "No, this is of more importance," and she went outside where the woman was sitting. She said to the woman, "My sister, what is the matter?"

"I am not your sister," was the reply.

Then the lady laid her hand on her, and said: "Yes, I am your sister, and I love you." So she spoke until the heart of the poor woman was touched.

The conversation lasted some time, and the company was waiting patiently. Ultimately, the lady brought the woman into the room. There was the poor, wretched, degraded creature, full of shame. She would not sit on a chair, but sat down on a stool beside the speaker's seat, and she let her lean against her, with her arms around the poor woman's neck, while she spoke to the assembled people. And that love touched the woman's heart; she had found one who really loved her, and that love gave access to the love of Jesus.

Praise God! There is love on earth in the hearts of God's children; but oh, that there were more!

O God, baptize our ministers with a tender love, and our missionaries, our Bible readers, our workers, and our young men's and young women's associations. Oh, that God would begin with us now and baptize us with heavenly love!

### LOVE INSPIRES INTERCESSION

Once again, it is only love that can equip us for the work of intercession.

I have said that love must equip us for our work. Do you know what the hardest and the most important work is that has to be done for this sinful world? It is the work of intercession, the work of going to God and taking time to lay hold of Him.

A man may be an earnest Christian, an earnest minister, and he may do good. But unfortunately, how often he has to confess that he knows little of what it is to tarry with God! May God give us the great gift of an intercessory spirit, a spirit of prayer and supplication! Let me ask you in the name of Jesus not to let a day pass without praying for all God's people.

I find that there are Christians who think little of this. I find that there are prayer groups where they pray for the members, and not for all believers. I urge you, take time to pray for the church of Christ. It is right to pray for the heathen, as I have already said. God help us to pray more for them. It is right to pray for missionaries and for evangelistic work and for the unconverted. But Paul did not tell people to pray for the heathen or the unconverted. Paul told them to pray for believers. Make this your first prayer every day: "Lord, bless Your people everywhere."

The state of Christ's church is indescribably low. Plead for God's people that He would visit them, plead for each other, plead for all believers who are trying to work for God. Let love fill your heart. Ask Christ to pour fresh love into you every day. Try to grasp this truth, by the Holy Spirit of God, "I am separated unto the Holy Spirit, and *'the fruit of the Spirit is love.'"* God help us to understand it.

May God grant that we learn day by day to wait more quietly upon Him. We must not wait upon God only for ourselves, or the power to do so will soon be lost. But we must give ourselves up to the ministry and the love of intercession, and pray more for God's people in general, for God's people around us, for the Spirit of love in ourselves and in them, and for the work of God we are connected with. The answer will surely come, and our waiting upon God will be a source of untold blessing and power. *"The fruit of the Spirit is love."*

Do you have a lack of love to confess before God? Then make confession and say before Him, "O Lord, my lack of heart, my lack of love—I confess it." And then, as you cast that lack at His feet, believe that the blood cleanses you, that Jesus comes in His mighty, cleansing, saving power to deliver you, and that He will give His Holy Spirit.

*"The fruit of the Spirit is love."*

chapter 3

# Separated unto the Holy Spirit

*Now in the church that was at Antioch there were certain prophets
and teachers: Barnabas, Simeon who was called Niger, Lucius of
Cyrene, Manaen...and Saul. As they ministered to the Lord and
fasted, the Holy Spirit said, "Now separate to Me Barnabas and
Saul for the work to which I have called them." Then, having
fasted and prayed, and laid hands on them, they sent them away.
So, being sent out by the Holy Spirit, they went down to Seleucia.*
—Acts 13:1–4

In the story contained in this Scripture passage, we find some
precious thoughts to guide us to what God wants for us, and
what God wants to do for us. The great lesson of the verses
quoted is this: the Holy Spirit is the director of the work of God
upon the earth. And what we should do, if we are to rightly work
for God, and if God is to bless our work, is to see that we stand
in a right relationship with the Holy Spirit. We must be sure
that we give Him the place of honor that belongs to Him everyday. In all our work and (what is more) in our private, inner
lives, the Holy Spirit must always have first place. Let me
point out to you some of the precious thoughts our passage
suggests.

## GOD'S PLANS FOR HIS KINGDOM

First of all, we see that God has His own plans with regard
to His kingdom. His church at Antioch had been established.
God had certain plans and intentions with regard to Asia and
with regard to Europe. He had conceived them; they were His,
and He made them known to His servants.

Our great Commander organizes every campaign, and His
generals and officers do not always know the great plans. They

often receive sealed orders, and they have to wait for Him to reveal their contents. God in heaven has wishes and a will in regard to any work that ought to be done, and to the way in which it has to be done. Blessed is the man who receives God's secrets and works under Him.

Some years ago, in Wellington, South Africa, we opened a Mission Institute—what is considered there to be a fine, large building. At our opening services, the principal said something that I have never forgotten. He remarked, "Last year we gathered here to lay the foundation stone, and what was there then to be seen? Nothing but rubbish and stones and bricks and ruins of an old building that had been pulled down. There we laid the foundation stone, and very few knew what the building was that was to rise. No one knew it perfectly in every detail except one man, the architect. In his mind it was all clear, and as the contractor and the mason and the carpenter came to do their work, they took their orders from him. The humblest laborer had to be obedient to orders. The structure rose, and this beautiful building has been completed. And just so," he added, "this building that we open today is simply laying the foundation of a work of which only God knows what is to become."

God has His workers and His plans clearly mapped out. Our position is to wait so that God may communicate to us as much of His will as is necessary.

We simply have to be faithful in obedience, carrying out His orders. God has a plan for His church on earth. But unfortunately, we too often make our own plans. We think that we know what ought to be done. We ask God to bless our feeble efforts, instead of absolutely refusing to go unless God goes before us. God has planned for the work and the extension of His kingdom. The Holy Spirit has had that work given to Him, to be under His control. *"The work to which I have called them."* May God, therefore, help us all to be afraid of touching *"the ark of God"* (2 Sam. 6:6), except as we are led by the Holy Spirit.

## God Reveals His Will

Second, God is willing and able to reveal to His servants what His will is.

Yes, blessed be God, communications still come down from heaven! As we read here what the Holy Spirit said, so the Spirit will still speak to His church and His people. In these latter days, He has often done it. He has come to individual men, and by His divine teaching He has led them out into fields of labor that others could not at first understand or approve. He has led them into ways and methods that did not appeal to the majority. But the Holy Spirit still, in our time, teaches His people. Thank God, in our foreign missionary societies and in our home missions, and in a thousand forms of work, the guiding of the Holy Spirit is known. But (we are all ready, I think, to confess) He is too little known. We have not learned to wait upon Him enough, and so we should make a solemn declaration before God: "O God, we need to wait more for You to show us Your will."

Do not ask God only for power. Many Christians have their own plans of working, but God must send the power. The man works in his own will, and God must give the grace—the one reason why God often gives so little grace and so little success. But let us all take our place before God and say, "What is done in the will of God, the strength of God will not be withheld from it. What is done in the will of God must have the mighty blessing of God."

And so let our first desire be to have the will of God revealed.

If you ask me, "Is it an easy thing to get these communications from heaven and to understand them?" I can give you the answer. It is easy to those who are in proper fellowship with heaven, and who understand the art of waiting on God in prayer.

We often ask, "How can a person know the will of God?" And people want, when they are in perplexity, to pray very earnestly so that God will answer them at once. But God can reveal His will only to a heart that is humble and tender and empty. God can reveal His will in perplexities and special difficulties only to a heart that has learned to obey and honor Him loyally in little things and in daily life.

## HEARTS SURRENDERED TO GOD

This brings me to the third thought. Note the disposition to which the Spirit reveals God's will.

What do we read in the beginning verses of Acts 13? There were a number of men ministering to the Lord and fasting, and the Holy Spirit came and spoke to them. Some people understand this passage as they would in reference to a missionary committee of our day. We see that there is an open field, and we have had our missions in other fields. We decide to enter that new field. We have virtually settled on this, and we pray about it. But the position was a very different one in those former days. I doubt whether any of them thought of Europe (for later on even Paul himself tried to go back into Asia, until the night vision called him by the will of God). Look at those men. God had done wonders. He had extended the church to Antioch, and He had given rich and large blessings. Now, here were these men ministering to the Lord, serving Him with prayer and fasting. What a deep conviction they had—"It must all come directly from heaven. We are in fellowship with the risen Lord; we must have a close union with Him, and somehow He will let us know what He wants." And there they were, empty, ignorant, helpless, glad, and joyful, but deeply humbled.

"O Lord," they seemed to say, "we are Your servants, and in fasting and prayer we wait upon You. What is Your will for us?"

Was it not the same with Peter? He was on the housetop, fasting and praying, and little did he think of the vision and the command to go to Caesarea. He was ignorant of what his work might be.

It is in hearts entirely surrendered to the Lord Jesus, separating themselves from the world and even from ordinary religious exercises, and giving themselves up in intense prayer to look to their Lord, that the heavenly will of God will be manifested.

The word *fasting* occurs a second time in the third verse: *"Having fasted and prayed."* When you pray, you love to go into your prayer closet, according to the command of Jesus, and shut the door (Matt. 6:6). You shut out business and company and pleasure and anything that can distract, and you want to be alone with God. But in one way, even the material world follows you there. You must eat. These men wanted to shut themselves out from the influences of the material and the visible, and they fasted. What they ate was simply enough to supply the needs of nature. In the intensity of their souls, they thought to give expression to their letting go of everything on earth by fasting before God. Oh, may God give us that intensity of desire—that separation from everything—because we want to wait upon God, so that the Holy Spirit may reveal to us God's blessed will.

## SEPARATION UNTO THE HOLY SPIRIT

The fourth thought is this: What is now the will of God as the Holy Spirit reveals it? It is contained in one phrase: separation unto the Holy Spirit. This is the keynote of the message from heaven.

"*'Separate to Me Barnabas and Saul for the work to which I have called them.'* The work is mine; I care for it. I have chosen these men and called them, and I want you who represent the church of Christ upon earth to set them apart unto Me."

Look at this heavenly message in its two aspects. The men were to be set apart to the Holy Spirit, and the church was to do this separating work. The Holy Spirit could trust these men to do it in a right spirit. There they were, abiding in fellowship with the heavenly. The Holy Spirit could say to them, "Do the work of separating these men." And these were the men the Holy Spirit had prepared, and He could say of them, "Let them be separated unto Me."

Here we come to the very root—the very life—of the need of Christian workers. The question is, "What is needed so that the power of God will rest on us more mightily? What is needed so that the blessing of God will be poured out more abundantly among those poor, wretched people and perishing sinners among whom we labor?" And the answer from heaven is, "I want men separated unto the Holy Spirit."

What does this imply? You know that there are two spirits on earth. Christ said, when He spoke about the Holy Spirit, *"The world cannot receive* [Him]" (John 14:17). Paul said, *"We have received, not the spirit of the world, but the Spirit who is from God"* (1 Cor. 2:12). This is the great need in every worker—the spirit of the world going out, and the Spirit of God coming in to take possession of the inner life and of the whole being.

I am sure there are workers who often cry to God for the Holy Spirit to come upon them as a Spirit of power for their work. When they feel that measure of power, and receive blessing, they thank God for it. But God wants something more and something higher. God wants us to seek the Holy Spirit as a Spirit of power in our own hearts and lives, to conquer self and cast out sin, and to work the blessed and beautiful image of Jesus into us.

There is a difference between the power of the Spirit as a gift and the power of the Spirit for the grace of a holy life. A man may often have a measure of the power of the Spirit, but if there is not a large measure of the Spirit as the Spirit of grace and holiness, the defect will be evident in his work. He may be the means of conversion, but he will never help people on to a higher standard of spiritual life. When he passes away, a great deal of his work may pass away, too. But a man who is separated unto the Holy Spirit is a man who is given up to say, "Father, let the Holy Spirit have full dominion over me, in my home, in my temperament, in every word of my tongue, in every thought of my heart, in every feeling toward my fellowmen. Let the Holy Spirit have entire possession."

Is this what has been the longing and the covenant of your heart with your God—to be a man or a woman separated and given up unto the Holy Spirit? I urge you to listen to the voice of heaven: *"Separate to Me,"* said the Holy Spirit. Yes, separated unto the Holy Spirit. May God grant that the Word may enter into the very depths of our beings to search us, and if we discover that we have not come out from the world entirely—if God discloses to us that self-life, self-will, and self-exaltation are there—let us humble ourselves before Him.

Man, woman, brother, sister, you are a worker separated unto the Holy Spirit. Is this true? Has this been your desire? Has this been your surrender? Has this been what you have expected through faith in the power of our risen and almighty Lord Jesus? If not, here is the call of faith, and here is the key of blessing—separated unto the Holy Spirit. May God write the word in our hearts!

I said that the Holy Spirit spoke to the church in Antioch as a church capable of doing that work. The Holy Spirit trusted them. God grant that our churches, our missionary societies, and all our directors and councils and committees may consist of men and women who are fit for the work of separating workers unto the Holy Spirit. We can ask God for that, too.

## A MATTER OF ACTION

Then comes my fifth thought: one's holy partnership with the Holy Spirit in this work becomes a matter of consciousness and of action.

These men in Antioch, what did they do? They set apart Paul and Barnabas, and then the two, being sent forth by the Holy Spirit, went to Seleucia. Oh, what fellowship—the Holy Spirit in heaven doing part of the work, men on earth doing the other part! After the ordination of the men on earth, it is written in God's inspired Word that they were sent forth by the Holy Spirit.

See how this partnership called them to new prayer and fasting. They had for a certain time been ministering to the Lord and fasting, perhaps for days. The Holy Spirit spoke, and they had to do the work and enter into partnership, and at once they came together for more prayer and fasting. This is the spirit in which they obeyed the command of their Lord. And this teaches us that it is not only in the beginning of our Christian work, but all along, that we need to have our strength in prayer. If there is one thought with regard to the church of Christ that at times comes to me with overwhelming sorrow; if there is one thought in regard to my own life of which I am ashamed; if there is one thought of which I feel that the church of Christ has not accepted and not grasped; if there is one thought that makes me pray to God, "Oh, teach us new things by Your grace"—it is the wonderful power that prayer is meant to have in the kingdom. We have so little availed ourselves of it.

You may have read the expression of Christian in Bunyan's great work, *The Pilgrim's Progress,* when he found he had the key that would unlock the dungeon. He said, "What a fool am I, thus to lie in a stinking dungeon, when I may as well walk at liberty! I have a key in my bosom, called Promise, that will, I am persuaded, open any lock in Doubting Castle." Similarly, we have the key that can unlock the dungeon of atheism and of heathendom. But, oh, we are far more occupied with our work than we are with prayer! We believe more in speaking to men than we believe in speaking to God. Learn from these men that the work that the Holy Spirit commands must call us to new fasting and prayer, to new separation from the spirit and the pleasures of the world, to new consecration to God and to His fellowship. Those men gave themselves up to fasting and prayer, and if in all our ordinary Christian work there were more prayer, there would be more blessing in our own inner lives. If we felt and proved and testified to the world that our only strength lay in keeping in contact with Christ, every minute allowing Him to work in us—if that were our spirit every minute, would not, by the grace of God, our lives be holier? Would they not be more abundantly fruitful?

I hardly know a more solemn warning in God's Word than that which we find in the third chapter of Galatians, where Paul asked, *"Having begun in the Spirit, are you now being made perfect by the flesh?"* (Gal. 3:3).

Do you understand what this means? A terrible danger in Christian work—just as in a Christian life that is begun with much prayer, begun in the Holy Spirit—is that it may be gradually diverted to the lines of the flesh. In the time of our first perplexity and helplessness, we prayed much to God. God answered and God blessed, and our organization became perfected. Our band of workers became larger. But gradually the organization and the work and the rush have so taken possession of us that the power of the Spirit—in which we began when we were a small company—has almost been lost. Oh, I urge you, note it well! It was with new prayer and fasting, with more prayer and fasting, that this company of disciples carried out the command of the Holy Spirit, *"My soul, wait silently for God alone"* (Ps. 62:5). This is our highest and most important work. The Holy Spirit comes in answer to believing prayer.

When the exalted Jesus had ascended to the throne, the footstool of the throne was the place where His waiting disciples cried to Him for ten days. And this is the law of the kingdom—the King on the throne, the servants on the footstool. May God find us there unceasingly!

## THE BLESSING OF THE SPIRIT-LED LIFE

Here is the final thought: what a wonderful blessing comes when the Holy Spirit is allowed to lead and to direct the work, and when it is carried on in obedience to Him!

You know the story of the mission on which Barnabas and Saul were sent out. You know what power there was with them. The Holy Spirit sent them, and they went on from place to place with large blessing. The Holy Spirit was their leader further on. You recall how it was by the Spirit that Paul was hindered from going again into Asia, and was led away over to Europe. Oh, the blessing that rested on that little company of men and on their ministry unto the Lord!

Let us learn to believe that God has a blessing for us. The Holy Spirit, into whose hands God has put the work, has been called "the Executive of the Holy Trinity." The Holy Spirit has not only power, but He also has the Spirit of love. He is brooding over this dark world and every sphere of work in it, and He is willing to bless. And why is there not more blessing? There can be only one answer. We have not honored the Holy Spirit as we should have done. Is there one who can say that this is not true? Is not every thoughtful heart ready to cry, "God forgive me that I have not honored the Holy Spirit as I should have, that I have grieved Him, that I have allowed self, the flesh, and my own will to work where the Holy Spirit should have been honored! May God forgive me that I have allowed self, the flesh, and the will to actually have the place that God wanted the Holy Spirit to have."

Oh, this sin is greater than we know! No wonder there is so much feebleness and failure in the church of Christ!

chapter 4

# Peter's Repentance

*And the Lord turned and looked at Peter. And Peter remembered*
*the word of the Lord, how He had said to him, "Before*
*the rooster crows, you will deny Me three times."*
*So Peter went out and wept bitterly.*
—Luke 22:61–62

This Scripture describes the turning point in the life of Peter. Christ had said to him, *"You cannot follow Me now"* (John 13:36). Peter was not in a fit state to follow Christ, because he had not been brought to an end of himself. He did not know himself, and he therefore could not follow Christ. But when he went out and wept bitterly, then came the great change. Christ previously said to him, *"When you have returned to Me, strengthen your brethren"* (Luke 22:32). Here is the point where Peter was converted from self to Christ.

I thank God for the story of Peter. I do not know a man in the Bible who gives us greater comfort. When we look at his character, so full of failures, and at what Christ made him by the power of the Holy Spirit, there is hope for every one of us. But remember, before Christ could fill Peter with the Holy Spirit and make a new man of him, he had to go out and weep bitterly; he had to be humbled. If we want to understand this, I think there are four points that we must look at. First, let us look at Peter, the devoted disciple of Jesus; next, at Peter as he lived the life of self; then, at Peter in his repentance; and last, at what Christ made of Peter by the Holy Spirit.

## PETER, THE DEVOTED DISCIPLE OF CHRIST

Christ called Peter to forsake his nets and follow Him. Peter did it at once, and afterward he could rightly say to the Lord, *"We have left all and followed You"* (Matt. 19:27).

211

Peter was a man of absolute surrender; he gave up all to follow Jesus. Peter was also a man of ready obedience. You remember Christ said to him, *"Launch out into the deep and let down your nets"* (Luke 5:4). Peter, the fisherman, knew there were no fish there, for they had been fishing all night and had caught nothing; but he said, *"At Your word I will let down the net"* (v. 5). He submitted to the word of Jesus. Furthermore, Peter was a man of great faith. When he saw Christ walking on the sea, he said, *"Lord, if it is You, command me to come to You"* (Matt. 14:28). At the voice of Christ, he stepped out of the boat and walked on the water.

Peter was also a man of spiritual insight. When Christ asked the disciples, *"Who do you say that I am?"* Peter was able to answer, *"You are the Christ, the Son of the living God."* And Christ said, *"Blessed are you, Simon Bar-Jonah, for flesh and blood has not revealed this to you, but My Father who is in heaven"* (Matt. 16:15–17). Then Christ spoke of him as the rock, and of his having the keys of the kingdom (vv. 18–19). Peter was a splendid man, a devoted disciple of Jesus, and if he were living now, everyone would say that he was an advanced Christian. And yet how much there was lacking in Peter!

## PETER, LIVING THE LIFE OF SELF

You recall that just after Christ had said to him, *"Flesh and blood has not revealed this to you, but My Father who is in heaven"* (Matt. 16:17), Christ began to speak about His sufferings, and Peter dared to say, *"Far be it from You, Lord; this shall not happen to You!"* (v. 22). Then Christ had to say, *"Get behind Me, Satan! You are an offense to Me, for you are not mindful of the things of God, but the things of men"* (v. 23).

There was Peter in his self-will, trusting his own wisdom, and actually forbidding Christ to go and die. Where did that come from? Peter trusted in himself and his own thoughts about divine things. We see later on, more than once, that the disciples questioned who should be the greatest among them. Peter was one of them, and he thought he had a right to the very first place. He sought his own honor above the others. The life of self was strong in Peter. He had left his boats and his nets, but not his old self.

When Christ had spoken to him about His sufferings, and said, *"Get behind Me, Satan!"* He followed it up by saying: *"If anyone desires to come after Me, let him deny himself, and take up his cross, and follow Me"* (Matt. 16:24). No man can follow Him unless he does this. Self must be utterly denied. What does this mean? We read that when Peter denied Christ, he said three times, *"I do not know Him"* (Luke 22:57). In other words, he said, "I have nothing to do with Him; He and I are not friends. I deny having any connection with Him." Christ told Peter that he must deny self. Self must be ignored, and its every claim rejected. This is the root of true discipleship. But Peter did not understand it and could not obey it. And what happened? When the last night came, Christ said to him, *"Before the rooster crows twice, you will deny Me three times"* (Mark 14:30).

But with self-confidence Peter said, *"Even if all are made to stumble, yet I will not be"* (v. 29). *"Lord, I am ready to go with You, both to prison and to death"* (Luke 22:33).

Peter meant it honestly, and he really intended to do it; but Peter did not know himself. He did not believe he was as bad as Jesus said he was.

We perhaps think of individual sins that come between us and God, but what are we to do with the self-life that is all unclean—our very natures? What are we to do with that flesh that is entirely under the power of sin? Deliverance from this is what we need. Peter did not know it, and therefore it was in self-confidence that he went forth and denied his Lord.

Notice how Christ used the word *deny* twice. He said to Peter the first time, *"Deny himself"* (Matt. 16:24); He said to Peter the second time, *"You will deny Me"* (Matt. 26:34). It is either of the two. There is no other choice for us; we must either deny self or deny Christ. There are two great powers fighting each other—the self-nature in the power of sin, and Christ in the power of God. One of these must rule within us.

It was self that made the Devil. He was an angel of God, but he wanted to exalt self. He became a devil in hell. Self was the cause of the fall of man. Eve wanted something for herself, and so our first parents fell into all the wretchedness of sin. We, their children, have inherited an awful nature of sin.

## PETER'S REPENTANCE

Peter denied his Lord three times, and then the Lord looked upon him. That look of Jesus broke Peter's heart. The terrible sin that he had committed, the terrible failure that had come, and the depth into which he had fallen suddenly opened up before him. Then, Peter *"went out and wept bitterly."*

Oh, who can tell what that repentance must have been? During the following hours of that night and the next day—when he saw Christ crucified and buried, and the next day, the Sabbath—oh, what hopeless despair and shame he must have felt!

"My Lord is gone; my hope is gone; and I denied my Lord. After that life of love, after that blessed fellowship of three years, I denied my Lord. God have mercy upon me!"

I do not think we can imagine the depth of humiliation Peter sank into then. But that was the turning point and the change. On the first day of the week, Christ was seen by Peter, and in the evening He met him with the others. Later on at the Sea of Galilee, He asked him, *"Do you love Me?"* (John 21:17). Peter was made sad by the thought that the Lord reminded him of having denied Him three times, and said in sorrow, but in uprightness, *"Lord, You know all things; You know that I love You"* (v. 17).

## PETER TRANSFORMED

Now, Peter was prepared for deliverance from self, and this is my last thought. You know that Christ took him with the others to the footstool of the throne and told them to wait there. Then, on the Day of Pentecost, the Holy Spirit came, and Peter was a changed man. I do not want you to think only of the change in Peter, in that boldness, that power, that insight into the Scriptures, and that blessing with which he preached that day. Thank God for that. But there was something deeper and better that happened to Peter. His whole nature was changed. The work that Christ began in Peter when He looked upon him was perfected when he was filled with the Holy Spirit.

If you want to see this, read the first epistle of Peter. You know where Peter's failings lay. When he said to Christ, in effect,

"You can never suffer; it cannot be," it showed he did not have an idea of what it was to pass through death into life. Christ said, "Deny yourself," and in spite of this he denied his Lord. When Christ warned him, *"You will deny Me"* (Matt. 26:34), and he insisted that he never would, Peter showed how little he understood what there was in himself. But when I read his epistle in which he said, *"If you are reproached for the name of Christ, blessed are you, for the Spirit of glory and of God rests upon you"* (1 Pet. 4:14), then I say that it is not the old Peter, but it is the very Spirit of Christ breathing and speaking within him.

I read again how Peter said, *"You were called [to suffer], because Christ also suffered for us"* (1 Pet. 2:21). I understand what a change had come over Peter. Instead of denying Christ, he found joy and pleasure in having self denied, crucified, and given up to the death. And therefore, we read in Acts that when he was called before the council he could boldly say, *"We ought to obey God rather than men"* (Acts 5:29), and that he could return with the other disciples and rejoice that they were counted worthy to suffer for Christ's name (v. 41).

You remember his self-exaltation; but now he had found out that *"the incorruptible beauty of a gentle and quiet spirit...is very precious in the sight of God"* (1 Pet. 3:4). Again he told us to be *"be submissive to one another, and be clothed with humility"* (1 Pet. 5:5).

Dear friend, I implore you, look at Peter utterly changed—the self-pleasing, the self-trusting, the self-seeking Peter, full of sin, continually getting into trouble, foolish and impetuous, now filled with the Spirit and the life of Jesus. Christ had done it for him by the Holy Spirit.

And now, what is the point in my having thus pointed to the story of Peter? This story must be the story of every believer who is really to be made a blessing by God. This story is a prophecy of what everyone can receive from God in heaven.

Now, let us just glance at what these lessons teach us.

The first lesson is this: you may be a very earnest, godly, devoted believer, in whom the power of the flesh is still very strong.

This is a very solemn truth. Peter, before he denied Christ, had cast out devils and had healed the sick. Yet the flesh had power, and the flesh had room in him. Oh, beloved, we have to realize that it is because there is so much of the self-life in us that the power of God cannot work in us as mightily as He desires it to work. Do you realize that the great God is longing to double His blessing, to give tenfold blessing through us? But there is something hindering Him, and that something is nothing but the self-life. We talk about the pride of Peter, and the impetuosity of Peter, and the self-confidence of Peter. It is all rooted in that one word, *self.* Christ had said, "Deny self," and Peter had never understood and never obeyed. Every failing came out of that.

What a solemn thought, and what an urgent plea for us to cry, "Oh God, show this to us so that none of us may be living the self-life!" It has happened to people who have been Christians for years; it has happened to people who have perhaps occupied prominent positions—God found them out and taught them to find out about themselves. They became utterly ashamed and fell broken before God. Oh, the bitter shame and sorrow and pain and agony that came to them, until at last they found that there was deliverance! Peter *"went out and wept bitterly."* There may be many godly people in whom the power of the flesh still rules.

My second lesson is this: it is the work of our blessed Lord Jesus to disclose the power of self.

How was it that Peter—the carnal Peter, self-willed Peter, Peter with the strong self-love—ever became a man of Pentecost and the writer of his epistles? It was because Christ placed him in charge, and Christ watched over him, and Christ taught and blessed him. The warnings that Christ had given him were part of the training. Last of all, there came that look of love. In His suffering, Christ did not forget him, but turned around and looked upon him, and Peter *"went out and wept bitterly."* And the Christ who led Peter to Pentecost is waiting today to take charge of every heart that is willing to surrender itself to Him.

Are there not some people saying, "Ah, that is the problem with me! It is always the self-life, self-comfort, self-consciousness, self-pleasing, and self-will. How am I to get rid of it?"

My answer is, It is Christ Jesus who can rid you of it. No one else but Christ Jesus can give deliverance from the power of self. And what does He ask you to do? He asks that you humble yourself before Him.

chapter 5

# Impossible with Man, Possible with God

*But He said, "The things which are impossible with men*
*are possible with God."*
—Luke 18:27

hrist had said to the rich young ruler, *"Sell all that you
have...and come, follow Me"* (Luke 18:22). The young
man went away sorrowful. Christ then turned to the disciples and said, *"How hard it is for those who have riches to enter
the kingdom of God!"* (v. 24). The disciples, we read, were
greatly astonished and answered, *"Who then can be saved?"* (v.
26). And Christ gave this blessed answer, *"The things which are
impossible with men are possible with God."*

The text contains two thoughts: first, that in the question of
salvation and of following Christ by a holy life, it is impossible
for man to do it; second, that what is impossible with man is
possible with God.

These two thoughts mark the two great lessons that one has
to learn in the Christian life. It often takes a long time to learn
the first lesson—that in the Christian life man can do nothing,
that salvation is impossible to man. And often a man learns this,
and yet he does not learn the second lesson—that what has been
impossible to him is possible with God. Blessed is the man or
woman who learns both lessons! The learning of them marks
stages in the Christian's life.

## MAN CANNOT

The one stage is when a man is trying to do his utmost and
fails, when a man tries to do better and fails again, when a man
tries much more and always fails. And yet, very often he does
not even then learn the lesson: with man it is impossible to

serve God and Christ. Peter spent three years in Christ's school, and he never learned that it is impossible, until he had denied his Lord and *"went out and wept bitterly"* (Luke 22:62). Then he learned it.

Just look for a moment at a person who is learning this lesson. At first, he fights against it. Then he submits to it, but reluctantly and in despair. At last, he accepts it willingly and rejoices in it. At the beginning of the Christian life, the young convert has no idea of this truth. He has been converted; he has the joy of the Lord in his heart; he begins to run the race and fight the battle. He is sure he can conquer, for he is earnest and honest, and God will help him. Yet somehow, very soon he fails where he did not expect it, and sin gets the better of him. He is disappointed, but he thinks, "I was not cautious enough. I did not make my resolutions strong enough." And again he vows, and again he prays, and yet he fails. He thinks, "Am I not a redeemed man? Have I not the life of God within me?" And he thinks again, "Yes, and I have Christ to help me. I can live the holy life."

At a later period, he comes to another state of mind. He begins to see such a life is impossible, but he does not accept it. There are multitudes of Christians who come to this point: "I cannot." They then think that God never expected them to do what they cannot do. If you tell them that God does expect it, it is a mystery to them. A good many Christians are living a low life—a life of failure and of sin—instead of rest and victory, because they began to say, "I cannot, it is impossible." And yet they do not understand it fully. So, under the impression of "I cannot," they give way to despair. They will do their best, but they never expect to get very far.

But God leads His children on to a third stage. A man comes to accept "it is impossible" in its full truth, and yet at the same time says, "I must do it, and I will do it. It is impossible for man, and yet I must do it." The renewed will begins to exercise its whole power, and in intense longing and prayer begins to cry to God, "Lord, what is the meaning of this? How am I to be freed from the power of sin?"

This is the state of the regenerate man in Romans 7. There you will find the Christian man trying his very utmost to live a holy life. God's law has been revealed to him as reaching down into the very depth of the desires of the heart. The man can dare to say, "'I delight in the law of God according to the inward man' (Rom. 7:22) 'To will [what is good] is present with me' (v. 18). My heart loves the law of God, and my will has chosen that law."

Can a man like this fail, with his heart full of delight in God's law and with his will determined to do what is right? Yes. This is what Romans 7 teaches us. There is something more needed. Not only must I delight in "the law of God according to the inward man" (v. 22) and will what God wills, but I need a divine omnipotence to work it in me. And this is what the apostle Paul taught in Philippians 2:13: "It is God who works in you both to will and to do for His good pleasure."

Note the contrast. In Romans 7, the regenerate man says, "To will is present with me, but how to perform what is good I do not find" (v. 18). But in Philippians 2, you have a man who has been led on farther. He is a man who understands that when God has worked the renewed will, He will give the power to accomplish what that will desires. Let us receive this as the first great lesson in the spiritual life: "It is impossible for me, my God. Let there be an end of the flesh and all its powers, an end of self, and let it be my glory to be helpless."

Praise God for the divine teaching that makes us helpless! When you thought of absolute surrender to God, were you not brought to an end of yourself? Did you not feel that you could see how you actually could live as a man absolutely surrendered to God every moment of the day—at your table, in your house, in your business, in the midst of trials and temptations? I pray that you will learn the lesson now. If you felt you could not do it, you are on the right road if you let yourselves be led. Accept this position, and maintain it before God: "My heart's desire and delight, O God, is absolute surrender, but I cannot perform it. It is impossible for me to live that life. It is beyond me." Fall down and learn that when you are utterly helpless, God will come to work in you not only to will, but also to do.

## God Can

Now comes the second lesson: the things that are impossible with men are possible with God.

I said a little while ago that there is many a man who has learned the lesson that it is impossible with men, and then he gives up in helpless despair. He lives a wretched Christian life, without joy or strength or victory. And why? Because he does not humble himself to learn that other lesson: with God all things are possible.

Your Christian life is to be a continuous proof that God works impossibilities. Your Christian life is to be a series of impossibilities made possible and actual by God's almighty power. This is what the Christian needs. He has an almighty God whom he worships, and he must learn to understand that he does not need a little of God's power. Rather—and I say this with reverence—he needs the whole of God omnipotence to keep him right and to live like a Christian.

The whole of Christianity is a work of God's omnipotence. Look at the birth of Christ Jesus. That was a miracle of divine power, and it was said to Mary, *"With God nothing will be impossible"* (Luke 1:37). It was the omnipotence of God. Look at Christ's resurrection. We are taught that it was according to the *"exceeding greatness of...His mighty power"* (Eph. 1:19) that God raised Christ from the dead.

Every tree must grow on the root from which it springs. An oak tree three hundred years old grows all the time on the one root from which it had its beginning. Christianity had its beginning in the omnipotence of God. In every soul, Christianity must have its continuance in that omnipotence. All the possibilities of the higher Christian life have their origin in a new understanding of Christ's power to work all God's will in us.

I want to call on you now to come and worship an almighty God. Have you learned to do it? Have you learned to deal so closely with an almighty God that you know omnipotence is working in you? In outward appearance there is often little sign of it. The apostle Paul said, *"I was with you in weakness, in fear, and in much trembling. And...my preaching [was] in demonstration of the Spirit and of power"* (1 Cor. 2:3–4). From the human side there was feebleness; from the divine side there was divine omnipotence. And this is true of every godly life. If we would only learn this lesson better, and give a wholehearted, undivided surrender to it, we would learn what blessedness there is in dwelling every hour and every moment with an almighty God. Have you ever studied in the Bible the attribute of God's omnipotence? You know that it was God's omnipotence that created the world, and created light out of darkness, and created man. But have you studied God's omnipotence in the works of redemption?

Look at Abraham. When God called him to be the father of the people out of which Christ was to be born, He said to him, *"I am Almighty God; walk before me and be blameless"* (Gen. 17:1). And God trained Abraham to trust Him as the omnipotent One. Whether it was his going out to a land that he did not know, or his faith as a pilgrim amid the thousands of Canaanites, his faith said, "This is my land." Whether it was his faith in waiting twenty-five years for a son in his old age, against all hope, or whether it was the raising up of Isaac from the dead on Mount Moriah when he was going to sacrifice him, Abraham believed God. He was *"strengthened in faith, giving glory to God, and being fully convinced that what He had promised He was also able to perform"* (Rom. 4:20–21).

The cause of the weakness of your Christian life is that you want to work it out partly, and to let God help you. And that cannot be. You must come to be utterly helpless, to let God work. He will work gloriously. This is what we need if we are indeed to be workers for God. I could go through Scripture and prove to you how Moses, when he led Israel out of Egypt—how Joshua, when he brought them into the land of Canaan—how all God's servants in the Old Testament counted on the omnipotence of God doing impossibilities. And this God lives today; this God is the God of every child of His. Yet some of us want God to give us a little help while we do our best, instead of coming to understand what God wants, and to say, "I can do nothing. God must and will do all." Have you said, "In worship, in work, in sanctification, in obedience to God, I can do nothing of myself, and so my place is to worship God, and to believe that He will work in me every moment"? Oh, may God teach us this! Oh, that God would by His grace show you what a God you have, and to what a God you have entrusted yourself—an omnipotent God. He is willing, with His whole omnipotence, to place Himself at the disposal of every child of His! Will we not take the lesson of the

Lord Jesus and say, "Amen; the things that are impossible with men are possible with God"?

Remember what I have said about Peter, his self-confidence, self-power, self-will, and how he came to deny his Lord. You feel, "Ah, there is the self-life; there is the flesh-life that rules in me!" And now, have you believed that there is deliverance from it? Have you believed that Almighty God is able to reveal Christ in your heart, to let the Holy Spirit rule in you so that the self-life will not have power or dominion over you? Have you coupled the two together and, with tears of repentance and with deep humiliation and feebleness, cried out, "O God, it is impossible to me; man cannot do it, but glory to Your name, it is possible with God"? Have you claimed deliverance? Do it now. Put yourself afresh in absolute surrender into the hands of a God of infinite love. His power to do it is as infinite as His love.

## GOD WORKS IN MAN

But again, we come to the question of absolute surrender and feel that that is lacking in the church of Christ. This is why the Holy Spirit cannot fill us, and why we cannot live as people entirely separated unto the Holy Spirit. This is why the flesh and the self-life cannot be conquered. We have never understood what it is to be absolutely surrendered to God as Jesus was. I know that many earnestly and honestly say, "Amen, I accept the message of absolute surrender to God." Yet they think, "Will that ever be mine? Can I count on God to make me one of whom it will be said in heaven, on earth, and in hell, 'He lives in absolute surrender to God'?" Brother, sister, *the things which are impossible with men are possible with God.* Believe that, when He takes charge of you in Christ, it is possible for God to make you a man or woman of absolute surrender. And God is able to maintain this. He is able to let you rise from bed every morning of the week with this blessed thought, directly or indirectly: "I am in God's care. My God is working out my life for me."

Some of you are weary of thinking about sanctification. You pray; you have longed and cried for it; and yet, it has appeared so far off! You are so conscious of how distant the holiness and humility of Jesus is. Beloved friends, the one doctrine of sanctification that is scriptural and real and effective is this: *"The things which are impossible with men are possible with God."* God can sanctify men. By His almighty and sanctifying power, God can keep them every moment. Oh, that we might get a step nearer to our God now! Oh, that the light of God might shine, and that we might know our God better!

I could go on to speak about the life of Christ in us—living like Christ, taking Christ as our Savior from sin, and as our life and strength. It is God in heaven who can reveal this in you. The prayer of the apostle Paul was, *"That He would grant you, according to the riches of His glory, to be strengthened with might through His Spirit in the inner man"* (Eph. 3:16). Do you not see that it is an omnipotent God working by His omnipotence in the heart of His believing children, so that Christ can become an indwelling Savior? You have tried to grasp it, to understand it, and to believe it, and it would not come. It was because you had not been brought to believe that *"the things which are impossible with men are possible with God."*

And so I trust that the word spoken about love may have brought many to see that we must have an inflowing of love in quite a new way. Our hearts must be filled with life from above—from the Fountain of everlasting love—if they are going to overflow all day. Then it will be just as natural for us to love our fellowmen as it is natural for the lamb to be gentle and the wolf to be cruel. When we are brought to such a state that the more a man hates and speaks evil of us—the more unlikable and unlovable a man is, we will love him all the more. When we are brought to such a state that obstacles, hatred, and ingratitude surround us, the power of love can triumph in us all the more. Until you are brought to see these, you are not saying: "It is impossible with men." But if you have been led to say, "This message has spoken to you about a love utterly beyond my power. It is absolutely impossible," then you can come to God and say, "It is possible with You."

Some people are crying to God for a great revival. I can say that this is the unceasing prayer of my heart. Oh, if God would only revive His believing people! I cannot think of the unconverted formalists of the church or of the infidels and skeptics or of all the wretched and perishing around me, without my heart pleading, "My God, revive Your church and people." It is not for a lack of reason that thousands of hearts yearn after holiness and consecration. It is a forerunner of God's power. God works to will and then He works to do (Phil. 2:13). These yearnings are a witness and a proof that God has worked to will. Oh, let us in faith believe that the omnipotent God will work to do among His people more than we can ask. Paul said, *"Now to Him who is able to do exceedingly abundantly above all that we ask or think, ...to Him be glory"* (Eph. 3:20–21). Let our hearts say this. Glory to God, the omnipotent One, who can do above what we dare to ask or think!

*"The things which are impossible with men are possible with God."* All around you there is a world of sin and sorrow, and Satan is there. But remember, Christ is on the throne; Christ is stronger; Christ has conquered, and Christ will conquer. But wait on God. My text casts us down—*"The things which are impossible with men"*—but it ultimately lifts us up high—*"are possible with God."* Get linked to God. Adore and trust Him as the omnipotent One, not only for your own life, but for all the souls that are entrusted to you. Never pray without adoring His omnipotence, saying, "Mighty God, I claim Your almightiness." And the answer to the prayer will come. Like Abraham you will become strong in faith, giving glory to God, because you know that He who has promised is able to perform (Rom. 4:20–21).

chapter 6

# Out of Bondage

*O wretched man that I am! Who will deliver me from this body of death? I thank God; through Jesus Christ our Lord!*
—Romans 7:24–25

Y ou know the wonderful location that this text has in the epistle to the Romans. It stands here at the end of the seventh chapter as the gateway into the eighth. In the first sixteen verses of the eighth chapter, the name of the Holy Spirit is found sixteen times. You have there the description and promise of the life that a child of God can live in the power of the Holy Spirit. This begins in the second verse: *"For the law of the Spirit of life in Christ Jesus has made me free from the law of sin and death"* (Rom. 8:2). From this, Paul went on to speak of the great privileges of the child of God who is led by the Spirit of God. The gateway into all this is found at the end of chapter seven: *"O wretched man that I am!"* Here you have the words of a man who has come to the end of himself. He had in the previous verses described how he had struggled and wrestled in his own power to obey the holy law of God, and had failed. But in answer to his own questions, he now found the true answer and cried out, *"I thank God; through Jesus Christ our Lord!"* From that he went on to speak of the deliverance that he had found.

From these words, I want to describe the path by which a man can be led out of the spirit of bondage into the spirit of liberty. You know how distinctly it is said, *"You did not receive the spirit of bondage again to fear"* (Rom. 8:15). We are continually warned that this is the great danger of the Christian life, to go again into bondage. I want to describe the path by which a man can get out of bondage into the glorious liberty of the children of God. Rather, I want to describe the man himself.

First, these words are the language of a regenerate man; second, of a weak man; third, of a wretched man; and fourth, of a man on the border of complete liberty.

## THE REGENERATE MAN

There is much evidence of regeneration from the fourteenth verse of chapter seven on to the twenty-third verse. *"It is no longer I who do it, but sin that dwells in me"* (Rom. 7:17). This is the language of a regenerate man—a man who knows that his heart and nature have been renewed, and that sin is now a power in him that is not himself. *"I delight in the law of God according to the inward man"* (v. 22). This, again, is the language of a regenerate man. He dares to say when he does evil, *"It is no longer I who do it, but sin that dwells in me."* It is of great importance to understand this.

In the first two sections of the epistle, Paul dealt with justification and sanctification. In dealing with justification, he lay the foundation of the doctrine in the teaching about sin. He did not speak of the singular *sin,* but of the plural *sins*—the actual transgressions. In the second part of the fifth chapter, he began to deal with sin, not as actual transgression, but as a power. Just imagine what a loss it would have been to us if we did not have this second half of the seventh chapter of the epistle to the Romans—if Paul had omitted from his teaching this vital question of the sinfulness of the believer. We would have missed the question we all want answered regarding sin in the believer. What is the answer? The regenerate man is one in whom the will has been renewed, and who can say, *"I delight in the law of God according to the inward man"* (v. 22).

## THE WEAK MAN

Here is the great mistake made by many Christian people: they think that when there is a renewed will, it is enough. But this is not the case. This regenerate man tells us, "I will to do what is good, but I do not have the power to perform." How often people tell us that if you set yourself determinedly, you can perform what you will! But this man was as determined as any man can be, and yet he made the confession: *"To will is present with me, but how to perform what is good I do not find"* (Rom. 7:18).

But, you ask, "How does God make a regenerate man utter such a confession? He has a right will, a heart that longs to do good, and he longs to do his very utmost to love God."

Let us look at this question. What has God given us our wills for? Did the angels who fell, in their own wills, have the strength to stand? Surely, no. The will of man is nothing but an empty vessel in which the power of God is to be manifested. Man must seek in God all that is to be. You have it in the second chapter of the epistle to the Philippians, and you have it here also, that God's work is to work in us both to will and to do of His good pleasure. Here is a man who appears to say, "God has not worked to do in me." But we are taught that God works both to will and to do. How is the apparent contradiction to be reconciled?

You will find that in this passage (Rom. 7:6–25), the name of the Holy Spirit does not occur once, nor does the name of Christ occur. The man is wrestling and struggling to fulfill God's law. Instead of the Holy Spirit and Christ, the law is mentioned nearly twenty times. This chapter shows a believer doing his very best to obey the law of God with his regenerate will. Not only this, but you will find the little words *I, me,* and *my* occur more than forty times. It is the regenerate *I* in its weakness seeking to obey the law without being filled with the Spirit. This is the experience of nearly every believer. After conversion, a person begins to do his best, and he fails. But if we are brought into the full light, we no longer need to fail. Nor do we need to fail at all if we have received the Spirit in His fullness at conversion.

God allows this failure so that the regenerate man will be taught his own utter inability. It is in the course of this struggle that the sense of our utter sinfulness comes to us. It is God's way of dealing with us. He allows man to strive to fulfill the law so that, as he strives and wrestles, he may be brought to say, "I am a regenerate child of God, but I am utterly helpless to obey His law." See what strong words are used all through the chapter to describe this condition: *"I am carnal, sold under sin"*

227

(Rom. 7:14); *"I see another law in my members,...bringing me into captivity"* (v. 23); and last of all, *"O wretched man that I am! Who will deliver me from this body of death?"* This believer who bows here in deep contrition is utterly unable to obey the law of God.

## THE WRETCHED MAN

Not only is the man who makes this confession a regenerate and a weak man, but he is also a wretched man. He is utterly unhappy and miserable. What is it that makes him so utterly miserable? It is because God has given him a nature that loves Himself. He is deeply wretched because he feels he is not obeying his God. He says, with brokenness of heart, "It is not I that do it, but I am under the awful power of sin, which is holding me down. It is I, and yet not I. Alas! It is myself; so closely am I bound up with it, and so closely is it intertwined with my very nature." Blessed be God; when a man learns to say, *"O wretched man that I am!"* from the depth of his heart, he is on the way to the eighth chapter of Romans.

There are many who make this confession an excuse for sin. They say that if Paul had to confess his weakness and helplessness in this way, who are they that they should try to do better? So the call to holiness is quietly set aside. Pray God that every one of us would learn to say these words in the very spirit in which they are written here! When we hear sin spoken of as the abominable thing that God hates, do not many of us wince before the word? If only all Christians who go on sinning and sinning would take this verse to heart. If ever you utter a sharp word say, *"O wretched man that I am!"* And every time you lose your temper, kneel down and understand that God never meant His child to remain in this state. If only we would take this word into our daily lives, and say it every time we see that we have sought our own honor! If only we would take it into our hearts every time we say sharp things, and every time we sin against the Lord God, and against the Lord Jesus Christ in His humility, obedience, and self-sacrifice! Pray God that we could forget everything else and cry out, *"O wretched man that I am! Who will deliver me from this body of death?"*

Why should you say this whenever you commit sin? Because it is when a man is brought to this confession that deliverance is at hand.

And remember, it was not only the sense of being weak and taken captive that made him wretched. It was, above all, the sense of sinning against his God. The law was doing its work, making sin exceedingly sinful in his sight. The thought of continually grieving God became utterly unbearable. It was this that brought forth the piercing cry, *"O wretched man!"* As long as we talk and reason about our inability and our failure, and only try to find out what Romans 7 means, it will profit us little. But when every sin gives new intensity to the sense of wretchedness, and we feel our whole state as one of not only helplessness, but actual and great sinfulness, we will be moved not only to ask, *"Who will deliver me?"* but also to cry, *"I thank God; through Jesus Christ my Lord!"*

## THE ALMOST-DELIVERED MAN

The man has tried to obey the beautiful law of God. He has loved it; he has wept over his sin; and he has tried to conquer. He has tried to overcome fault after fault, but every time he has ended in failure.

What did he mean by *"this body of death"*? Did he mean, "my body when I die"? Surely not. In the eighth chapter, you have the answer to this question in the words, *"If by the Spirit you put to death the deeds of the body, you will live"* (Rom. 8:13). This is the body of death from which he is seeking deliverance.

And now he is on the brink of deliverance! In the twenty-third verse of the seventh chapter, we have the words, *"I see another law in my members, warring against the law of my mind, and bringing me into captivity to the law of sin which is in my members."* It is a captive who cries, *"O wretched man that I am! Who will deliver me from this body of death?"* He is a man who feels himself bound. But look to the contrast in the second verse of the eighth chapter: *"The law of the Spirit of life in Christ Jesus has made me free from the law of sin and death."* This is the deliverance through Jesus Christ our Lord, the liberty to the captive that the Spirit brings. Can you keep captive any longer a man made free by the *"law of the Spirit of life in Christ Jesus"?*

But you say that the regenerate man did not have the Spirit of Jesus when he spoke in the sixth chapter. Yes, he did not know what the Holy Spirit could do for him.

God does not work by His Spirit as He works by a blind force in nature. He leads His people on as reasonable, intelligent beings. Therefore, when He wants to give us the Holy Spirit whom He has promised, He first brings us to the end of self. He brings us to the conviction that although we have been striving to obey the law, we have failed. When we have come to the end of that, then He shows us that in the Holy Spirit we have the power of obedience, the power of victory, and the power of real holiness.

God works to will, and He is ready to work to do, but many Christians misunderstand this. They think because they have the will, it is enough, and that now they are able to do. This is not so. The new will is a permanent gift, an attribute of the new nature. The power to do is not a permanent gift, but must be received each moment from the Holy Spirit. It is the man who is conscious of his own weakness as a believer who will learn that by the Holy Spirit he can live a holy life. This man is on the brink of that great deliverance; the way has been prepared for the glorious eighth chapter. I now ask this solemn question: Where are you living? With you, is it, *"O wretched man that I am! Who will deliver me?"* with a little experience of the power of the Holy Spirit every now and then? Or is it, *"I thank God; through Jesus Christ!...The law of the Spirit...has made me free from the law of sin and of death"?*

What the Holy Spirit does is to give the victory. *"If by the Spirit you put to death the deeds of the body, you will live"* (Rom. 8:13). It is the Holy Spirit who does this—the third person of the Godhead. It is He who, when the heart is opened wide to receive Him, comes in and reigns there, and mortifies the deeds of the body, day by day, hour by hour, and moment by moment.

I want to bring this to a point. Remember, dear friend, what we need is to come to decision and action. In Scripture there are two very different sorts of Christians; one is led by the flesh, the other by the Spirit. The Bible speaks in Romans, Corinthians, and Galatians about yielding to the flesh, and this is the life of tens of thousands of believers. All their lack of joy in the Holy Spirit, and their lack of the liberty He gives, is just owing to the flesh. The Spirit is within them, but the flesh rules the life. To be led by the Spirit of God is what they need. If only I could make every child of His realize what it means that the everlasting God has given His dear Son, Christ Jesus, to watch over you every day, and that what you have to do is to trust. If only I could make His children understand that the work of the Holy Spirit is to enable you every moment to remember Jesus and to trust Him! The Spirit has come to keep the link with Him unbroken every moment. Praise God for the Holy Spirit! We are so accustomed to thinking of the Holy Spirit as a luxury for special times or for special ministers and men. But the Holy Spirit is necessary for every believer, every moment of the day. Praise God that you have Him, and that He gives you the full experience of the deliverance in Christ as He makes you free from the power of sin.

Who longs to have the power and the liberty of the Holy Spirit? Oh, brother or sister, bow before God in one final cry of despair: "O God, must I go on sinning this way forever? Who will deliver me, O wretched man that I am, from this body of death?"

Are you ready to sink before God in that cry and to seek the power of Jesus to live and work in you? Are you ready to say, *"I thank God; through Jesus Christ"*?

What good does it do that we go to church or attend conventions, that we study our Bibles and pray, unless our lives are filled with the Holy Spirit? This is what God wants. Nothing else will enable us to live a life of power and peace. How sad that many Christians are content with the question, *"Who will deliver me from this body of death?"* but never give the answer. Instead of answering, they are silent. Instead of saying, *"I thank God; through Jesus Christ our Lord,"* they are forever repeating the question without the answer. If you want the path to the full deliverance of Christ and the liberty of the Spirit—the glorious liberty of the children of God—take it through the seventh chapter of Romans. Then say, *"I thank God; through Jesus Christ our Lord!"* Do not be content to remain ever groaning, but say,

"I, a wretched man or woman, thank God through Jesus Christ. Even though I do not see it all, I am going to praise God."

Here is deliverance; here is the liberty of the Holy Spirit. The kingdom of God is *"joy in the Holy Spirit"* (Rom. 14:17).

chapter 7

# Living in the Spirit

*This only I want to learn from you: Did you receive the Spirit by the works of the law, or by the hearing of faith? Are you so foolish? Having begun in the Spirit, are you now being made perfect by the flesh?*
—Galatians 3:2–3

W hen we speak of the quickening or the deepening or the strengthening of the spiritual life, we are speaking of something that is feeble and wrong and sinful. It is a great thing to take our place before God with the confession. "O God, my spiritual life is not what it should be!" May God work that in your heart, dear reader.

As we look at the church, we see so many indications of feebleness, failure, sin, and shortcoming. They compel us to ask, Why is it? Is there any necessity for the church of Christ to be living in such a low state? Or is it actually possible that God's people should be living always in the joy and strength of their God?

Every believing heart must answer, It is possible.

Then comes the great question, How is it to be accounted for, that God's church as a whole is so feeble, and that the great majority of Christians are not living up to their privileges? There must be a reason for it. Has God not given Christ His almighty Son to be the Keeper of every believer, to make Christ an ever-present reality, and to impart and communicate to us all that we have in Christ? God has given His Son, and God has given His Spirit. How is it that believers do not live up to their privileges?

In more than one of the epistles, we find a very solemn answer to this question. There are epistles, such as the first to the Thessalonians, where Paul wrote to the Christians, in effect, "I want you to grow, to abound, to increase more and more." They were young, and there were things lacking in their faith. But their state was so far satisfactory, and gave him such great joy, that he wrote time after time, *"We urge and exhort in the Lord Jesus that you should abound more and more"* (1 Thess. 4:1); *"We urge you, brethren, that you increase more and more"* (v. 10). But there are other epistles where he took a very different tone, especially the epistles to the Corinthians and to the Galatians, and he told them in many different ways what the one reason was that they were not living as Christians ought to live: many were under the power of the flesh. Our text verse is one example. Paul reminded them that they had received the Holy Spirit by the preaching of faith. He had preached Christ to them; they had accepted Christ and had received the Holy Spirit in power.

But what happened? They tried to perfect the work that the Spirit had begun in the flesh by their own efforts. We find the same teaching in the epistle to the Corinthians.

Now, we have here a solemn revelation of what the great need is in the church of Christ. God has called the church of Christ to live in the power of the Holy Spirit. But the church is living, for the most part, in the power of human flesh, and of will and energy and effort apart from the Spirit of God. I do not doubt that this is the case with many individual believers. And oh, if God will use me to give you a message from Him, my one message will be this: If the church will acknowledge that the Holy Spirit is her strength and her help, and if the church will give up everything and wait on God to be filled with the Spirit, her days of beauty and gladness will return. We will see the glory of God revealed among us. This is my message to every individual believer: Nothing will help you unless you come to understand that you must live every day under the power of the Holy Spirit.

God wants you to be a living vessel in whom the power of the Spirit is manifested every hour and every moment of your life. God will enable you to be this.

Now, let us try to learn what this word to the Galatians teaches us—some very simple thoughts. It shows us, first, that the beginning of the Christian life is receiving the Holy Spirit.

Second, it shows us what great danger there is of forgetting that we are to live by the Spirit and not live according to the flesh. It shows us, third, what are the fruits and the proofs of our seeking perfection in the flesh. And then it suggests to us, finally, the way of deliverance from this state.

## RECEIVING THE HOLY SPIRIT

First of all, Paul said, *"Having begun in the Spirit."* Remember, the apostle not only preached justification by faith, but he preached something more. He preached—the epistle is full of it—that justified men cannot live except by the Holy Spirit, and that therefore God gives to every justified man the Holy Spirit to seal him. The apostle said to them, in effect, more than once, "How did you receive the Holy Spirit? Was it by the preaching of the law, or by the preaching of faith?"

He could point back to that time when there had been a mighty revival under his teaching. The power of God had been manifested, and the Galatians were compelled to confess, "Yes, we have the Holy Spirit; we accepted Christ by faith, and by faith we received the Holy Spirit."

Now, it is to be feared that there are many Christians who hardly know that when they believed, they received the Holy Spirit. A great many Christians can say, "I received pardon, and I received peace." But if you were to ask them, "Have you received the Holy Spirit?" they would hesitate. And many, if they were to say yes, would say it with hesitation. They would tell you that they hardly know what it is, since that time, to walk in the power of the Holy Spirit. Let us try to take hold of this great truth: the beginning of the true Christian life is to receive the Holy Spirit. And the work of every Christian minister is that which was the work of Paul—to remind his people that they received the Holy Spirit, and must live according to His guidance and in His power.

If those Galatians who received the Holy Spirit in power were tempted to go astray by that terrible danger of perfecting in the flesh what had been begun in the Spirit, how much more danger those Christians run who hardly ever know that they have received the Holy Spirit. How much more danger there is for those who, if they know it as a matter of belief, hardly ever think of the gift of the Holy Spirit, and hardly ever praise God for it!

## NEGLECTING THE HOLY SPIRIT

But now look, in the second place, at the great danger of forgetting that we are to live by the Holy Spirit.

You may know what shunting is on a railway. A locomotive with its train may be traveling in a certain direction, and the points at some place may not be properly opened or closed, and it is shunted off to the right or to the left. And if this takes place, for instance, on a dark night, the train goes in the wrong direction, and the people might never know it until they have gone some distance.

Similarly, God gives Christians the Holy Spirit with this intention—that every day, all their lives, should be lived in the power of the Spirit. A man cannot live one hour of a godly life unless he lives by the power of the Holy Spirit. He may live a proper, consistent life, as people call it—an irreproachable life, a life of virtue and diligent service. But to live a life acceptable to God, in the enjoyment of God's salvation and God's love, to live and walk in the power of the new life—he cannot do it unless he is guided by the Holy Spirit every day and every hour.

But now pay attention to the danger. The Galatians received the Holy Spirit, but what was begun by the Spirit they tried to perfect in the flesh. How? They fell back again under Judaizing teachers who told them they must be circumcised. They began to seek their religion in external observances. And so Paul used that expression about those teachers who had them circumcised so *"that they may boast in your flesh"* (Gal. 6:13).

Sometimes I hear the expression "religious flesh" used. What is meant by this? It is simply an expression made to give utterance to these thoughts: my human nature and my human will and my human effort can be very active in religion. After being converted, and after receiving the Holy Spirit, I may begin in my own strength to try to serve God.

I may be very diligent and do a great deal, and yet all the time it is more the work of human flesh than of God's Spirit.

What a solemn thought, that person can, without noticing, be shunted off from the line of the Holy Spirit onto the line of the flesh.

How solemn it is that man can be most diligent and make great sacrifices, and yet it is all in the power of the human will! Ah, the great question for us to ask of God in self-examination is that we may be shown whether our Christian lives are lived more in the power of the flesh than in the power of the Holy Spirit. A man may be a preacher and may work most diligently in his ministry; a man may be a Christian worker, and others may say of him that he makes great sacrifices, and yet you can sense there is something lacking. You sense that he is not a spiritual man; there is no spirituality about his life. How many Christians there are about whom no one would ever think of saying, "What a spiritual man he is!" Ah, here is the weakness of the church of Christ. It is all in this one word—*flesh*.

Now, the flesh may manifest itself in many ways. It may be manifested in fleshly wisdom. My mind may be most active about Christianity. I may preach or write or think or meditate, and delight in being occupied with things in God's Book and in God's kingdom. Yet the power of the Holy Spirit may be notably absent. I fear that if you take the preaching throughout the church of Christ and ask why there is so little converting power in the preaching of the Word, why there is so much work and often so little result for eternity, why the Word has so little power to build up believers in holiness and in consecration— the answer will be that the power of the Holy Spirit is absent. And why is this? There can be no other reason except that the flesh and human energy have taken the place that the Holy Spirit ought to have. This was true of the Galatians; it was true of the Corinthians. Paul said to them, *"I...could not speak to you as to spiritual people but as to carnal"* (1 Cor. 3:1).

And you know how often in the course of his epistle he had to reprove and condemn them for strife and for divisions.

## LACKING THE FRUIT OF THE HOLY SPIRIT

A third thought is this: what are the proofs or indications that a church like the Galatians, or a Christian, is serving God in the power of the flesh—is perfecting in the flesh what was begun in the Spirit? The answer is very easy. Religious self-effort always ends in sinful flesh. What was the state of those Galatians? They were striving to be justified by the works of the law. And yet they were quarreling and in danger of devouring one another. Count the number of expressions that the apostle used to indicate their lack of love. You will find more than twelve: envy, jealousy, bitterness, strife, and all sorts of others. Read in the fourth and fifth chapters what he said about this. You see how they tried to serve God in their own strength, and they failed utterly. All this religious effort resulted in failure. The power of sin and the sinful flesh got the better of them. Their whole condition was one of the saddest that could be thought of.

This comes to us with unspeakable solemnity.

There is a complaint everywhere in the Christian church of the lack of a high standard of integrity and godliness, even among the professing members of Christian churches. I remember a sermon that I heard preached on commercial morality. But let us not speak only of the commercial morality or immorality; let us go into the homes of Christians. Think of the life to which God has called His children, and that He enables them to live by the Holy Spirit. Think of how much there is of unlovingness, temper, sharpness, and bitterness. Think how often there is strife among the members of churches, and how much there is of envy, jealousy, oversensitivity, and pride. Then we are compelled to say, "Where are marks of the presence of the Spirit of the Lamb of God?" Lacking, sadly lacking!

Many people speak of these things as though they were the natural result of our feebleness and cannot be helped. Many people speak of these things as sins, yet have given up the hope of conquering them. Many people speak of these things in the church around them, and do not see the least prospect of ever having the things changed. There is no prospect until there is a radical change, until the church of God begins to see that every sin in the believer comes from the flesh—from a fleshly life amid our Christian activities, from a striving in self-effort to serve God. We will fail until we learn to make confession, and until we begin to see that we must somehow or other get God's Spirit in power back to His church. Where did the church begin at Pentecost? They began in the Spirit. But how the church of the next century went off into the flesh! They thought they could perfect the church in the flesh.

Do not let us think, because the Reformation restored the great doctrine of justification by faith, that the power of the Holy Spirit was then fully restored. If it is our belief that God is going to have mercy on His church in these last ages, it will be because the doctrine and the truth about the Holy Spirit will not only be studied, but sought after with a whole heart. It is not only because this truth will be sought after, but because ministers and congregations will be found bowing before God in deep abasement with one cry: "We have grieved God's Spirit. We have tried to be Christian churches with as little as possible of God's Spirit. We have not sought to be churches filled with the Holy Spirit."

All the feebleness in the church is owing to the refusal of the church to obey its God.

And why is this so? I know your answer. You say, "We are too feeble and too helpless, and we vow to obey, but somehow we fail."

Ah, yes, you fail because you do not accept the strength of God. God alone can work out His will in you. You cannot work out God's will, but His Holy Spirit can. Until the church and believers grasp this, cease trying by human effort to do God's will, and wait upon the Holy Spirit to come with all His omnipotent and enabling power, the church will never be what God wants her to be. It will never be what God is willing to make of her.

## YIELDING TO THE HOLY SPIRIT

I come now to my last thought, the question, What is the way to restoration?

Beloved friend, the answer is simple and easy. If that train has been shunted off, there is nothing for it to do but to come back to the point at which it was led away. The Galatians had no other way of returning except to come back to where they had gone wrong. They had to come back from all religious effort in their own strength, and from seeking anything by their own work, and to yield themselves humbly to the Holy Spirit. There is no other way for us as individuals.

Is there any brother or sister whose heart is saying, "My life has little of the power of the Holy Spirit"? I come to you with God's message—that you can have no idea of what your life would be in the power of the Holy Spirit. It is too high, too blessed, and too wonderful. But I bring you the message that just as truly as the everlasting Son of God came to this world and did His wonderful works, just as truly as on Calvary He died and brought about your redemption by His precious blood, so can the Holy Spirit come into your heart. With His divine power, He may sanctify you, enable you to do God's blessed will, and fill your heart with joy and strength.

We have forgotten, we have grieved, we have dishonored the Holy Spirit; and He has not been able to do His work. But I bring you the message that the Father in heaven loves to fill His children with His Holy Spirit. God longs to give each one individually, separately, the power of the Holy Spirit for daily life. The command comes to us individually, unitedly. God wants us as His children to arise and place our sins before Him, and to call on Him for mercy. Oh, are you so foolish? Are you perfecting in the flesh what was begun in the Spirit? Let us bow in shame and confess before God how our fleshly religion, our self-effort, and our self-confidence have been the cause of every failure.

I have often been asked by young Christians, "Why do I fail so? I did so solemnly vow with my whole heart, and did desire to serve God. Why have I failed?"

To such I always give this answer, "My dear friend, you are trying to do in your own strength what Christ alone can do in you."

And when they tell me, "I am sure I knew Christ alone could do it; I was not trusting in myself," my answer is, "You were trusting in yourself, or you could not have failed. If you had trusted Christ, He could not fail."

Oh, this perfecting in the flesh what was begun in the Spirit runs far deeper through us than we know. Let us ask God to show us that it is only when we are brought to utter shame and emptiness that we will be prepared to receive the blessing that comes from on high.

And so I come with these two questions. Are you living, beloved brother or sister—I ask it of every minister of the Gospel—under the power of the Holy Spirit? Are you living as an anointed, Spirit-filled man or woman in your ministry and your life before God? Oh, friends, our place is an awesome one. We have to show people what God will do for us, not in our words and teaching, but in our lives. God help us to do it!

I ask every member of Christ's church and every believer, Are you living a life under the power of the Holy Spirit day by day? Or are you attempting to live without His power? Remember, you cannot. Are you consecrated, given up to the Spirit to work in you and to live in you? Oh, come and confess every failure of temper, every failure of the tongue, however small. Confess every failure owing to the absence of the Holy Spirit and the presence of the power of self. Are you consecrated, are you given up to the Holy Spirit?

If your answer is no, then I come with a second question: Are you willing to be consecrated? Are you willing to give yourself up to the power of the Holy Spirit?

You well know that the human side of consecration will not help you. I may consecrate myself a hundred times with all the intensity of my being, and it will not help me. What will help me is this—that God from heaven accepts and seals the consecration.

And now, are you willing to give yourselves up to the Holy Spirit? You can do it now. A great deal may still be dark and dim, and beyond what we understand. You may feel nothing, but come. God alone can bring about the change. God alone, who gave us the Holy Spirit, can restore the Holy Spirit in power into our lives. God alone can strengthen us *"with might through His Spirit in the inner man"* (Eph. 3:16). And to every waiting heart that will make the sacrifice, give up everything, and give time to cry and pray to God, the answer will come. The blessing is not far off. Our God delights in helping us. He will enable us to perfect, not in the flesh, but in the Spirit, what was begun in the Spirit.

chapter 8

# The Keeping Power of God

*Blessed be the God and Father of our Lord Jesus Christ, who...has
begotten us again to a living hope through the resurrection of Jesus
Christ from the dead, to an inheritance incorruptible...
reserved in heaven for you, who are kept by the power
of God through faith for salvation.*
—1 Peter 1:3–5

H ere we have two wonderful, blessed truths about the
way a believer is kept unto salvation. One truth is *"kept
by the power of God,"* and the other truth is *"kept...
through faith."* We should look at the two sides—at God's side
and His almighty power, offered to us to be our Keeper every
moment of the day; and at the human side, on which we have
nothing to do but in faith to let God do His keeping work. We
are born again to an inheritance kept in heaven for us. We are
kept here on earth by the power of God. We see there is a double
keeping—the inheritance kept for me in heaven, and I on earth
kept for the inheritance there.

Now, as to the first part of this keeping, there is no doubt
and no question. God keeps the inheritance in heaven very wonderfully and perfectly, and it is waiting there safely. And the
same God keeps me for the inheritance. This is what I want to
examine in this chapter.

It is very foolish for a father to take great trouble to have an
inheritance for his children, and to keep it for them, if he does
not keep them for it. Think of a man spending all of his time and
making every sacrifice to amass money, and as he gets his tens
of thousands, you ask him why he sacrifices himself so. His answer is, "I want to leave my children a large inheritance, and I
am keeping it for them." If you were then to hear that that man
takes no trouble to educate his children, that he allows them to

run wild on the streets and to go in paths of sin and ignorance and foolishness, what would you think of him? Would you not say, "Poor man! He is keeping an inheritance for his children, but he is not keeping or preparing his children for the inheritance"? And there are so many Christians who think, "My God is keeping the inheritance for me," but they cannot believe, "My God is keeping me for that inheritance." The same power, the same love, the same God is doing the double work.

Now, I want to write about a work God does upon us—keeping us for the inheritance. I have already said that we have two very simple truths: the one, the divine side, is that we are *"kept by the power of God"*; the other, the human side, is that we are *"kept...through faith."*

## KEPT BY THE POWER OF GOD

Look at the divine side: Christians are *"kept by the power of God."*

### • KEEPING INCLUDES ALL

Think, first of all, that this keeping is all-inclusive. What is kept? You are kept. How much of you? The whole being. Does God keep one part of you and not another? No. Some people have an idea that this is a sort of vague, general keeping, and that God will keep them in such a way that when they die they will get to heaven. But they do not apply the word *"kept"* to everything in their beings and natures. And yet this is what God wants.

Suppose I have a watch and that this watch had been borrowed from a friend. Suppose the friend said to me, "When you go to Europe, I will let you take it with you, but make sure you keep it safely and bring it back."

Suppose I damaged the watch—the hands are broken, the face is defaced, and some of the wheels and springs are spoiled—and took it back to my friend in that condition. He would say, "Ah, but I gave you that watch on the condition that you would keep it."

"Have I not kept it? Here is the watch."

"But I did not want you to keep it in that general way, so that you would bring me back only the shell of the watch, or the remains. I expected you to keep every part of it."

Similarly, God does not want to keep us in this general way, so that at the last, somehow or other, we will be saved as by fire, and just get into heaven. But the keeping power and the love of God applies to every part of our beings.

Some people think God will keep them in spiritual things, but not in temporal things. The latter, they say, lies outside of His realm. Now, God sends you to work in the world, but He did not say, "I must now leave you to go and earn your own money, and to get your livelihood for yourself." He knows you are not able to keep yourself. But God says, "My child, there is no work you are to do, and no business in which you are engaged, and not a cent you are to spend, but I, your Father, will take that up into My keeping." God not only cares for the spiritual, but also for the temporal. The greater part of many people's lives must be spent, sometimes eight or nine or ten hours a day, amid the temptations and distractions of business. But God will care for you there. The keeping of God includes all.

Other people think, "Ah, in time of trial God keeps me. But in times of prosperity I do not need His keeping; then I forget Him and let Him go." Others, again, think the very opposite. They think, "In time of prosperity, when things are smooth and quiet, I am able to cling to God. But when heavy trials come, somehow or other my will rebels, and God does not keep me then."

Now, I bring you the message that in prosperity as in adversity, in the sunshine as in the dark, your God is ready to keep you all the time.

Then again, others think of this keeping in this way: "God will keep me from doing very great wickedness, but there are small sins I cannot expect God to keep me from. There is the sin of a bad temper. I cannot expect God to conquer that."

When you hear of some man who has been tempted and gone astray or fallen into drunkenness or murder, you thank God for His keeping power.

"I might have done the same as that man," you say, "if God had not kept me." And you believe He kept you from drunkenness and murder.

And why do you not believe that God can keep you from outbreaks of temper? You thought that this was of less importance.

You did not remember that the great commandment of the New Testament is, *"Love one another; as I have loved you"* (John 13:34). And when your temper and hasty judgment and sharp words came out, you sinned against the highest law—the law of God's love. And yet you say, "God does not keep me from that." You perhaps say, "He can; but there is something in me that cannot attain it, and that God does not take away."

I want to ask you, Can believers live a holier life than is generally lived? Can believers experience the keeping power of God all day, to keep them from sin? Can believers be kept in fellowship with God? And I bring you a message from the Word of God, in these words: *"Kept by the power of God."* There is no qualifying clause to them. The meaning is this: if you will entrust yourself entirely and absolutely to the omnipotence of God, He will delight in keeping you.

Some people think that they can never reach the point at which every word of their mouths would be to the glory of God. But it is what God wants of them; it is what God expects of them. God is willing to set a watchman at the door of their mouths (Ps. 141:3). If God will do that, can He not keep their tongues and their lips? He can. This is what God is going to do for those who trust Him. God's keeping is all-inclusive. Let everyone who desires to live a holy life think about all his needs, his weaknesses, his shortcomings, and his sins, and say deliberately, "Is there any sin that my God cannot keep me from?" And the heart will have to answer, "No, God can keep me from every sin."

### • KEEPING REQUIRES POWER

Second, if you want to understand this keeping, remember that it is not only an all-inclusive keeping, but also an almighty keeping.

I want to get this truth burned into my soul. I want to worship God until my whole heart is filled with the thought of His omnipotence. God is almighty, and the almighty God offers Himself to work in my heart—to do the work of keeping me. I want to get linked with omnipotence, or rather, linked to the omnipotent One—the living God—and to have my place in the hollow of His hand. You read the Psalms, and you think of the wonderful thoughts in many of the expressions that David used. For instance, he spoke about our God being our *"fortress"* (Ps. 18:2), our *"refuge"* (Ps. 28:8), our *"strong tower"* (Ps. 61:3), our *"strength"* (Ps. 18:1), and our *"salvation"* (Ps. 27:1). David had wonderful views of how the everlasting God is Himself the hiding place of the believing soul. David had a beautiful understanding of how God takes the believer and keeps him in the very hollow of His hand—in the secret of His pavilion (Ps. 27:5)—under the shadow of His wings (Ps. 17:8), under His very feathers (Ps. 91:4). David lived there. And we, who are the children of Pentecost, who have known Christ, His blood, and the Holy Spirit sent down from heaven, why do we know so little of what it is to walk step by step with the almighty God as our Keeper?

Have you ever thought that, in every action of grace in your heart, you have the whole omnipotence of God engaged to bless you? When I come to a man and he gives me a gift of money, I get it and go away with it. He has given me something of his. He keeps the rest for himself. But it is not this way with the power of God. God can part with nothing of His own power, and therefore I can experience the power and goodness of God only so far as I am in contact and fellowship with Him. And when I come into contact and fellowship with Him, I come into contact and fellowship with the whole omnipotence of God. I have the omnipotence of God to help me every day.

Suppose that a son has a very rich father, and as the former is about to commence business the father says, "You can have as much money as you want for your undertaking." All the father has is at the disposal of the son. This is the way with God, your almighty God. You can hardly take it in; you feel like such a little worm. His omnipotence is needed to keep a little worm! Yes, His omnipotence is needed to keep every little worm that lives in the dust, and also to keep the universe. Therefore, His omnipotence is much more needed in keeping your soul and mine from the power of sin.

Oh, if you want to grow in grace, learn to begin here. In all your judgings and meditations and thoughts and deeds and questions and studies and prayers, learn to be kept by your almighty God. What is the almighty God not going to do for the child who trusts Him? The Bible says He will do *"above all that we ask or think"* (Eph. 3:20). It is omnipotence you must learn to know and trust. Then you will live as a Christian ought to live. How little we have learned to study God, and to understand that a godly life is a life full of God. It is a life that loves God and waits on Him, trusts Him, and allows Him to bless it! We cannot do the will of God except by the power of God. God gives us the first experience of His power to prepare us to desire more, and to come and claim all that He can do. God helps us to trust Him every day.

### • KEEPING IS CONTINUOUS

Another thought is that this keeping is not only all-inclusive and omnipotent, but also continuous and unbroken.

People sometimes say, "For a week or a month God has kept me very wonderfully. I have lived in the light of His countenance, and I can say what joy I have had in fellowship with Him. He has blessed me in my work for others. He has given me souls, and at times I felt as if I were carried heavenward on eagles' wings. But it did not continue. It was too good; it could not last." And some say, "It was necessary that I should fall to keep me humble." And others say, "I know it was my own fault, but somehow you cannot always live up in the heights."

Oh, beloved, why is it? Can there be any reason why the keeping of God should not be continuous and unbroken? Just think; all life is in unbroken continuity. If my life were stopped for half an hour, I would be dead, and my life would be gone. Life is a continuous thing, and the life of God is the life of His church. The life of God is His almighty power working in us. And God comes to us as the almighty One, and without any condition He offers to be my Keeper. His keeping means that day by day, moment by moment, God is going to keep us.

If I were to ask you the question, "Do you think God is able to keep you one day from actual transgression?" you would answer, "I not only know He is able to do it, but I think He has done it. There have been days in which He has kept my heart in His holy presence. There have also been days when, though I have always had a sinful nature within me, He has kept me from conscious, actual transgression."

Now, if He can do that for an hour or a day, why not for two days? Oh, let us make God's omnipotence as revealed in His Word the measure of our expectations. Has God not said in His Word, *"I, the LORD, keep it, I water it every moment"* (Isa. 27:3)? What can this mean? Does *"every moment"* mean every moment? Did God promise of that vineyard that every moment He would water it so that the heat of the sun and the scorching wind might never dry it up? Yes.

Will our God, in His tenderhearted love toward us, not keep us every moment when He has promised to do so? Oh, if we once got hold of the thought that our entire spiritual lives are to be God's doing! *"It is God who works in you both to will and to do for His good pleasure"* (Phil. 2:13). Once we get faith to expect this from God, God will do all for us.

The keeping is to be continuous. Every morning, God will meet you as you wake. It is not a question of, "If I forget to wake in the morning with the thought of Him, what will come of it?" If you trust your waking to God, God will meet you in the mornings as you wake with His divine sunshine and life. He will give you the consciousness that, throughout the day, you have God to continually take charge of you with His almighty power. And God will meet you the next day and every day. Never mind if, in the practice of fellowship, failure sometimes comes. If you maintain your position and say, "Lord, I am going to expect You to do Your utmost, and I am going to trust You day by day to keep me absolutely," your faith will grow stronger and stronger. You will know the keeping power of God in unbrokenness.

## KEPT THROUGH FAITH

And now we come to the other side, which is believing. *"Kept by the power of God through faith."* How must we look at this faith?

### • FAITH IMPLIES HELPLESSNESS

Let me say, first of all, that this faith means utter inability and helplessness before God.

At the bottom of all faith, there is a feeling of helplessness. If I have a bit of business to transact, perhaps to buy a house, the lawyer must do the work of getting the transfer of the property in my name. He must make all the arrangements. I cannot do that work, and, in trusting that agent, I confess I cannot do it. Similarly, faith always means helplessness. In many cases it means, "I can do it with a great deal of trouble, but another can do it better." But in most cases it is utter helplessness: "Another must do it for me." And this is the secret of the spiritual life. An individual must learn to say, "I give up everything. I have tried and longed and thought and prayed, but failure has come. God has blessed me and helped me, but still, in the long run, there has been so much sin and sadness." What a change comes when a person is thus broken down into utter helplessness and self-despair, and says, "I can do nothing!"

Remember Paul. He was living a blessed life, and he had been taken up into the third heaven. Then the thorn in the flesh came, *"a messenger of Satan to buffet me"* (2 Cor. 12:7). And what happened? Paul could not understand it, and three times he prayed to the Lord to take it away. But the Lord said, in effect, "No, it is possible that you might exalt yourself. Therefore, I have sent you this trial to keep you weak and humble."

And Paul then learned a lesson that he never forgot—to rejoice in his infirmities. He said that the weaker he was, the better it was for him. For when he was weak, he was strong in his Lord (v. 10).

Do you want to enter what people call "the higher life"? Then go a step lower down. I remember Dr. Boardman telling how once he was invited by a gentleman to go to a factory where they made fine shot. I believe the workmen did so by pouring down molten lead from a great height. This gentleman wanted to take Dr. Boardman up to the top of the tower—to see how the work was done. The doctor came to the tower, he entered by the door, and began going upstairs. But when he had gone a few steps, the gentleman called out, "That is the wrong way. You must come down this way. That stair is locked up."

The gentleman took him downstairs a good many steps, and there an elevator was ready to take him to the top. He said, "I have learned a lesson that going down is often the best way to get up."

Ah, yes, God will have to bring us down very low. A sense of emptiness and despair and nothingness will have to come upon us. When we sink down in utter helplessness, the everlasting God will reveal Himself in His power. Then our hearts will learn to trust God alone.

What is it that keeps us from trusting Him perfectly?

Many say, "I believe what you say, but there is one difficulty. If my trust were perfect and always abiding, all would come right, for I know God will honor trust. But how am I to get that trust?"

My answer is, By the death of self. The great hindrance to trust is self-effort. As long as you have your own wisdom and thoughts and strength, you cannot fully trust God. But when God breaks you down, when everything begins to grow dim before your eyes and you see that you understand nothing, then God is coming near. If you will bow down in nothingness and wait on God, He will become all.

As long as we are something, God cannot be all. His omnipotence cannot do its full work. This is the beginning of faith—utter despair of self, a ceasing from man and everything on earth, and finding our hope in God alone.

### • FAITH IS REST

And then, next, we must understand that faith is rest.

In the beginning of the faith-life, faith is struggling. But as long as faith is struggling, faith has not attained its strength. But when faith in its struggling gets to the end of itself, and throws itself upon God and rests on Him, then joy and victory come.

Perhaps I can make it plainer if I tell the story of how the Keswick Convention began. Canon Battersby was an evangelical clergyman of the Church of England for more than twenty years. He was a man of deep and tender godliness, but he did not have the consciousness of rest and victory over sin. He was often deeply saddened by the thought of stumbling and failure and sin. When he heard about the possibility of victory, he felt it was desirable, but it was as if he could not attain it. On one occasion, he heard an address on "Rest and Faith" from the story of the nobleman who came from Capernaum to Cana to ask

Christ to heal his child. In the address, it was shown that the nobleman believed that Christ could help him in a general way. But he came to Jesus a good deal by way of an experiment. He hoped Christ would help him, but he did not have any assurance of that help. But what happened? When Christ said to him, *"Go your way; your son lives"* (John 4:50), the man believed the word that Jesus spoke. He rested in that word. He had no proof that his child was well again, and he had to walk back seven hours' journey to Capernaum. He walked back, and on the way met his servant, and got the first news that the child was well. The servant told him that at one o'clock on the afternoon of the previous day, at the very time that Jesus spoke to him, the fever left the child. That father rested on the word of Jesus and His work, and he went down to Capernaum and found his child well. He praised God, and he and his whole house became believers and disciples of Jesus.

Oh, friends, that is faith! When God comes to me with the promise of His keeping, and I have nothing on earth to trust in, I say to God, "Your word is enough. I am kept by the power of God." That is faith; that is rest.

When Canon Battersby heard that address, he went home that night, and in the darkness of the night he found rest. He rested on the word of Jesus. And the next morning, in the streets of Oxford, he said to a friend, "I have found it!" Then he went and told others, and asked that the Keswick Convention might commence. He said that those at the convention, along with himself, should simply testify to what God had done.

It is a great thing when a man comes to rest on God's almighty power for every moment of his life. It is also great when he does so in the midst of temptations to haste and anger and unlovingness and pride and sin. It is a great thing in the face of these to enter into a covenant with the omnipotent Jehovah—not on account of anything that any man says, or of anything that my heart feels—but on the strength of the Word of God. *"Kept by the power of God through faith."*

Oh, let us say to God that we are going to prove Him to the very utmost. Let us say, "We ask You for nothing more than You can give, but we want nothing less." Let us say, "My God, let my life be a proof of what the omnipotent God can do." Let these be the two dispositions of our souls every day—deep helplessness and simple, childlike rest.

## • FAITH NEEDS FELLOWSHIP

This brings me to just one more thought in regard to faith—faith implies fellowship with God.

Many people want to take the Word and believe it, but do not think it is so necessary to fellowship with God. Ah, no! You cannot separate God from His Word. No goodness or power can be received apart from God. If you want to get into this life of godliness, you must take time for fellowship with God.

People sometimes tell me, "My life is one of such scurry and bustle that I have no time for fellowship with God." A dear missionary said to me, "People do not know how we missionaries are tempted. I get up at five o'clock in the morning, and there are the natives waiting for their orders for work. Then I have to go to the school and spend hours there. Then there is other work, and sixteen hours rush along. I hardly get time to be alone with God."

Ah, there is the need. I urge you, remember two things. I have not told you to trust the omnipotence of God as a thing, and I have not told you to trust the Word of God as a written book. I have told you to go to the God of omnipotence and the God of the Word. Deal with God as that nobleman dealt with the living Christ. Why was he able to believe the word that Christ spoke to him? Because in the very eyes and tone and voice of Jesus, the Son of God, he saw and heard something that made him feel that he could trust Him. And this is what Christ can do for you and me. Do not try to stir and arouse faith from within. How often I have tried to do that, and made a fool of myself! You cannot stir up faith from the depths of your heart. Leave your heart, and look into the face of Christ. Listen to what He tells you about how He will keep you. Look up into the face of your loving Father, and take time every day with Him. Begin a new life with the deep emptiness and poverty of a man who has nothing and who wants to get everything from Him—with the deep restfulness of a man who rests on the living God, the omnipotent Jehovah. Try God, and prove Him if He will not open the windows of heaven and pour out a blessing that there will not be room to receive it (Mal. 3:10).

I close by asking if you are willing to fully experience the heavenly keeping for the heavenly inheritance? Robert Murray McCheyne has said, "Oh, God, make me as holy as a pardoned sinner can be made." And if this prayer is in your heart, come now, and let us enter into a covenant with the everlasting and omnipotent Jehovah afresh. In great helplessness, but in great restfulness, let us place ourselves in His hands. And then, as we enter into our covenant, let us have the one prayer—that we may fully believe that the everlasting God is going to be our Companion. Let us believe that He will hold our hands every moment of the day. He is our Keeper, watching over us without a moment's interruption. He is our Father, delighting to reveal Himself in our souls always. He has the power to let the sunshine of His love be with us all day.

Do not be afraid that because you have your business you cannot have God with you always. Learn the lesson that the natural sun shines on you all day, and you enjoy its light. Wherever you are, you have the sun; God makes certain that it shines on you. God will make certain that His own divine light shines on you, and that you will abide in that light, if you will only trust Him for it. Let us trust God to do this with a great and entire trust. Here is the omnipotence of God, and here is faith reaching out to the measure of this omnipotence. We can say, "All that this omnipotence can do, I am going to trust my God for." Are not the two sides of this heavenly life wonderful? God's omnipotence covers me, and my will in its littleness rests in that omnipotence, and rejoices in it!

> Moment by moment, I'm kept in His love;
> Moment by moment, I've life from above;
> Looking to Jesus, the glory doth shine;
> Moment by moment, Oh, Lord, I am thine!

# chapter 9

# The Blessings of Branch-Life

## AN ADDRESS TO CHRISTIAN WORKERS

*I am the vine, you are the branches.*
—John 15:5

Everything depends on our being right in Christ. If I want good apples, I must have a good apple tree. If I care for the health of the apple tree, the apple tree will give me good apples. It is just the same with our Christian life and work. If our lives with Christ are right, all will come out right. Instruction and suggestion and help and training in the different departments of the work may be needed; all of these have value. But in the long run, the greatest essential is to have the full life in Christ—in other words, to have Christ in us, working through us. I know how much there is to disturb us, or to cause anxious questionings. But the Master has such a blessing for every one of us and such perfect peace and rest. He has such joy and strength if we can only come into, and be kept in, the right attitude toward Him.

Look carefully at our text verse: *"I am the vine, you are the branches."* Look especially at the second part of the verse: *"You are the branches."* What a simple thing it is to be a branch—the branch of a tree, or the branch of a vine! The branch grows out of the vine, or out of the tree, and there it lives and grows and, in due time, bears fruit. It has no responsibility except to receive sap and nourishment from the root and stem. And if only we knew, by the Holy Spirit, about our relationship to Jesus Christ, our work would be changed into the brightest and most heavenly thing on earth. Instead of there ever being soul-weariness or exhaustion, our work would be like a new experience, linking us to Jesus as nothing else can. For is it not true that often our work comes between us and Jesus? What foolishness! The very work that He has to do in me, and I for Him, I take up in such a way that it separates me from Christ. Many a laborer in the vineyard has complained that he has too much work and not enough time for close communion with Jesus. He complains that his usual work weakens his inclination for prayer, and that his many conversations with men darken the spiritual life. Sad thought, that the bearing of fruit should separate the branch from the vine! That must be because we have looked on our work as something other than the branch bearing fruit. May God deliver us from every false thought about the Christian life.

Now, let's examine a few thoughts about this blessed branch-life.

## ABSOLUTE DEPENDENCE

In the first place, it is a life of absolute dependence. The branch has nothing; it depends on the vine for everything. Absolute dependence is one of the most solemn and precious of thoughts. A great German theologian wrote two large volumes some years ago to show that the whole of Calvin's theology is summed up in this one principle of absolute dependence upon God, and he was right. Another great writer has said that absolute, unalterable dependence upon God alone is the essence of the religion of angels. It should also be that of men. God is everything to the angels, and He is willing to be everything to the Christian. If I can learn to depend on God every moment of the day, everything will come right. You will receive the higher life if you depend absolutely on God.

Now, here we find it with the vine and the branches. Every vine you ever see, or every bunch of grapes that comes to your table, let it remind you that the branch is absolutely dependent on the vine. The vine has to do the work, and the branch enjoys the fruit of it.

What does the vine have to do? It has to do a great work. It has to send its roots out into the soil and hunt under the ground—the roots often extend a long way out—for nourishment, and to drink in the moisture. Put some manure in certain directions, and the vine sends its roots there. Then, its roots or stems turn the moisture and manure into the special sap that makes the fruit that is borne. The vine does the work, and the branch has just to receive the sap from the vine. The sap is then changed into grapes. I have been told that at Hampton Court, London, there was a vine that sometimes bore a couple of thousand bunches of grapes. People were astonished at its large growth and rich fruitage. Afterward, the cause was discovered. The Thames River flows nearby, so the vine had stretched its roots hundreds of yards under the ground until it had come to the riverside. There, in all the fertile slime of the riverbed, it had found rich nourishment and obtained moisture. The roots had drawn the sap all that distance up and up into the vine. As a result, there was the abundant, rich harvest. The vine had the work to do, and the branches had just to depend on the vine and receive what it gave.

Is this literally true of my Lord Jesus? Must I understand that when I have to work, when I have to preach a sermon or address a Bible class or go out and visit the poor or neglected ones, that all the responsibility of the work is on Christ?

This is exactly what Christ wants you to understand. Christ desires that in all your work, the very foundation should be the simple, blessed consciousness that Christ must care for all.

And how does He fulfill the trust of that dependence? He does it by sending down the Holy Spirit—not now and then only as a special gift. But remember, the relationship between the vine and the branches is such that the living connection is maintained hourly, daily, unceasingly. The sap does not flow for a time, then stop, and then flow again. Instead, moment to moment, the sap flows from the vine to the branches. Similarly, my Lord Jesus wants me to take that blessed position as a worker. Morning by morning and day by day and hour by hour and step by step—in every work—I have to go out to abide before Him in the simple, utter helplessness of one who knows nothing. I must be as one who is nothing and can do nothing. Oh, beloved workers, study that word *nothing*. You sometimes sing, "Oh, to be nothing, nothing," but have you really studied that word and prayed every day and worshipped God in the light of it? Do you know the blessedness of that word *nothing?*

If I am something, then God is not everything; but when I become *nothing,* God can become *all.* The everlasting God in Christ can reveal Himself fully. This is the higher life. We need to become nothing. Someone has well said that the seraphim and cherubim are flames of fire because they know they are nothing, and they allow God to put His fullness and His glory and brightness into them. Oh, become nothing in deep reality, and, as a worker, study only one thing—to become poorer and lower and more helpless, so that Christ may work all in you.

Workers, here is your first lesson: learn to be nothing, to be helpless. The man who has something is not absolutely dependent. But the man who has nothing is absolutely dependent. Absolute dependence on God is the secret of all power in work. The branch has nothing but what it gets from the vine. You and I can have nothing but what we get from Jesus.

## DEEP RESTFULNESS

Second, the life of the branch is not only a life of entire dependence, but also of deep restfulness.

That little branch, if it could think, feel, and speak, and if we could say, "Come, branch of the vine, I want to learn from you how I can be a true branch of the living Vine," what would it answer? The little branch would whisper, "Man, I hear that you are wise, and I know that you can do a great many wonderful things. I know you have much strength and wisdom given to you, but I have one lesson for you. With all your hurry and effort in Christ's work, you never prosper.

The first thing you need is to come and rest in your Lord Jesus. That is what I do. Since I grew out of that vine, I have spent years and years, and all I have done is just to rest in the vine. When the time of spring came I had no anxious thought or care. The vine began to pour its sap into me, and to give the bud and leaf. And when summer came, I had no care; and in the great heat, I trusted the vine to bring moisture to keep me fresh. And in the time of harvest, when the owner came to pluck the grapes, I had no care. If there was anything in the grapes not good, the owner never blamed the branch; the blame was always on the vine. And if you want to be a true branch of Christ, the living Vine, just rest on Him. Let Christ bear the responsibility."

You say, "Won't that make me slothful?"

I tell you it will not. No one who learns to rest on the living Christ can become slothful. The closer your contact with Christ, the more the Spirit of His zeal and love will be borne in upon you. But, oh, begin to work in the midst of your entire dependence by adding deep restfulness to it. A man sometimes tries and tries to be dependent on Christ, but he worries himself about this absolute dependence. He tries and he cannot get it. But let him sink down into entire restfulness every day.

> In Thy strong hand I lay me down.
> So shall the work be done;
> For who can work so wondrously
> As the Almighty One?

Workers, take your place every day at the feet of Jesus, in the blessed peace and rest that come from the knowledge—

> I have no care, my cares are His!
> I have no fear, He cares for all my fears.

Come, children of God, and understand that it is the Lord Jesus who wants to work through you. You complain of the lack of fervent love. It will come from Jesus. He will give the divine love in your heart with which you can love people. That is the meaning of the assurance, *"The love of God has been poured out in our hearts by the Holy Spirit"* (Rom. 5:5), and of that other word, *"The love of Christ compels us"* (2 Cor. 5:14). Christ can give you a fountain of love so that you cannot help loving the most wretched and the most ungrateful, or those who have wearied you.

Rest in Christ, who can give wisdom and strength. You do not know how that restfulness will often prove to be the very best part of your message. You plead with people and you argue, and they get the idea, "This is someone arguing and striving with me." But if you will let the deep rest of God come over you—the rest in Christ Jesus, the peace and the rest and holiness of heaven—that restfulness will bring a blessing to the heart, even more than the words you speak.

## MUCH FRUITFULNESS

Third, the branch teaches a lesson of much fruitfulness.

The Lord Jesus Christ repeated the word *fruit* often in the Parable of the Vine and the Branches. He spoke, first, of *"fruit"* (John 15:2), then of *"more fruit"* (v. 2), and then of *"much fruit"* (v. 5). Yes, you are ordained not only to bear fruit, but to bear *"much fruit."* *"By this My Father is glorified, that you bear much fruit"* (v. 8). In the first place, Christ said, *"I am the true vine, and My Father is the vinedresser"* (v. 1). God will watch over the connection between Christ and the branches. It is in the power of God through Christ that we are to bear fruit.

Oh, Christians, you know this world is perishing for lack of workers. And it lacks more than workers. Many workers are saying, some more earnestly than others, "We need not only more workers, but we need our workers to have a new power—a different life—so that we workers will be able to bring more blessing."

Children of God, I appeal to you. You know what trouble you take, say, in a case of sickness. Suppose you have a beloved friend apparently in danger of death, and nothing can refresh that friend so much as a few grapes. But they are out of season. Still, what trouble you will take to get the grapes that are to be the nourishment of this dying friend! Likewise, there are people around who never go to church, and so many who go to church but do not know Christ. And yet the heavenly grapes—the grapes of the heavenly Vine—are not to be had at any price unless the child of God bears them out of his inner life in fellowship with Christ. Unless the children of God are filled with the sap of the heavenly Vine, unless they are filled with the Holy Spirit and the love of Jesus, they cannot bear much of the real heavenly grape. We all confess there is a great deal of work, a great deal of preaching, teaching, and visiting, and a great deal of earnest effort of every kind. But there is not much manifestation of the power of God in it.

What is missing? The close connection between the worker and the heavenly Vine is lacking. Christ, the heavenly Vine, has blessings that He could pour on tens of thousands who are perishing. Christ, the heavenly Vine, has power to provide the heavenly grapes. But *"you are the branches,"* and you cannot bear heavenly fruit unless you are in close connection with Jesus Christ.

Do not confuse work and fruit. There may be a good deal of work for Christ that is not the fruit of the heavenly Vine. Do not seek only work. Study this question of fruit-bearing. It means the very life, power, spirit, and love within the heart of the Son of God. It means the heavenly Vine Himself coming into your hearts and mine.

You know there are different sorts of grapes, each with a different name. Every vine provides exactly the aroma and juice that gives the grape its particular flavor and taste. In a similar manner, there is in the heart of Christ Jesus a life, a love, a Spirit, a blessing, and a power for men, that are entirely heavenly and divine, and that will come down into our hearts. Stand in close connection with the heavenly Vine and say, "Lord Jesus, nothing less than the sap that flows through You, nothing less than the Spirit of Your divine life is what we ask. Lord Jesus, I pray, let Your Spirit flow through me in all my work for You."

I tell you again that the sap of the heavenly Vine is nothing but the Holy Spirit. The Holy Spirit is the life of the heavenly Vine. What you must get from Christ is nothing less than a strong inflow of the Holy Spirit. You need it exceedingly, and you need nothing more than this. Remember this. Do not expect Christ to give a bit of strength here, a bit of blessing there, and a bit of help over there. As the vine does its work in giving its own sap to the branch, so expect Christ to give His own Holy Spirit into your heart. Then you will bear *"much fruit"* (John 15:5). Perhaps you have only begun to bear fruit, and you are listening to the word of Christ in the parable—*"more fruit"* (v. 2), *"much fruit"* (v. 5). Remember that in order for you to bear more fruit, you just require more of Jesus in your life and heart.

We ministers of the Gospel are in danger of getting into a condition of work, work, work! We pray over it, but the freshness, buoyancy, and joy of the heavenly life are not always present. Let us seek to understand that the life of the branch is a life of much fruit because it is a life rooted in Christ, the living, heavenly Vine.

## CLOSE COMMUNION

Fourth, the life of the branch is a life of close communion.

Let us again ask, What does the branch have to do? You know the precious, inexhaustible word that Christ used—*"abide"* (John 15:4). Your life is to be an abiding life. And how is the abiding to be? It is to be just like the branch in the vine, abiding every minute of the day. The branches are in close communion, in unbroken communion, with the vine, from January to December. And can I not live every day—it is to me an almost terrible thing that we should ask the question—in abiding communion with the heavenly Vine?

You say, "But I am so occupied with other things."

You may have ten hours' hard work daily, during which your brain has to be occupied with temporal things. God has ordered things to be so. But the abiding work is the work of the *heart,* not of the brain. It is the work of the heart clinging to and resting in Jesus, a work in which the Holy Spirit links us to Christ Jesus. Oh, believe that deeper down than the brain, deep down in the inner life, you can abide in Christ, so that every moment you will know, "Blessed Jesus, I am still in You."

If you will learn for a time to put aside other work and to get into this abiding contract with the heavenly Vine, you will find that fruit will come.

How can we apply this abiding communion to our lives? What does it mean?

It means close fellowship with Christ in secret prayer. I am sure there are Christians who long for the higher life, and who sometimes have received a great blessing. I am sure there are those who have at times found a great inflow of heavenly joy and a great outflow of heavenly gladness. Yet after a time, it has passed away. They have not understood that close, personal communion with Christ is an absolute necessity for daily life. Take time to be alone with Christ. Nothing in heaven or earth can free you from the necessity for this, if you are to be happy and holy Christians.

Oh, how many Christians look on it as a burden and a tax, a duty and a difficulty, to often be alone with God! This is the great hindrance to our Christian lives everywhere. We need more quiet fellowship with God. I tell you in the name of the heavenly Vine that you cannot be healthy branches—branches into which the heavenly sap can flow—unless you take plenty of time for communion with God. If you are not willing to sacrifice time to get alone with Him, to give Him time every day to work in you, and to keep up the link of connection between you and Himself, He cannot give you the blessing of His unbroken fellowship. Jesus Christ asks you to live in close communion with Him. Let every heart say, "O Christ, it is this I long for. It is this I choose." And He will gladly give it to you.

## ABSOLUTE SURRENDER

Finally, the life of the branch is a life of absolute surrender.

The words *absolute surrender* are great and solemn. I believe we do not fully understand their meaning. Yet the little branch preaches it.

"Have you anything to do, little branch, besides bearing grapes?"

"No, nothing."

"Are you fit for nothing?"

Fit for nothing! The Bible says that a bit of vine cannot even be used as a pen. It is fit for nothing but to be burned.

"And now, what do you understand, little branch, about your relationship to the vine?"

"My relationship is just this: I am utterly given up to the vine, and the vine can give me as much or as little sap as it chooses. Here I am, at its disposal, and the vine can do with me what it likes."

Oh, friends, we need this absolute surrender to the Lord Jesus Christ. The more I write, the more I feel that this is one of the most difficult points to make clear. It is also one of the most important and necessary points to explain what this absolute surrender is. It is often an easy thing for a man or a number of men to come out and offer themselves up to God for entire consecration, saying, "Lord, it is my desire to give myself up entirely to You." This is of great value, and often brings very rich blessing. But the one question they ought to study quietly is, What is meant by absolute surrender?

It means that, as literally as Christ was given up entirely to God, we are given up entirely to Christ. Is that too strong? Some think so. Some think that this can never be. They cannot believe that, just as entirely and absolutely as Christ gave up His life to do nothing but seek the Father's pleasure, and depend on the Father absolutely and entirely, we are to do nothing but to seek the pleasure of Christ. But this is actually true. Christ Jesus came to breathe His own Spirit into us. He came to help us find our very highest happiness in living entirely for God, just as He did. Oh, beloved brethren, if this is the case, then we ought to say, "Yes, as true as it is of that little branch of the vine, by God's grace, I desire it to be true of me. I desire to live day by day so that Christ may be able to do with me what He will."

Ah, here comes the terrible mistake that lies at the bottom of so much of our own Christianity. A man thinks, "I have my business and family duties, and my responsibilities as a citizen. All this I cannot change. And now alongside all this, I am to take Christianity and the service of God as something that will keep me from sin. God help me to perform my duties properly!"

This is not right. When Christ came, He bought the sinner with His blood. If there was a slave market here and I were to buy a slave, I would take that slave away to my own house from his old surroundings. He would live at my house as my personal property, and I could order him about all day. And if he were a faithful slave, he would live as having no will and no interests of his own. His one care would be to promote the well-being and honor of his master. And in like manner, we, who have been bought with the blood of Christ, have been bought to live every day with the one thought, "How can I please my Master?"

Oh, we find the Christian life so difficult because we seek God's blessing while we live in our own wills. We desire to live the Christian life according to our own liking. We make our own plans and choose our own work. Then we ask the Lord Jesus to come in and make sure that sin will not conquer us too much, and that we will not go too far wrong. We ask Him to come in and give us so much of His blessing. But our relationship to Jesus ought to be such that we are entirely at His disposal. Every day we are to come to Him humbly and straightforwardly and say, "Lord, is there anything in me that is not according to Your will, that has not been ordered by You, or that is not entirely given up to You?"

Oh, if we could wait patiently, I tell you what the result would be. A relationship between us and Christ would spring up. It would be so close and so tender that afterward we would be amazed at how we formerly could have lived with the idea, "I am surrendered to Christ." We would feel how distant our fellowship with Him had previously been. We would understand that He can, and does indeed, come and take actual possession of us, and give us unbroken fellowship all day. The branch calls us to absolute surrender.

Now, I do not speak so much about the giving up of sins. There are people who need this—people who have violent tempers, bad habits, and actual sins that they commit from time to time and that they have never given up into the very heart of the Lamb of God. I urge you, if you are branches of the living Vine, do not keep one sin back. I know there are a great many difficulties about this question of holiness. I know that not everyone thinks exactly the same with regard to it. To me, this would be a matter of comparative indifference if I could see that all are honestly longing to be free from every sin. But I am afraid that unconsciously there are often compromises in hearts, with the idea that we cannot be without sin. There are those who think that we must sin a little every day; we cannot help it. Oh, that people would actually cry to God, "Lord, keep me from sin!" Give yourself utterly to Jesus, and ask Him to do His very utmost for you in keeping you from sin.

There is a great deal in our work, in our churches, and in our surroundings that we found in the world when we were born into it. It has grown all around us, and we think that it is all right, that it cannot be changed. We do not come to the Lord Jesus and ask Him about it. Oh, I advise you, Christians, bring everything into relationship with Jesus, and say, "Lord, everything in my life has to be in most complete harmony with my position as a branch of You, the blessed Vine."

Let your surrender to Christ be absolute. I do not understand the word *surrender* fully. It gets new meanings every now and then. It enlarges immensely from time to time. But I advise you to speak it out: "Absolute surrender to You, Christ, is what I have chosen." And Christ will show you what is not according to His mind, and He will lead you on to deeper and higher blessedness.

In conclusion, let me gather up everything in one sentence. Christ Jesus said, *"I am the vine, you are the branches."* In other words, "I, the living One who have so completely given Myself to you, am the Vine. It is impossible to trust Me too much. I am the almighty Worker, full of a divine life and power."

You are the branches of the Lord Jesus Christ. If there is in your heart the consciousness that you are not a strong, healthy, fruit-bearing branch—not closely linked with Jesus, not living in Him as you should be—then listen to Him say, "I am the Vine; I will receive you. I will draw you to Myself; I will bless you. I will strengthen you; I will fill you with My Spirit. I, the Vine, have taken you to be My branches. I have given Myself utterly to you; children, give yourselves utterly to Me. I have surrendered Myself as God absolutely to you. I became man and died for you so that I might be entirely yours. Come and surrender yourselves entirely to be Mine."

What will our answer be? Oh, let it be the prayer from the depths of our hearts, that the living Christ may take each one of us and link us closely to Himself. Let our prayer be that He, the living Vine, will so link each of us to Himself that we will go away with our hearts singing, "He is my Vine, and I am His branch. I want nothing more, now that I have the everlasting Vine." Then, when you get alone with Him, worship and adore Him; praise and trust Him; love Him and wait for His love. "You are my Vine, and I am Your branch. It is enough; my soul is satisfied."

Glory to His blessed name!

# Book Four

# The Secret of
# Spiritual Strength

# chapter 1

# Knowing Jesus

*Their eyes were opened and they knew Him.*
—Luke 24:31

I t is very possible to have Jesus Himself with you and not know it. It is very possible to listen to all the truth about Jesus, and even to preach about it, and yet not know Him. This fact has made a deep impression on me.

This was the case of the disciples who met Jesus on the road to Emmaus after He was resurrected. Their hearts burned within them as they talked with Him about all the events of His crucifixion and the reports of His resurrection (Luke 24:32). These disciples spent a very blessed time with Jesus, but if they had gone away before He revealed Himself that evening, they never would have been sure that it was Jesus, for they had been prevented from recognizing Him.

This, I am sorry to say, is the condition of a great number of people in the church of Christ. They know that Christ has risen from the dead. They believe in Him; they frequently have blessed experiences that come from the risen Christ. Very often, at a Bible conference or in a time of silent Bible reading or when God gives His grace to them in a special way, their hearts burn within them. Yet it can be said of many Christians, whose hearts are burning within them, that they do not know it is Jesus Himself who is with them.

If you were to ask me what great blessing we should seek from God, my answer would be this: Not only should we think about Jesus Himself and speak about Him and believe in Him, but we should come to the point at which the disciples in the text arrived: *"They knew Him."* Everything is to be found in this.

## FOUR STAGES OF THE CHRISTIAN LIFE

In the story of the disciples on the road to Emmaus, I recognize four stages of the Christian life. First, there is the stage of the sad and troubled heart. Then there is the time in which the heart is slow to believe. This is followed by the period of the burning heart. But the highest level we are to reach is the stage of the satisfied heart.

### • THE SAD AND TROUBLED HEART

Imagine how the disciples were feeling that morning as they started on their journey. Their hearts were sad and troubled because they thought that Jesus was dead. They did not know that He was alive, and this is the way it is with a large number of Christians. They look to the Cross and they struggle to trust Christ, but they have never yet learned the blessedness of believing that there is a living Christ who will do everything for them. The words that the angel spoke to the women who came to Christ's tomb on the morning of the Resurrection were striking: *"Why do you seek the living among the dead?"* (Luke 24:5). What is the difference between a dead Christ, whom the women had gone to anoint, and a living Christ? The difference is that I must do everything for a dead Christ, but a living Christ does everything for me.

The disciples began the morning with a sad heart. It is very possible that they had spent a sleepless night. What a terrible disappointment they had experienced. They had hoped that Christ would be the Deliverer of Israel, yet they had seen Him die an accursed death. Their bitter sadness cannot possibly be expressed. Again, the lives of many Christians are much the same. They try to believe in Jesus and to trust Him and to hope in Him, but they have no joy. Why? They do not know that there is a living Christ who can be revealed to them.

### • SLOW TO BELIEVE

The second stage is taken from the words that Christ spoke to the disciples when He told them that they were *"slow of heart to believe"* (v. 25). They had heard the message from the women, and they told the Stranger who walked with them, *"Certain*

*women of our company, who arrived at the tomb early, aston-*
*ished us. When they did not find His body, they came saying that*
*they had also seen a vision of angels who said He was alive"* (vv.
22–23).

And Christ replied to them, *"O foolish ones, and slow of*
*heart to believe"* (v. 25). Yes, there are many Christians today
who have heard the Gospel and who know that they must not
only believe in a crucified Christ but in a living Christ, and they
try to grasp it and take it in, but it does not bring them a blessing. Why? They do not receive the blessing because they want to
feel it and not to believe it. They want to work for it and to receive it through their own efforts, instead of just quietly humbling themselves and believing that Christ, the living Jesus, will
do everything for them.

Therefore, this is the second stage. The first stage is one of
ignorance, and the second stage is one of unbelief. The doubting
heart cannot take in the wonderful truth that Jesus lives.

## • THE BURNING HEART

The third stage of the Christian life is the burning heart. Jesus came to the two disciples, and after He had reproved them,
He began to interpret the Scriptures for them and to tell them of
all the wonderful things the prophets had taught. Then their eyes
were opened, and they began to understand the Scriptures. They
saw that it was true that it had been prophesied that Christ must
rise. And as the Living Risen One talked, a mighty spiritual
power emanated from Him. It rested upon them, and they began
to feel their hearts burn with joy and gladness.

You may be saying, "This is the final stage at which we need
to arrive." Yet God forbid that you should stop there. You may
arrive at this third stage, yet something will still be lacking: the
revelation of Christ. The disciples had had a blessed experience
of His divine power, but He had not revealed Himself. Our
hearts often burn within us at Bible conferences, in churches, in
meetings, and in blessed fellowship with God's people. These are
precious experiences of the working of God's grace and Spirit,
and yet there is something lacking. What is it?

Jesus Himself has been working in us and the power of His
risen life has touched us, but we have not been able to say, "I

271

have met Him. He has made Himself known to me." There is a great difference between a burning heart, which becomes cold after a while, and which comes and goes, and the blessed revelation of Jesus Himself as my Savior who takes charge of me and blesses me and keeps me every day!

### • THE SATISFIED HEART

The final stage, which I have just described, is the stage of the satisfied heart. I pray that you will arrive at this stage. I am sure that you are praying for this, as well. I am certainly praying that I will arrive at this stage in my own life. Lord Jesus, may we know You in Your divine glory as the Risen One, our Jesus, our Beloved, and our Mighty One.

## HOW TO KNOW JESUS

If you are sad and unable to comprehend or accept this, and if you are saying, "I have never yet known the joy of faith," read the following words carefully, because I am going to tell you how you can know it. Everything centers on one thing. Just as a little child lives day by day in the arms of his mother and grows up year after year under his mother's loving eye, it is possible for you to live every day and hour of your life in fellowship with the holy Jesus. Let your sad heart begin to hope. You may be asking, "Will He really reveal Himself?" He did it for the disciples, and He will do it for you.

Perhaps you have arrived at the stage of the burning heart and can relate many blessed experiences that you have had, but somehow there is a worm at the root. The experiences do not last, and your heart is very changeable. Come, beloved believer, and follow Christ. Say, "Jesus, reveal Yourself so that I may know You personally. I am not only asking to drink the living water, I want the Fountain. I am not only asking to bathe myself in the light, I want the *'Sun of righteousness'* (Mal. 4:2) within my heart. I am not only asking to know You, who have touched me and warmed my heart and blessed me, but I want to know that I have the unchangeable Jesus dwelling within my heart and remaining with me forever."

It may be that you have gotten beyond the stage of the sad heart, but you still feel that you do not have what you want. If you will throw open your heart and give up everything, except believing and allowing Him to do what He wants, it will come. Praise God, it will come!

## To Whom Does Jesus Reveal Himself?

The main question I want to address is, What are the conditions under which our blessed Lord reveals Himself? Or, to put it another way, To whom will Jesus reveal Himself? We find the answer in the way Jesus responded to the disciples on the road to Emmaus.

### • Those Who Give Up Everything for Him

First of all, I think we can conclude from our text that Christ revealed Himself to those disciples who had given up everything for Him. He had said to them, *"Deny [yourself], and take up [your] cross, and follow Me"* (Matt. 16:24), and they had done it. With all their unfaithfulness and with all their weaknesses, they had followed Christ to the end. He had said to them, *"You are those who have continued with Me in My trials. And I bestow upon you a kingdom, just as My Father bestowed one upon Me"* (Luke 22:28–29).

They were not perfect men, but they would have died for Him. They had loved Him, obeyed Him, followed Him. They had left everything, and for three years they had been following Christ earnestly. You say, "Tell me what Christ wants from me so that I may have His wonderful presence. Tell me the kind of person to whom Christ will reveal Himself in this highest and fullest way." My answer is, "He will reveal Himself to the one who is ready to give up everything and to follow Him." If Christ is to give Himself wholly to me, He must know that I am wholly committed to Him. I trust that God will give us grace, so that these words I have written about consecration and surrender— not only of all evil, but of many lawful things, and even, if necessary, of life itself—may lead us to understand the demand that Jesus makes upon us.

A motto that is often quoted is, "God first." In one sense, this is a beautiful motto, and yet I am not always satisfied with it because it is a motto that is often misunderstood. "God first" may mean "I" second, something else third, and something else fourth. In this hierarchy, God is first in order, but He still is one of a series of authorities, and this is not the place God wants. The true meaning of the phrase "God first" is "God all, God everything," and this is what Christ wants. To be willing to give up everything, to submit to Christ so that He may teach you what to say and what to do, is the first characteristic of the person to whom Christ will come. Are you ready to take this step and to say, "Jesus, I do give up everything. Now that I have surrendered to You, I ask You to reveal Yourself"?

Do not hesitate to do this. Speak it from your heart, and let this be the time in which a new sacrifice is laid at the feet of the blessed Lamb of God.

## • THOSE CONVICTED OF THEIR UNBELIEF

The first step, as I have described, is to turn away from everything else and to follow Him, to give up everything in submission to Him, and to live a life of simple love and obedience. But there is a second thing that is needed in a person who is to have this full revelation of Christ: he must be convicted of his unbelief.

*"O foolish ones, and slow of heart to believe in all that the prophets have spoken!"* (Luke 24:25). If we could only see the amount of unbelief in the hearts of God's children, which bars the doors of their hearts, closing them against Christ, we would be astonished and ashamed! Yet where there is faith instead of unbelief, Christ cannot help coming in. He cannot help coming where there is a living faith. When the heart is opened and prepared, when it is full of faith, then Christ will come as naturally as water runs into a hollow place.

What is it that continues to hinder some earnest believers who say, "I have given myself to the Lord Jesus. I have done it often, and by His grace I am doing it every day. God knows how earnestly and genuinely I am doing it. I have the assurance of God's Word, and I know God has blessed me"? Even though they are trying to yield to God, they are hindered because they have not been convicted of their unbelief. *"O foolish ones, and slow of heart to believe."*

Do you want the Lord Jesus to give you a full revelation of Himself? Are you willing to acknowledge that you are a fool for never having believed in Him? Then pray, "Lord Jesus, it is my own fault. You are right here, longing to have possession of me. You have always been here with Your faithful promises, waiting to reveal Yourself."

Have you ever heard of a person who did not desire to make himself known to someone he loved? Christ desires to reveal Himself to us, but He cannot do so because of our unbelief. May God convict us of this unbelief so that we may become utterly ashamed and broken down, and cry out to Him, "Oh, my God, what is this unbelief that actually throws a barrier across the door of my heart so that Christ cannot come in, that blinds my eyes so that I cannot see Jesus, even though He is so near? He has been near me for ten or twenty years, and from time to time He has given me a burning heart. I have enjoyed the experience of a little of His love and grace, and yet I have not had the revelation of Him in which He takes possession of my heart and remains with me in unbroken communion."

Oh, may God convict us of unbelief. Let us make sure that we believe, because *"all things are possible to him who believes"* (Mark 9:23). This is God's promise, and the blessing of receiving the revelation of Jesus can come only to those who learn to believe and trust Him.

### • THOSE WHO PERSEVERE IN SEEKING THE REVELATION

There is another characteristic of those to whom this special revelation of Christ will come: they do not rest until they obtain it. When the disciples were talking with Jesus on the road to Emmaus, their hearts were burning. As they drew close to their destination, Christ acted as if He were going farther. He put them to the test, and if they had allowed Him to go on quietly, if they had been content with the experience of the burning heart, they would have lost something infinitely better. But they were not content with it. They were not content to go home to the other disciples that night and say, "What a blessed afternoon we have had. What wonderful teaching we have had!" No. The burning heart and the blessed experience made them say, "Sir, *'Abide with us'*" (Luke 24:29), and they compelled Him to come in with them.

This always reminds me of the story of Jacob, who wrestled with a man all night and then said, *"I will not let You go unless You bless me!"* (Gen. 32:26). This is the quality that prepares us for the revelation of Jesus. My dear friend, has this been the attitude in which you have looked upon the wonderful blessing of the presence of Jesus? Have you said, "My Lord Jesus, though I do not understand it, though I cannot grasp it, though my struggles do not accomplish anything, I am not going to let You go. If it is possible for a sinner on earth to have You dwelling in his heart in resurrection power every day, every hour, and every moment—shining within him, filling him with love and joy— then I want it"? Is this truly what you want? Then come and say, "Lord Jesus, I cannot let You go unless You bless me."

## THE NEED FOR A REVELATION OF CHRIST

The question is often asked, What is the reason for the weak spiritual lives of so many Christians? This is an excellent question, for it is remarkable how little the church responds to Christ's call, how little the church is what Christ wants her to be. What is really the matter? What is actually needed? Various answers may be given, but there is one answer that includes them all: each believer needs the full revelation of a personal Christ as an indwelling Lord, as a satisfying portion.

When the Lord Jesus was here on earth, what was it that distinguished His disciples from other people? The answer is that Jesus took them away from their fishnets and their homes. He gathered them around Himself, and they knew Him. He was their Master; He guarded them, and they followed Him. And what is supposed to make the difference today between Christ's disciples—not those who are just hoping to get to heaven, but Christ's wholehearted disciples—and other people? It is this: fellowship with Jesus every hour of the day. When Christ was on earth, He was able to keep the disciples with Him for three years, day after day. Now that Christ is in heaven, He is able to do what He could not do when He was on earth—to keep in the closest fellowship with every believer throughout the whole world. Praise God for this.

You may know the verse in Ephesians that says, *"He who descended is also the One who ascended far above all the heavens, that He might fill all things"* (Eph. 4:10). Why was our Lord Jesus taken up to heaven, away from the life of earth? He ascended to heaven because the life of earth is confined to localities, but the life of heaven has no limits, no boundaries, and no localities. Christ was taken up to heaven so that, in the power of God, the omnipresent God, He might be able to fill every one of His followers on earth and be with every individual believer in a personal way.

This is what my heart wants to experience by faith. It is a possibility, it is a promise, it is my birthright, and I want to have it. By the grace of God, I want to say, "Jesus, I will not rest until You have revealed Yourself fully to me."

Oftentimes, people have very blessed experiences during the stage of the burning heart. One of the major characteristics of this stage is that believers delight in God's Word. How did the disciples receive their burning hearts? It was through the way in which Christ opened the Scriptures to them. He made it all look different and new, and they saw what they had never seen before. They could not help feeling how wonderful and how heavenly the teaching was.

There are many Christians who discover that the best time of the day is when they can read and explore their Bibles, and they love nothing more than to get a new spiritual insight. As a person who mines diamonds rejoices when he has found a diamond, or someone who digs for gold when he has found a nugget, they delight when they get some new thought from the Bible, and they feed upon it. Yet even with all their interest in God's Word, and with all the joy that is stirred in their hearts, when they go to their work or attend to their daily duties, they find that there is still something missing in their lives.

From time to time, we must leave all the many and diverse blessings that Jesus gives us and come to the one blessing that encompasses them all: the blessing that Jesus makes Himself known, that Jesus is willing to make Himself known to us. If I were to ask, "Is this not exactly what you and I need, and what many of us have been longing for?" I am sure you would answer, "Yes, this is what I want!" Think of the blessedness that will come from it.

> Oh, the peace my Savior gives!
> Peace I never knew before,
> And my way has brighter grown,
> Since I've learnt to trust Him more.

I recently received a letter from someone who wrote what a wonderful comfort and strength the above poem had been in the midst of difficulties and troubles. But how can a person maintain peace in his life? It was the presence of Christ that brought the peace; therefore, peace must be sustained through the continual presence of Jesus. Remember that when the storm on the sea was threatening to swallow up the disciples, it was the presence of Christ Himself that brought the peace.

Do you want peace and rest? Then you must have Jesus Himself. You talk of purity, you talk of cleansing, you talk of deliverance from sin. Praise God, the deliverance and the cleansing come when the living Jesus comes and gives power. Then you have the resurrected Christ, the heavenly Christ who sits on the throne, making Himself known to you. Surely this is the secret of purity and the secret of strength.

## THE NEED FOR A FRIENDSHIP WITH JESUS

Where does the strength of so many believers come from? It comes from the joy of a personal friendship with Jesus. If those disciples had gone back with their burning hearts to the other disciples, they could have told them wonderful things about a man who had explained the Scriptures and the promises to them, but they could not have said, "We have seen Jesus." They might have said, "Jesus is alive; we are sure of that," but this would not have satisfied the others. Yet now they could go back and say, "We have seen Jesus Himself. He has revealed Himself to us."

Most believers are happy to work for Christ; however, there is a common complaint throughout the church, from the ministers in the pulpit to the least-noticed Christian workers, of a lack of joy and a lack of experiencing the blessings of God. Let us try to find out whether or not the secret of joy may be found where the Lord Jesus comes and shows Himself to us as our Master, and then speaks to us. When you have Jesus with you, and when you take every step with the thought that it is Jesus who wants you to go, that it is Jesus who sends you and is helping you, then there will be brightness in your testimony. Your experience will help other believers, and they will begin to understand, too. They will say, "I see why I have failed. I received the Word, I received the blessing, and I thought I was living the life of Christ, but I did not allow the living Jesus to be a constant, daily presence in my life."

Perhaps you may now be asking, "How will this revelation of Christ come?" This is the secret that no one can know, that Jesus keeps to Himself. It will come in the power of the Holy Spirit. The disciples on the road to Emmaus had a revelation of the living, risen Christ. The Scripture says, *"They knew Him."* He revealed Himself, and then He vanished from their sight.

Was that vision of Christ worth much? It was gone in a moment, yet it was worth heaven, eternity, everything. Why? From that time on, Christ's disciples were no longer to relate to Him in an earthly way. From then on, Christ was to live in the life of heaven. When Christ was resurrected, He entered into a new life. His resurrection life is entirely different from what His life had been before His death. He is now in the power of the Spirit who fills heaven, in the power of the Spirit who is the power of the Godhead, in the power of the Spirit who fills our hearts.

Thank God, Christ can reveal Himself to each one of us by the power of the Holy Spirit. Yet how He does so is a secret thing between Christ and each individual believer. Take this assurance, *"Their eyes were opened and they knew Him,"* and believe that it was written for you.

You may be able to say, "I have known the other three stages. I have experienced the stage of the sad heart, when I mourned that I did not know the living Christ. I have known the stage of the heart that is slow to believe, when I struggled with my lack of faith. And now I know the stage of the burning heart, in which I experience great times of joy and blessed-ness."

If you can say this, then come and know the stage of the satisfied heart. You will have a heart that has been made glad for eternity, a heart that cannot keep in its joy but goes back to other believers, as the disciples went back to the believers in Jerusalem, and says, "It is true. Jesus has revealed Himself. I know it. I feel it."

Beloved, how will this revelation come? Jesus will tell you. Just come to the Lord Jesus and say a simple, childlike prayer. You need to come to Jesus yourself. My work is done. I have pointed you to the Lamb of God, to the Risen One. You must now enter into the presence of the Holy One and begin to plead, "Oh, Savior, I have come so that I might have this blessedness with me at all times—Jesus Himself, my portion forever."

# chapter 2

# The Secret of the Christian Life

*Lo, I am with you always, even to the end of the age.*
—Matthew 28:20

I am aware of the numerous struggles, difficulties, and failures of which many Christians complain, and I know that many are trying to make a new effort to begin a holy life. I know that their hearts are continually afraid that they might fail again, because they experience so many difficulties and temptations, and because of the natural weakness of their characters. My heart longs to be able to tell them the secret of the Christian life in words so simple that a little child could understand them.

But even so, I ask myself, "Can I venture to hope that I will be able to describe the glorious, heavenly Lord Jesus to these believers so that they can see Him in His glory? Can I open their eyes to see that there is a divine, almighty Christ who does actually come into people's hearts, who faithfully promises, *'If anyone loves Me, he will keep My word; and My Father will love him, and We will come to him and make Our home with him'* (John 14:23), and *'I will never leave you nor forsake you'"* (Heb. 13:5)? No, my words are not adequate for that.

However, my Lord Jesus can use me, as a simple servant, to encourage and help struggling Christians. I can say, "I urge you to come into the presence of Jesus and to wait on Him, and He will reveal Himself to you." I pray that God may use His precious Word to encourage you in this.

The secret of the Christian's strength and joy is simply the presence of the Lord Jesus. When Christ was on earth, He was physically present with His disciples. They walked around together all day, and at night they met together and often ate together and stayed at the same house. They were continually together. The presence of Jesus was the training school of His disciples. They were united to Him by this wonderful communion of love for three long years; in their fellowship with Christ, they learned to know Him, and He instructed and corrected them and prepared them for what they were to receive at a later time. After His resurrection, just before He ascended to heaven, He said to them, *"Lo, I am with you always, even to the end of the age."*

What a promise! Christ was with Peter in the boat, and Christ sat with John at the Last Supper, yet I can have Christ with me in just as real a way. In fact, I can have Him in a more complete way, for, before Christ's resurrection, they knew Him as a human being, an individual who was separate from them, but I may know Christ as the One who is glorified in the power of the throne of God—the omnipotent Christ, the omnipresent Christ.

Yes, what a promise! You may be asking, "How is this possible?" It is possible because Christ is God and because Christ, after having been made a human being, went up into the throne and life of God. And now, this blessed Christ Jesus, with His loving, pierced heart; this blessed Christ Jesus, who lived on earth; this same Christ who was glorified into the glory of God, can be in me and can be with me every day.

You may be saying, "Is having the constant presence of the Lord Jesus really possible for someone in business or for someone who has the responsibility of a large and demanding household or for a poor man who is occupied with his problems? Is it possible? Can I always be thinking of Jesus?" Thank God, you do not need to be constantly thinking of Him. You may be the manager of a bank, and your whole attention may be required to carry out the business that you have to do. However, while you have to think of your business, Jesus will think of you, and He will come in and take charge of you.

When a three-month-old baby sleeps in his mother's arms, he lies there helplessly. He hardly knows his mother; he does not think of her, but the mother thinks of the child. And this is the blessed mystery of love: Jesus, the God-man, waits to come to me in the greatness of His love; and when He gets possession of my heart, He embraces me in those divine arms and tells me,

"My child, I, the Faithful One, I, the Mighty One, will remain with you. I will watch over you and keep you every day." He tells me that He will come into my heart so that I can be a happy Christian, a holy Christian, a useful Christian. You say, "Oh, if only I could believe this, if only I could believe that it is possible to have Christ constantly taking charge of me and keeping me every hour and every moment!"

Yet this is exactly my message to you. When Jesus said to His disciples, *"Lo, I am with you always,"* He meant it in the fullness of the divine omnipresence, in the fullness of divine love, and He longs to reveal Himself to you and to me as we have never seen Him before.

And now, just think for a moment what a blessed life it must be to have the continual presence of Jesus. Is this not the secret of peace and happiness? Many people are saying, "If I could just arrive at the point at which every day and all day I believed that Jesus was watching over me and continually keeping me. What peace I would have in the thought, 'I have no care if He cares for me, and I have no fear if He provides for me.'"

Your heart says that this is too good to be true, and that it is too glorious to be possible for you. Still, you acknowledge that it must be a very blessed way to live. Fearful one, mistaken one, anxious one, I bring you God's promise; it is for me and for you. Jesus will do it. As God, He is able, and Jesus is willing and longing as the Crucified One to keep you in perfect peace. This is a wonderful fact, and it is the secret of unspeakable joy.

This is also the secret of holiness. Instead of indwelling sin, there is an indwelling Christ who conquers it. Instead of indwelling sin, there is the indwelling life and light and love of the blessed Son of God. He is the secret of holiness. Christ *"became for us...sanctification"* (1 Cor. 1:30).

Always remember that it is Christ Himself who is our holiness. The experience of having Christ come into you, take charge of your whole being, and rule all things—your nature and your thoughts and your will and your emotions—will make you holy. Christians talk about holiness, but do you know what holiness is? You have as much of holiness as you have of Christ, for it is written, *"Both He who sanctifies and those who are being sanctified are all of one"* (Heb. 2:11). Christ sanctifies us by bringing God's life into us.

We read in Judges, *"The Spirit of the LORD came upon Gideon"* (Judg. 6:34); that is, Gideon was clothed with the Spirit. But in the New Testament there is an equally wonderful text in which we read, *"Put on the Lord Jesus Christ"* (Rom. 13:14). We are to clothe ourselves with Christ Jesus. What does this mean? It not only means that we are given a righteousness outside of ourselves, but that we are to clothe ourselves with the living character of the living Christ, with the living love of the living Christ.

## PUT ON THE LORD JESUS

This is a tremendous calling. I cannot put on Christ unless I believe and understand that I have to put Him on like a garment that covers my whole being. I have to put on a living Christ who has said, *"Lo, I am with you always."* Just pull the folds of that robe of light closer around you, the robe with which Christ wants to dress you. Just acknowledge that Christ is with you, on you, in you. Be clothed with Christ completely!

Examine one characteristic of His after another, and hear God's word, *"Let this mind be in you which was also in Christ Jesus"* (Phil. 2:5). This passage of Scripture tells you that He was obedient to the point of death. When you respond and put on this Jesus, then you have received and put on Christ the Obedient One, Christ whose whole life was obedience. He becomes your life, and His obedience rests upon you until you learn to whisper, as Jesus did, *"My Father,...Your will be done"* (Matt. 26:42), and *"Behold, I have come to do Your will, O God"* (Heb. 10:9).

This, too, is the secret of power for witness and work. Why is it so difficult to be obedient, and why do we sin so often? People sing, "Oh, to be wholly Yours," and they sing it from their hearts. Then why are they disobedient again? Where does the disobedience come from? They are disobedient because they are trying to obey a distant Christ, and therefore His commands do not come to them with power.

What does God's Word tell us about all this? When God wanted to send any man to do His will, He met with him and talked with him and encouraged him, time after time. God appeared to Abraham seven or eight times and gave him one command after another. In this way, Abraham learned to obey Him perfectly. God appeared to Joshua and to Gideon, and they obeyed. Why are we not obedient? It is because we have so little of this close communion with Jesus.

However, if we knew the blessed, heavenly secret of having the presence of Christ with us every day, every hour, every minute, what a joy it would be to obey! We could not live with the conscious thought, "My Lord Jesus is with me and around me," and not obey Him. Are you beginning to long for this and to say, "I must have the ever abiding presence of Jesus"?

There are some Christians who try not to be disobedient, who serve God very faithfully on Sundays and during the week, who pray for grace and blessing, but who complain that they have very little blessing and power. Why? They are not allowing the living Jesus to fill their hearts completely.

I sometimes think of this as an extremely solemn truth. There is a great diversity of gifts among ministers and others who teach and preach. However, I am sure of this: a person's gifts are not the measure of his real power. God can see what neither you nor I can see, though sometimes people can sense it to some degree. Yet to the extent that a person has—not as a feeling or a desire or a thought, but in reality—the very Spirit and presence of Jesus upon him, an unseen silent influence comes out from him. That secret influence is the holy presence of Jesus.

I hope that what I have written to this point has shown you what a desirable thing it is to have the continual presence of Jesus, and what a blessed thing it is to live for. Let me now give you an answer to a question that arises in many people's hearts: "How can I obtain this blessed, constant presence of Jesus, and how can I always keep it? I think that if I were to have this, I would have everything. The Lord Jesus has come very near to me. I have tried to turn away from everything that can hinder my relationship with my Lord, and He has been very close to me. But how can I know that He will always be with me?"

## CONTINUAL BELIEF

My reply to this is, If you were to ask the Lord, "Oh, my blessed Lord Christ, what must I do? How can I enjoy Your never failing presence?" His first response would be, "Only believe. I have said it often, and you have only partly understood it, but I will say it again. My child, only believe."

We believe by faith. We sometimes speak of faith as trust, and it is a very helpful thing to tell people that faith is trust. However, when people say, as they sometimes do, that faith is nothing but trust, that is not the case. *Faith* is a much broader word than *trust*. It is by faith that I learn to know the invisible God, and it is by faith that I see Him. Faith is my spiritual eyesight for what is unseen and heavenly.

You often try hard to trust God, and you fail. Why? It is because you have not first taken time to see God. How can you trust God fully until you have met Him and until you have come to know Him? You ask, "Where should I begin?" Begin with believing, with presenting yourself before God in an attitude of silent worship and asking Him to let a sense of His greatness and His presence come upon you. You must ask Him to let your heart be covered with His holy presence. You must seek to know in your heart the presence of an almighty and all-loving God, an unspeakably loving God. Take time to worship Him as the omnipotent God, to feel that the very power that created the world, the very power that raised Jesus from the dead, is working in your heart at this moment.

We do not often experience this fellowship with God because we do not believe. We must take time to believe. Jesus is saying to you, "My child, shut your eyes to the world, shut out of your heart all your thoughts about religion, and begin to believe in God Himself." This is the true meaning of the first part of the Apostles' Creed, "I believe in God."

By believing, I open my heart to receive this glorious God, and I bow and worship. Then, as I believe in who He is, I look up and see the Lamb on the throne, and I believe that the almighty power of God is in Jesus for the very purpose of revealing His presence to my heart.

Why are there Two on the throne? Is it not enough for God the Father to be there? The Lamb of God is on the throne for our benefit. The Lamb upon the throne is Christ Himself; He has the power, as God, to take possession of us.

Do not think that this will never be a reality for you, or do not think of it as something that is within your reach only for the present moment. Cultivate the habit of faith. Say, "Jesus, I believe in Your glory; I believe in Your omnipotence; I believe in Your power working within me; I believe in Your living, loving presence with me, revealing itself in divine power."

Do not be occupied with feelings or experiences. You will find it far simpler and easier just to trust and to say, "I am sure He is taking care of me completely." Put yourself aside for the time being. Do not think or speak about yourself, but think about who Jesus is.

And then remember that you are always to believe. I sometimes feel that I cannot find the words to explain that God wants His people to believe from morning until night. Every breath ought to be spent just believing. Yes, it is indeed true; the Lord Jesus loves for us to be continually believing from morning until evening, and you must begin to make this the chief thing in life. In the morning, when you wake up, go out to your day with a strong faith in His presence; and in the watches of the night, let this thought be present with you: "My Savior, Jesus, is around me and near me." At any point of the day or night, you can look to Jesus and say, "I want to trust You always."

You know what trust is. It is so sweet to trust. But now, can you trust Jesus, this Presence, this keeping Presence? He lives for you in heaven. You are marked with His blood, and He loves you. Can you say, "My King is with me every day"? Trust Jesus to fulfill His own promises.

## CONTINUAL OBEDIENCE

There is a second answer that I think Christ would give if you were to come to Him in faith and say, "Is there anything more, my blessed Master?" I think I can hear His answer: "My child, always obey."

Do not fail to understand the lesson contained in this. You must distinctly and definitely receive the words *obey* and *obedience,* and learn to say for yourself, "Now I have to obey, and by the grace of God I am going to obey in everything."

When Cecil Rhodes was the prime minister of South Africa, he went to an event, thinking he had the amount of the entrance fee in his pocket. When he got to the gate, however, he found that he did not have enough money, and he said to the attendant, "I am Mr. Rhodes. Let me in, and I will make sure that the ticket is paid for." However, the man said, "I cannot help that, sir, I have my orders," and he refused to let Mr. Rhodes in. The prime minister had to borrow the money from a friend and pay the fee before he could go through the gate. At a dinner afterward, Mr. Rhodes spoke about it, and he said it was a real joy to see a man stick to his orders like that. This is exactly the point I am trying to make. The man had his orders and that was enough for him, and whoever came to the gate had to pay the fee before he could enter. God's children ought to be like soldiers and be ready to say, "I must obey."

What a wonderful thing it would be to have this thought in our hearts: "Jesus, I love to obey You." Personal communion with the Savior will be followed by the joy of personal service and allegiance. Are you ready to obey in all humility and weakness and reverence? Can you say, "Yes, Lord Jesus, I will obey"? If so, give yourself up to Him completely. Then your thinking will be, "I am not going to speak one word if I think that Jesus would not like to hear it. I am not going to have an opinion of my own, but my whole life is going to be covered with the purity of Christ's obedience to the Father and His self-sacrificing love for me. I want Christ to have my whole life, my whole heart, my whole character. I want to be like Christ and to obey." Give yourself up to this loving obedience.

## CLOSE DAILY FELLOWSHIP WITH CHRIST

Third, if you were to say, "My Master, blessed Savior, tell me everything. I will believe, and I will continue to obey. Is there anything more that I need in order to secure the enjoyment of Your continual presence?" I believe this would be His answer: "My child, you need close fellowship with Me every day."

The fault of many who try to obey and try to believe is that they do it in their own strength. They do not know that if the Lord Jesus is to reign in their hearts, they must have close daily communion with Him. You cannot do all that He desires, but Jesus will do it for you. There are many Christians who fail at this point, and for this reason they do not understand what it is to have fellowship with Jesus.

Let me try to impress upon you that God has given you a loving, living Savior, but how can He bless you if you do not meet with Him? The joy of friendship is found in fellowship, and Jesus asks for this fellowship every day so that He may have time to influence you, to tell you of Himself, to teach you, to breathe His Spirit into you, and to give you new life and joy and strength.

Remember, fellowship with Jesus does not mean just spending half an hour or an hour reading your Bible and praying. A person may study his Bible or his Bible commentary carefully; he may look up all the parallel passages in the chapter, and he may be able to tell you all about it; yet he may never have met Jesus at all during the time that he spent studying. You may be praying for five or ten minutes a day, and yet you may never have met Jesus.

And so, we must remember that, although the Bible is very precious and reading it is very blessed and necessary, Bible reading and prayer, in themselves, are not fellowship with Jesus. What we need is to meet with Jesus every morning and to say, "Lord, here is a new day again, and I am just as weak in myself as I ever was. Please come this morning and feed me with Yourself and speak to my soul." My friend, it is not your faith that will keep you standing, but it is a living Jesus with whom you meet every day in fellowship and worship and love. Wait in His presence, no matter how cold and faithless you feel. Wait before Him, and say, "Lord, helpless as I am, I believe and rest in the blessed assurance that You will do for me what You have promised."

## WORK FOR JESUS

If you were to ask the Master once again, "Lord Jesus, is that all?" His answer would be, "No, my child. There is one thing more."

"And what is that? You have told me to believe and to obey and to stay close to You. What additional thing would You like?"

"Work for Me, my child. Remember, I have redeemed you for My service. I have redeemed you so that I may have a witness to go out into the world and tell others about Me."

Friend, do not hide your spiritual treasure, and do not think that if Jesus is with you, you can hide it. One of two things will happen—either you must give up all of your treasure, or it will have to be revealed. Perhaps you have heard of the little girl who, after attending one of evangelist D. L. Moody's meetings, started singing hymns at home. The child's parents were in a good position in society, and when the mother heard the little girl singing hymns in the living room, she forbade her to continue doing so. One day, the girl was singing a hymn with the words, "Oh, I'm so glad that Jesus loves me," and her mother said, "My child, why are you singing this when I have forbidden it?" She replied, "Oh, Mother, I cannot help it. It comes out by itself."

If Jesus Christ is in a person's heart, He will be revealed in the person's life. The reason for this is that it is our duty to witness about Him (it is our duty, yet it is much more than that); if you do not tell others about Christ, it is just an indication that you have not given yourself up completely to Jesus: your character, your reputation, your all. It means you are holding back from Him. You must confess Jesus in the world, in your home, and, in fact, everywhere. You know the Lord's command, *"Go into all the world and preach the gospel to every creature"* (Mark 16:15). He has also said, *"I am with you,"* meaning, "If anyone works for Me, I will be with him." This is true of the minister, the missionary, and every believer who works for Jesus. The presence of Jesus is intimately connected with work for Him.

You may be saying, "I never thought of that before. I work for Him on Sunday, but during the week I am not working for Him." You cannot have the presence of Jesus and let this continue to be the case. I do not believe that you can have the presence of Jesus all week and yet do nothing for Him. Therefore, my advice is, work for Him who is worthy, and His blessing and His presence will be found in the work. It is a blessed privilege to work for Christ in this perishing world. Oh, why is it that our hearts often feel so cold and closed up, and that so many of us say, "I do not feel called to Christ's work"? Be willing to yield yourself for the Lord's service, and He will reveal Himself to you.

## CHRIST IS COMPLETELY FOR US

Christ comes with His extraordinary promise, and He says to all believers: *"Lo, I am with you always.'* This is My promise. This is what I can do in My power. This is what I faithfully pledge to do. Will you receive it? I give Myself to you."

To each person who comes to Him, Christ says, "I give Myself to you, to be absolutely and wholly yours every hour of every day, to be with you and in you every moment, to bless you and sustain you, and to give you the continual knowledge of My presence. I will be wholly, wholly, wholly yours."

## WE ARE TO BE COMPLETELY FOR CHRIST

The other side of it is that He wants us to be wholly His. Are you ready right now to take this as your motto: "Wholly for God"? Let us fall down at His feet in true humility and heartfelt worship. O God, breathe Your presence into our hearts so that You may shine forth from our lives.

A missionary from Africa said that he has often been touched by seeing how the native Christians, when they give their hearts to Jesus, do not stand or kneel in prayer, but lie down with their foreheads to the ground and cry out to God with loud voices. I sometimes wish that more Christians would do this. However, we do not need to do it literally. Let us do it in spirit, for the everlasting Son of God has come into our hearts.

Are you going to receive Him and cherish Him in your heart, to give Him glory and let Him have His way? Say, "I will seek You with my whole heart. I am wholly Yours." Yield yourself entirely to Him so that He can have complete possession of you. He will take you and keep you in His possession. Jesus delights in the worship of His beloved. Our entire lives can become one continuous act of worship and work, filled with love and joy, if we will only remember and value what Jesus has said: *"Lo, I am with you always, even to the end of the age."*

chapter 3

# The Power of the Cross

*Christ, who through the eternal Spirit offered*
*Himself without spot to God.*
*—Hebrews 9:14*

Once we fully commit our lives to Jesus, to live completely for Him, we need to understand a new dimension of life in Christ: the power of the Cross.

The Cross of Christ is the highest expression of the Spirit of Christ. The obedience and self-denial that Christ demonstrated when He endured the Cross are His chief characteristics. They are what distinguish Him from everyone in heaven and earth, and what give Him His glory as Mediator on the throne throughout eternity. Until we truly know the Spirit who led Christ to the Cross, we neither truly know Christ nor the Cross.

Moreover, once we have come to know the nature of the Spirit who led Christ to the Cross, we will see that this knowledge is only one aspect of the great subject of the Spirit of the Cross. We will see how the Holy Spirit of Pentecost and the Spirit of the Cross are one and the same. The Holy Spirit led Christ to the Cross, and He also flows forth from the Cross to us as its purchase, and to whom its power is given.

We will then further find that as the Spirit led Christ to the Cross, and the Cross led to the giving of the Spirit, so the Spirit will always lead back to the Cross again, because He alone can reveal its meaning and communicate its fellowship. In other words, the Spirit led Christ to the Cross, and the Cross leads Christ and us to the outpouring of the Spirit, and the Spirit leads us back to the Cross.

## THE CROSS, OUR LIFE

The Scriptures do not teach us that when Christ bore the Cross and fulfilled the Atonement, the meaning of the Cross was exhausted. They do not indicate that when we trust in the finished work of the Cross, our only relationship to it is one of grateful confidence in what it has accomplished for us. No, the Word of God tells us that in the most intimate spiritual fellowship, the way of the Cross is to be our life. We are to live as if we have been *"crucified with Christ"* (Gal. 2:20), which we have been. We are to walk as those who have crucified the flesh and who can conquer it in no other way but by continually regarding it as crucified. We are to take up our cross day by day, and to glory in it. Every moment of our lives, our relationship to the world is to be that of those who are crucified to it, and who know and believe that the world is crucified to them.

Therefore, if the nature of the Cross is to produce and characterize the only true Christian life, and if we are to have the same attitude toward the Cross that Jesus had, we need to know what it was that made the Spirit of the Cross the only power by which Christ could gain life for us or by which we can possess and enjoy life in Him.

In the first place, the path in which Jesus Christ walked did not derive its value from the amount of suffering it required or from His actual surrender to death, but from the mindset that motivated Him. That mindset was not something strange or different that came to Him in His last hour. It was what motivated and inspired Him throughout the whole course of His earthly life. And it is only as this perspective becomes the animating principle of the life of the believer that the thought of being *"crucified with Christ"* can have any true meaning. How did our Lord have *"this mind"* (Phil. 2:5) that was in Him, and the power to carry it out at any cost? We have the answer in our text for this chapter: *"Who through the eternal Spirit offered Himself without spot to God."*

It was this eternal Spirit who was in Christ from His birth, and who taught Him to say words that contained the seeds of His obedience and self-denial on the cross: *"I must be about My Father's business"* (Luke 2:49). It was this Spirit who led Christ to humble Himself and be treated as a sinner by being baptized in the Jordan River by John (Matt. 3:13–15). It was this Spirit who descended on Jesus like a dove to prepare Christ for the death for which He was set apart (vv. 16–17). It was this Spirit who led our Lord into the wilderness to resist and overcome and begin the struggle that ended on Calvary (Matt. 4:1). It was through this Spirit that He was led, step by step, to speak of and to face and to bear all He had to suffer.

Through the prophets, *"the Spirit of Christ...testified beforehand the sufferings of Christ"* (1 Pet. 1:11). In the same way, it was through the eternal Spirit that all was fulfilled and accomplished. The Spirit of God, dwelling in flesh, leads inevitably and triumphantly to the Cross.

The Cross is the perfect expression of the mind of the Spirit —of what He asks and works. When God took possession of human nature to free it from sin and fill it with Himself, the only way He could do it was by slaying it. In the whole universe, there is no possibility of freedom from the power of sin except by personal separation from it through entire death to it. What God demands, the Spirit works. He worked His will in the Man Christ Jesus, the spotless Holy One who, because of His union with us and because He was our forerunner in the path of life, needed to die to sin. He works His will now as the Spirit of Christ who dwells in each believer.

## THE CRUCIFIXION SPIRIT

Let us who desire to be filled with the Spirit consider the nature of the Spirit of the Cross. The Spirit leads us to a death that is characterized by the Cross. Since He had nothing higher than this to accomplish for us in Christ before He raised Jesus from the dead, He also has no higher work He can do for us than to lead us into the perfect fellowship of the Cross. Pray to know what this means. Have you truly yielded to the Spirit so that He may lead you, as He led Christ, in the path of the Cross? Are you seeking the fullness of the Spirit in total agreement with His one purpose: to manifest in you the obedience and self-denial of Christ? For you, as it was for Jesus, the path of the Cross is the sure path, the only path, to glory.

## DENY YOURSELF AND TAKE UP YOUR CROSS

There is a deep and intimate connection between taking up one's cross and following Christ. An additional aspect of crossbearing may be drawn from the words of Christ:

*If anyone desires to come after Me, let him deny himself, and take up his cross daily, and follow Me. For whoever desires to save his life will lose it, but whoever loses his life for My sake will save it.* (Luke 9:23–24)

A believer must *"deny himself"* before he can take up his cross and follow Christ. The deepest root of crossbearing and following Christ is exposed in this passage of Scripture. Even while the Christian is striving earnestly to follow Christ, and in some measure to take up his cross, there is a secret power that resists and opposes and prevents him. The very person who is praying and vowing and struggling to follow fully what his desire and will and heart are apparently set on, in his innermost self, refuses the cross to which his Lord has called him. Self, the real center of his being, the controlling power, refuses to accept it. And so, Christ teaches us that we must begin with the total denial of self.

## THE CROSS MEANS SURRENDER

Taking up one's cross means accepting and surrendering to death. Self, the real inner life of a person, must die. For us to attempt to take up our cross and follow Jesus will mean unceasing failure unless we start with Christ's words: *"Let him deny himself, and take up his cross....Whoever loses his life for My sake will save it"* (Luke 9:23–24).

Christ calls me to love nothing more than I love Him, to lose my life, to disallow what gives life its own value, to disclaim what I am in my own person—to deny myself. Why must I first carry my cross and then be "crucified" on it? And why, if Jesus has already died for me on the cross and won life for me, must I still die, deny myself, and take up my cross daily?

## WHY THE CROSS?

The answer is simple, and yet it is not easy to comprehend. The real spiritual answer will be revealed only to the person who consents to obey Jesus before he understands what it all means. Through the sin of Adam, the life of mankind fell from its high position. It had been a vessel in which God caused His power and blessedness to work. But man fell under the power of the world, in which the god of this world has his rule and dominion.

Therefore, man has become a creature who has a strange, unnatural, worldly life. The will of God, heaven, and holiness, for which man was created, have become darkened and lost to him. The pleasures of the flesh and of the world and of self, which are the dark, accursed workings of the Evil One, have become natural and attractive. People do not see, they do not know, how sinful, wretched, and deadly they are—that they are alienated from God and that they bear within them the very seeds of hell. And this self, this innermost root of man's life, which he loves so much, is really the concentration of all that is not of God but is of the Evil One. Exhibiting a great deal of what is naturally beautiful and seemingly good, the power of self and its pride corrupt everything. They are the very seat of sin and death and hell.

Yet once a person has consented to a life of the entire denial of self, he will welcome and love the cross. He will recognize it as the appointed power of God for freeing him from the evil power that is the only thing hindering him from being fully conformed to the image of God's Son—from loving and serving the Father as Christ did. To deny self is a work of the inner spirit. Taking up the cross is the manifestation of this work.

*"Let him deny himself, and take up his cross daily, and follow Me"* (Luke 9:23). When we receive insight into what the denial of self means, it becomes clear why the cross must be taken up daily. Taking up one's cross is not only called for during a time of special trial or suffering. During times of quiet and prosperity, the need is even more urgent. Self is the enemy that is always near and always seeking to regain its power.

For example, when the apostle Paul came down from the third heaven (see 2 Corinthians 12:2–7), he was in danger of being prideful. The danger of pride is always with us. Denying self and bearing the cross are to be everyday attitudes. When Paul said, *"I have been crucified with Christ"* (Gal. 2:20) and *"God forbid that I should boast except in the cross of our Lord Jesus Christ, by whom the world has been crucified unto me, and I to the world"* (Gal. 6:14), he spoke of himself as living the crucifixion life each moment of the day.

There used to be a picture of a hand holding a cross, with the motto, *Teneo et Tenem*—"I hold and am held," or to use a looser translation, "I bear and am borne." The words Jesus used before His death, *"Take up [your] cross"* (Luke 9:23), reflect the first idea of the motto, "I hold." Accept your cross and bear it. Paul's words in Galatians, which were inspired by the Holy Spirit after Christ had been glorified—*"crucified with Christ"* (Gal. 2:20)—point more to the second part of the motto: believe that His Cross, rather, that He, the Crucified One, bears you.

Before the work of the Cross was actually finished, the idea was to take up one's cross. Now that the finished work has been revealed, that is, taken up and transformed into the higher idea of being crucified with Christ, the concept is that I both bear the cross and am borne by Christ. *"I have been crucified with Christ"* and *"Christ lives in me"* (Gal. 2:20). It is only in the power of being borne by Christ that I can bear the cross.

## FOCUS ON CHRIST

What was first a condition that we had to fulfill if we were to follow Jesus, became the blessed fruit of following Him. When we hear the call, *"Follow Me"* (Matt. 4:19), we think chiefly of all it implies for us. It is necessary that we do so, but it is not the chief thing. As we think of denying ourselves and taking up our cross daily, we realize how little we know of what it all means, and how little we are able to perform even what we do know.

A trusted leader takes all the responsibility for the journey and makes every provision. We need to focus our hearts on Jesus, who calls us to take up our cross and to follow Him. On Calvary, He opened the way for us and led us even to the throne of God's power. Yes, let us focus our hearts on Him. As He led His disciples, He will lead us.

The Cross is a mystery. Taking up one's cross is a deep mystery. To be *"crucified with Christ"* (Gal. 2:20) is the deepest mystery of redemption. The hidden wisdom of God is a mystery. Let us follow Christ with a true desire to let Him lead us. Let us live as fully as He did, to the glory of the Father. And let us enter with Christ through death into the fullness of life.

chapter 4

# Drawing Near to God

*For Christ also suffered once for sins, the just for the unjust,*
*that He might bring us to God.*
—1 Peter 3:18

I n the previous chapter, I described how the way of the Cross is the pathway to life in Christ. Now I want to show you how the Cross enables us to draw near to God.

The Cross speaks of sin. It is only by comprehending the evil of sin, and fully admitting that it is hatred against God, that man can come to God. The Cross speaks of the Curse, which is God's judgment against sin. As long as man does not accept and affirm that God's judgment is righteous, there can be no thought of his being restored to God's presence. The Cross speaks of suffering. When we suffer, it is only as we accept the will of God and give up everything to that will that we can have union with God. The Cross speaks of death. It is only as man is ready to completely part with his whole present life—to die to it—that he can enter into, or fully receive to himself, the life and glory of God. Christ Himself did all this. His whole life was animated by the crucifixion spirit.

When Christ bore the Cross and entered into God's holy presence, He opened up a way in which we, too, could draw near to God. When He bore God's judgment for sin by His death, He *"put away sin"* (Heb. 9:26); He made an end of sin. By bearing the Curse, death, and condemnation, He carried away sin. He broke and abolished the power of the Devil, who had the power of death, and He set us free from Satan's prison.

The Cross and the blood and the death of Christ are God's assurance to the sinner that there is immediate acquittal and everlasting admission to God's favor and friendship for each one who will accept and entrust himself to the Savior. All the claims

299

that God's law had against us and all the power that sin and Satan had over us are at an end. The death of Jesus destroyed sin and death. The path of the Cross is the path Christ has opened for us; in it, we have full freedom and power to draw near to God.

The path of the Cross is the only way that mankind can come to God. It is the path in which Christ Himself walked, the path that He opened for us, the path in which we, too, walk, and the only path in which we can lead others.

## THE WAY OF THE CROSS

The way of the Cross was the way in which Jesus, as Man, personally walked throughout His whole life, so that, as our Forerunner, He might enter in and appear before God for us. *"Though He was a Son, yet He learned obedience by the things which He suffered. And having been perfected, He became the author of eternal salvation to all who obey Him"* (Heb. 5:8–9).

The Cross was the path to God even for Jesus Himself. If there was no path to God for Christ except through death, the entire giving up of His life, how much more must this be the only path in which a sinner can come to be filled with the life of God. And now that Christ's death is an accomplished fact, the death and the life that we receive in Him are the power of His absolute surrender working in us, and this leads to the blessed indwelling of the Spirit. It is this kind of faith that enables a believer to say joyfully, *"I have been crucified with Christ"* (Gal. 2:20), and *"God forbid that I should boast except in the cross of our Lord Jesus Christ, by whom the world has been crucified to me, and I to the world"* (Gal. 6:14).

The crucifixion spirit, with its protest against and separation from the world, its sacrifice of all self-interest, and its absolute surrender to God, even to the death, characterizes the whole life and walk of a Christian. Daily bearing and glorying in the cross becomes, indeed, the path to God.

## THE WAY TO BLESS OTHERS

In this path, we can win others for Christ and bless them. It was as the Crucified One, giving His life for men, that Christ won the power to bless people. It was Peter's full acceptance of the sufferings that Christ underwent on His way to glory, of which he spoke in his first epistle, that filled the apostle with boldness to testify for his Lord. It was the intensity of Paul's desire for perfect conformity to his Lord's sufferings that gave him his power as an apostle.

The power of God's Spirit will work through the church in the measure in which God's people give themselves to Him as a sacrifice for men. It is Christ crucified who saves men. It is Christ crucified, living, and breathing in us who can and will use us for His saving work. Jesus living and working in us means precisely that we, like Him, are ready to give our lives for others. This means that we are to forget ourselves, to sacrifice ourselves, to suffer anything so that the lost may be won.

## LIFE OUT OF DEATH

At first, when a person enters into the truth of being *"crucified with Christ"* (Gal. 2:20) and of *"always carrying about in the body the dying of the Lord Jesus"* (2 Cor. 4:10), his chief thought is one of personal sanctification. He regards death to sin, death to the world, and death to self as the path of life and blessing.

But these desires cannot truly lead him to trust in Christ as the only One in whom death, and the life that arises out of this death, may be known and found, unless he understands another truth. He must also allow Christ to teach him the secret that every aspect of His obedience to the Father and His victory over sin was not for any personal glorification but was for the purpose of saving others around Him. The believer learns that the path of the cross cannot truly be followed by any who are not willing to work and to give their lives for others. The believer also learns, on the other hand, that the only true power to bless others comes when the cross, that is, death to the world and self, becomes the guiding principle of his daily life.

The Cross was Christ's way to God—for Himself and for us. The cross is our way to God—for ourselves and for others. The cross is the way for us, so that it may be the way for others, too.

301

The church is continually speaking of needing to find the secret of power for its ministry of calling others to faith in Christ. People do not truly understand that the church only has power over the world when she is crucified to the world. The power is *"Christ crucified"* (1 Cor. 1:23); it is a *"stumbling block"* and *"foolishness"* (v. 23) to men, but it is gloried in by those who can say, *"I have been crucified with Christ"* (Gal. 2:20). The power of God manifests itself in preaching that proclaims the Cross of Christ, with its message of crucifixion to the world and self, and victory over sin and death.

## THE ENEMY OF THE CROSS

*"Now thanks be to God who always leads us in triumph in Christ, and through us diffuses the fragrance of His knowledge in every place"* (2 Cor. 2:14).

When God created the earth, He placed Adam in Paradise, not only to work it, but to take care of it. It is evident that there must have been some evil power that Adam had to watch for and guard against. Since everything God created during the six days was very good, the evil must have been in existence previously. Scripture does not reveal how the evil came to exist or where it came from. It is enough for us to know that it existed and that it threatened the very center of the new creation—the Garden of God and the dwelling of man—with danger and destruction. It is as true today as it was then that God seeks to rob this evil of its power, and He purposes to do so through the medium of man.

The idea naturally suggests itself that man may have been created for the very purpose of conquering the evil that had existed before him. It is this perspective that establishes our apparently insignificant earth as the historic center of the universe. Satan, whose evil power had probably caused the formlessness (Gen. 1:2) or chaos of the earth, still sought to maintain his kingdom—in the very world that had been raised out of the ruins of his previous kingdom. It was on earth that man was created to conquer evil and to cast it out. This is what makes the world of such great importance in the eyes of God and His angels; it is the battlefield where heaven and hell meet in deadly conflict.

302

The terrible history of mankind can never be correctly understood until we allow Scripture to teach us the following fact: even as God's purposes rule over all, there is, on the other hand, amid what appears to be nothing but natural growth and development, an organized system and evil kingdom that rules over men, keeps them in darkness, and uses them in its war against the kingdom of God's Son. On a scale that we can hardly imagine, through the slow length of ages that God's patience endures, amid all the freedom of human will and action, there is an unceasing contest going on. Though the outcome is not in question, the struggle is long and destructive. And in the history of that struggle, the Cross is the turning point.

## THE CROSS IS A TRIUMPH

[Christ has] *wiped out the handwriting of requirements that was against us, which was contrary to us. And He has taken it out of the way, having nailed it to the cross. Having disarmed principalities and powers, He made a public spectacle of them, triumphing over them in it.* (Col. 2:14–15)

The above Scripture wonderfully clarifies what the redemption of the Cross means. Having thrown off from Himself the principalities and powers, Christ made a show of them openly, triumphing over them in His Cross. The powers of darkness had made their onslaught in the darkness of the Cross; together, they had pressed on Him with everything that is terrible in their power, surrounding Him with the very darkness and misery of hell. They had formed a cloud so thick and dark that the very light of God's face was hidden from Him. But He defeated them; He beat back His enemies and overcame the temptation. He made a show of them openly; throughout the entire spiritual realm, before angels and devils, it was known that He had conquered.

When Christ died on the cross, the very grave gave up its dead (Matt. 27:52–53). And so He triumphed over our enemy, death. In the spiritual world, the Cross is the symbol of victory. In triumph, Christ led the principalities and powers as prisoners. Their power was broken forever, the gate of the prison in which they held men captive was broken open, and freedom was proclaimed to all their prisoners.

The prince of this world has been cast out. He no longer has power to hold in bondage those who long for deliverance. He now only rules over those who consent to be his slaves. There is now a perfect deliverance for all who yield themselves to Christ and His Cross.

The great lesson of the second chapter of Colossians is that the Cross is a triumph. It began when Christ cried, *"It is finished!"* (John 19:30). This was the beginning of a triumphal procession in which Christ moves on through the world in hidden glory, leading *"captivity captive"* (Eph. 4:8), leading His ransomed ones into liberty. And the believer can now continually rejoice, *"Now thanks be to God who always leads us in triumph in Christ"* (2 Cor. 2:14). Every thought of the Cross, every step we take under the Cross, every proclamation of the Cross ought to have the tone of divine triumph: *"Death is swallowed up in victory....Thanks be to God, who gives us the victory through our Lord Jesus Christ"* (1 Cor. 15:54, 57).

Without this mindset, our understanding of the meaning of the Cross and our experience of the power of the Cross will be defective. We will find this to be true both in our personal lives and in our work for others. In our personal lives, we will consider the cross to be a burden. The call to carry the cross will seem like a law that is hard to obey. Our attempts to live the crucifixion life will be a failure. The thought of a daily death will be wearisome. Crucifying the flesh demands such unceasing watchfulness and self-denial that we will give it up as a hopeless or fruitless task.

It cannot be otherwise until we know, in some measure, that the Cross is a triumph. We do not have to crucify the flesh. This has been accomplished in Christ. The act of crucifixion on Calvary is a finished transaction; the life and Spirit that go forth from the Crucifixion work with unceasing power. Our calling is to believe, to *"be of good cheer"* (John 16:33). Nothing less than His death can meet our need; nothing less than His death is at our disposal. *"Thanks be to God who always leads us in triumph in Christ"* (2 Cor. 2:14).

It is of no less importance, in our service in the world, that we believe in the triumph of the Cross over the powers of darkness. Nothing except insight into this truth can teach us to know the supernatural strength and spiritual subtlety of our Enemy. Nothing else can teach us what our purpose must be as we *"wrestle...against the rulers of the darkness of this age"* (Eph. 6:12). This purpose is to bring men out of the world and away from the power of its prince.

Nothing except this insight into the triumph that the Cross has won, and continually gives, can make us take our true position as the instruments and servants of our conquering King, servants whose one hope is to be led in triumph in Him. And nothing else can keep alive in us the courage and the hope that we need in our helplessness, as the mighty powers of the Enemy continually force themselves on us.

In faith, we must learn to say, through all our service and warfare, *"Thanks be to God who always leads us in triumph in Christ"* (2 Cor. 2:14). The Cross, with its foolishness (1 Cor. 1:18) and weakness, its humiliation and shame, is the everlasting sign of the victory that Christ has won by mighty weapons that are spiritual, not carnal (2 Cor. 10:4). It is also the symbol of the victory that the church and every servant of Christ can continually win as we enter more deeply into the character of our crucified Lord, and, in this way, yield more fully to Him.

# chapter 5

# Called into His Light

*But God forbid that I should boast except in the cross of
our Lord Jesus Christ, by whom the world has been
crucified to me, and I to the world.*
—Galatians 6:14

There is no question that is of greater interest to the
church today than that which deals with her relationship
to the world. The meaning of the word *world,* as Christ
used it, is simple. He used the expression to describe mankind in
its fallen state and its alienation from God. He regarded it as an
organized system or kingdom, the very opposite and mortal enemy of His kingdom. A mighty, unseen power, the *"god of this
world"* (2 Cor. 4:4 KJV), rules it; and a spirit, the *"spirit of the
world"* (1 Cor. 2:12), pervades it and gives it strength.

More than once, Christ revealed this as His special characteristic: *"I am not of this world"* (John 8:23). He also clearly
taught His disciples, *"You are not of the world"* (John 15:19). He
warned them that because they were not of the world, the world
would hate them as it had hated Him (vv. 18–19). Of His sufferings, He said, *"The ruler of this world is coming, and he has
nothing in Me"* (John 14:30); *"This is* [the] *hour, and the power
of darkness"* (Luke 22:53); and *"Be of good cheer, I have overcome the world"* (John 16:33).

In the hatred that nailed Him to the cross, the world revealed its true spirit, which is under the power of its god. In the
Cross, Christ revealed His Spirit and His rejection of the world
with all its threats and promises. The Cross is the confirmation
of His word—that His kingdom *"is not of this world"* (John
18:36). The more we love the Cross and live by it, the more we
will know what the world is and be separate from it.

The difference and antagonism between the two kingdoms is irreconcilable. No matter how much the world might be externally changed by Christian influence, its nature will remain the same. No matter how close and apparently favorable the alliance between the world and the church might become, the peace will be merely hollow and will last for only a time. When the Cross is fully preached—with its revelation of sin and the Curse, with its claim to be accepted and taken up—the enmity may quickly be seen. No one can overcome the world unless he is *"born of God"* (1 John 5:4).

## GLORYING IN THE CROSS

In Galatians 6:14, we see how clearly Paul recognized the enmity between the Cross and the world, and how boldly he proclaimed it: *"But God forbid that I should boast except in the cross of our Lord Jesus Christ, by whom the world has been crucified to me, and I to the world."* He identified himself so strongly with the Cross that its relationship to the world was also his. The Cross separated Paul from the world.

The Cross is the sign that the world has condemned Christ. Paul accepted this; the world was crucified to him, and he was crucified to the world. The Cross is God's condemnation of the world. Paul understood that the world is condemned and under the Curse. The Cross forever separated Paul from the world in its evil nature. The Cross alone could be their meeting place and reconciliation. It was for this reason that he gloried in the Cross and preached that it was the only power that could draw men out of the world to God.

The view that many Christians take is the opposite of the perspective of Christ and John and Paul. These Christians speak as if in some way the Curse has been taken off the world, and that the nature of the world has somehow been softened. They think of educating and winning the world—by meeting it more than halfway—with offers of friendship. They believe that the work of the church is to permeate the world with a Christian spirit and to take possession of it. They do not see that the spirit of the world permeates the church and takes possession of it to a far greater extent. As a result of this, *"the offense of the cross"*

(Gal. 5:11) is done away with, and the Cross is adorned with the flowers of earth so that the world is quite content to give it a place among its idols.

## WAR WITH THE ENEMY

In war, there is no greater danger than to underestimate the power of the enemy. We must remember that the work of the church is a war, an unceasing battle: *"For we do not wrestle against flesh and blood, but against principalities, against powers, against the rulers of the darkness of this age, against spiritual hosts of wickedness in the heavenly places"* (Eph. 6:12).

The world is made up of sinful humanity, not a mere collection of individuals who are led on in their sin by blind chance. It is an organized force that is unknowingly animated by one evil power that fills it with its spirit; it is a power of darkness, led on by one leader, the *"god of this world"* (2 Cor. 4:4 KJV). *"You once walked according to the course of this world, according to the prince of the power of the air, the spirit who now works in the sons of disobedience"* (Eph. 2:2).

It is only when the church accepts this truth in all its ramifications that she becomes capable of understanding the meaning of the Cross and how it was designed to draw men out of the world. And it is only in this awareness and acceptance that she will have the courage to believe that nothing but the persistent preaching of the Cross, in all its divine mystery, is what can overcome the world and save men out of it. The powers of the other world, the *"spiritual hosts of wickedness in the heavenly places"* (Eph. 6:12), working on earth in men, can only be conquered and brought into subjection by a higher power, the power of Christ, who, *"having disarmed principalities and powers,...made a public spectacle of them, triumphing over them in* [the Cross]*"* (Col. 2:15). It is the Cross, with its victory over sin and the Curse and death, with its love and life and triumph, that alone is the power of God.

## BLINDED MINDS

The great power of the world lies in its darkness. The Scriptures tell us, *"The god of this world hath blinded the minds of them which believe not"* (2 Cor. 4:4 KJV), and *"We do not wrestle against flesh and blood, but against principalities, against powers, against the rulers of the darkness of this age"* (Eph. 6:12). If anything of the spirit of this world is found in individual believers—or in the church—then, to the same extent, they will be incapable of seeing things in the light of God. They will judge spiritual truth with hearts that are prejudiced by the spirit of the world that is in them.

No person, no matter how honest his intentions are, no matter how earnest his thoughts are, no matter how much intellectual power he has, can understand and receive God's truth any farther than the Spirit of Christ and the Cross has expelled—or is truly sought after to expel—the spirit of the world in him. The Holy Spirit, when He is carefully waited on and yielded to, is the only Light that can open the eyes of the heart to see and to know what is of the world and what is of God. Moreover, we only truly yield to the Holy Spirit when the path of the Cross, with its crucifixion of the flesh and the world, becomes the law of our lives. The Cross and the world are diametrically and unchangeably opposed to one other.

Sin brought about destruction and ushered in the spirit of the world. Man was to have lived on earth in the power of the heavenly life, in fellowship with God, and in obedience to His will. When man sinned, he fell entirely under the power of this *"present evil age"* (Gal. 1:4), which *"the god of this world"* (2 Cor. 4:4 KJV) rules and uses as a means of temptation and sin. Man's eyes were closed to eternal and spiritual things, and so things related to time and the physical world mastered and ruled him.

Some Christians speak as if the Cross of Christ has taken away the Curse and the power of sin in the world in such a way that the believer is now free to enter into the enjoyment of the world without danger. They believe that the church now has the calling and power of appropriating the world—of taking possession of it for God.

This is certainly not what Scripture teaches. The Cross removes the Curse from the believer, not from the world. Whatever has sin in it has the Curse on it as much as ever. What the believer is to possess of the world and its goods must first be *"sanctified by the word of God and prayer"* (1 Tim. 4:5).

Nothing except an understanding of the evil of the spirit of the world, and our deliverance from it by the Cross and the Spirit of Christ—nothing except the Spirit and power of the Cross animating us, separating and freeing us from the spirit of the world—can keep us so that we are in the world but not of it. To conquer the world by the Cross, it cost Christ His agony in the Garden of Gethsemane, where He sweat blood; it cost Him His awful struggle with death and the sacrifice of His life. Nothing less than a full and wholehearted entrance into fellowship with Him in His crucifixion can save us from the spirit of the world.

## CRUCIFIED WITH CHRIST

In the epistle to the Galatians, there are several passages that refer to the Cross of Christ, but only one of them speaks definitely of the Atonement: *"Christ has redeemed us from the curse of the law, having become a curse for us"* (Gal. 3:13). The other passages in Galatians pertain to fellowship with the Cross and its relationship to our inner life. When Paul said, *"I have been crucified with Christ; it is no longer I who live, but Christ lives in me"* (Gal. 2:20); *"Those who are Christ's have crucified the flesh"* (Gal. 5:24); and *"The world has been crucified to me, and I to the world"* (Gal. 6:14), he spoke of a life, an inward disposition, a spiritual experience, in which the same Spirit and power that sustained Christ when He bore the Cross are maintained and manifested in the believer.

There are many who claim to boast, or glory, in the Cross (v. 14). They consider their faith in the righteousness of Christ as man's justification before God to be the great proof of their faithfulness to Scripture. Yet in their toleration of things that are of the spirit of this world, and through their wholehearted enjoyment and participation in them, they prove that they do not really glory in a Cross that crucifies the world. To them, the Cross that atones and the world that crucified the Savior are at peace with one another. They do not know anything about walking the path of the Cross, which crucifies the world for being an accursed thing and keeps us crucified to it.

310

## THE CROSS WILL PROVE ITS POWER

If the preaching of the Cross—not only for forgiveness but for holy living, not only for pardon from sin but for power over the world and an entire freedom from its spirit—is to be of central importance to the church today, as it was with the apostle Paul, we must implore God to reveal what He means by the world and what He means by the power of the Cross. It is in the lives of believers who are actually and obviously crucified to the world and all that is of it, that the Cross will prove its power.

# Book Five

# Experiencing the
# Holy Spirit

# Preface

In all our studies of the work of the blessed Spirit, and in our pursuit of a life in His fullness, we will always find the sum of Christ's teaching in these wonderful words: *"He who believes in Me, as the Scripture has said, out of his heart will flow rivers of living water"* (John 7:38). As we are convicted of the defectiveness of our faith in Christ and as we understand that believing in Him means a yielding of the whole heart, life, and will, we can confidently count on receiving the Holy Spirit's power and presence. When Christ becomes all that God has made Him to be for us, the Holy Spirit can then flow from Christ to do His blessed work of leading us back to know Him better and to believe in Him more completely.

The book of Hebrews speaks of Christ in His heavenly glory and power as the object of our faith. The Holy Spirit reveals the way into the Holiest by the blood of Christ and invites us by faith in Christ to have our life there. As we yield our hearts to the leading of the Spirit to know Christ and to believe in what is revealed, the Spirit can take possession of us. The Spirit is given to reveal Christ, and every fully accepted revelation of Christ gives the Spirit room to dwell and work within us. This promise will surely then be fulfilled: *"He who believes in Me,...out of his heart will flow rivers of living water."* May God lead us to this simple and full faith in Christ, our great High Priest and King in the heavens, and so into a life in the fullness of the Spirit.

ANDREW MURRAY

# Introduction

This book brings a simple but solemn message. The one thing needed for the church in its search for spiritual excellence is to be filled with the Spirit of God. In order to secure attention to this message and attract the hearts of my readers to its blessing, I have laid particular emphasis on certain main points:

- The will of God for every one of His children is that they live entirely and unceasingly under the control of the Holy Spirit.
- Without being filled with the Spirit, it is impossible for an individual Christian or a church to ever live or work as God desires.
- In the life and experience of Christians, this blessing is little used and little searched for.
- God waits to give us this blessing, and in our faith we may expect it with the greatest confidence.
- The self-life and the world hinder and usurp the place that Christ ought to occupy.
- We cannot be filled with the Spirit until we are prepared to yield ourselves to be led by the Lord Jesus—to forsake and sacrifice everything for this *"pearl of great price"* (Matt. 13:46).

We have such a poor idea of the unspiritual and sinful state that prevails in the church that, unless we take time to devote our hearts and our thoughts to the real facts of the case, the promise of God can make no deep impression on us. I have presented the subject in various aspects to prepare the way for the conviction that this blessing is in truth the one thing needed; and to get possession of this one thing, we ought to say good-bye to everything else we hold dear. Owing to the prevailing lack of the presence and operation of the Spirit, it takes a long time before these spiritual truths concerning the need, the fullness, and the reality of the Spirit's power can obtain mastery over us.

Every day ought to be a Pentecostal season in the church of Christ. Christians cannot live according to the will of God without this blessing. I cannot exhort you, my readers, strongly enough to continue this search for spiritual excellence by calling on God in the confidence that He will answer.

When we read the book of Acts, we see that the filling with the Spirit and His mighty operation was always obtained by prayer. Recall, for example, what took place at Antioch. When the Christians were engaged in fasting and prayer, God regarded them as prepared to receive the revelation that they must separate Barnabas and Saul. It was only after they had once more fasted and prayed that these two men went forth, sent by the Holy Spirit. (See Acts 13:2–3.) These servants of God felt that the blessing they needed could come only from above.

To obtain the blessing we so greatly need, we, in like manner, must liberate ourselves as far as possible from the demands of the earthly life. Let us never become weary or discouraged but ask that the Holy Spirit may again assume His rightful place and exercise full dominion in us. In addition, let us pray that He may again have His true place in the church, be held in honor by all, and in everything reveal the glory of our Lord Jesus. To the soul who diligently searches and prays in sincerity according to His Word, God's answer will surely come.

Nothing searches and cleanses the heart like true prayer. It teaches one to ask such questions as these: Do I really desire what I pray for? Am I willing to cast out everything to make room for what God is prepared to give me? Is the prayer of my lips really the prayer of my life? Am I willing to wait on Him, in quiet trust, until He gives me this supernatural gift—His own Spirit?

Let us pray continually, coming before God with supplications and strong crying as His priests and the representatives of His church. We can depend on Him to hear us.

Believer, you know that the Lord is a God who often hides Himself. He desires to be trusted. He is often very near to us without our knowing it. He is a God who knows His own time. Though He tarries, wait for Him. He will surely come. (See Habakkuk 2:3.)

chapter 1

# How the Blessing Is to Be Taught

*And it happened...that Paul...came to Ephesus. And finding some disciples he said to them, "Did you receive the Holy Spirit when you believed?"*
—Acts 19:1–2

About twenty years after the outpouring of the Holy Spirit, this incident took place. In the course of his journey, Paul came to Ephesus and found in the Christian church some disciples in whom he observed that there was something lacking in their belief or experience. Accordingly he asked them the question, *"Did you receive the Holy Spirit when you believed?"* Their reply was that they had not even heard of the Holy Spirit. They had been baptized by disciples of John the Baptist with the baptism of repentance, with a view to faith in Jesus as One who was to come, but they were still unacquainted with the great event of the outpouring of the Spirit or the significance of it. They came from a region of the country into which the full Pentecostal preaching of the exalted Savior had not yet penetrated.

Paul took them at once under his care and told them about the full Gospel of the glorified Lord who had received the Spirit from the Father and had sent Him down to this world so that every one of His believing disciples might also receive Him. Hearing this good news and agreeing with it, they were baptized into the name of this Savior who baptizes with the Holy Spirit. Paul then laid his hands on them and prayed, and they received the Holy Spirit. They obtained a share in the Pentecostal miracle and spoke with other tongues.

In these chapters, it is my desire to bring to the children of God the message that there is a twofold Christian life. The one is that in which we experience something of the operations of the Holy Spirit, just as many did under the old covenant, but we do not yet receive Him as the Pentecostal Spirit, as the personal indwelling Guest. On the other hand, there is a more abundant life, in which the indwelling just referred to is known and experienced. When Christians come to fully understand the distinction between these two conditions, they will find the will of God concerning them.

Therefore, it is a possible experience for each believer, having confessed the sinfulness and inconsistency that still marks our lives, to dare to hope that the Christian community will once more be restored to its Pentecostal power. With our focus on this distinction, let's ponder the lessons presented in this incident at Ephesus.

## Do Not Rest Prematurely

For a healthy Christian life, it is indispensable that we be fully conscious that we have received the Holy Spirit to dwell in us.

Had it been otherwise, Paul would never have asked the question, *"Did you receive the Holy Spirit when you believed?"* These disciples were recognized as believers. This position, however, was not enough for them. The disciples who walked with the Lord Jesus on earth were also true believers, yet He commanded them not to rest satisfied until they had received the Holy Spirit from Himself in heaven. Paul, too, had seen the Lord in His heavenly glory and was by that vision led to conversion. Yet even in his case, the spiritual work the Lord required to have done in him was not completed. Ananias had to go to him and lay his hands on him so that he might receive the Holy Spirit. Only then could he become a witness for Christ.

All these facts teach us that there are two ways in which the Holy Spirit works in us. The first is the preparatory operation in which He simply acts on us but does not yet take up His abode within us, though He leads us to conversion and faith and ever urges us to all that is good and holy. The second is the higher and more advanced phase of His working, when we receive Him as an abiding gift, as an indwelling Person who assumes responsibility for our whole inner beings. This is the ideal of the full Christian life.

## WHERE DO WE STAND?

There are disciples of Christ who know little or nothing of this conscious indwelling of the Holy Spirit.

It is of the utmost importance to understand this statement. The more fully we come under the conviction of its truth, the better we will understand the condition of the church in our times and be enabled to discover where we really stand.

The condition I refer to becomes very plain to us when we consider what took place at Samaria. Philip the evangelist had preached there. Many had been led to believe in Jesus and were baptized into His name, and there was great joy in that city. When the apostles heard this news, they sent down Peter and John, who, when they came to Samaria, prayed that these new converts might receive the Holy Spirit. (See Acts 8:16–17.) This gift was something quite different from the working of the Spirit that led them to conversion, faith, and joy in Jesus as a Savior. It was something higher; for now from heaven and by the glorified Lord Himself, the Holy Spirit was imparted in power with His abiding indwelling to consecrate and fill their hearts.

If this new experience had not been given, the Samaritan disciples would still have been Christians, but they would have remained weak. Thus it is that in our own days, there are still many Christians who know nothing of this gift of the Holy Spirit. Amid much that is good and amiable, even with much earnestness and zeal, the lives of such Christians are still hampered by weakness, stumbling, and disappointment simply because they have never been brought into vitalizing contact with power from on high. Such souls have not received the Holy Spirit as the Pentecostal gift to be possessed, kept, and filled by Him.

## CAN WE WORSHIP WITH SINCERITY?

It is the great work of the gospel ministry to lead believers to the Holy Spirit.

It was the great aim of the Lord Jesus, after He had educated and trained His disciples for three years, to lead them to the point of waiting for the promise of the Father and receiving the Holy Spirit sent down from heaven. This was the chief objective of Peter on the Day of Pentecost, when, after summoning those who were convicted in their hearts to repent and be baptized for the forgiveness of sins, he assured them that they should then receive the Holy Spirit. (See Acts 2:38.)

Paul aimed at this when he asked his fellow Christians if they did not know that they were each a temple of the Holy Spirit. He reminded them that they had to be filled with the Holy Spirit. (See Ephesians 5:18.)

Yes, the supreme need of the Christian life is to receive the Holy Spirit and, when we have it, to be conscious of the fact and live in harmony with it. An evangelical minister must not merely preach about the Holy Spirit from time to time, but also direct his efforts toward teaching his congregation that there can be no true worship except through the indwelling and unceasing operation of the Holy Spirit.

To lead believers to the Holy Spirit, the great lack in their lives must be pointed out to them.

This was the intention in Paul's question, *"Did you receive the Holy Spirit when you believed?"* Only those who are thirsty will drink water with eagerness, and only those who are sick will desire a physician. In the same way, it is only when believers are prepared to acknowledge the defective and sinful character of their spiritual condition that the preaching of the full blessing of Pentecost will find an entrance into their hearts.

Many Christians imagine that the only thing lacking in their lives is more earnestness or more strength and, if they only obtain these benefits, they will become all they ought to be. This makes the preaching of a full salvation of little avail. Only when the discovery is made that they are not standing in a right attitude toward the Holy Spirit, that they have only His preparatory operations but do not yet know Him in His indwelling, will the way to something higher ever be open or even be desired.

For this discovery, it is indispensable that the question should be put to each individual as pointedly and as personally as possible: *"Did you receive the Holy Spirit when you believed?"* When the answer takes the shape of a deeply felt and utterly sincere concern, then the time of revival is not far off.

## HELP TO TAKE HOLD OF THIS BLESSING

In the Acts of the Apostles we read often about the laying on of hands and prayer. Even a man like Paul—whose conversion was due to the direct intervention of the Lord—had to receive the Spirit through laying on of hands and prayer on the part of Ananias. (See Acts 9:17.)

This implies that there must be among ministers of the Gospel, and believers in general, a power of the Spirit that makes them the channel of faith and courage to others. Those who are weak must be helped to take hold of the blessing for themselves. But those who have this blessing, as well as those who desire to have it, must realize and acknowledge their absolute dependence on the Lord and expect all from Him.

The gift of the Spirit is imparted only by God Himself. Every fresh outpouring of the Spirit comes from above. There must be frequent personal dealing with God. The minister of the Spirit whom God is to use for communicating the blessing, as well as the believer who is to receive it, must meet with God in immediate and close communion. *"Every good gift...is from above"* (James 1:17). Faith in this truth will give us courage to expect, with confidence and gladness, that the full Pentecostal blessing may be looked for and that a life under the continual leading of the Holy Spirit is within our reach.

The proclamation and the taking hold of this blessing will restore the Christian community to the primary Pentecostal power.

On the Day of Pentecost, speaking *"with other tongues"* (Acts 2:4) and prophesying were the results of being filled with the Spirit. Here at Ephesus, twenty years later, the very same miracle was again witnessed as the visible token and pledge of the other glorious gifts of the Spirit. We may depend on it that where the reception of the Holy Spirit and the possibility of being filled with Him are proclaimed and taken hold of, the blessed life of the Pentecostal community will be restored in all its fresh power.

An increasing acknowledgement of the lack of power in the church exists today. In spite of the multiplication of the means of grace, there is neither the power of the divine salvation in believers nor the power for conversion in preaching. Little conflict exists in the church between worldliness and unbelief.

This complaint is justified. If the expression of it became strong enough, the children of God might be led to cast themselves on the great truth that the Word of God teaches. When faith in the full Pentecostal blessing is found in the Christian church again, the members will find their strength and be able to do their first works.

## THE CHURCH NEEDS MEN WHO TESTIFY

We need more pastors and teachers who preach Christ Jesus as John the Baptist did—as the One who baptizes with the Holy Spirit. It is only the minister who stands forth as a personal witness and living proof of the ministry of the Spirit whose word will have full entrance into the hearts of the people and exercise full sway over them. The first disciples obtained the baptism on their knees, and on their knees they obtained it for others. It will be on our knees also that the full blessing will be won today. Let this be the attitude in which we await the full blessing of our God.

Have you received the Holy Spirit since you believed? To be filled with the Holy Spirit of God and to have the full enjoyment of the Pentecostal blessing is the will of God concerning us. Judge your life and your work before the Lord in the light of this question, and present your answer to God.

Do not be afraid to confess before your Lord what is still lacking in you. Do not hold back, although you do not as yet fully understand what the blessing is or how it comes. The early disciples called on their Lord and waited with prayer and supplication.

Let your heart be filled with a deep conviction of what you lack, a desire for what God offers, and a willingness to sacrifice everything for it. Then you may rest assured that the marvel of Jerusalem and Samaria, of Caesarea and Ephesus, will once again be repeated. We may and we will be filled with the Spirit.

# chapter 2

# How Glorious the Blessing Is

*They were all filled with the Holy Spirit.*
—Acts 2:4

Whenever we speak of being filled with the Holy Spirit and desire to know precisely what it is, our thoughts always turn back to the Day of Pentecost. How glorious the blessing is that is brought from heaven by the Holy Spirit!

One fact makes the great event of the Day of Pentecost doubly instructive—namely, that, by their three-year relationship with the Lord Jesus, we have learned to know intimately the men who were then filled with the Spirit. Their weaknesses, defects, sins, and perversities all stand open to our view.

The blessing of Pentecost brought about a complete transformation. They became entirely new men, so that one could say of them with truth, *"Old things have passed away; behold, all things have become new"* (2 Cor. 5:17). Close study of them and their example will help us in more than one way. It shows us to what weak and sinful men the Spirit will come. It teaches us how they were prepared for the blessing. It teaches us also—and this is the principal thing—how mighty and complete the transformation is when the Holy Spirit is received in His fullness. It lets us see how glorious is the grace that awaits us if we diligently search for spiritual excellence through the full blessing of Pentecost.

## BLESSINGS OF THE PENTECOSTAL LIFE

The ever-abiding presence and indwelling of the Lord Jesus is the first and principal blessing of the Pentecostal life. In the course of our Lord's dealings with His disciples on earth, He spared no pains to teach and train them or to renew and sanctify them. In most respects, however, they remained just what they were. The reason was that, up to this point, He was still nothing more than an external Christ who stood outside of them and from the outside sought to work on them by His word and His personal influence.

With the advent of Pentecost, this condition was entirely changed. In the Holy Spirit, He came down as the indwelling Christ to become the life of their lives. He had promised this in the words, *"I will not leave you orphans; I will come to you....At that day you will know that I am in My Father, and you in Me, and I in you"* (John 14:18, 20).

This was the source of all the other blessings that came with Pentecost. Jesus Christ, the Crucified, came in spiritual power to impart to them the ever-abiding presence of their Lord in a way that was intimate and all-powerful. Him whom they had had in the flesh, living with them on earth, they now received by the Spirit in His heavenly glory within them. Instead of an outward Jesus near them, they now obtained the inward Jesus with them.

From this first and principal blessing sprang the second: the Spirit of Jesus came into them as the life and the power of sanctification. Often the Lord had to rebuke the disciples for their pride and exhort them to humility. It was all of no avail. Even on the last night of His earthly life, at the table of the Holy Supper, there was strife among them as to which of them should be the greatest. (See Luke 22:24.)

The outward teaching of the outward Christ, whatever other influences it may have exercised, was not sufficient to redeem them from the power of indwelling sin. This could be achieved only by the indwelling Christ. Only when Jesus descended into them by the Holy Spirit did they undergo a complete change. They received Him in His heavenly humility and subjection to the Father and in His self-sacrifice for others. From that point, all was changed. From that moment on, they were animated by the spirit of the meek and lowly Jesus.

Many Christians keep their minds occupied only with the external Christ on the cross. They wait for the blessing of His teaching and His working without understanding that the blessing of Pentecost brings Him *into us*. This is why they make so little progress in sanctification. Christ Himself is our sanctification (1 Cor. 1:30).

## LIVING THE LIFE OF LOVE

A heart overflowing with the love of God is also a part of the blessing of Pentecost. Next to pride, a lack of love was the sin for which the Lord had often rebuked His disciples. These two sins have the same root: the desire for pleasing self. The new commandment that He gave them, by which all men would know that they were His disciples, was their love for one another.

This was gloriously manifested on the Day of Pentecost when the Spirit of the Lord poured out His love in the hearts of His own. (See Romans 5:5.) *"The multitude of those who believed were of one heart and one soul"* (Acts 4:32). All things they possessed were held in common. No one said that anything he had was his own. The kingdom of heaven, with its life of love, had come down to them. The spirit, the disposition, and the wonderful love of Jesus filled them because He Himself had come into them.

The mighty working of the Spirit and the indwelling of the Lord Jesus are bound together with a life of love. This appears in the prayer of Paul on behalf of the Ephesians. He asked that they might be strengthened with power by the Spirit in order that Christ might dwell in their hearts (Eph. 3:17). Then he quickly made this addition: *"That you, being rooted and grounded in love, may be able to comprehend with all the saints …the love…which passes knowledge"* (vv. 17–19).

The filling with the Spirit and the indwelling of Christ bring a life that has its root, its joy, its power, and its evidence in love because Christ is love. If the filling with the Spirit was recognized as the blessing that the Father promised us, the love of God would fill the church, and the world would be convinced she has received a heavenly element into her life.

## OBTAINING COURAGE AND POWER

We know how Peter denied his Lord and how all the disciples fled and forsook Him. Their hearts were really attached to the Lord, and they were sincerely willing to do what they had promised and go to die with Him. But when it came to the crisis, they had neither the courage nor the power. After the blessing of the Spirit of Pentecost, it was no longer a matter of willing apart from performing. By Christ dwelling in us, God works both the willing and the doing (Phil. 2:13).

On the Day of Pentecost, Peter preached about Jesus to thousands of hostile Jews. With boldness and in opposition to the leaders of the people, he was able to say, *"We ought to obey God rather than men"* (Acts 5:29). With courage and joy, Stephen, Paul, and many others were enabled to encounter threats, suffering, and death. They did this triumphantly because the Spirit of Christ—the Victor, Christ Himself—had been glorified and now dwelt within them. The joy of the blessing of Pentecost gives courage and power to speak for Jesus because it fills the whole heart with Him.

The blessing of Pentecost makes the Word of God new. We see this fact distinctly in the case of the disciples. As with all the Jews of that age, their ideas of the Messiah and the kingdom of God were external and carnal. All the instruction of the Lord Jesus throughout three long years could not change their way of thinking. They were unable to comprehend the doctrine of a suffering and dying Messiah or the hope of His invisible spiritual dominion. Even after His resurrection, He had to rebuke them for their unbelieving spirit and their inability to understand the Scriptures.

With the coming of the Day of Pentecost, an entire change took place. Their ancient Scriptures opened up before them. The light of the Holy Spirit in them illuminated the Word. In the preaching of Peter and Stephen and in the addresses of Paul and James, we see how a divine light had shone on the Old Testament. They saw everything through the Spirit of this Jesus who had made His abode within them.

So it will be with us. It is necessary to meditate on the Scriptures and keep the Word of God in our thoughts, hearts, and daily walks. Let us, however, constantly remember that only when we are filled with the Spirit can we fully experience the spiritual power and truth of the Word. He is *"the Spirit of truth"* (John 16:13). He alone guides us into all truth when He dwells in us.

## POWER TO BLESS OTHERS

The divine power of the exalted Jesus to grant repentance and the forgiveness of sins is exercised by Him through His servants. The minister of the Gospel who desires to preach repentance and forgiveness through Jesus and have success in winning souls must do the work in the power of the Spirit of Jesus. Much preaching of conversion and pardon is fruitless because these elements of truth are presented only as a doctrine.

Some preachers try to reach the hearts of their audience in the power of mere human earnestness, reasoning, and eloquence. But little blessing is won by these means. The man whose chief desire is to be filled with the Spirit of the indwelling Christ can be assured that the glorified Lord will speak and work in him. He will obtain the blessing—not always in the same manner, but it will always certainly come.

In preaching and in the daily life of a servant of Christ, the full blessing of Pentecost is the sure way of becoming a blessing to others. Jesus said, *"He who believes in Me,...out of his heart will flow rivers of living water"* (John 7:38). This refers to the Holy Spirit. A heart filled with the Spirit will overflow with the Spirit.

It is the blessing of Pentecost that will make the church what God wants her to be.

I have spoken of what the Spirit will do in individual believers. Think of what the blessing will be when the church as a whole answers her calling to be filled with the Spirit and exhibits the life, the power, and the very presence of her Lord to the world. We must not only seek and receive this blessing, each person for himself, but we must also remember that the full manifestation of the blessing cannot be given until the whole body of Christ receives it. *"If one member suffers, all the members suffer with it"* (1 Cor. 12:26).

If many members of the church of Christ are content to remain without this blessing, the whole church will suffer. Even in individual disciples, the blessing will not come to its full manifestation. Therefore, it is of the utmost importance that we not only think of what being filled with the Spirit means for ourselves, but also consider what it will do for the church.

## WILL YOU SEPARATE YOURSELF?

Recall the morning of the Day of Pentecost. At that time, the Christian church in Jerusalem consisted only of one hundred and twenty disciples, most of them poor, uneducated fishermen, tax collectors, and humble women, an insignificant and despised gathering. Yet it was by these believers that the kingdom of God had to be proclaimed and extended, and they did it.

By them and those who were added to them, the power of Jewish prejudice and of pagan hardness of heart was overcome, and the church of Christ won glorious triumphs. This grand result was achieved simply and only because the first Christian church was filled with the Spirit. The members of it gave themselves wholly to their Lord. They allowed themselves to be filled, consecrated, governed, and used only by Him. They yielded themselves to Him as instruments of His power. He dwelt in them and used them for all His wondrous deeds.

It is to this same experience that the church of Christ in our age must be brought back. This is the only thing that will help her in the conflict with sin and the world. She must be filled with the Spirit.

Beloved fellow Christians, this call comes to you and the whole church of the Lord. This one thing is needed: we have to be filled with the Spirit. Do not imagine that you must understand it all before you seek and find it. For those who wait on Him, God will do more than they can imagine. You must taste the happiness and know by personal experience the blessedness of having Jesus in your heart. Then His Spirit of holiness and humility, of love and self-sacrifice, and of courage and power will become as natural as your own spirit.

If you have the Word of God in you, you will be able to carry it as a blessing to others. If you desire to see the church of Christ arrayed in her first splendor, then separate yourselves from everything that is evil, cast it out of your hearts, and focus your desire on this one thing: to be filled with the Spirit of God. Receive this blessing as your rightful heritage. Take hold of it and hold on to it by faith. It will certainly be given to you.

chapter 3

# How the Blessing Was Bestowed from Heaven

*If you love Me, keep My commandments. And I will pray the Father, and He will give you another Helper, that He may abide with you forever; the Spirit of truth.*
—John 14:15–17

A tree always lives according to the nature of the seed from which it grew. Every living being is always guided and governed by the nature that it received at its birth. The church received the promise and her growth by the Holy Spirit on the day of her birth. It is important for us to turn back often to the Day of Pentecost and not to rest until we thoroughly understand, receive, and experience what God did for His people on that Day. The hearts of the disciples were ready to receive the Spirit. Now we know what we must do to enjoy the same blessing. The first disciples serve as our examples on the way to the fullness of the Spirit.

What enabled them to become the recipients of these heavenly gifts? What made them acceptable vessels for the habitation of God? The right answer to these questions will help us on the way to being filled with the Holy Spirit.

## A PERSONAL RELATIONSHIP

First, the disciples were deeply attached to the Lord Jesus. The Son of God came into the world in order to unite the divine life, which He had with the Father, with the life of man. In this way, the life of God could penetrate the life of the creature. When He had completed the work by His obedience, death, and resurrection, He was exalted to the throne of God on high. This was done in order that, in spiritual power, His disciples and church might participate in His very own life. We read that the Holy Spirit *"was not yet given, because Jesus was not yet glorified"* (John 7:39). It was only after His glorification that the Spirit of the complete indwelling of God in man could be given. It is the Spirit of the glorified Jesus that the disciples received on the Day of Pentecost. His Spirit penetrated all the members of His body.

If the fullness of the Spirit dwells in Jesus, a personal relationship with Him is the first condition for the reception of the full gift of the Comforter. It was to attain this end that the Lord Jesus kept the disciples in close fellowship with Himself. He desired to attach them to Himself. He wanted them to truly feel at one with Him. He wanted them to identify themselves with Him, as far as this was possible. By knowledge, love, and obedience, they became inwardly knit to Him. This was the preparation for participating in the Spirit of His glorification.

The lesson that is taught here is extremely simple, but it is one of profound significance. Many Christians believe in the Lord, are zealous in His service, and eagerly desire to become holy, yet they do not succeed in their endeavor. It often seems as if they could not understand the promise of the Spirit. The thought of being filled with the Spirit exercises little influence on them.

The reason is obvious. They lack the personal relationship to the Lord Jesus, the inward attachment to Him, the perfectly natural reference to Him as their best and nearest Friend, as the beloved Lord, that was so characteristic of the disciples. This is absolutely indispensable. Only a heart that is entirely occupied with the Lord Jesus and depends entirely on Him can hope for the fullness of the Spirit.

## THEY LEFT ALL FOR JESUS

"Nothing for nothing." This proverb contains a deep truth. A thing that costs me nothing may nevertheless cost me much. It may bring me under an obligation to the giver and so cost me more than it is worth. I may have so much trouble in taking hold of it and keeping it that I may pay much more for it than the price that should be asked for it. "Nothing for nothing."

This maxim also holds good in the life of the kingdom of heaven. The parables of the *"treasure hidden in a field"* (Matt. 13:44) and the *"pearl of great price"* (v. 46) teach us that, in order to obtain possession of the kingdom within us, we must sell all that we have. This is the renunciation that Jesus literally demanded of the disciples who followed Him. This is the requirement He so often repeated in His preaching: *"Whoever of you does not forsake all that he has cannot be My disciple"* (Luke 14:33).

The two worlds between which we stand are in direct conflict with one another. The world we live in exercises such a mighty influence over us that it is often necessary for us to withdraw from it. Jesus trained His disciples to long for what is heavenly. Only then could He prepare them to desire and receive the heavenly gift with an undivided heart.

The Lord has left us no outward directions as to how much of the world we are to abandon or in what manner we are to do so. In His Word He teaches us that without sacrifice, without a deliberate separation from the world, we will never make much progress in grace. The spirit of this world has penetrated into us so deeply that we do not observe it. We share in its desire for comfort and enjoyment, for self-pleasing and self-exaltation, without our knowing how impossible these things make it for us to be filled with the Spirit.

Let us learn from the early disciples that, to be filled from the heavenly world with the Spirit, we must be entirely separate from the children of this world or from worldly Christians. We must be willing to live as entirely different people, who literally represent heaven on earth, because we have received the Spirit of the King of heaven.

## RECOGNIZING YOUR ENEMIES

Man has two great enemies by whom the Devil tempts him and with whom he has to contend. The one is the world outside, and the other is the self-life within. This last, the selfish ego, is much more dangerous and stronger than the first. It is quite possible for a man to have made much progress in forsaking the world while the self-life retains full dominion within him.

You see this fact illustrated in the case of the disciples. Peter could say with truth, *"See, we have left all and followed You"* (Matt. 19:27). Yet how manifestly did the selfish ego, with its self-pleasing and its self-confidence, still retain its full sway over him.

The Lord led the disciples to the point of forsaking their outward possessions and following Him. He also began to teach them that a disciple must deny himself and lose his own life if he wishes to be worthy of receiving His life. It was man's love for his self-life that hindered the Lord Jesus from doing His work in man's heart. It cost man more to be redeemed from the selfish ego within him than to withdraw from the world around him. The self-life is the natural life of sinful man. He can be liberated from it by nothing except death—that is, by first dying to it and then living in the strength of the new life that comes from God.

The forsaking of the world began at the outset of the three years' discipleship. At the end of that period, at the Cross of Jesus, dying to the self-life first took place. When they saw Him die, they learned to despair of themselves and of everything on which they had previously based their hope. Whether they had thought of their Lord and the expected redemption or of themselves and their shameful unfaithfulness toward Him, they tended to be filled with despair over everything. Little did they know that this despair would break up their hard hearts, mortifying their self-life and confidence in themselves. This death to self enabled them to receive something entirely new—namely, a divine life through the Spirit of the glorified Jesus in the innermost depths of their souls.

Oh, that we understood better that nothing hampers us as much as secret reliance on ourselves. On the other hand, nothing brings as much blessing as entire despair of ourselves and all that is on the earth, teaching us to turn our hearts wholly to heaven and partake of the heavenly gift.

## THE UNHEARD-OF WONDER

The disciples received and held fast the promise of the Spirit given by the Lord Jesus.

In His farewell address, Jesus comforted His disciples in their sorrow over His departure with one great promise—namely, the mission of the Holy Spirit from heaven. Better than His bodily presence among them, it would be to them the full fruit and the power of His redemption. The divine life—He Himself with the Father—was to make its abode within them. They were to know they were in Him and He in them. At His ascension from the Mount of Olives, this promise of the Spirit was the last subject He addressed to them.

It is evident the disciples had little idea of what this promise signified. But however defective their understanding was, they held it fast; or rather, the promise held them fast and would not let them go. They all had only one thought: "Something has been promised to us by our Lord; it will give us a share in His heavenly power and glory; we know for certain that it is coming." What the thing itself was or what their experience of it was to be, they could give no account. It was enough for them that they had the word of the Lord. He would make it a blessed reality within them.

The same disposition is needed now. To us also, even as to them, has the word of the Lord come concerning the Spirit who is to descend from the throne in the power of His glorified life.

*"He who believes in Me,...out of his heart will flow rivers of living water"* (John 7:38). For us also the one thing needed is to hold fast to that word, to set our whole desire on the fulfillment of it, and to lay aside all else until we inherit the promise. The word from the mouth of Jesus, concerning the reception of the Spirit in such measure that we will be endued with power from on high, must fill us with strong desire and with firm, joyful assurance.

They waited on the Father until the fulfillment of the promise came and they were filled with the Spirit.

The ten days of waiting were for them days in which they were continually praising and blessing God and continuing in prayer and supplication. It is not enough for us to try to strengthen desire and to hold fast our confidence. The principal thing is to set ourselves in close and abiding contact with God. The blessing must come from God; God Himself must give it to us. We are to receive the gift directly from Him. What is promised to us is a wonderful work of divine omnipotence and love. What we desire is the personal occupancy and indwelling of God the Holy Spirit. God Himself must give this personally to us.

A man gives another a piece of bread or a piece of money. He gives it away and has nothing further to do with it. It is not so with God's gift of the Holy Spirit. No, the Spirit is God. God is in the Spirit who comes to us, even as He was in the Son. The gift of the Spirit is the most personal act of the Godhead. It is the gift of Himself to us. We have to receive it in the closest, personal contact with God.

The clearer the insight we obtain into this principle, the more deeply we will feel how little we can do to grasp the blessing by our own desiring or believing. The goodness of God alone must give it. His omnipotence must work it into us. Our disposition must be one of silent assurance that the Father desires to give it to us and will not keep us waiting one moment longer than is absolutely necessary. Every soul that persists in waiting will be filled with the glory of God.

Every tree grows from the root out of which it first sprang. The Day of Pentecost was the planting of the Christian church, and the Holy Spirit became the power of its life. Let us turn back to that experience and learn from the disciples what is really necessary. Attachment to Jesus, the abandonment of everything in the world for Him, despair of self and of all help from man, holding on to the word of promise, and then waiting on the living God—this is the sure way of living in the joy and power of the Holy Spirit.

# chapter 4

# How Little the Blessing Is Enjoyed

*My speech and my preaching were not with persuasive words of
human wisdom, but in demonstration of the Spirit and of power,
that your faith should not be in the wisdom of men but
in the power of God.*
—1 Corinthians 2:4–5

P aul spoke here of two kinds of preaching and two kinds of
faith. The spirit of the preacher will determine the faith of
the congregation. When the preaching of the Cross is given
only in the words of human wisdom, then the faith of the hearers will be in the wisdom of men. When the preaching is in demonstration of the Spirit and of power, the faith of the Christian
people will also be firm and strong in the power of God.
Preaching in the demonstration of the Spirit will bring the double blessing of power in the Word and in the faith of those who
receive that Word. If we desire to know the measure of the
working of the Spirit, we must consider the preaching and the
faith that spring from it. In this way alone can we see whether
the full blessing of Pentecost is truly manifested in the church.

Very few individuals are prepared to say this is really the
case. Everywhere among the children of God, we hear complaints of weakness and sin. Among those who do not complain
is reason to fear that their silence is ascribed to ignorance or
self-satisfaction. It is important that we concentrate on this fact
until we come under the full conviction that the condition of the
church is marked by powerlessness and that nothing can restore
her except the return to a life in the full enjoyment of the
blessing of Pentecost. The more deeply we feel our deficiency,
the more speedily we will desire and obtain restoration. It will ·
help to awaken longing for this blessing if we earnestly consider

how little it is enjoyed in the church and how far the church is from being what her Lord has power to make her.

## POWER OVER SIN

Think, for example, what little power over sin there is among the children of God.

The Spirit of Pentecost is the Holy Spirit, the Spirit of God's holiness. When He filled the hearts of the disciples, a transformation was brought about in them. Their carnal thoughts were changed into spiritual insight, their pride into humility, their selfishness into love, their fear of man into courage and fidelity. Sin was cast out by the inflowing of the life of Jesus and of heaven.

The life that the Lord has prepared for His people is a life of victory. It is not victory to such an extent that there will be no temptation to evil or inclination to sin. But there is to be victory of such a kind that the indwelling power of the Spirit who fills us, the presence of the indwelling Savior, will keep sin in subjection as the light subdues the darkness.

Yet to what a small extent we see power for victory over sin in the church! Even among earnest Christians we see untruthfulness and lack of honor, pride and self-esteem, selfishness and lack of love. How little are the traces of the image of Jesus—obedience, humility, love, and entire surrender to the will of God—even among the people of God! The truth is that we have become so accustomed to the confession of sin and unfaithfulness, of disobedience and backsliding, that it is no longer regarded as a matter of shame.

We make the confession before each other; and then after the prayer, we rest comforted and contented. Brothers and sisters, let us feel humbled and mourn over it! It is because so little of the full blessing of the Spirit is enjoyed or sought that the children of God still commit so much sin and have so much to confess.

Let every sin, whether in ourselves or others, serve as a call to notice how much the Spirit of God is lacking among us. Let every instance of failure, in the fear of the Lord, in love, holiness, and entire surrender to the will of God, urge us to call on God to bring His Spirit to full dominion over the church once more.

## SEPARATION FROM THE WORLD

When the Lord Jesus promised the Comforter, He said, *"Whom the world cannot receive"* (John 14:17). The spirit of this world, which is devotion to the visible, is in irreconcilable antagonism with the Spirit of Jesus in heaven, where God and His will are everything. The world has rejected the Lord Jesus; and, to whatever extent it may now usurp the Christian name, the world is still the same untamable enemy.

For this reason Jesus said of His disciples, *"They are not of the world, just as I am not of the world"* (John 17:16). This, too, is the reason why Paul said, *"We have received, not the spirit of the world, but the Spirit who is from God"* (1 Cor. 2:12). The two spirits, the spirit of the world and the Spirit of God, are engaged in a life-and-death conflict with one another.

This is why God has always called on His people to separate themselves from the world and to live as pilgrims whose treasure and hearts are in heaven. But is this what is really seen among Christians? Who will dare to say so? When they have attained a measure of unblamableness in their walk and assurance of heaven, most Christians consider that they are at liberty to enjoy the world as fully as others. Little is seen of true heavenly mindedness in conversation and walk or in disposition and endeavor. Is this not the case because the search for spiritual excellence is so little enjoyed and sought?

Light drives out darkness. The Spirit of heaven expels the spirit of the world. Where a man does not surrender himself to be filled with the Spirit of Jesus and the Spirit of heaven, though he may be very Christian, he must come under the power of the spirit of the world. Listen to the piercing cry that rises from the whole church, "Who will rescue us from the power of this spirit of the world?" Your answer should be, "Nothing, no one, except the Spirit of God. You must be filled with the Spirit."

## ARE WE STEADFAST?

Those who labor for the salvation of souls complain that there are many who are full of zeal for a time and then fall away. When professing Christians enter into another circle of influence and are put to the test of prosperity or temptation, they cease to persevere. What produces this unfortunate result? It comes from preaching with the wisdom of persuasive words rather than in demonstration of the Spirit and of power. Hence their faith also stands in the wisdom and work of man rather than in the power of God.

As long as such people have the benefit of earnest and instructive preaching, they will continue to stand. If they lose it, they will begin to backslide. Because current preaching shows little demonstration of the Spirit, souls are not brought into contact with the living God. For the same reason, far too much of the current faith is not in the power of God.

The Word, preaching, and means of grace will become a hindrance instead of a help if they are not in demonstration of the Spirit. All external means of grace are things that inevitably change and fade. The Spirit alone works a faith that stands in the power of God and so remains strong and unwavering.

Why are there so many who do not continue to stand? The answer of God is a grave lack of the demonstration of the Spirit. Let every sad example serve as a summons to us to acknowledge that the full blessing of Pentecost is lost. This is what we long for and must have from God. Let all that is within us begin to thirst and cry out, "Come from the four winds, Spirit of God, and breathe on these dead souls so that they may live." Think how little there is of power for service among the unconverted.

What an immense host of workers there is in Christian countries. How varied and unceasing is the preaching of the Word. Sunday school teachers are numbered by hundreds of thousands. Large numbers of Christian parents make their children acquainted with the Word of God and also bring them to the Lord as Savior. Yet how little fruit springs from all this work.

Many who hear and are by no means indifferent never make a definite choice for salvation. Many who from youth to old age are familiar with the Word of God are never seized by it in the depths of their hearts. They find it good, pleasing, and instructive to attend church, but they have never felt the power of the Word as a hammer, a sword, or a fire. The reason they are so little disturbed is that the preaching they listen to is so little in demonstration of the Spirit and of power. This is evidence enough that there is a great lack of the full blessing of Pentecost.

Does the blame for this issue belong to preachers or to congregations? I feel it belongs to both. Preachers are the offspring of the Christian community. Through children we are enabled to see whether parents are spiritually healthy or not. Likewise, preachers are dependent on the life that is in their congregations.

When a congregation finds satisfaction in the merely acceptable and instructive preaching of a young minister, it encourages him to go forward on the same path. He should rather be helped by its more advanced believers to seek earnestly the demonstration of the Spirit. When a minister does not lead his congregation to expect everything from the Spirit of God, then he is tempted to put confidence in the wisdom of man and the work of man.

The great cause of all worldliness and impenitence is the lack of the full blessing of Pentecost. This alone gives power from on high that can break down and revive the hard hearts of men.

## A SOURCE OF COURAGE

Think how little preparedness there is for self-sacrifice on behalf of the extension of the kingdom of God.

When the Lord Jesus promised the Holy Spirit at His ascension, it was given as a power in us to work for Him. *"You shall receive power when the Holy Spirit has come upon you; and you shall be witnesses to Me in Jerusalem, and in all Judea and Samaria, and to the end of the earth"* (Acts 1:8). The aim of the Pentecostal blessing from the King in heaven was simply to complete the equipping of His servants for His work as King on the earth. No sooner did the Spirit descend on them than they began to witness for Him. The Spirit filled them with the desire, impulse, courage, and power to brave all hostility and danger and to endure all suffering and persecution in making Jesus known as a Savior. The Spirit of Pentecost was the true missionary spirit that seeks to win the whole world for Jesus Christ.

It is often said in our days that the missionary spirit is on the increase. Yet when we reflect carefully how little effort is expended on the missionary enterprise in comparison with the time spent on our own interests, we will see at once how feebly this question is still kindled in our hearts: "What more can I still sacrifice for Jesus? He offered Himself for me. I will offer myself wholly for Him and His work."

It has been well said that the Lord measures our gifts not according to what we give, but according to what we retain. He who stands beside the treasury and observes what is cast into it still finds many who, like the widow, cast in their entire living. (See Mark 12:41–44.)

So many people have given only what they could never miss and what costs them little or no sacrifice. How different it would be if the full blessing of Pentecost began to flow in. How the hearts of men would burn with love for Jesus and, out of sheer joy, be impelled to give everything so that He might be known as Savior and so that all might know His love.

Brother or sister, contemplate the condition of the church on earth, of the Christian community around you, and of your own heart. Then see why there is grave reason for the cry, "The full blessing of Pentecost—how little it is known!" Ponder the present lack of sanctification, of separation from the world, of steadfastness among professing Christians, of conversions among the unsaved, and of self-sacrifice for the kingdom of God. Let the sad reality deepen in your soul the conviction that the church is at present suffering from one great evil, and this is her lack of the blessing of Pentecost. There can be no healing of her breaches, no restoration from her fall, and no renewing of her power except by this one remedy—namely, her being filled with the Spirit of God.

Never cease to speak, think, mourn, and pray over this trouble until this one necessary thing becomes the one thing that occupies our hearts. Restoration is not easy. It may not come all at once. It may not come quickly. The disciples of Jesus required every day with Jesus for three long years to prepare them for it.

Let us not be unduly discouraged if the transformation we long for does not take place immediately. Let us feel the need and take it to heart. Let us continue to be steadfast in prayer. Let us stand fast in faith.

The blessing of Pentecost is the birthright of the church, the pledge of our inheritance, and something that belongs to us here on earth. Faith can never be put to shame. Cleaving to Jesus with purpose of heart can never be in vain. The hour will surely come when, if we believe perseveringly in Him, out of our hearts *"will flow rivers of living water"* (John 7:38).

# chapter 5

# How the Blessing Is Hindered

*Then Jesus said to His disciples, "If anyone desires to
come after Me, let him deny himself, and take up his cross,
and follow Me. For whoever desires to save his life
will lose it, but whoever loses his life for
My sake will find it."*
—Matthew 16:24–25

M any people earnestly seek the full blessing of Pentecost and yet do not find it. Often the question is
asked as to what may be the cause of this failure. To
this inquiry more than one answer may be given. Sometimes
the solution to the problem points in the direction of one or
another sin that is still permitted. Worldliness, lovelessness,
lack of humility, and ignorance of the secret of walking in the
way of faith, and indeed many more causes, may also be often
mentioned in truth.

Many people think they have come to the Lord and sincerely
confessed these failures and put them away. Yet they complain
that the blessing does not come. It is necessary to point out that
there still remains one great hindrance—namely, the root from
which all other hindrances have their beginning. This root is
nothing less than the individual self, the hidden life of *self* with
its varied forms of self-seeking, self-pleasing, self-confidence,
and self-satisfaction.

The more earnestly anyone strives to obtain the blessing
and desires to know what prevents him, the more certainly he
will be led to the discovery that it is here the great evil lies. He
himself is his worst enemy. He must be liberated from himself,
and the self-life to which he clings must be utterly lost. Only
then can the life of God entirely fill him.

## A FULL UNDERSTANDING OF THE CROSS

This is what is taught in the words of the Lord Jesus to Peter. Peter had uttered such a glorious confession of his Lord that Jesus said to him, *"Blessed are you, Simon Bar-Jonah, for flesh and blood has not revealed this to you, but My Father who is in heaven"* (Matt. 16:17). But when the Lord began to speak of His death by crucifixion, the same Peter was seduced by Satan to say, *"Far be it from You, Lord; this shall not happen to You!"* (v. 22).

The Lord said to him that not only must He Himself lay down His life, but also this same sacrifice was to be made by every disciple. Every disciple must deny himself and take up his cross in order that he himself may be crucified and put to death on it. He who wishes to save his life will lose it, and he who is prepared to lose his life for Christ's sake will find it.

You see, then, what the Lord teaches and requires. Peter had learned through the Father to know Christ as the Son of God, but he did not yet know Him as the Crucified One. Of the absolute necessity of the death on the cross, he as yet knew nothing. It may be so with the Christian. He knows the Lord Jesus as his Savior; he desires to know Him better, but he does not yet understand that he must have a deeper discernment of the death of the cross as a death which he himself must die. He must actually deny and lose his life—his whole life and being in the world—before he can receive the full life of God.

This requirement is hard and difficult. And why is this so? Why should a Christian be called on always to deny himself, his own feelings, will, and pleasure? Why must he part with his life? The answer is very simple. It is because that life is so completely under the power of sin and death that it has to be utterly denied and sacrificed. The self-life must be wholly taken away to make room for the life of God. He who wishes to have the full, overflowing life of God must utterly deny and lose his own life.

Only one great stumbling block lies in the way of the full blessing of Pentecost. It is the fact that two opposing things cannot at the same time occupy the very same place. Your own life and the life of God cannot fill the heart at the same time. Your life hinders the entrance of the life of God. When your own life is cast out, the life of God will fill you. As long as I myself am still something, Jesus Himself cannot be everything. My life must be expelled; then the Spirit of Jesus will flow in.

Let every seeker of the full blessing of Pentecost accept this principle and hold on to it. The subject is of such importance that I would like to make it still clearer by pointing out the chief lessons that these words of the Lord Jesus teach us.

## SELF AND THE POWER OF SIN

When God created the angels and man, He gave them a separate personality, a power over themselves, with the intention that they would, of their own free will, present and offer up that life to Him in order that He in turn might fill them with His life and His glory. To be a vessel filled with the life and the perfection of God was to be the highest blessedness of the creature.

The fall of angels and men alike consisted of nothing but the perversion of their lives, their wills, and their personalities, away from God, in order to please themselves. This self-exaltation was the pride that cast them out of heaven and into hell. This pride was the infernal poison that the Serpent breathed into the ears and the heart of Eve.

Man turned himself away from God to delight in himself and the world. His life, his whole individuality, was perverted and withdrawn from the control of God so that he might seek and serve himself.

You must utterly lose that life before the full life of the Spirit of God can be yours. To the minutest details, always and in everything, you must deny that self-life! *"If anyone desires to come after Me, let him deny himself, and take up his cross, and follow Me."*

A deep conviction of the entire corruption of our human nature is an experience that is still lacking in many people. It appears to them both strange and harsh when we say that in nothing is the Christian free to follow his own feelings. Self-denial is a requirement that must prevail in every sphere of life and without any exceptions. The Lord has never withdrawn His words: *"Whoever of you does not forsake all that he has cannot be My disciple"* (Luke 14:33).

## Is Your Heart Open?

At the time of his conversion, the young Christian has little understanding of this requirement. He receives the seed of the new life into his heart while the natural life is still strong. It was this way with Peter when the Lord addressed to him the above words. He was a disciple but an incomplete one. When his Lord was to die, instead of denying himself, he denied his Lord. But this grievous failure brought him at last to despair of himself and prepared him for losing his own life entirely and for being wholly filled with the life of Jesus.

We must all eventually come to this point. As long as a Christian imagines that in some things—for example, in his eating and drinking, in the spending of his time or money, or in his thinking and speaking about others—he has the right and the liberty to follow his own wishes, to please himself, and to maintain his own life, he cannot possibly attain the full blessing of Pentecost.

My dear readers, it is an unspeakably holy and glorious thing that a man can be filled with the Spirit of God. It demands inevitably that the present occupant and governor of the heart, the individual self, be cast out and everything be surrendered into the hands of the new inhabitant, the Spirit of God. If only we could understand that the joy and power of being filled with the Spirit will come once we comply with the first and principal condition—namely, that He alone be acknowledged as our Life and our Leader.

## Who Performs This Transformation?

At no stage of our spiritual careers are the power and the deceitfulness of the individual self and the self-life more manifest than in the attempt to grasp the full blessing of Pentecost. Many people endeavor to take hold of this blessing by a great variety of efforts. They do not succeed and are not able to discover the reason why. They forget that self-will can never cast out self-will and that self can never really mortify itself. Happy is the man who is brought to the point of acknowledging his helplessness and powerlessness. He will especially need to deny himself here and cease to expect anything from his own life and strength. He will rather lay himself down in the presence of the Lord as one who is powerless and dead, so that he may really receive the blessing from Him.

It was not Peter who prepared himself for the Day of Pentecost or brought down the Pentecostal blessing from heaven. It was his Lord who did all this for him. His part was to despair of himself and yield himself to his Lord to accomplish in him what He had promised.

It is your part, believer, to deny yourself, to lose your own life, and in the presence of the Lord to sink down in your nothingness and powerlessness. Accustom yourself to set your heart before Him in deep humility, silent patience, and childlike submission. The humility that is prepared to be nothing, the patience that will wait for Him and His time, and the submission that will yield itself wholly so that He may do what seems good are all that you can do to show that you are ready to lose your life.

Jesus summons you to follow Him. Remember how He first sacrificed His will. He laid down His life into the hands of the Father, went down into the grave, and waited until God raised Him to life again. In like manner, you are to be ready to lay down your life in weakness, assured that God will raise it up again in power with the fullness of the Spirit. Forfeit the strength of mere personal efforts and abandon the dominion of your own power. *"Not by might nor by power, but by My Spirit,' says the LORD"* (Zech. 4:6).

## DENY YOURSELF DAILY

You of course say at once, "Who is sufficient for these things? Who can sacrifice everything and die and lay down his life utterly as Jesus did? Is such a surrender impossible?" My reply is that it is indeed so. But *"with God all things are possible"* (Matt. 19:26). You cannot literally follow Jesus down into death and the grave. That will always remain beyond your power. Never will our individual selves yield themselves up to death or rest quietly in the grave.

But hear the glad tidings. In Christ you have died and have been buried. The power of His dying, of His willing surrender of

347

His spirit into the hands of the Father, and of His silent resting in the grave works in you. By faith in this working of the spirit and the power of the death and the life of the Lord Jesus, give yourself willingly to lose your life.

For this end, begin to regard the denying of yourself as the first and most necessary work of every day. Accept the message I bring you. The great hindrance in the way of the life of Pentecost is the self-life. Believe in the sinfulness of that life, not because of its gross external sins, but because it sets itself in the place of God. It seeks, pleases, and honors itself more than God.

Recognize your own life as your own worst enemy and as the enemy of God. Begin to see what the full blessing is that Jesus has prepared for you and that He bestowed at Pentecost— namely, His own indwelling. Count nothing too precious or too costly to give as an exchange for this *"pearl of great price"* (Matt. 13:46).

Believer, are you really sincere about being filled with the Spirit of God? Is it your great desire to know what hinders you from obtaining it? Take the word of our Lord and keep it in your heart. Go to Him with it. He is able to make you understand and experience it. It is He who baptizes with the Holy Spirit.

Let everything in you that belongs to self be sacrificed to Him. He, who by His death obtained the Spirit, who prepared Peter for Pentecost in *"the fellowship of His sufferings"* (Phil. 3:10), has your guidance in His hands. Trust your own Jesus. He baptizes with the Spirit beyond doubt or question.

Deny yourself and follow Him. Lose your own life and find His. Let Him impart Himself in the place you have up to this time retained for yourself. From Him there *"will flow rivers of living water"* (John 7:38).

# chapter 6

# How the Blessing Is Obtained by Us

*Do not be drunk with wine, in which is dissipation;*
*but be filled with the Spirit.*
—Ephesians 5:18

The command to be filled with the Spirit is just as authoritative as the prohibition not to be drunken with wine. As truly as we are not at liberty to be guilty of the vice are we bound not to be disobedient to the positive command. The same God who calls on us to live in sobriety urges us with equal earnestness to be filled with the Spirit. His command is tantamount to a promise. It is a sure pledge that He Himself will give what He desires us to possess.

With full confidence in this fact, let us ask in all simplicity for the way in which we should live in the will of God, as those who wish to be filled with the Spirit. I suggest to those who really long for this blessing some steps by which they may obtain what is prepared for them.

## THE FIRST PRINCIPLE

There are many of God's children who do not believe that the fullness of the Holy Spirit is their inheritance. They imagine that the Day of Pentecost was only the birthday feast of the church and that it was a time of blessing and of power that was not destined to endure. They do not reflect on the command to be filled with the Spirit. The result is that they never seek to receive the full blessing. They remain content with the weak and defective life in which the church of the day exists.

Is this the case with you, my reader? In order to carry on her work in the world, the church requires the full blessing. To please your Lord and to live a life of holiness, joy, and power, you, too, have need of it. To manifest His presence, indwelling, and glory in you, Jesus considers it necessary that you be filled with the Spirit. Believe firmly that the full blessing of Pentecost is a sacred reality. A child of God must have it.

Take time to contemplate it and to allow yourself to be fully possessed by the thought of its glorious significance and power. A firm confidence that the blessing is actually within our reach is the first step toward obtaining it and a powerful impulse in the pursuit.

## A SECOND STEP

Admitting that you do not have this blessing is the second step toward it. Perhaps you ask why it should be necessary to cherish this conviction. I will tell you briefly the reason why I consider it of importance.

First, many Christians think that they already have the Holy Spirit, and that all that is required is to be more faithful in their endeavor to know and to obey Him. They think they are already standing in God's grace and that they only need to make a better use of the life they possess. They imagine that they have all that is necessary for continued growth.

On the contrary, it is my deep conviction that such souls are in an unhealthy state and that they have need of a healing. Accordingly, just as the first condition for recovery from disease is the knowledge that one is sick, so it is absolutely necessary for them to acknowledge that they do not walk in the fullness of the Spirit. Being filled with the Spirit is indispensable for them if they are to please God in everything.

Once this first conviction is made thoroughly clear to them, they will be prepared for another consideration—namely, that they ought to acknowledge the guiltiness of their condition. They ought to see that if they have not yet rendered obedience to the command to *"be filled with the Spirit,"* this defect is to be ascribed to sluggishness, self-satisfaction, and unbelief. Once the confession that they have not yet received the full blessing is deeply rooted in them, there will spring from it a stronger impulse to attain it.

## Is This Blessing for You?

I have spoken of those who suppose that the full blessing of Pentecost was only for the first Christian community. Others are willing to acknowledge that it was intended also for the church of later times but still think that all are not entitled to expect it. They might quite reasonably say, "My unfavorable circumstances, my unfortunate disposition, my lack of real ability, and similar difficulties make it impossible for me to realize this ideal. God will not expect this of me. He has not destined me to obtain it."

Do not permit yourself to be deceived by such shallow views. All the members of a body, even to the very least, must be healthy before the body as a whole can be healthy. The indwelling, the fullness of the Spirit is the health of the entire body of Christ. Even if you are the most insignificant member of it, the blessing is for you. In this the Father makes no exceptions.

A great distinction prevails regarding gifts, callings, and circumstances. But there can be no distinction in the love of the Father and His desire to see every one of His children in full health and in the full enjoyment of the Spirit of adoption.

Learn, then, to express and to repeat over again the conviction, "This blessing is for me. My Father desires to have me filled with His Spirit. The blessing lies before me, to be taken with my full consent. I will no longer refuse by unbelief what falls to me as my birthright. With my whole heart, I will say, 'This blessing is for me.'"

## Obtaining the Blessing

When a Christian begins to strive for this blessing, he generally makes a variety of efforts to search for the faith, obedience, humility, and submission that are the conditions of obtaining it. When he does not succeed, he is tempted to blame himself. If he does not become utterly discouraged, he rouses himself to still stronger effort and greater zeal.

All this struggling is not without its value and its use, however. It does the very work that the law does. It brings us to the knowledge of our entire powerlessness. It leads us to that despair of ourselves where we become willing to give God the place that belongs to Him. This lesson is entirely indispensable. "I can neither bestow this blessing on myself nor take it. It is God alone who must work it in me."

The blessing of Pentecost is a supernatural gift, a wonderful act of God in the soul. The life of God in every soul is as truly a work of God as when that life was first manifested in Jesus Christ. A Christian can do as little to bring the full life of the Spirit to fruition in his soul as the Virgin Mary did to conceive her supernatural child. (See Luke 1:38.) Like her, he can only receive it as the gift of God.

The impartation of this heavenly blessing is as entirely an act of God as the resurrection of Christ from the dead was His divine work. Christ Jesus had to go down to death and lay aside the life He had in order to receive a new life from God. Likewise, the believer must abandon all power and hope of his own to receive this full blessing as a free gift of divine omnipotence. This acknowledgment of our utter powerlessness, this descent into true self-despair, is indispensable if we wish to enjoy this supreme blessing.

## THE PEARL OF GREAT PRICE

The full blessing of Pentecost is to be obtained at no small price. He who desires to have it must sell all and forsake all. Every faculty of our natures, every moment of our lives, and every religious work of our bodies, souls, and spirits must be surrendered to the power of the Spirit of God. In nothing can independent control or independent force have a place. Everything must be under the leading of the Spirit. One must indeed say, "Cost what it may, I am determined to have this blessing." Only the vessel that is utterly empty of everything can be full and overflowing with this living water.

We know that there is often a great gulf between the will and the deed. Even when God has endued the willing, the doing does not always come at once. But it will come wherever a man surrenders himself to the will that God has worked and openly expresses his consent in the presence of God. This, accordingly, is what must be done by the soul who intends to be sincerely ready to part with everything, even though he feels that he has no power to accomplish it.

The selling price is not always paid at the moment of the sale; nevertheless, the purchaser may become the possessor as soon as the sale is concluded and security is given for the payment.

Oh, believer, this very day speak the word, "Cost what it may, I will have this blessing." Jesus is surety that you will have power to abandon everything. Express your decision in the presence of God with confidence and perseverance. Repeat it before your own conscience and say, "I am a purchaser of the pearl of great price. I have offered everything to obtain the full blessing of Pentecost. I have said to God that I must, I will have it. I stand by this decision."

There is a great difference between taking hold of a blessing by faith and the actual experience of it. Christians often become discouraged when they do not at once experience the feeling and the enjoyment of what is promised them. When you have said that you forsake all and count it but loss for the full blessing of Pentecost, then from that moment you have to believe that He receives your offer and that He bestows on you the fullness of the Spirit.

Yet it may easily be that you cannot at that time trace any noticeable change in your experience. It is as if everything in you remained in its old condition. Now, however, is the very time to persevere in faith. Learn by faith to be as sure as if you had seen it written in heaven that God has accepted your surrender of everything as a certain and completed transaction.

In faith look on yourself as a person who is known to God as one who has sold everything to obtain this heavenly treasure. Believe that God has given you the fullness of the Spirit. Regard yourself as on the way to knowing the full blessing in feeling as well as in experience. Believe that God will order this blessing to break forth and be revealed in you. In faith let your life be a life of joyful thanksgiving and expectation. God will not disappoint you.

## WAIT FOR THE MANIFESTATION

Faith must lead you to the actual inheritance of the promise and to the experience and enjoyment of it. Do not rest content with a belief that does not lead to experience. Rest in God by faith in the full assurance that He can make Himself known to you in a manner that is truly divine. At times the whole process may appear to you too great and too wonderful and really impossible.

Do not be afraid. The more clearly you discern the fact that you have said to God that He may take you and fill you with His Holy Spirit, the more you will feel what a miracle of the grace of God it is. There may be in you things you are not aware of that hinder the breaking forth of the blessing. God is bent on putting them aside. Let them be consumed in the fire. Let them be annihilated in the flame of God's countenance and His love. Let your expectation be fixed on the Lord your God.

He who raised up the dead Jesus to the life of glory will just as miraculously bring this heavenly blessing to fruition in you. Then you may be filled with the Holy Spirit and know, not by reasoning but by experience, that you have actually received the Holy Spirit.

God desires to make you full of the Holy Spirit. He desires to have your whole nature and life under the power of the Holy Spirit. He asks if you really desire to have it. Let there be in your answer no uncertainty, but let all that is within you cry out, "Yes, Lord, with all my heart." Let this promise of your God become the chief element in your life, the most precious, the only thing you seek. Do not be content to think and pray over it, but this very day enter into a transaction with God that will allow no doubt concerning the choice you have made.

When you have made this choice, cleave firmly to the faith that expects this blessing as a miracle of divine omnipotence. The more earnestly you exercise that faith, the more it will teach you that your heart must be entirely emptied and set free from every fetter, to be filled with the Spirit. You may take it for granted that it will surely come.

# chapter 7

# How the Blessing May Be Strengthened

T his blessing of Pentecost is entrusted to us as a talent that must be used, and only by use does it become strong. The Lord Jesus, after He was baptized with the Holy Spirit, was perfected by obedience and submission to the leading of the Spirit. Likewise, the Christian who has received the blessing of Pentecost must guard safely the deposit entrusted to him.

When we inquire how we can grow spiritually, Scripture points us to the fact that we can confidently entrust our spiritual life to the Lord. *"He is able to keep what I have committed to Him....That good thing which was committed to you, keep by the Holy Spirit who dwells in us"* (2 Tim. 1:12, 14). After saying, *"Keep yourselves in the love of God"* (Jude 21), Jude added the doxology, *"To Him who is able to keep you...be glory"* (vv. 24–25).

The main secret of success in the development of the blessing is the exercise of a humble dependence on the Lord who keeps us and on the Spirit by whom we ourselves are kept in close fellowship with Him. This blessing, as the manna that fell in the wilderness, must be renewed from heaven every day. The new heavenly life, as with the life we live on earth, must be drawn in every moment in sustaining fresh air from without and from above. Let us see how this ever-abiding, uninterrupted keeping takes place.

Jesus is the Keeper of Israel. This is His name and His work. God not only created the world but also keeps and upholds it. Jesus is not content with merely giving the blessing of Pentecost. He will also maintain it every moment. The Holy Spirit is not a power that in any sense is subordinate to us, entrusted to us, or to be used by us. He is an energizing power that is over and above us, carrying forward His work from moment to moment. Our right place and our proper attitude must always be that of the deepest dependence in our own nothingness and powerlessness. Our chief concern is to let Jesus do His work within us.

As long as the soul does not discern this truth, there will always be a certain dread of receiving the full blessing. Such a one will be inclined to say, "I will not be able to continue in that holy life. I will not be able to dwell on such a lofty plane all the time." But these thoughts only show what a feeble grasp one has of the great reality. When Jesus comes by the Spirit to dwell in my heart and to live in me, He will actually work out the maintenance of the blessing and regard my whole inner life as His special care.

The joy of the blessing of Pentecost, while it can never be relieved of the necessity of watchfulness, is a life that is freed from anxiety and ought to be characterized by continual gladness. The Lord has come into His holy temple. There He will abide and work out everything. He desires only that the soul will know and honor Him as its faithful Shepherd and Almighty Keeper.

## Jesus Will Keep the Blessing

The law that prevails at every stage in the progress of the kingdom of God is, *"According to your faith let it be to you"* (Matt. 9:29). The faith that you had when you first received the Lord Jesus was as small as a grain of mustard seed. It must, in the course of the Christian life, become so enlarged that it will see and enjoy more of the fullness that is in the Lord.

Paul wrote to the Galatians, *"It is no longer I who live, but Christ lives in me; and the life which I now live in the flesh I live by faith in the Son of God"* (Gal. 2:20). His faith was as broad and boundless as were the needs of his life and work.

In everything and at all times, without ceasing, he trusted in Jesus to do all. Paul's faith was as wide and abundant as the energy that flows from Jesus. He had given his whole life to Jesus, and he himself lived no longer. By a continuous and unrestricted faith, he gave Jesus the liberty of energizing his life without ceasing and without limitation.

The fullness of the Spirit is not a gift that is given once for all as a part of the heavenly life. Rather, it is a constantly flowing stream of the river of the water of life that issues from beneath the throne of God and of the Lamb (Rev. 22:1). It is an uninterrupted communication of the life and the love of Jesus, the most personal and intimate association of the Lord with His own on the earth. Jesus will certainly do His work of keeping if faith discerns this truth and cleaves to it with joy.

## CLOSER FELLOWSHIP WITH JESUS

Jesus keeps this blessing in fellowship with Himself. The single aim of the blessing of Pentecost is to reveal Jesus as Savior, so that He may exhibit His power to redeem souls in us and by us here in the world. The Spirit did not come merely to occupy the place of Jesus, but to unite the disciples with their Lord more completely than when He was on earth.

The power from on high did not come as a power that they were henceforth to consider as their own. The power was inseparably bound up with the Lord Jesus and the Holy Spirit. Every operation of the power was a direct working of God in them.

The fellowship that the disciples had with Jesus on earth—following Him, receiving His teaching, doing His will, and participating in His suffering—was still to be their experience, only in greater measure.

It is no different with us. The Spirit in us will always glorify Jesus and make it known that He alone is to be Lord. Close communion with God in the inner chamber, faithfulness in searching His Word and seeking to know His will in the Scriptures, sacrificing time and business to bring us into touch with the Savior are all indispensable for the enrichment of the blessing. He who loves His fellowship above everything will have the experience of His keeping.

## FOR THE OBEDIENT

When the Lord Jesus promised to send the Holy Spirit, He said three times that the blessing was for the obedient. *"If you love Me, keep My commandments. And I will pray the Father, and He will give you another Helper, that He may abide with you forever"* (John 14:15–16). Peter spoke of *"the Holy Spirit whom God has given to those who obey Him"* (Acts 5:32).

Of our Lord Himself we read that He *"became obedient to the point of death....Therefore God also has highly exalted Him"* (Phil. 2:8–9). Obedience is what God demands. Obedience attains what was lost by the Fall. Jesus came to restore the power of obedience. It is His own life. Apart from obedience, the blessing of Pentecost can neither come nor abide.

There are two kinds of obedience. One that is very defective is like that of the disciples prior to Pentecost. They desired from the heart to do what the Lord said, but they did not have the power. Yet the Lord accounted their desire and purpose as obedience. On the other hand, there is a more abundant life that comes with the fullness of the Spirit, where new power is given for full obedience.

The characteristic of the full blessing of Pentecost is a surrender to obedience in the minutest details. To listen to the voice of Jesus Himself, to the voice of the Spirit, and to the voice of conscience is the way Jesus leads us. The method of making the life of Pentecost within us sure and strong is to know Jesus, to love Him, and to receive Him in the aspect that made Him well-pleasing to the Father—namely, as the Obedient One.

The exercise of this obedience gives the soul a wonderful firmness, confidence, and power to trust God and to expect all from Him. A strong will is necessary for a strong faith, and it is in obedience that the will is strengthened to trust God to the uttermost. This is the only way in which the Lord can lead us to ever richer blessing.

## One Body, One Spirit

At the outset of his seeking the full blessing, a Christian may think primarily of himself. Even after he receives the blessing as a new experience, he is still rather disposed to see merely how he can keep it safely for himself. But very speedily the Spirit will teach him that a member of the body cannot enjoy the flow of healthy life in a state of separation from others. He begins to understand that there is one body and one Spirit. The unity of the body must be realized to enjoy the fullness of the Spirit.

This principle teaches us some very important lessons about the condition in which the blessing should be maintained. All that you have belongs to others and must be used for their service. All that they have belongs to you and is indispensable for you. The Spirit of the body of the Lord can work effectively only when the members of it work in unison.

You should confess to others what the Lord has done for you, ask their intercession, seek their fellowship, and help them with what the Lord has given you. You should take to heart the unhappy condition of the enfeebled Christian church in our days. It should not be done in the spirit of judgment or bitterness, but rather in the spirit of humility and prayer.

Jesus will teach you what is meant by the saying that love is the greatest. By the very intensity of your surrender to the welfare of His church, He will increase the blessing in you.

The very name of Jesus Christ involves entire consecration to God's work of rescuing souls. It was for this end that He lived on earth and for this cause that He lives in heaven. How can anyone ever dream of having the Spirit of Christ except as a Spirit that aims at the work of God and the salvation of souls? It is an impossibility. Therefore, from the outset we must keep these two aspects of the Spirit's operation closely knit together. What the Spirit works in us is for the sake of what He works by us. We must present ourselves to be used by the Spirit to do His work.

## ONE MORE THOUGHT

Whenever mention is made of Jesus as our Keeper, it is often difficult to believe that we who are on the earth can really know ourselves to be always, without interruption, in His hands and under His power. How much clearer and more glorious the truth becomes when the Spirit reveals to us that Christ is in us. He is in us, not only as a tenant in a house or as water in a glass, but rather as the soul is in the body, moving every part and never being separated from each other.

Yes, Christ dwells in us, penetrating our entire natures with His nature. The Holy Spirit came for the purpose of making Jesus deeply present within us. The sun is high in the firmament above me and yet, by its heat, penetrates my bones and marrow and quickens my whole life. Likewise, the Lord Jesus, who is exalted high in heaven, penetrates my whole nature by His Spirit until all my willing, thinking, and feeling are moved by Him.

Once this fact is fully grasped, we no longer think of an external keeping through a person outside of us in heaven. We become convinced that our lives are quickened by One who, in a divine manner, occupies the heart. Then we see how natural, how certain, and how blessed it is that the indwelling Jesus keeps the blessing and always maintains the fullness of the Spirit.

Brothers and sisters, is there anyone among you who is longing for this life in the fullness of blessing, yet is afraid to enter into it because he does not know how to persevere? Jesus will make this blessing continuous and sure. Is there any one of you who longs for it and cannot understand where the secret lies? The blessing is this: as Jesus Christ was with His disciples daily in bodily fashion, so He will, by His Spirit, daily live His life in you. No one can fully understand how things look on the top of a mountain until he himself has been there.

Although you do not understand everything, believe that the Lord Jesus has sent His Spirit with no other purpose than to keep you in His divine power. Trust Him for this. Let all burdens be laid aside to receive this blessing from Him as a fountain that He Himself will cause to spring up in you unto everlasting life.

chapter 8

# How Your Blessing May Be Increased

*He who believes in Me shall never thirst.*
—John 6:35

*He who believes in Me,...out of his heart will*
*flow rivers of living water.*
—John 7:38

Can the full blessing of Pentecost be still further increased? Can anything that is full become still fuller? Yes, undoubtedly. It can become so full that it always overflows, especially this blessing of Pentecost.

The above words of our blessed Lord Jesus point us to a double blessing. First, Jesus says that he who believes in Him will never thirst. He will always have the satisfaction of having his needs met. Then, He speaks of something that is grander and more glorious. Whoever believes in Him, *"out of his heart will flow rivers of living water"* to quench the thirst of others. It is the distinction between full and overflowing. A vessel may be full and yet have nothing left over for others. When it remains full and has something for others, there must be in it an over-brimming, ever-flowing supply. This is what our Lord promises to His believing disciples. At the outset, faith in Him gives them the blessing that they will never thirst. But as they advance and become stronger in the faith, it makes them a fountain of water out of which streams flow to others. The Spirit who at first only fills us will overflow out of us to souls around us.

The rivers of living water can be compared with many fountains on earth. When we begin to open them, the stream is weak. The more the water is used, and the more deeply the source is opened up, the stronger the water flows. In the realm of the spiritual life, let us discover what is necessary to secure the fullness of the Spirit constantly flowing from us. Several simple steps may help us in reaching this knowledge.

## HOLD FAST TO WHAT YOU HAVE

First, see to it that you do not misunderstand the blessing God has given you. Be sure that you do not form any wrong ideas of what the full blessing is. Do not imagine that the joy and power of Pentecost must be felt and seen immediately. No, the church at present is in a dead-and-alive condition, and restoration often comes slowly.

At first, one receives the full blessing only as a seed. The quickened soul has longed for it; he has surrendered himself unreservedly for it; he has believed in silence that God has accepted his consecration and fulfilled His promise. In this faith he goes on his way, silent and happy, saying to himself, "The blessing of the fullness of the Spirit is for me."

But the actual experiences of the blessing did not come as he had anticipated. The result was that he began to fear that his surrender was not a reality, only a transient emotion. He feared the real blessing was something greater and more powerful than he had yet received. The result is that very soon the blessing becomes less instead of greater. Through discouragement, he moves farther back rather than forward.

The cause of this condition is simply lack of faith. We are bent on judging God and His work in us by sight and feeling. We forget that the whole process is the work of faith. Even in its highest revelations in Christians who have made the greatest progress, faith rests not on what is to be seen of the work of God or on the experiences of it, but on the work of God as spiritual, invisible, deeply hidden, and inconceivable.

Do you desire in this time of discouragement to return to the true life according to the promise? My advice is this: if you know that you have given yourself to God with a perfect heart, then rest in silence before Him and hold fast your integrity. Do this, and you will know God.

If you are sure that you have set yourself before God as an empty, purified vessel, then continue to regard yourself so and keep silent before Him. If you have believed that God has received you to fill you as a purified vessel—purified through Jesus Christ and by your entire surrender to Him—then abide in this attitude day by day. You may expect the blessing to grow and begin to flow. *"Whoever believes...will not be put to shame"* (Rom. 9:33).

## PERSEVERE IN SELF-DENIAL

In your surrender you have said in truth and uprightness that you are prepared to sacrifice and forsake everything in order to win this pearl of the kingdom of heaven. This consecration was acceptable to God. But you have not yet fully understood the importance of the words you have used. The Lord still has much to teach you concerning what the individual self is, how deeply rooted it is in your nature, and how utterly corrupt as well as deeply hidden it is.

Be willing to make room for the Spirit by a constant, daily denial of the self-life. You may be sure that He will always be willing to come and fill the empty place. You have forsaken and sacrificed everything as far as you know, but keep your mind open to the teaching of the Spirit. He will lead you farther on and let you see that when the sacrifice of everything becomes the rule in His church, then the blessing will again break forth like an overflowing stream.

It is surprising how sometimes a very little thing may hinder the continuance in the increase of the blessing. It may, for example, be a little disagreement between friends, where they are not willing to forgive and bear with one another at once according to the law of Christ. Or it may be some unobserved yielding to oversensitiveness or to ambition that is not prepared to take the lowest place. Or it may be the possession or use of earthly property as if it were our own.

It may also be in connection with things that are lawful and in themselves innocent, which, however, do not harmonize with us in our claim of being led by the Spirit of God. For here, like the Lord Jesus in His poverty, we are bound to show that the heavenly portion we possess is itself sufficient to satisfy all our desires. Or it may be in connection with questionable things, in which we give way too easily to the lust of the flesh.

Christian, do you really desire to enjoy the full measure of the blessing of the Spirit? Then, before temptation comes, train yourself to understand the fundamental law of the imitation of Jesus and of full discipleship, and forsake all. Allow yourself to be strengthened and drawn into the observance of it by the sure promise of the "hundredfold in this life." (See Matthew 19:29.) A full blessing will be given you, a measure *"shaken together, and running over"* (Luke 6:38).

## SACRIFICE AND GIVING

*"God is love"* (1 John 4:8). His whole being is nothing but a surrender of Himself in love to be the life of the creature and to make the creature participate in His holiness and blessedness. He blesses and serves all who live. His glory as God is that He puts all that He has at the disposal of His creatures.

Jesus Christ is the Son of God's love, the Bearer, Bringer, and Dispenser of the love. What God is as invisible in heaven, He was as visible on earth. He came, He lived, He suffered, and He died only to glorify the Father, to let it be seen how glorious the Father is in His love. He came to show that in the Godhead there is no other purpose than to bless men, to make them happy, and to show that the highest honor and blessedness of any being is to give and to sacrifice.

The Holy Spirit came as the Spirit of the Father and the Son to make us partakers of this divine nature. The Spirit pours out the love of God in our hearts (Rom. 5:5) to secure the indwelling of the Son and His love to such an extent that Christ may be formed within us, and our whole inner man will bear the imprint of His likeness.

Hence, when any soul seeks and receives the fullness of the Spirit, is it not perfectly evident that he can enjoy this blessing only as he is prepared to give himself to a life in the service of love? The Spirit comes to expel the life of self and self-seeking. The fullness of the Spirit presupposes a willingness to consecrate ourselves to the blessing of others as the servants of all. The Spirit is the outflowing of the life of God. If we will only yield ourselves to Him, He will become the river of living water, flowing from the depths of our hearts.

Christian, if you want the blessing increased, begin to live only so that the love of God may work through you. Love everyone around you with the love of God that is in you through the Spirit. Love the children of God cordially, even the weakest and most perverse. Exercise and exhibit your love in every possible way. Love the unsaved. Present yourself to the Spirit to love Him. Then love will constrain you to speak, to work, to give, and to pray.

If there is no open door for working, or if you do not have the strength for it, the door of prayer is always open, and power can be obtained at the mercy seat. Embrace the whole world in your love, because Christ, who is in your heart, belongs also to the unsaved. The Spirit is the power of Christ for redeeming them. Like God and Jesus and the Spirit, live wholly to bless others. Then the blessing will stream forth and become overflowing.

## LET JESUS CHRIST BE EVERYTHING

You know what the Scripture says: *"All the promises of God in Him are Yes, and in Him Amen, to the glory of God through us"* (2 Cor. 1:20). When the Lord spoke of *"rivers of living water,"* He connected the promise with faith in Himself: *"He who believes in Me,...out of his heart will flow rivers."* If we only understood that word *"believes"* rightly, we would require no other answer than this to the question as to how the blessing may be increased.

Faith is primarily a seeing by the Spirit that Jesus is nothing but a flowing fountain of divine love. The Spirit Himself always flows from Him as the Bearer of the life that this love brings and that always streams forth in love. Then it is an embracing of the promise, a taking hold of the blessing as it is provided in Christ, a resting in the certainty of it, and a thanking God for what He is yet to do.

Thereafter, faith is keeping the soul open so that Christ can come in with the blessing, take possession, and fill all. Faith becomes the most fervent and unbroken communion between the soul and Christ, who obtains His place and is enthroned in the heart.

Learn the lesson that, if you believe, you will see the glory of God. Let every doubt, every weakness, every temptation find you trusting, rejoicing, and counting on Jesus always to work all in you.

A believer can encounter and strive against sin in two ways. One is to endeavor to ward it off with all his might, seeking his strength in the Word and in prayer. In this form of conflict, we use the power of the will. The other is to turn at the very moment of the temptation to the Lord Jesus in the silent exercise of faith and say to Him, "Lord, I have no strength. You are my Keeper."

This is the method of faith. *"This is the victory that has overcome the world; our faith"* (1 John 5:4). Jesus, who is in Himself the one thing needed, can maintain the work of His Spirit in us. When we exercise faith without ceasing, the blessing will flow in us without ceasing.

Christ must be all to us every moment. It is of no avail to me that I have life on earth unless that life is renewed every moment by my breathing fresh air. Similarly, God must actually renew and strengthen the divine life in me every moment. He does this for me in my union with Christ. Christ is simply the fullness of God, the life of God, and the love of God prepared for us and communicating themselves to us. The Spirit is simply the fullness of Christ, the life of Christ, and the self-communicating love of Christ surrounding us as the air surrounds the body.

Let us believe that we are in Christ, who surrounds us in His heavenly power, longing to make the rivers of His Spirit flow forth through us. Let us endeavor to obtain hearts filled with the joyful assurance that the almighty Lord will fulfill His word with power. Our only choice is to see Him, to rejoice in Him, to sacrifice all for Him. Then His word will become true: *"He who believes in Me,...out of his heart will flow rivers of living water."*

# chapter 9

# In Search of the Full Manifestation

*For this reason I bow my knees to the Father*
*of our Lord Jesus Christ.*
*—Ephesians 3:14*

Paul, in writing to the church at Ephesus, wished to make it clear to them that he desired several things for their spiritual growth. Thus, he wrote, *"I bow my knees to the Father,"* for the following reasons:

- *"That He would grant you...to be strengthened with might through His Spirit in the inner man"* (Eph. 3:16).
- *"That Christ may dwell in your hearts through faith"* (v. 17).
- *"That you, being rooted and grounded in love, may...know the love of Christ which passes knowledge"* (vv. 17–19).
- *"That you may be filled with all the fullness of God"* (v. 19).

Every blessing God gives is like a seed with the power of an indissoluble life hidden in it. Do not imagine that to be filled with the Spirit is a condition of perfection that leaves nothing more to be desired. In no sense can this be true. After the Lord Jesus was filled with the Spirit at His baptism, He had to go forth to be still further perfected by temptations and the learning of obedience. (See Matthew 4:1–11.)

When the disciples were filled with the Spirit on the Day of Pentecost, this equipping with *"power from on high"* (Luke 24:49) was given to them so that they might have victory over sin in their own lives.

The Spirit is the Spirit of truth, and He must guide us into it (John 16:13). He will lead us into the eternal purpose of God, into the knowledge of Christ, into true holiness, and into full fellowship with God. The fullness of the Spirit is simply the full preparation for living and working as a child of God.

When we consider the matter from this point of view, we see at a glance how entirely indispensable it is for every child of God to aim at obtaining this blessing. We also understand why Paul offered this prayer on behalf of all believers without distinction. He did not regard it as a spiritual distinction or special luxury that was intended only for those who were prominent or favored among the children of God. No, he prayed for all, without distinction, who at their conversion had by faith received the Holy Spirit.

His request was that, by the special work of the Spirit, God would bring them to their true destiny—to be *"filled with all the fullness of God"* (Eph. 3:19). Paul's prayer is regarded as one of the most glorious representations of what the life of a Christian ought to be. Let us endeavor to learn what the full revelation and manifestation of this blessing of the Spirit may become.

## STRENGTHENED WITH POWER

That these Christians had received the Spirit when they believed in Christ is clear from a previous statement in the epistle. But Paul saw that they did not yet know or have all that the Spirit could do for them. He realized there was a danger that, by their ignorance, they might make no further progress.

Hence he bowed his knees and prayed without ceasing on their behalf, that the Father would strengthen them with might by His Spirit in the inner man. This powerful strengthening with the Spirit is equivalent to being filled with the Spirit, and it is indeed another aspect of this same blessing. It is the indispensable condition of a healthy, growing, and fruitful life.

Paul prayed that the Father would grant this gift. He asked for a new, definite operation of God. He requested that God would do this according to the riches of His glory. It is surely not any common, trifling thing that he asked. He desired that God would remember and bring into play all the riches of His grace and strengthen these believers with might by His Spirit in the inner man.

Oh, Christian, learn at this point that your life daily depends on God's will, on God's grace, and on God's omnipotence. Yes, every moment God must work in your inner life and strengthen you by His Spirit; otherwise, you cannot live as He desires you to live. Just as no creature in the natural world can exist for a moment if God does not work in it to sustain its life, so the gift of the Holy Spirit is the pledge that God Himself is to work everything in us from moment to moment.

Learn to know your entire, blessed dependence on God. Recognize the claim you have on Him as your heavenly Father to begin in you a life in the mighty strengthening of the Spirit and to maintain it without the interruption of a single moment.

Paul told these believers what he prayed for on their behalf in order that they might know what they had need of and ask for it themselves. Expect everything from God alone. Bow your knees, ask, and expect from the Father His manifestation to you of the riches of His glory. Ask and expect that He will strengthen you with might by His Spirit who is already in you as an unknown, hidden, and slumbering seed.

Let this become the desire and confidence of your soul: "God will fill me with the Spirit; God will strengthen me through the Spirit with His almighty energy." Let your whole life be daily permeated by this prayer and this expectation.

## WHAT IS GOD'S AIM?

This is the glorious fruit of the divine strengthening with might in the inner man by the Spirit. The great work of the Father in eternity is to bring forth the Son.

In Him alone the good pleasure of God is realized. The Father can have no fellowship with the creature except through the Son. He can have no joy in it except as He beholds His Son in it. His great work in redemption is to reveal His Son in us so that our lives will be visible expressions of the life of Jesus.

This indwelling of Christ is not like that of a man who abides in a house and is in no sense identified with it. No, His indwelling is a possession of our hearts that is truly divine, quickening, and penetrating our innermost being with His life. The Father strengthens us inwardly with might by His Spirit

(Eph. 3:16), so that the Spirit animates our wills and brings them, like the will of Jesus, into entire sympathy with His own.

The result is that our hearts, like the heart of Jesus, then bow before Him in humility and surrender, seeking only His honor. Our entire souls thrill with desire and love for Jesus. This inward renewal makes the heart fit to be a dwelling place of the Lord. By the Spirit He is revealed within us, and we come to know that He is actually in us as our Life in a deep, divine unity—He is one with us.

Believer, God longs to see Jesus in you. He is prepared to work mightily in you so that Christ may dwell in you. The Spirit has come, and the Father is willing to work mightily by Him so that the living presence of His Son may always abide in you. Jesus loves you dearly and longs intensely for you. He cannot rest until He makes His abode in your heart. This is the supreme blessing that the fullness of the Spirit brings you.

By faith, you receive and know the indwelling of the Spirit and the operation of the Father by Him. By faith, which discerns invisible things as clearly as the sun, you receive and know the living Jesus in your heart. As constantly as He was with His disciples on earth—yes, even more constantly than with them—He will be in you and will grant you the enjoyment of His presence and His love.

Dear reader, pray that the Father will strengthen you with might by the Spirit and open your heart for the fullness of the Spirit. Then at last you will know what it means to have Christ dwelling in your heart by faith.

## Love Is...

*"That you, being rooted and grounded in love, may...know the love of Christ which passes knowledge"* (Eph. 3:17–19). Here is the glorious fruit of the indwelling of Christ in the heart. By the Spirit, the love of God is poured out in the heart (Rom. 5:5). By Christ, who dwells in the heart, the love with which God loved Him comes into us. Just as life in God—between Father, Son, and Spirit—is only infinite love, so the life of Christ in us is nothing but love.

Thus we become *"rooted and grounded in love."* We are planted in the soil of love, and we strike our roots into heavenly love; henceforth, we have our being in it and draw our strength from it. Love is the supreme element in our spiritual lives. The Spirit in us and the Son in us bring us nothing but the love of God.

Love is the first and the chief among the streams of living water that are to flow from us.

*"Love is the fulfillment of the law"*; it *"does no harm to a neighbor"* (Rom. 13:10). It *"does not seek it own"* (1 Cor. 13:5). It causes us to *"lay down our lives for the brethren"* (1 John 3:16). Our hearts become ever larger and larger.

Our friends, our enemies, the children of God, and the children of the world are worthy to be loved. Those who are the hated, the ransomed and the lost, the world as a whole, and every individual creature in particular are all embraced in the love of God.

Our happiness lies in sacrificing our honor, our advantage, and our comfort in favor of others. Love takes no account of sacrifice. It is blessed to love.

We are able to love only because the Father, with His Spirit, works mightily within us and because His Son dwells in us. He, who is crucified love, has filled our hearts completely with Himself. We are rooted in love. In accordance with the nature of the root, God produces the fruit—love.

Dear readers, listen to the Word: *"God is love"* (1 John 4:8). He has provided everything so that you may know love fully. It is with this aim that Christ desires to have your whole hearts. Begin to pray that the Father will strengthen you with might by the Spirit, and that you may know the love of Christ.

## FILLED WITH THE FULLNESS

Filled with the fullness of God—this is the experience to which the fullness of the Spirit is intended to bring us and will bring us.

God has made provisions for our enlightenment. In Christ Jesus we see a man full of God, a man who was perfected by suffering and obedience, filled with all the fullness of God. He was a man, who in the solitariness and poverty of an ordinary human life, with all its needs and infirmities, has nevertheless let us see on earth the life enjoyed by the inhabitants of heaven. The will and the honor, the love and the service of God were always visible in Him. God was everything to Him.

When God called the world into existence, it was in order that it might reveal Him. In it His wisdom, might, and goodness were to dwell and be visibly manifested. We say continually that nature is full of God. God can be seen in everything by the believing eye. The seraphim sing, and *"the whole earth is full of His glory"* (Isa. 6:3). When God created man after His image, it was in order that He Himself might be seen in man, that man would simply serve as a reflection of His likeness. The image of a man never serves any other purpose than to represent the man. As the image of God, man was destined simply to receive the glory of God in his own life, to bear it and make it visible. Man was to be full of God.

This divine purpose has been frustrated by sin. Instead of being full of God, man became full of himself and the world. Sin has blinded us to such an extent that it appears an impossibility ever to become full of God again. Even many Christians see nothing desirable in this fullness. Yet Jesus came to redeem us and bring us back to this blessing. God is prepared to work mightily within us by His Spirit. This is no less the result for which the Son of God desires to dwell in our hearts and which He will bring to accomplishment.

Yes, this is the highest aim of the Pentecostal blessing. To attain this, we can count on the Spirit to make sure of our reaching it. He will open the way for us and guide us in it. He will work in us the deep humility of Jesus, who always said, *"I can of Myself do nothing"* (John 5:30); *"not to do My own will"* (John 6:38); *"the words that I speak to you I do not speak on My own authority"* (John 14:10). Amid this self-emptying and sense of dependence, He will work in us the assurance and the experience that, for the soul that is nothing, God is surely *all*. By our faith He will reveal Jesus to us, who is full of God. He will cause us to be rooted in the love in which God gives all, and we will take God as all. Thus it will be with us as with Jesus: man is nothing, and God's honor, His will, His love, and His power are everything.

Christian, I beg of you by the love of God not to say that this is too high an experience for you or that it is not for you. No, it is in truth the will of God concerning you—the will of His commandment and of His promise. He Himself will work it out. Today, in humility and faith, take this word, *"Filled with all the fullness of God"* (Eph. 3:19), as the purpose and the watchword of your life, and see what it will do for you.

It will become to you a mighty lever to raise you out of the self-seeking that is quite content with only being prepared for blessing. It will urge you to enter into and become firmly rooted in the love of God. It will convince you that nothing less than Christ Himself dwelling in your heart can keep such a love abiding in you. It will make the fullness of God a reality within you.

Go down on your knees and summon to your aid the wealth of God's glory. Continue to do this until your heart is able to utter the response, "Yes, being filled with the fullness of God is what my God has prepared for me."

With this glorious prospect before you, join with the apostle in the doxology: *"Now to Him who is able to do exceedingly abundantly above all that we ask or think, according to the power that works in us* [the power of His might], *to Him be glory"* (Eph. 3:20–21). Desire nothing less than these riches of the glory of God. Today, if you have never done it before, *"be filled with all the fullness of God"* (v. 19).

When God said to Abraham, *"I am God Almighty"* (Gen. 35:11), He invited him to trust His omnipotence to fulfill His promise. When Jesus went down into the grave, it was in the faith that God's omnipotence could lift Him to the throne of His glory. That same omnipotence waits to work out God's purpose in those who believe in Him to do so. Let our hearts say, *"Now to Him who is able to do exceedingly abundantly above all that we ask or think,...to Him be glory"* (Eph. 3:20–21).

chapter 10

# How Fully It Is Assured to Us by God

*If you then, being evil, know how to give good gifts to your children, how much more will your heavenly Father give the Holy Spirit to those who ask Him!*
—Luke 11:13

When Jairus came to the Lord Jesus to entreat His help for his dying daughter, he had already learned that she had died. Jesus said to him, *"Do not be afraid; only believe"* (Luke 8:50). Face to face with a trial in which man was utterly helpless, the Lord called on him to put his trust in Him. One thing could help him: *"Only believe."*

Thousands of times this word has been the strength of God's children. Where man was concerned, all hope was lost and success appeared to be impossible. Here again, in seeking the full Pentecostal blessing, we have need of this word. The wonder-working power of God can make this exceeding grace a reality within us. Be silent before God. Hear the voice of Jesus saying to us, *"'Do not be afraid; only believe.'* God will do it for you."

God will give the Holy Spirit to those who ask Him much more readily than an earthly father will give his children bread. We must have firm confidence in the Father to give His child His full heritage. *"God is Spirit"* (John 4:24). He desires in His eternal love to obtain full possession of us, but He can do this in no other manner than by giving us His Spirit. Child of God, as surely as He is God, He will fill you with His Holy Spirit.

Without this faith you will never succeed in your quest for this blessing. This faith will give you the victory over every difficulty. Therefore, *"do not be afraid; only believe"* (Luke 8:50). Hear the voice of Jesus: *"Did I not say to you that if you would believe you would see the glory of God?"* (John 11:40).

374

## HOW DOES THIS BLESSING COME?

Preliminary questions arise at once in connection with this subject and tempt us to understand everything about it before we expect the blessing.

The first question is, Where does this blessing come from, from within or from above? Some earnest Christians will say at once that it must come from within. The Holy Spirit descended on the earth on the Day of Pentecost and was given to the Christian community. At the moment of conversion, He comes into our hearts. Therefore, we no longer have to pray that He may be given to us. We have simply to recognize and use what we already have. We do not have to seek more of the Spirit because we have Him in the fullness of the gift as it is. It is rather the Holy Spirit who must have more of us. As we yield ourselves entirely to Him, He will entirely fill us from within. The fountain of living water is already there. It has only to be open and every obstruction cleared, and the water will stream forth from within.

On the other hand, a few may say, "No, it must come from above." When, on the arrival of the Day of Pentecost, the Father freely gave the Spirit, He did not give Him away beyond His own control. The fullness of the Spirit still remains in God. God gives nothing apart from Himself to work without or independently of His will. He Himself works only through the Spirit, and every new and greater manifestation of the Spirit's power comes directly from above. Long after the Day of Pentecost, the Spirit came down again from heaven at Samaria and Caesarea. In His fullness He is in heaven still, and it is from God in heaven that the fullness of the Spirit is to be waited for.

Christian, pray. Do not linger until by reasonings of your own you have decided which of these representations is the right one. God can bless people in both ways. When the Flood came, all the fountains of the abyss were broken up and the floodgates of heaven were opened. It came simultaneously from beneath and from above. God is prepared to bless people in both of these methods. He desires to teach us to know and honor the Spirit who is already within us. He desires to bring us to wait on Himself in a spirit of utter dependence.

I entreat you not to allow yourself to be held back by such a question as this. God understands your petition. He knows what you need. Believe that God is prepared to fill you with His Spirit. Let your faith look up to Him with unceasing prayer and confidence, and He will give the blessing.

The other question is, Does this blessing come gradually or at once? Will it manifest itself in the shape of a silent, unobserved increase of the grace of the Spirit or as a momentary, immediate outpouring of His power? It must suffice for me to say here again that God has already sent this blessing in both modes and will continue to do so.

There must be a definite resolution, however, to place one's whole life unreservedly under the control of the Spirit and a conviction of faith that God has accepted this surrender. In the majority of cases, this is done at once. Perhaps after a long course of seeking and praying, the soul must come to the place at which it will present itself to God for this blessing in one definite, irrevocable act and believe that the offering is then sanctified and accepted on the altar. Whether the experience of the blessing comes at once and with power or quietly and gradually, the soul must maintain its act of self-dedication and simply look to God to do His own work.

Thus, in dealing with all such questions, the chief concern is this: *"Only believe"* (Luke 8:50), and rest in the faithfulness of God. Hold fast this one principle: God has given us a promise that He will fill us with His Spirit. It is His work to make His promise an accomplished fact. Thank God for the promise even as you would thank Him for the fulfillment of it. In the promise, God has already pledged Himself to you. Rejoice in Him and in His faithfulness. Do not be held back by any questions whatsoever. Set your heart on what God will do and on Him from whom the blessing must come. The result will be certain and glorious.

## MORE OF THE SPIRIT

It is sad that so many in the church are content with things just as they are. They have no desire to know more of this seeking for the reality of the Spirit's power. They point to the present purity of doctrine, to the prevailing earnestness of preaching, to the generous gifts that are made for the maintenance of religious works and the enterprises of philanthropy. They look to the interest manifested in education and missions, and they say that it is better to give God thanks for the good we see around us. Such people would condemn the language of Laodicea and would refuse to say that they were *"rich, and increased with goods, and* [had] *need of nothing"* (Rev. 3:17 KJV).

Yet there are some traces of this spirit in what they say. They do not consider the command to be filled with the Spirit. They have forgotten the command to prophesy to the Spirit and say, *"Come from the four winds, O breath, and breathe on these slain, that they may live"* (Ezek. 37:9). When you speak of these things, you will receive little encouragement from these people. They do not understand what you mean. They believe indeed in the Holy Spirit, but their eyes have not been opened to the fact that more of the Spirit is the one thing needed for the church.

There are others who will agree with you when you speak of this need and yet will really give you even less encouragement. They have often thought and prayed over the matter, but no benefit has resulted from their effort. They have made no real progress. They urge you to look to the church of earlier times and say that it was not much different than it is now.

These people belong to the generation of the ten spies who were sent to spy out Canaan. The land is glorious, but the enemy in possession is too strong. We are too weak to overcome them. Lack of consecration and of willingness to surrender everything for this blessing is the root of the unbelief and has made them incapable of exercising the courage of Caleb when he said, *"Let us go up at once and take possession, for we are well able to overcome it"* (Num. 13:30).

If you wish to be filled with the Spirit, do not allow yourself to be held back by such reasonings. Only believe and strengthen yourself in the omnipotence of God. Do not say, "Is God able?" Say, rather, "God is able." The God who was able to raise Christ from the dead (Rom. 8:11) is still mighty in the midst of His people and is able to reveal His divine life with power in your heart.

Hear His voice saying to you as to Abraham, *"I am Almighty God; walk before Me and be blameless"* (Gen. 17:1). Set your heart without distraction on what God has said that He will do and then on the omnipotence that is prepared to bring the promise to accomplishment.

Pray to the Father that He will grant you to be strengthened with might by His Spirit (Eph. 3:16). Adore Him who is able to do for us *"exceedingly abundantly above all that we ask and think"* (v. 20), and give Him the glory.

Let faith in the omnipotence of God fill your soul, and you will be full of the assurance that, however difficult, however improbable, however impossible it may seem, God can fill us with His Spirit. *"Only believe"* (Mark 5:36).

## HE WILL WORK IT IN YOU

When one prays for this blessing of being filled with the Spirit, the thought will spring up uninvited of what one's life as a Christian has already been. The believer thinks of all the workings of divine grace in his heart and of the incessant striving of the Spirit. He thinks of all his efforts and prayers, of his past attempts at entire surrender, and of the taking hold of faith. He then looks on what he is at the moment, on his unfaithfulness and sin and helplessness, and he becomes dispirited. In the span of many years, little progress has been made. The past testifies only of failure and unfaithfulness.

If all his praying and believing of earlier days have been of so little avail, why should he now dare to hope that everything is to be transformed at once? He presents to himself the life of a man full of the Holy Spirit, and alongside it he sets his own life as he has learned to know it. It becomes impossible for him to imagine that he will ever be able to live as a man full of the Spirit. For such a task he is unfit and feels no courage to make the attempt.

Christian, when such thoughts as these crowd in on you, there is only one bit of advice to follow, and that is, *"Only believe."* Cast yourself into the arms of your Father who gives His children the Holy Spirit much more readily than an earthly father gives bread. Only believe and count on the love of God. All your self-dedication and surrender, all your faith and integrity, are not works by which you have to move God or make Him willing to bless you. Far from it.

God desires to bless you and will Himself work everything in you. God loves you as a Father and sees that, to be able to live in perfect health and happiness as His child, you have need of nothing but this one thing—to be full of His Spirit. Jesus has by His blood opened up the way to the full enjoyment of this love.

Enter into this love, abide in this love, and by faith acknowledge that it shines on and surrounds you, even as the light of the sun illuminates and animates your body. Begin to trust this love. I do not say trust in its willingness, but in its unspeakable longing to fill you entirely with itself. Your Father's love waits to make you full of His Spirit. He Himself will do it for you.

And what does He crave at your hands? Simply this, that you yield yourself to Him in utter unworthiness, nothingness, and powerlessness to let Him do this work in you. Taking charge of all the preparatory work, God will help you by His Spirit. He will strengthen you with might in the inner man, silently and hiddenly, to abandon everything that has to be given up to receive this treasure. He will help you to rest in His Word and to wait for Him in faith. He will hold Himself responsible for all the future. He will make provision that you will be able to walk in the fullness of this blessing.

Perhaps you have already formed a very high idea of what a man must be who is filled with the Spirit of God, and you see no chance of your being able to live in such a fashion. Or it may be that you have not been able to form any idea of it whatsoever and are, on that account, afraid to strive for a life that is so unknown to you. Christian, abandon all such thoughts. The Spirit alone, once He is in you, will Himself teach you what that life is, for He will work it in you. God will take upon Himself the responsibility of making you full of the Spirit, not as a treasure that you must carry and keep, but as a power that is to carry and keep you. Therefore, *"only believe"* (Mark 5:36). Count on the love of your Father.

In His promise of the blessing and the power of the Spirit, the Lord Jesus always pointed to God the Father. He called it *"the Promise of My Father"* (Luke 24:49). He directed us to the faithfulness of God. *"He who promised is faithful"* (Heb. 10:23). He directed us to the power of God. The Spirit was, as power from on high, to come from God Himself. (See Acts 1:8.) He directed us to the love of God. It is as a Father that God is to give this gift to His children.

Let every thought of this blessing and every desire for it only lead us to God. Here is something that He must do, that He must give, that He, He alone, must work. Let us in silent adoration set our hearts on God. Let us joyfully trust in Him. He is able to do abundantly above all praying and thinking.

His love will willingly bestow a full blessing on us. God will make you full of the Spirit. Say humbly, "Behold the servant of the Lord. Let Him do to me what is good in His sight. Be it unto me according to Your Word." (See Luke 1:38.) *"He who calls you is faithful, who also will do it"* (1 Thess. 5:24).

chapter 11

# Finding the Blessing

*Then I will sprinkle clean water on you, and you shall be clean;*
*I will cleanse you from all your filthiness and from all your idols. I*
*will...put a new spirit within you....I will put My Spirit within you*
*and cause you to walk in My statutes, and you will keep*
*My judgments and do them.*
—Ezekiel 36:25–27

T he full Pentecostal blessing is for all the children of God. *"As many as are led by the Spirit of God, these are sons of God"* (Rom. 8:14). God does not give a half portion to any one of His children. To every one He says, *"Son, you are always with me, and all that I have is yours"* (Luke 15:31). Christ is not divided (see 1 Corinthians 1:13); he who receives Him receives Him in all His fullness. Every Christian is destined by God and is actually called to be filled with the Spirit.

In the preceding chapters I have had in view especially those who are to some extent acquainted with these things and have been already in search of the truth. They have already been led, after conversion, to make a more complete renunciation of sin and to yield themselves wholly to the Lord. But it is quite conceivable that among those who read this book, there may be Christians who have heard little of the full Pentecostal blessing and in whose hearts the desire has arisen to obtain a share in it. They do not, however, understand that they are willing to have pointed out to them where they are to begin and what they have to do in order to succeed in their desire. They are prepared to acknowledge that their lives are full of sin and that it seems to them as if they will have to strive long and earnestly before they can become full of the Spirit.

I would like to inspire them with fresh courage and to direct them to the God who has said, *"I, the LORD, will hasten it in its time"* (Isa. 60:22). I would like to take them and guide them to the place where God will bless them and to point to them out of His Word what the attitude must be in which they can receive this blessing.

## PUTTING AWAY SIN

In the message of Ezekiel, God first promised, *"I will cleanse you,"* and then, *"I will put My Spirit within you."* A vessel into which anything precious is to be poured must always first be cleansed. So, if the Lord is to give you a new and full blessing, a new cleansing must also take place.

Your conversion was a confession and putting away of sin. After conversion you endeavored to overcome sin, but the effort did not succeed because you did not know the purity and holiness the Lord desired.

This new cleansing must come through new confession and discovery of sin. The old leaven cannot be purged unless it is first searched for and found. Do not say that you already know sufficiently well that your Christian life is full of sin. Sit down in silent meditation with the specific purpose of seeing what your life as a Christian has been. How much pride, self-seeking, worldliness, self-will, and impurity has been in it? Can such a heart receive the fullness of the Spirit? It is impossible.

Look into your home life. Do hastiness of temper, anxiety about yourself, bitterness, harsh or unbecoming words testify to how little you have been cleansed?

Look into the current life of the church. How much religion is there that is merely intellectual, formal, and pleasing to men, without real humiliation of spirit? It lacks real desire for the living God, real love for Jesus, and real subjection to the Word—things that constitute worship in spirit and in truth.

Look into your general course of conduct. Consider whether the people around you can testify that they have observed, by your honorable spirit and freedom from worldly-mindedness, that you are one who has been cleansed from sin by God. Contemplate all this in the light of what God expects from you and has offered to work in you, and take your place as a guilty, helpless soul that must be cleansed before God can bestow the full blessing on you.

## Not in Our Own Strength

Following this discovery is the actual putting away and casting out of what is impure. This is something that you are simply bound to do. You must come with these sins, especially with those that are most strictly your own troublesome sins. You must acknowledge them before God in confession and make renunciation of them.

You must be brought to the conviction that your life is a guilty and shameful life. You are not at liberty to take comfort in the consideration that you are so weak or that the majority of Christians live no higher life than you. It must become a matter of earnest resolution with you that your life is to undergo a complete transformation. The sins that still cleave to you are to be cast off and done away with.

Perhaps you may say in reply that you find yourself unable to do away with them or cast them off. I tell you that you are quite able to do this. You can give these sins up to God. If there happens to be anything in my house that I wish to have taken away and I am unable to carry, I call for men who will do it for me. I give it over into their hands, saying, "Look here, take that away," and they do it. So I am able to say that I have put the thing out of my house.

In like manner, you can give up to God those sins of yours against which you feel yourself utterly powerless. You can give them up to Him to be dealt with as He desires, and He will fulfill His promise: *"I will cleanse you from all your filthiness."*

There should be a definite understanding between you and the Lord. You on your part must confess your sin and bid it everlasting farewell. Wait on Him until He assures you that He has taken your heart and life into His own hands to give you complete victory.

## Experiencing Christ

If the knowledge of sin at conversion is superficial, so also is the faith in Jesus. Our faith, our reception of Jesus, never goes further or deeper than our insight into sin. If since your conversion you have learned to know the inward, invincible power of sin in your life, you are now prepared to receive from God a discovery of the inward, invincible power of the Lord Jesus in your heart as you have never known it before.

If you really long for a complete deliverance from sin, to be able to live in obedience to God, God will reveal the Lord Jesus to you as a complete Savior. He will make you know that although the flesh, with its inclination to evil, always remains in you, the Lord Jesus will so dwell in your heart so that the power of the flesh will be kept in subjection by Him. Then you will no longer do the will of the flesh.

Through Jesus Christ, God will cleanse you from all unrighteousness so that, day by day, you may walk before God with a pure heart. What you really need is the discovery that He is prepared to work this change in you. You may receive it by faith here and now.

This is what Jesus Christ desires to work in you by the Holy Spirit. He came to put away sin—not the guilt and punishment of it only, but sin itself. He has not only mastered the power and dominion of the law and its curse over you, but He has also completely broken and taken away the power and dominion of sin. He has completely rescued you as a newborn soul from beneath the power of sin. He lives in His heavenly authority and all-pervading presence in order to work out this deliverance in you.

In this power, He will live in you and carry out His work in you. As the indwelling Christ, He is bent on maintaining and manifesting His redemption in you. The sins that you have confessed—the pride, the lovelessness, the worldly-mindedness, and uncleanness—He will by His power take out of your heart.

Although the flesh may tempt you, the choice and the joy of your heart must abide in Him and in His obedience to God's will. Yes, you may indeed become more than a conqueror through Him who loves you. (See Romans 8:37.) As the indwelling Christ, He will overcome sin in you.

What, then, is required on our side? When the soul sees it to be true that Jesus will carry out this work, it will then open the door before Him and receive Him into the heart as Lord and King. Yes, this can be done at once. A house that has remained closely shut for twenty years can be penetrated by the light in a moment if the doors and windows are thrown open. In like manner, a heart that has remained enveloped in darkness and powerlessness for twenty years, because it did not know that Jesus was willing to take the victory over sin into His own hands, can have its whole experience changed in a moment.

When I acknowledge my sinful condition, yield myself to God, and trust the Lord to do this work, then I may firmly believe that it is done and that Jesus takes all that is in me into His own hands. This is an act of faith that must be held fast. When doors and windows are thrown open and the light streaming in drives out the darkness, we discover at once how much dust and impurity there is in the house. But the light shines in order that we may see how to take it away.

When we receive Christ into the heart, everything is not yet perfected. Light and gladness are not seen and experienced at once, but by faith the soul knows that He who is faithful will keep His Word and will surely do His work. The faith that has, up to this moment, only sought and wrestled, now rests in the Lord and His Word.

It knows that what was begun by faith must be carried forward only by faith. It says, "I abide in Jesus; I know that He abides in me and that He will manifest Himself to me." As Jesus cleansed the lepers with a word, so He cleanses us by His Word. He who firmly holds to this fact in faith will see the proof of it.

## PREPARING YOUR SOUL

The Lord gave the promise, *"I will cleanse you."* Then He gave the second promise, *"I will put My Spirit within you."* The Holy Spirit cannot come with power or fill the heart and continue to dwell in it, unless a special and complete cleansing first takes place within it.

The Spirit and sin are engaged in mortal combat. The only reason why the Spirit works so feebly in the church is sin, which is all too little known or dreaded or cast out. Men do not believe in the power of Christ to cleanse; therefore, He cannot do His work of baptizing with the Spirit.

It is from Christ that the Spirit comes and to Christ the Spirit returns again. The heart that gives Christ liberty to exercise dominion in it will inherit the full blessing.

Reader, if you have done what has been suggested, if you have believed in Jesus as the Lord who cleanses you, be assured that God will certainly fulfill His Word: *"I will cleanse you...* [and] *put My Spirit within you."* Cling to Jesus, who cleanses you. Let Him be all within you. God will see to it that you are filled with the Spirit.

Do not be surprised if your heart does not at once feel as you would like it to feel immediately after your act of surrender. Rest assured that if you present yourself to God as a pure vessel, cleansed by Christ, to be filled with the Spirit, God will take you at your word and say to you, *"Receive the Holy Spirit"* (John 20:22). He will manifest it to you more gloriously than ever before.

Keep in mind the purpose for which the Spirit is given. God said He would put His Spirit within you and cause you to walk in His statutes and keep His judgments and do them. The fullness of the Spirit must be sought and received with the direct aim that you will now simply and wholly live to do God's will and work on the earth. Yes, you will be able to live like the Lord Jesus and to say with Him, *"Behold, I have come...to do Your will, O God"* (Heb. 10:7).

If you cherish this disposition, the fullness of the Spirit may be positively expected. Be full of courage and yield yourself to walk in God's statutes and to keep His judgments and do them, and you may trust God to keep His Word that He will cause you to keep and do them. He, the living God, will work in you. Even before you are aware how the Spirit is in you, He will enable you to experience the full blessing.

Have you been seeking for a long while without finding the fullness of the Spirit? Here you have at last the sure method of winning it. Acknowledge the sinfulness of your condition as a Christian, and make renunciation of it once and for all by yielding it up to God. Acknowledge that the Lord Jesus is ready and able to cleanse your heart from its sin, to conquer these sins by His entrance into it, and to set you free.

Take Him now as your Lord, at once and forever. Be assured that He will do it. Permit Him to begin, and let Him do it in you now.

chapter 12

# The Key to the Secret

*Then the Son Himself will also be subject to Him who put all things under Him, that God may be all in all.*
—1 Corinthians 15:28

When we speak of entire consecration, we are frequently asked what the precise distinction is between the ordinary doctrine of sanctification and the preaching of the gracious work that has begun to prevail in the church in recent years. One answer that may be given is that the distinction lies solely in the little word *"all."* This word is the key to the secret. The ordinary method of proclaiming the necessity of holiness is true as far as it goes, but sufficient emphasis is not laid on this one point of the *"all."*

Why, then, is the fullness of the Spirit not more widely enjoyed? That little word *"all"* suggests the explanation. As long as the *"all"* of God, of sin, of Christ, of surrender, of the Spirit, and of faith is not fully understood, the soul cannot enjoy all that God wants it to be.

Let us consider the full Pentecostal blessing from this standpoint. Do this in a spirit of humble waiting on God and with the prayer that He will make us, by His Spirit, feel where the evil lies and what the remedy is. Then we will be ready to give up everything in order to receive nothing less than everything.

## THE ALL OF GOD

The answer lies in the very being and nature of God that He must be all. *"Of Him and through Him and to Him are all things"* (Rom. 11:36). As God, He is the life of everything.

Everything that exists serves as a means for the manifestation of the goodness, wisdom, and power of God in His direct and continuous operation.

Sin consists in nothing but the fact that man determined to be something and would not allow God to be everything. The redemption of Jesus has no other aim than that God should again become everything in our hearts and lives. In the end, even the Son will be subjected to the Father so that God may be all in all. Nothing less than this is what redemption is to secure. Christ Himself has shown in His life what it means to be nothing and to allow God to be everything. As He once lived on the earth, so does He still live in the hearts of His people. According to the measure in which they receive the truth that God is all, the fullness of the blessing will be able to find its way into their lives.

The all of God—this is what we must seek. In His will, His honor, and His power, He must be everything for us. There should be no word of our lips, no movement of our hearts, no satisfying of the needs of our physical lives, that is not the expression of the will, glory, and power of God. Only the man who discerns this and consents to it can rightly understand what the fullness of the Spirit must bring about and why it is necessary for us to forsake everything if we desire to obtain it. God must be not merely something, not merely much, but literally all.

## THE ALL OF SIN

What is sin? It is separation from God. Where man is guided by his own will, his own honor, or his own power; where the will, the honor, and the operation of God are not manifested, sin must be at work. Sin is death and misery because it is a turning away from God to the creature.

Sin is in no sense a thing that may exist in man along with other things that are good. No, as God was once everything, so has sin in fallen man become everything. It now dominates and penetrates his whole being, even as God should have been allowed to do. Every part of his nature is corrupt. We still have our natural existence in God. All is in sin and under the influence of sin.

The all of sin—some small measure of the knowledge of this fact was necessary even at the time of conversion. This, however, was still very imperfect. If a Christian is to make progress and become fully convinced of the necessity of being filled with the Spirit, his eyes must be opened to the extent in which sin dominates everything within him.

Everything in him is tainted with sin, and therefore the omnipotence of God must take in hand the renewal of everything by the Holy Spirit. Man is utterly powerless to do what is good in the highest sense. He can do no more of what is good than what the Spirit actually works in him at any moment. He learns also to see the all of sin just as distinctly in the world around him. Everything must be sacrificed and given over to death.

All of God must expel the all of sin. God must again live wholly and entirely within us and continually take the place that sin usurped. He who desires this change will rightly understand and desire the fullness of the Spirit, and as he believes he will certainly receive it.

## THE ALL OF CHRIST

The Son is the revelation of the Father—the all of God is exhibited to our view and made accessible to us in the Son. On this account, the all of Christ is just as necessary and infinite as that of God. Christ is God come upon the earth to undo the all of sin, to win back and restore in man the lost all of God. To this end we must thoroughly know the all of Christ.

The idea that most believing disciples have of the all of Christ is that He alone does everything in the atonement and the forgiveness of sin. This is indeed the glorious beginning of His redemptive work, but still only the beginning. God has given in Him all that we have need of life and grace. Christ Himself desires to be our life and strength, the Indweller of our hearts, who animates our hearts and makes them what they ought to be before God. To know the all of Christ and to understand how Christ is prepared to be everything in us is the secret of true sanctification. He who discerns the will of God in this principle and yields himself to its operation has found the pathway to the full blessing of Pentecost.

Acknowledge the all of Christ in humble, joyful thanksgiving. Confess that everything has been given by God in Him. Receive with firm confidence the fact that Christ is all and the promise that He will work all, yes, all in you. Consent from the heart that this must be so, and confirm it by laying everything at His feet and offering it up to Him. The two things go together: let Him be and do all, and let Him reign and rule over all. Let there be nothing in which He does not rule and operate. It is not impossible for you to accomplish this change. Let Him be everything; let Him have everything in order that by His almighty energy He may fill everything with Himself.

## THE ALL OF SURRENDER

Leave all, sell all, forsake all—this was the Lord's requirement when He was here on earth. The requirement is still in force. The chief hindrance of the Christian life is that, because men do not believe that Christ is all, they consequently never think of the necessity of giving Him all.

Everything must be given to Him, because everything is under sin. He cannot cleanse and keep a thing when it is not yielded up to Him so that He can take full possession of it and fill it. All must be given up to Him, because He alone can bring the all of God to its rightful supremacy within us. Even what appears useful or lawful or innocent becomes defiled by the stain of our selfishness when it is held fast in our own possession and for our own enjoyment. We must surrender it into the hands and the power of Christ; only there can it be sanctified.

The all of surrender—it is because Christians are so ignorant of this requirement that all their praying and hearing avail so little. If you are really prepared to turn to God for the fullness of the Spirit and to have your heart purified and kept pure, then be assured that it is your blessed privilege to regard and deal with everything—everything that you have to strive for or do—as given up to Him. The all of surrender will be the measure of your experience of the all of Christ.

In a preceding chapter we have seen that surrender may be carried out at once and as a whole. Let us not merely think of this, but actually do it. Yes, this very day, let the all of Christ be the power of a surrender on our part that will be immediate, complete, and everlasting.

## THE ALL OF THE SPIRIT

The all of God and the all of Christ demand as a necessary consequence the all of the Spirit. It is the work of the Spirit to glorify the Son as dwelling in us and by Him to reveal the Father. How can He do this if He Himself is not all and does not penetrate all with His own power? To be filled with the Spirit, to let the Spirit have all, is indispensable to a true, healthy Christian life.

It is a source of great loss in the life of Christendom today that the truth is not discerned that the triune God must have all. Even the professing Christian often makes it his very first aim to find out what he is and what he desires, what pleases him and makes him happy. Then he brings in God in the second place to secure this happiness. The claim of God is not the primary or main consideration. He does not discern that God must have him at His disposal even in the most trivial details of his life in order to manifest His divine glory in him. He is not aware that this entire filling with the will and the operation of God would prove to be his highest happiness. He does not know that the very same Christ, who once lived on the earth entirely surrendered to the will of the Father, is prepared to abide and work in like manner in his heart and life now. It is on this account that he can never fully comprehend how necessary it is that the Spirit must be all and must fill him completely.

If these thoughts have had any influence with you, allow yourself to be brought to the acknowledgment that the Spirit must be all in you. Say from the heart, "I am not at liberty to make any, even the least, exception—the Spirit must have all." Then add to this confession the simple thought that Christ has come to restore the all of God, and the Spirit has been given to reveal the all of Christ within us. Remember that the love of the Father is eagerly longing to secure again His own supreme place with us. Then your heart will be filled with the sure confidence that the Father actually gives you the fullness of the Spirit.

## THE ALL OF FAITH

*"All things are possible to him who believes"* (Mark 9:23). *"Whatever things you ask when you pray, believe that you receive them, and you will have them"* (Mark 11:24). The preceding sections of this chapter have taught us to understand why it is that faith is all. It is because God is all. It is because man is nothing and has nothing good in him except the capacity for receiving God. When he becomes a believer, what God reveals becomes of itself a heavenly light that illuminates him. He sees then what God is prepared to be for him, and he keeps his soul silent before God and open to God. He gives God the opportunity to work all by the Spirit. The more unceasingly and undividedly he believes, the more fully the all of God and Christ can prevail and work in him.

The all of faith—how little it is understood in the church that the one and only thing I have to do is to keep my soul open before God so that He may be free to work in me. This faith, as the willing acceptance and expectation of God's working, receives all and can achieve all. Every glance at my own powerlessness or sin, every glance at the promise of God and His power to fulfill it, must rouse me to the gladness of faith that God is able to work all.

Let such a faith look on Christ today and move you to renounce every known sin and receive Him as One who purifies you. Oh, that faith might receive the all of Christ and take Him with all that He is! Oh, that your faith might see that the all of the Spirit is your rightful heritage and that your hope is sure that the full blessing has been bestowed on you by God Himself!

If the all of God, the all of Christ, and the all of the Spirit are so immeasurable, if the dominion and power of the terrible all of sin is so unlimited, if the all of your surrender to God and your decision to live wholly for Him is so real, then let your faith in what God will do for you also be unlimited. *"He who believes in Me,...out of his heart will flow rivers of living water"* (John 7:38).

Reader, there is something that can be done today. The Holy Spirit says, *"Today, if you will hear His voice: do not harden your hearts"* (Ps. 95:7–8). I cannot promise that you will immediately overflow with the light and joy of the Holy Spirit. I do not promise you that you will today feel very holy and truly blessed. But what can take place is this: today you may receive Christ as One who purifies, baptizes, and fills you with the Spirit.

Yes, today you may surrender your whole being to Him to be forever wholly under the mastery of the Spirit. Today you may acknowledge and take hold of the all of the Spirit as your personal possession. Today you may submit to the requirement of the all of faith and begin to live only and wholly in the faith of what Christ will do in you through the Spirit.

This you may do; this you ought to do. Kneel down at the mercy seat and do it. Read once more the earlier chapter that deals with what Christ is prepared to do, and surrender yourself this very hour as an empty vessel to be filled with the Spirit. In His own time, God will certainly accomplish it in you.

There is also something, however, that He on His part is prepared to do. Today He is ready to give you the assurance that He accepts your surrender and to seal on your heart the conviction that the fullness of the Spirit belongs to you. Wait on Him to give you this today!

Pay close attention to my last words. The all of God summons you. The all of sin summons you. The all of Christ summons you. The all of the surrender that Jesus requires summons you. The all of the Spirit, His indispensableness and His glory, summons you. The all of faith summons you. Come and let the love of God conquer you. Come and let the glorious salvation master you. Do not back away from the glorious tidings that the triune God is prepared to be your all. Be silent and listen to it until your soul becomes constrained to give the answer, "Even in me God will be all." Take Christ anew today as One who has given His life so that God may be all. Yield your life for this supreme end. God will fill you also with His Holy Spirit.

# Book Six

# Daily Experience
# with God

# Preface

The daily need for a time of solitude and quiet to pray and read God's Word is of utmost importance. This time spent in fellowship with God will bring a blessing, strengthen our spiritual lives, and prepare us to meet the world. Then we will be equipped for service in God's kingdom in soul-winning and intercession. In this book I have attempted to systematically discuss the various aspects of the inner life. I hope that these lessons will help you in the cultivation of the hidden life and your relationship with God.

In the country of South Africa, there are various diseases that affect the orange trees. One of them is popularly known as root disease. A tree may be bearing fruit, and an ordinary observer may not notice anything wrong. However, an expert can see the beginning of a slow death. This disease also affects the vineyards, and only one cure has been found. That is to take out the old roots and provide new ones. The old vine is grafted onto a new root. In time you will have the same stem and branches and fruit as before, but the roots are new and able to resist the disease. The disease comes in the part of the plant that is hidden from sight, and that is where healing must also take place.

The church of Christ and the spiritual life of thousands of its members suffer from root disease—the neglect of secret communion with God. It is the lack of secret prayer, the neglect of the maintenance of a hidden life *"rooted and grounded in love"* (Eph. 3:17), that explains the inability of the Christian life to resist the world and its failure to produce fruit abundantly. Nothing can change this except the restoration of the inner chamber in the life of the believer. As Christians learn to daily sink their roots deeper into Christ and to make secret personal fellowship with God their main priority, true godliness will flourish. *"If the root is holy, so are the branches"* (Rom. 11:16). If the morning hour is made holy to the Lord, the day with its duties will also be holy. If the root is healthy, the branches will be, too. I pray that God may bless this book to His children who are in pursuit of the deeper and more fruitful life, the life *"hidden with Christ in God"* (Col. 3:3).

ANDREW MURRAY

# chapter 1

# The Morning Hour

*My voice You shall hear in the morning, O LORD;*
*in the morning I will direct it to You, and I will look up.*
—Psalm 5:3

*The Lord GOD...awakens me morning by morning, He*
*awakens my ear to hear as the learned.*
—Isaiah 50:4

Morning has always been considered the time best suited for personal worship by God's servants. Most Christians regard it as a duty and a privilege to devote some portion of the beginning of the day to seek fellowship with God. Many Christians observe the morning watch, while others speak of it as the quiet hour, the still hour, or the quiet time. All these, whether they think of a whole hour or half an hour or a quarter of an hour, agree with the psalmist when he said, *"My voice You shall hear in the morning, O LORD."*

## THE IMPORTANCE OF THE MORNING WATCH

In speaking of the extreme importance of this daily time of quiet for prayer and meditation on God's Word, a well-known Christian leader has said, "Next to receiving Christ as Savior and claiming the baptism of the Holy Spirit, we know of no act that brings greater good to ourselves or others than the determination to keep the morning watch, and spend the first half hour of the day alone with God." At first glance this statement appears too strong. The firm determination to keep the morning watch hardly appears sufficiently important to be compared to receiving Christ and the baptism of the Holy Spirit. However, it is true that it is impossible to live our daily Christian life, or maintain a walk in the leading and power of the Holy Spirit, without daily, close fellowship with God. The morning watch is the key to the position in which the surrender to Christ and the Holy Spirit can be unceasingly and fully maintained.

The morning watch must not be regarded as an end in itself. Although it gives us a blessed time for prayer and Bible study and brings us a certain measure of refreshment and help, this is not enough. It is to serve to secure the presence of Christ for the whole day.

Personal devotion to a friend or to a pursuit means that they will always hold a place in our hearts, even when other people and things occupy our attention. Personal devotion to Jesus means that we allow nothing to separate us from Him for a moment. To abide in Him and His love, to be kept by Him and His grace, to be doing His will and pleasing Him—this cannot possibly be an irregular practice if we are truly devoted to Him.

"I need Thee every hour," "Moment by moment I'm kept in His love"—these lines from two hymns are the language of life and truth. *"In Your name they rejoice all day long"* (Ps. 89:16). *"I, the LORD, keep it, I water it every moment"* (Is. 27:3). These are words of divine power. The believer cannot stand for one moment without Christ. Personal devotion to Him refuses to be content with anything less than to abide always in His love and His will. This is the true scriptural Christian life. The importance and blessedness and true aim of the morning watch can only be realized as our personal devotion becomes its chief purpose.

## SECURING HIS PRESENCE

The clearer the objective of our pursuit, the better we will be able to adapt to attain it. I consider the morning watch as the means to securing the presence of Christ all day long, to do nothing that can interfere with it. I feel that my success during the day will depend upon my time spent alone with Him in the morning. Meditation and prayer and the Word are secondary to the purpose of renewing the link for the day between Christ and me in the morning hour.

Concern for the day ahead, with all its possible cares, pleasures, and temptations, may seem to disturb the rest I have enjoyed in my quiet devotion. This is possible, but it will be no loss. True Christianity aims at having the character of Christ so formed in us that, in our most ordinary activities, His temperament and attitudes reveal themselves. The Spirit and the will of Christ should so possess us that, in our relationships with people, in our leisure time, and in our daily business, it will be second nature for us to act like Him. All this is possible because Christ Himself, as the Living One, lives in us.

Do not be disturbed if at first this goal appears too difficult and occupies too much of your time in the hour of private prayer. The time you allot to bring your daily concerns to the Lord will be richly rewarded. You will return to prayer and Scripture reading with new purpose and new faith. As the morning watch begins to have its effects on the day, the day will respond to its first half hour, and fellowship with Christ will have new meaning and power.

## WHOLEHEARTED DETERMINATION

As we seek to have this unbroken fellowship with God in Christ throughout the day, we will realize that only a definite meeting time with Christ will secure His presence for the day. The one essential thing to having this daily quiet time is wholehearted determination, whatever effort or self-denial it may cost to win the prize. In academic study or in athletics, every student needs determined purpose to succeed. Christianity requires, and indeed deserves, not less but more intense devotion. If anything, surely the love of Christ needs the whole heart.

It is this fixed decision to secure Christ's presence that will overcome every temptation to be unfaithful or superficial in the keeping of our pledges. This determination will make the morning watch itself a mighty force in strengthening our characters and giving us boldness to resist self-indulgence. It will enable us to enter the inner chamber and shut the door for our communion with Christ. From the morning watch on, this firm resolution will become the keynote of our daily lives.

In the world it is often said, "Great things are possible to any man who knows what he wills and wills it with all his heart." The believer who has made personal devotion to Christ his watchword will find in the morning hour the place where, day by day, the insight into his holy calling is renewed. During this quiet time, his will is fortified to walk worthy of his calling (Eph. 4:1). His faith is rewarded by the presence of Christ who is waiting to meet him and take charge of him for the day. *"We are more than conquerors through Him who loved us"* (Rom. 8:37). A living Christ waits to meet us.

# chapter 2

# Fellowship with the Father

*When you pray, go into your room, and when you have shut*
*your door, pray to your Father who is in the secret place.*
*—Matthew 6:6*

Man was created for fellowship with God. God made him in His own image and likeness, so that he would be capable of understanding and enjoying God, entering into His will, and delighting in His glory. Because God is the everywhere-present and all-pervading One, man could have lived in the enjoyment of this unbroken fellowship.

Sin robbed us of this fellowship. Nothing but this fellowship can satisfy the heart of either man or God. It was this fellowship that Christ came to restore—to bring back to God His lost creature, and to bring man back to all he was created for. Fellowship with God is the consummation of all blessedness on earth as it is in heaven. This blessing comes when we experience the promise, *"I will never leave you or forsake you"* (Heb. 13:5), and when we can say, "The Father is always with me."

This fellowship with God is meant to be ours all day long, whatever our condition or the circumstances surrounding us. The ability to maintain close and glad fellowship with God all day long will depend entirely upon the intensity with which we seek Him in the hour of secret prayer. The one essential thing in the morning watch or the quiet hour is fellowship with God.

## MEET THE FATHER

Our Lord teaches us the inner secret of prayer: *"Shut your door, [and] pray to your Father who is in the secret place."* When you are in secret, you have the Father's presence and attention. You know that He sees and hears you. Of more importance than all your requests is this one thing: the childlike, living assurance that your Father sees you and that you have now met Him face to face. With His eyes on you and yours on Him, you are now enjoying actual fellowship with Him.

Christian, there is a terrible danger to which you stand exposed in your inner chamber of prayer. You are in danger of substituting prayer and Bible study for living fellowship with God.

Fellowship is the living interchange of giving Him your love, your heart, and your life and receiving from God His love, His life, and His Spirit. Your needs and their expression, your desire to pray humbly, earnestly, and believingly, may so occupy your mind that the light of His countenance and the joy of His love cannot enter you. Your Bible study may so interest you that the very Word of God may become a substitute for God Himself. The greatest hindrance to fellowship is anything that keeps the soul occupied instead of leading it to God Himself. We go out into the day's work without the power of an abiding fellowship because the blessing was not secured in our morning devotions.

## GIVE HIM YOUR DAY

What a difference it would make in the lives of many Christians if everything in the closet were subordinate to this one decision: "I want to walk with God throughout the day, and my morning hour is the time when my Father enters into a definite relationship with me and I with Him." What strength would be imparted to us if we could say, "God has taken charge of me; He is going with me Himself; I am going to do His will all day in His strength; I am ready for all that may come." Yes, what a change would come into our lives if secret prayer were not only an asking for knowledge or strength, but also the giving of our lives for one day into the safekeeping of a faithful God.

*"Pray to your Father who is in the secret place; and your Father who sees in secret will reward you openly"* (Matt. 6:6). When secret fellowship with the Father is maintained in spirit and in truth, our public lives before people will carry the reward. The Father *"who sees in secret"* takes charge and rewards *"openly."* Separation from others, in solitude with God—this is the sure, the only way to live in harmony with people in the power of God's blessing.

chapter 3

# Unbroken Fellowship

*When you fast, anoint your head and wash your face, so that*
*you do not appear to men to be fasting, but to your Father*
*who is in the secret place; and your Father who sees in*
*secret will reward you openly.*
—Matthew 6:17–18

*When they saw the boldness of Peter and John,...*
*they realized that they had been with Jesus.*
—Acts 4:13

*Now it was so, when Moses came down from Mount Sinai...that*
*Moses did not know that the skin of his face shone while he talked*
*with Him. So when Aaron and all the children of Israel saw Moses,*
*behold, the skin of his face shone, and they were afraid to come*
*near him....When Moses had finished speaking with them,*
*he put a veil on his face.*
—Exodus 34:29–30, 33

The transition from fellowship with God in the morning hour to interaction with our fellowmen is often difficult. If we have met God, we long to maintain the sense of His presence and our surrender to Him. Yet when we go out to the breakfast table, the atmosphere is suddenly different. As the presence of our families and material things take over, we begin to lose what we gained in our quiet time.

## MAINTAINING THE GLOW

Many young Christians have wondered how to keep their hearts filled with the truth when they do not have the liberty or the opportunity to speak to others. Even in religious circles, it is not always easy to communicate what will give us the greatest profit and pleasure. Let us strive to learn how our conversations with people may be, instead of a hindrance, a help to the maintenance of a life of continual fellowship with God.

The story of Moses with the veil on his face teaches us an important lesson. Close and continued fellowship with God will in due time leave its mark and manifest itself to those around us. Just as Moses did not know that his face shone, we ourselves will be unaware of the light of God shining from us. Instead, it will deepen the sense of our being an earthen vessel. (See 2 Corinthians 4:6–7.) The sense of God's presence in a person may often cause others to feel ill at ease in his company. However, the true believer will know what it is to veil his face and prove by humility and love that he is indeed a man like those around him. And yet, there will be the proof that he is a man of God, who lives in and has dealings with an unseen world.

This same lesson was taught by our Lord when He spoke about fasting. Jesus said we should not draw attention to ourselves when we are fasting, *"so that you do not appear to men to be fasting."* Expect God, who has seen you in secret, to reward you openly and to make others know that His grace and light are upon you.

The story of Peter and John confirms the same truth: they had been with Jesus not only while He was on earth, but as He entered into the heavenlies and poured out His Spirit. They simply acted out what the Spirit of Christ taught them. Even their enemies could see by their boldness *"that they had been with Jesus."*

## UNBROKEN FELLOWSHIP

The blessing of communion with God can easily be lost by entering too deeply into communion with people. The spirit of the inner chamber must be carried over into a holy watchfulness throughout the day. We do not know at what hour the Enemy will come. This continuance of the morning watch can be maintained by quiet self-restraint, by not giving the reins of our lives over to our natural impulses.

This spirit of watchfulness can be encouraged by the other members of the family. Around the breakfast table, each person in turn may quote a verse pertaining to a certain subject. This practice will provide an easy opportunity for spiritual and godly conversation. When the abiding sense of God's presence has become the aim of the morning hour, then with deep humility and in loving conversation with those around us, we will pass on into the day's duties with the continuity of unbroken fellowship. It is a great thing to enter the inner chamber, shut the door, and meet the Father in secret. It is a greater thing to open the door again and go out in an enjoyment of God's presence that nothing can disturb.

To some, such a life does not seem necessary. They feel one can be a good Christian without this continual fellowship with the Father. If we are to influence the church and the world around us, we must be full of God and His presence. Everything else must be secondary to this one question: How can we have the power of Christ resting on us all day long?

chapter 4

# Prayer and the Word of God

In regard to the connection between prayer and the Word in our private devotion, this expression has often been quoted: "When I pray, I speak to God; when I read the Bible, God speaks to me." There is a verse in the history of Moses in which this thought is beautifully brought out. We read in Numbers 7:89, *"Now when Moses went into the tabernacle of meeting to speak with Him, he heard the voice of One speaking to him from above the mercy seat...thus He spoke to him."* When Moses went in to pray for himself or his people and to wait for instructions, he found One waiting for him. What a lesson for our morning watch!

## A PRAYERFUL SPIRIT

A prayerful spirit is the spirit to which God will speak. A prayerful spirit will be a listening spirit, waiting to hear what God says. In true communion with God, His presence and the part He takes must be as real as my own. We need to ask how our Scripture reading and praying can become true fellowship with God.

### • GET INTO THE RIGHT PLACE
Moses went into the tabernacle to speak with God. He separated himself from the people and went where he could be alone with God. He went to the place where God was to be found. Jesus has told us where that place is. He calls us to enter into our closet, shut the door, and pray to the Father who is in secret (Matt. 6:6). Any place where we are really alone with God can be for us the secret of His presence. To speak with God requires separation from all else. It needs a heart intently set upon and

in full expectation of meeting God personally and having direct dealings with Him. Those who go there to speak to God will hear the voice of One speaking to them.

### • GET INTO THE RIGHT POSITION

Moses heard the voice of One speaking from the mercy seat. Bow before the mercy seat, where the awareness of your unworthiness will not hinder you, but will be a real help in trusting God. At the mercy seat, you can have the assurance that your upward look will be met by His eyes, that your prayer can be heard, that His loving answer will be given. Bow before the mercy seat, and be sure that the God of mercy will see and bless you.

### • GET INTO THE RIGHT FRAME OF MIND

Have a listening attitude. Many people are so occupied with how much or how little they have to say in their prayers that the voice of One speaking is never heard, because it is not expected or waited for. *"Thus says the LORD: 'Heaven is My throne, and earth is My footstool....But on this one will I look: on him who is poor and of a contrite spirit, and who trembles at My word'"* (Isa. 66:1–2). Let us enter the closet and prepare ourselves to pray, with a heart that humbly waits to hear God speak. In the Word we read that we will indeed hear the voice of One speaking to us. The greatest blessing in prayer will be our ceasing to pray and our listening for God to speak.

## PRAYER AND THE WORD

Prayer and the Word are inseparably linked together; power in the use of either depends upon the presence of the other. The Word gives me *matter* for prayer, telling me what God will do for me. It shows me the *path* of prayer, telling me how God wants me to come to Him. It gives me the *power* for prayer, the assurance that I will be heard. And it brings me the *answer* to prayer, as it teaches what God will do for me. Prayer prepares the heart for receiving the Word from God Himself, for the teaching of the Spirit to give the spiritual understanding of it, for the faith that is made partaker of its mighty working.

It is clear why this is so. Prayer and the Word have one common center—God. Prayer seeks God; the Word reveals God. In prayer, man asks God; in the Word, God answers man. In prayer, man rises to heaven to dwell with God; in the Word, God comes to dwell with man. In prayer, man gives himself to God; in the Word, God gives Himself to man.

In prayer and the Word, God must be all. Make God the center of your heart, the one object of your desire. Prayer and the Word will be a blessed fellowship with God, the interchange of thought and love and life, a dwelling in God and God in us. Seek God and live!

chapter 5

# Learning How to Pray

Moses was the first man appointed to be a teacher and leader of men. In his life we find wonderful illustrations of the place and power of intercession in the servant of God.

## THE PRAYERS OF MOSES

From the time God first called him in Egypt, Moses prayed. He asked God what he was to say to the people. (See Exodus 3:11–13.) Moses told Him all of his weaknesses and pleaded with God to be relieved of his mission (Exod. 4:1–13). When the people accused him of increasing their burdens, he went and told God (Exod. 5:22). He made all his fears known to God (Exod. 6:12).

Out of this time of training, his power in prayer was born. Time after time, Pharaoh asked him to entreat the Lord for him, and deliverance came at Moses' request. (See Exodus 8–10.) Study these passages until you understand the importance of prayer in Moses' work and God's redemption.

At the Red Sea, Moses cried to God along with the people, and the answer came (Exod. 14:15). In the wilderness when the people thirsted, and when Amalek attacked them, it was also prayer that brought deliverance (Exod. 17:4, 11).

At Sinai, when Israel made the golden calf, it was prayer that averted the threatened destruction (Exod. 32:11, 14). It was more prayer that secured God's presence to go with them (Exod. 33:13–14). Once again it was prayer that brought the revelation of God's glory (vv. 18–19). When that had been given, it was fresh prayer that received the renewal of the covenant (Exod. 34:9–10).

In Deuteronomy we have a wonderful summary of all Moses' prayers. We see with what intensity he prayed, and we see how in one case it was for forty days and forty nights that he fell on his face before the Lord. (See Deuteronomy 9:18–26.)

In Numbers we read of Moses' prayer quenching the fire of the Lord and obtaining the supply of meat. (See Numbers 11:2, 11–13, 31–32.) Moses prayed for Miriam (Num. 12:13). Prayer again saved the nation when they refused to go up to Canaan (Num. 14:17–20). Prayer brought down judgment on Korah. When God was going to consume the whole congregation, prayer made atonement (Num. 16:15, 46). Prayer brought water out of the rock (Num. 20:1–11), and in answer to prayer the bronze serpent was given (Num. 21:7–8). In answer to prayer, God's will was made known, and Joshua was selected as Moses' successor. (See Numbers 27.)

Study all these passages until your whole heart is filled with the part that prayer must play in the life of a person who wants to be God's servant to his fellowmen.

## A MAN OF PRAYER

As we study Moses' life, he will become a living model for our prayer lives. We will learn what we need to become intercessors. Here are the lessons we can learn from Moses' life.

Moses was a man given up to God; zealous, yes, he was even jealous for God's honor and will. He was also a man absolutely given to his people, ready to sacrifice himself, so that they might be saved. Moses was a man conscious of a divine calling to act as a mediator, to be the link, the channel of communication and of blessing, between a God in heaven and men on earth. His life was so entirely possessed by this mediatorial consciousness that nothing was simpler and more natural than to expect that God would hear him.

In answer to the prayers of one man, God saves and blesses those He has entrusted to him and does what He would not do without prayer. The whole government of God has taken prayer into its plan as one of its constituent parts. Heaven is filled with the life and power and blessing earth needs, and the prayer of earth is the power to bring that blessing down.

Prayer is an index of the spiritual life, and its power depends on my relationship with God and the awareness of my being His representative. He entrusts His work to me. The simpler and more complete my devotion to His interests, the more natural and certain becomes the assurance that He hears me.

Think of the place God had in Moses' life, as the God who had sent him and the God to whom he was completely devoted. He was the God who promised to be with him and who would always help him when he prayed.

## LEARNING TO PRAY

How can we learn to pray as Moses did? We cannot secure this gift by an act of the will. Our first lesson must be the sense of our own weakness. Then grace can work in us, slowly and surely, if we give ourselves its training. The training will be gradual, but there is one thing that can be done at once. We can decide to give ourselves to this life and assume the right position. Do this now; make the decision to live entirely to be a channel for God's blessing to flow through you to the world. Take the step. Accept the divine appointment and concentrate on some particular object of intercession.

Take time, say a week, and get a firm hold on the elementary truths that Moses' example teaches. Just as a music teacher insists upon practicing the scales—only practice makes perfect—determine to learn and to apply these important first lessons.

God is looking for people through whom He can bless the world. Say definitely, "Here I am; I will give my life to this calling." Cultivate your faith in the simple truth, "God hears prayer; God will do what I ask."

Give yourself to others as completely as you give yourself to God. Open your eyes to sense the needs of a perishing world. Take up your position in Christ and in the power that His name and life and Spirit give you. And go on practicing definite prayer and intercession.

chapter 6

# Becoming a Man or Woman of God

*Moses the man of God blessed the children of Israel.*
—Deuteronomy 33:1

T*he man of God*"! How much this name means! He is a man who comes from God, chosen and sent by Him. He walks with God, lives in His fellowship, and carries the mark of His presence. He is man who lives for God and His will. His whole being is ruled by the glory of God, and he involuntarily and unceasingly causes men to think of God. In his heart the life of God has taken its rightful place as the all in all. His one desire is that God should have that place of prominence in men's hearts throughout the world.

## WANTED: MEN AND WOMEN OF GOD

Such men and women of God are what the world needs. God seeks these individuals so that He may fill them with Himself and send them into the world to help others to know Him. Moses was such a man of God that people naturally spoke of him this way—*"Moses the man of God."* Every servant of God should strive to be a living witness of what God is to him, and what He claims to be in all.

In a previous chapter I said that man was to have fellowship with God. This fellowship is to be the privilege of daily life and should be our highest priority during our morning time of devotions. I mainly referred to our personal needs and how the power of a happy, godly life can influence others. The thought of a man like Moses leads us beyond our own personal needs. He was so closely linked to God that men instinctively gave this as his chief characteristic—*"the man of God."* This thought brings

414

us out into public life and suggests the idea of the impression we make upon others. We can be so full of God's holy presence that, when others see us or think of us, this name will come to mind—*"the man of God."*

These are the kind of men and women the world and God equally need. Why is this? Because the world, by sin, has fallen away from God. Because in Christ the world has been redeemed for God. God has no way of showing people what they ought to be except through men and women of God, in whom His life, His spirit, and His power are working. Man was created for God, so that God might live, work, and show forth His glory in him and through him. God was to be his all in all.

The indwelling of God was to be as natural and delightful as it is strange and incomprehensible. When the redemption of Christ was completed in the descent of the Holy Spirit into the hearts of men, this indwelling was restored, and God regained possession of His home. A person can give himself completely to the presence of the Holy Spirit, not only as a power working in him, but also as God dwelling in him. Then he can become, in the deepest meaning of the word, *"a man of God."* (See John 14:16, 20, 23 and 1 John 4:13, 16.)

## A COMPLETE MAN

Paul told us that it is through the power of the Holy Scriptures that the man of God is complete. This suggests that with some people, the life is imperfect and needs to be made perfect. *"All Scripture is given by inspiration of God, and is profitable for doctrine, for reproof, for correction, for instruction in righteousness, that the man of God may be complete, thoroughly equipped for every good work"* (2 Tim. 3:16–17).

This brings us again to the morning watch as the chief time for personal Bible study. We must yield our hearts and lives to the Word, for its teaching, its reproof, its correction, its instruction to search and form our entire lives. In this way we will come under the direct operation of God, into full communion with Him, so that the man of God will be complete—*"equipped for every good work."*

Oh, to be truly a man or woman of God—one who knows and proves these three things: God is all, God claims all, and God works all. A man of God has seen the place God has in His universe and in men—He is the all in all! A man of God has understood that God asks for and must have all. He lives only to give God His due and glory. A man of God has discovered the great secret that God works all. And like the Son of God, he seeks to live in the unceasing, blessed dependence of the Father.

## BE A MAN OR WOMAN OF GOD

Brother or sister, seek to be a man or woman of God! Let God be all to you in the morning watch. Let God be all to you during the day. And let your life be devoted to one thing—to bring men to God, and God to men. Let it be your desire that, in His church and in the world, God may have the place due to Him.

*"If I am a man of God, then let fire come down from heaven"* (2 Kings 1:10). Thus answered Elijah when the captain called him to come down. The true God is the God who answers by fire. And the true man of God is he who knows how to call down the fire because he has power with the God of heaven. Whether the fire is that of judgment or the Holy Spirit, the work of the man of God is to bring fire down to earth. What the world needs is the man of God who knows God's power and his power with God.

It is in the secret prayer habit of daily life that we learn to know our God, His fire, and our power with Him. May we know what it is to be a man or woman of God and what it implies.

In Elijah, as in Moses, we see that being a man of God means a separation from every other interest, an entire identification with the honor of God. He is no longer a man of the world, but a man of God.

There is a secret feeling that all this brings more strain and sacrifice, difficulty and danger, than we are ready for. This is only true as long as we have not seen how absolute God's claim is, how blessed it is to yield to it, and how certain that God Himself will work it in us.

416

Turn back now and look at Moses, the man of prayer and of the Word. See how Moses grew out of these to be the man of God. See the same in the life of Elijah—the harmony between our hearing God's Word and His hearing ours. See the way in which it becomes divinely possible to be and live as a man or woman of God. Then study how you can apply these lessons to your own life.

chapter 7

# The Power of God's Word

*The word of God, which also effectively works*
*in you who believe.*
—1 Thessalonians 2:13

T he value of a man's words depends upon what I know about him. If a man promises to give me half of all he has, it greatly matters whether he is a poor man or a millionaire. One of the first requirements for fruitful Bible study is the knowledge of God as the Omnipotent One and of the power of His Word.

## CREATIVE POWER

The power of God's Word is infinite. *"By the word of the LORD the heavens were made....For He spoke, and it was done; He commanded, and it stood fast"* (Ps. 33:6, 9). God's power works in His Word. God's Word has creative power and calls into existence the very thing of which it speaks.

The Word of the living God is a living Word, and it gives life. It can call into existence and make alive again what is dead. Its quickening power can raise dead bodies, can give eternal life to dead souls. All spiritual life comes through it, for we are born of incorruptible seed *"through the Word of God which lives and abides forever"* (1 Pet. 1:23).

This is one of the deepest secrets of the blessing of God's Word—the faith in its creative and quickening energy. The Word will work in me the very character that it commands or promises. *"The word of God...effectively works in you who believe."* Nothing can resist its power when received into the heart through the Holy Spirit because it works effectively in those who believe. Everything depends upon learning the art of receiving that Word into the heart. And in learning this art the first step is faith—faith in its living, its omnipotent, its creative power. By His Word, God *"calls those things which do not exist as though they did"* (Rom. 4:17).

## HIDDEN POWER

As true as this is of all God's mighty deeds from creation to the resurrection of the dead, it is also true of every word spoken to us in His Holy Book. Two things keep us from believing this as we should. The one is the terrible experience of the Word being made ineffective by human wisdom, unbelief, or worldliness. The other is the neglect of the scriptural teaching that the Word is a seed. Seeds are small and may be long dormant; seeds have to be hidden; and when they sprout, they are of slow growth.

Because the action of God's Word is hidden and unobserved, we do not believe in its power. Let us make this one of our first lessons. The Word I study is *"the power of God to salvation"* (Rom. 1:16); it will work in me all that I need, all that the Father asks.

## POWER TO CHANGE US

What a prospect this kind of faith will open up for our spiritual lives! We will see that all the treasures and blessings of God's grace are within our reach. The Word has power to illuminate our darkness; in our hearts it will bring the light of God, the sense of His love, and the knowledge of His will. The Word can fill us with courage to conquer every enemy and to do whatever God asks us to do. The Word will cleanse, sanctify, and work in us faith and obedience. It will become in us the seed of every trait in the likeness of our Lord. Through the Word, the Spirit will lead us into all truth (John 16:13). It will make all that is in the Word true in us and so prepare our hearts to be the habitation of the Father and the Son.

What a change would come over our relationship with God's Word and to the morning watch if we really believed this simple truth! Let us begin our training for that ministry of the Word by proving its power in our own experience. Let us begin to seek to learn the great faith lesson, the mighty power of God's Word.

The Word of God is true because God Himself will make it true in us. We have much to learn regarding what hinders that power, much to overcome to be freed from these hindrances, and much to surrender to receive that power. But all will be right if we study our Bibles with the determination to believe that God's Word has omnipotent power in our hearts to accomplish every blessing of which it speaks.

# chapter 8

# The Word Is a Seed

I think it may be confidently said that in all of nature, the best illustration for the Word of God is that of the seed. The points of resemblance between the two are quite evident. There is the apparent insignificance of the seed—a little thing as compared with the tree that springs from it. There is the life, enclosed and dormant within a husk. There is the need for suitable soil, without which growth is impossible. There is the slow growth, with its length of time calling for the long patience of the farmer. And there is the fruit, in which the seed reproduces and multiplies itself. In all these respects, the seed teaches us precious lessons as to our use of God's Word.

## LESSONS FROM THE SEED

### • THE LESSON OF FAITH

Faith does not look at appearances. As far as we can judge, it looks most improbable that the Word of God can give life to the soul, can transform our whole characters, and can fill us with strength. And yet it does. When we have learned to believe that the Word can do what it says, then we have found one of the chief secrets of Bible study. We will then receive each word as the pledge and the power of God's working on our behalf.

### • THE LESSON OF LABOR

The seed needs to be gathered, kept, and put into the prepared soil. In the same way, the mind has to gather from Scripture, understand, and pass on to the heart the words that will meet our needs. We cannot give life or growth to the words. Nor do we need to; it is already there. But we can hide the Word in our hearts and keep it there, waiting for the sunshine that comes from above.

### • THE LESSON OF PATIENCE

The effect of the Word on the heart is in most cases not immediate. It needs time to send out roots and grow up. Christ's words must abide in us. We must day by day increase our reserve of Bible knowledge—this is like gathering the grain in a barn. We must also watch over the words of command or promise that have special meaning for us and allow them to spread both roots and branches in our hearts. We need to know what kind of seed we have sowed and to cultivate a watchful but patient expectancy. In due time we will reap if we do not faint.

### • THE LESSON OF FRUITFULNESS

However insignificant that little seed from the Word of God appears, no matter how trying the slowness of its growth may be to our patience, be sure the fruit will come. The very truth and life and power of God's Word will grow and ripen within you. A seed bears a fruit that contains the same seed for new reproduction. In the same way, the Word will not only bring you the fruit it promised, but that fruit will become a seed that you carry to others to give life and blessing.

## THE SEED IN YOUR HEART

Not only the Word, but *"the kingdom of heaven is like a...seed"* (Matt. 13:31). The kingdom's attributes come as a hidden seed in the heart of the regenerate person. Christ is a seed. The Holy Spirit is a seed. The exceeding greatness of the power (Eph. 1:19) that works in us is a seed. The hidden life is there in the heart, but it is not always felt in its power. The divine glory is there, to be counted on and acted on even when not felt, to be waited for in its springing forth and its growth.

As this central truth is firmly grasped and held as the law of all heavenly life on earth, the study of God's Word becomes an act of faith, surrender, and dependence on the living God. I believe humbly, almost tremblingly, in the divine seed that is in the Word, and I believe in the power of God's Spirit to make it true in my life and experience. I yield my heart hungrily and entirely to receive this divine seed. I wait on God in absolute dependence and confidence to give the increase in a power above anything we can ask or think (Eph. 3:20).

chapter 9

# Knowing and Doing God's Word

*[Jesus] said, "More than that, blessed are those who
hear the word of God and keep it!"*
—Luke 11:28

*If anyone wants to do His will, he shall know.*
—John 7:17

S ome time ago I received a letter from an earnest Christian
asking me for some hints to help him in Bible study. He
wanted some guidelines as to how to begin and how to go
on, so that he could better understand and know the Bible. The
very first thing I said to him, the thing that comes before all
else, is this: In your Bible study everything will depend on the
spirit in which you approach it.

## THE OBJECTIVE OF BIBLE STUDY

In worldly things a man is ruled and urged on by the goals
he sets for himself. It is no different with the Bible. If your aim
is simply to know the Bible well, you will be disappointed. If you
think that thorough knowledge of the Bible will necessarily be a
blessing, you are mistaken. To some it is a curse. To others it is
powerless; it does not make them either holy or happy. To some
it is a burden; it depresses them instead of quickening them or
lifting them up.

What should be the real objective of the Bible student? Because God's Word is food, bread from heaven, the first reason
for Bible study is a great hunger for righteousness—a great desire to do all God's will. The Bible is a light (Ps. 119:105), and
the first condition to its enjoyment is a sincere longing to walk
in God's ways.

This is what the Bible teaches us: *"Blessed are those who hear the word of God and keep it!"* There is no blessedness in hearing or knowing God's Word apart from keeping it. The Word is nothing if it is not kept, obeyed, done. *"If anyone wants to do His will, he shall know."* According to this saying of our Lord, all true knowledge of God's Word depends upon there first being the will to do it. God will unlock the real meaning and blessing of His Word only to those whose will is definitely set upon doing it. I must read my Bible with one purpose: *"Whatever He says to you, do it"* (John 2:5).

## THE IMPORTANCE OF WORDS

Words stand between the will and the deed. Suppose a man wills to do something for you. Before he does it, he expresses his thought or purpose in words. Then he fulfills the words by doing what he has promised. This is also the way God works. His words have their value from what He does. In creation His Word was with the power; He spoke and it was done.

God always does what He says. David prayed, *"Do as You have said"* (2 Sam. 7:25). Solomon also said at the consecration of the temple, *"Who has fulfilled with His hands what He spoke with His mouth"* (2 Chron. 6:4); *"The LORD has fulfilled His word which He spoke"* (v. 10); *"You have kept what You promised...; You have both spoken with Your mouth and fulfilled it with Your hand....Keep what You promised"* (vv. 15–16).

In the writings of the prophets, God says, *"I, the LORD, have spoken it, and I will do it."* (Ezek. 36:36). And the prophets have said, *"What You have spoken has happened"* (Jer. 32:24). The truth and the worth of what God promises consist in the fact that He does it. His word of promise is meant to be done.

## DOING GOD'S WORD

This is no less true of His words of command, of things that He wants us to do. If we seek to know them, if we admire their beauty and praise their wisdom, but do not do them, we delude ourselves. They are meant to be done. It is only as we do them that their real meaning and blessing can be revealed to us. It is only as we do them that we really can grow in the divine life. *"Walk worthy of the Lord, fully pleasing Him, being fruitful in every good work and increasing in the knowledge of God"* (Col. 1:10). We must approach God's words with the same objective God had in mind—that they should be done.

This principle is true in any pursuit of knowledge or in any kind of business. The pupil or apprentice is expected to put the lessons he receives into practice. Only then is he prepared for further teaching. In the Christian life, Bible study should be more than mere theory, more than a pleasing exercise of mind and imagination. Bible study has little value for a life of true holiness or Christlikeness until the student makes God's purpose his very own and listens when He says, *"Do all that I speak"* (Exod. 23:22).

This was the distinguishing mark of the Old Testament men of faith. *"So Abram departed as the LORD had spoken to him"* (Gen. 12:4). *"Thus Moses did; according to all that the LORD had commanded him, so he did"* (Exod. 40:16), is the description of the man who as a servant was faithful in all his house. And of David we read, *"I have found...a man after My own heart, who will do all My will"* (Acts 13:22). In Psalm 119, we hear him speaking with God about His Word and praying for divine light and teaching, always accompanied by the vow of obedience or some other expression of love and delight. The doing of God's will, as it was with God's own Son, is the one secret of entrance into the favor and the mind of God.

Young Christian, when you ask God to lead you into the treasures of His Word, do it as one who presents himself *"a living sacrifice"* (Rom. 12:1), ready to do whatever God says. Seek this with deep humility. To enjoy your food you must first be hungry. The first requirement for Bible study is a simple longing to find out what God wants you to do and the determination to do it. *"If anyone wants to do His will, he shall know"*—the Word of God will be opened to him.

# chapter 10

# Becoming a Doer of the Word

*Be doers of the word, and not hearers only, deceiving
yourselves....Not a forgetful hearer but a doer of the work, this
one will be blessed in what he does.*
—James 1:22, 25

I t is a terrible delusion to delight in hearing the Word and yet
not do it. Multitudes of Christians listen to the Word of God
regularly and yet do not do it. If their own children were to
hear but not do what they said, they would be greatly disturbed.
However, the delusion is so complete that some never know they
are not living good Christian lives. What deludes us in this way?

## HEARING BUT NOT DOING

One cause for this delusion is that people often mistake
hearing the Word for religion or worship. The mind delights in
having truth explained, and their imaginations are pleased with
clever illustrations. To an active mind, knowledge gives pleasure. A man may study some branch of science—say, electricity—
for the enjoyment the knowledge gives him, without the least
intention of applying it practically. Some people go to church,
enjoy the preaching, and yet do not do what God asks. The unconverted and the converted man alike are content to continue
listening and saying, yet still doing the things they should not
do.

Another cause for this delusion is the false teaching that we
are unable to do good. The grace of Christ to enable us to obey,
to keep us from sinning, and to make us holy is so little believed
that people think sinning is a part of the Christian life. They
think God could not possibly expect perfect obedience from
them because He knows they will fail. This error erodes away

any determined purpose to do all that God has said. It closes the heart to any earnest desire to believe and experience all that God's grace can do in us. It keeps men self-contented in the midst of sin.

## DUTY BUT NOT DELIGHT

Another reason for this delusion centers on our private Bible reading. The hearing or reading of the Bible is often regarded as a duty. We spend our five or ten minutes in the morning, reading thoughtfully and attentively trying to understand what we have read. It is a duty faithfully performed that eases the conscience and gives us a sense of satisfaction. We do not realize how this attitude of duty can cause us to become hardened toward God's Word. To avoid this delusion, we must approach our daily Bible reading with the desire to do and be all that God would have us to be. *"Be doers of the word, and not hearers only, deceiving yourselves."*

This delusion must be fought and conquered during our morning quiet time. This new approach may disturb our regular Bible reading and cause us to get behind in our scheduled selections. However, the important thing is that we decide to do what we read. Our Lord Jesus said, *"If anyone wants to do His will, he shall know concerning the doctrine, whether it is from God"* (John 7:17). If we delight in God's law and set our wills on doing it, then we can receive divine illumination on the teachings of Christ. Without this will to do, our knowledge has little value. It is simply head knowledge.

In all of life, whether science, art, or business, the only way of truly knowing is doing. What a man cannot do, he does not thoroughly know. The only way to know God is to do His will. By doing His will, I prove whether it is a God of my own sentiment and imagination that I confess, or the true and living God who rules and works over all. It is only by doing His will that I prove I love His will and accept it as my own. The only way to be united to God is to do His will.

The self-delusion of hearing and not doing is conquered in the quiet of my inner chamber. During my private Bible reading, I must decide that I am going to do whatever God says.

## DOING GOD'S WORD

It may help us if we take a portion of God's Word and see how we can accomplish this new resolution.

Let us take the Sermon on the Mount. The first beatitude says, *"Blessed are the poor in spirit"* (Matt. 5:3). I ask myself, What does this mean? Am I earnestly seeking day by day to maintain this attitude? As I realize how proud and self-confident my nature is, am I willing to wait, pray, and believe that He can work it in me? Am I going to do this—be *"poor in spirit"*? Or will I be a hearer and not a doer?

In this manner, I can go through the beatitudes and the whole sermon with its teachings on meekness and mercy, on love and righteousness. As I read about trusting Him and doing His will, I must ask myself, verse by verse, Do I know what this means? Am I living it? Am I doing what He says? By asking these questions, I will realize the need for a change in my attitudes and my behavior. I must ask myself if the vow, "Whatever He says, I am going to do," has taken the place in my Bible reading and my life that He demands that it should have.

Before I know it, such questions will give me an entirely new insight into my need for Christ, who will breathe in me His own life and work in me all He speaks. I will have courage to say by faith, *"'I can do all things through Christ who strengthens me'* (Phil. 4:13). Whatever He says in His Word, I will do."

chapter 11

# Keeping Christ's Commandments

*If you know these things, blessed are you if you do them.*
—John 13:17

The joy and the blessing of God's Word is only to be known by doing it. This subject is of such supreme importance in the Christian life, and therefore in our Bible study, that I must ask you to return to it once more. Let us this time just take the one expression "keeping the Word," or "keeping the commandments."

## KEEP HIS COMMANDMENTS

In Jesus' farewell address to His disciples, He emphasized the importance of keeping His commandments.

*If you love Me, keep My commandments. And...He will give you another Helper* (John 14:15–16).

*He who has My commandments and keeps them, it is he who loves Me. And he...will be loved by My Father* (v. 21).

*If anyone loves Me, he will keep My word; and My Father will love him* (v. 23).

*If you abide in Me, and My words abide in you, you will ask what you desire, and it shall be done for you* (John 15:7).

*If you keep My commandments, you will abide in My love* (v. 10).

*You are My friends if you do whatever I command you* (v. 14).

Study and compare these passages, until the words enter your heart and work the deep conviction that keeping Christ's commandments is the essential condition of all spiritual blessing. It is necessary for the coming of the Holy Spirit and His actual indwelling, for the enjoyment of the Father's love, and for the manifestation of Christ in our lives.

Power in prayer, the abiding in Christ's love, and the enjoyment of His friendship depend on the keeping of the commandments. The power to claim and enjoy these blessings in faith day by day also requires obedience. The will of God, delighted in and done, is the only way to the heart of the Father and His only way to our hearts. Keep the commandments—this is the way to every blessing.

## PROVING OUR LOVE FOR HIM

All this is confirmed by what we find in John's first epistle: *"Now by this we know that we know Him, if we keep His commandments. He who says, 'I know Him,' and does not keep His commandments, is a liar....But whoever keeps His word, truly the love of God is perfected in him"* (1 John 2:3–5). The only proof of a true, living, saving knowledge of God; the only proof of not being self-deceived in our religion; the only proof of God's love not being part of our imagination, but a possession, is keeping His Word.

*"If our heart does not condemn us, we have confidence toward God. And whatever we ask we receive from Him, because we keep His commandments....Now he who keeps His commandments abides in Him"* (1 John 3:21–22, 24). Keeping the commandments is the secret of confidence toward God, and the secret of true intimate fellowship with Him.

*"For this is the love of God, that we keep His commandments....For whatever is born of God overcomes the world"* (1 John 5:3–4). Our profession of love is worthless unless it is proved to be true by the keeping of His commandments in the power of a life born of God. Knowing God, having the love of God perfected in us, having boldness with God, abiding in Him, being born of Him and loving Him—all is dependent upon one thing: keeping the commandments.

## THE KEY TO BLESSING

When we realize the prominence Christ and Scripture give to keeping His commandments, we will learn to give it the same prominence in our lives. It will become to us one of the keys to true Bible study. The person who reads his Bible with the determined purpose to search out and to obey every commandment of God and of Christ is on the right track to receiving all the blessing the Word was ever meant to bring. He will especially learn two things. First, he must wait for the teaching of the Holy Spirit to lead him into all God's will. Second, there is joy in performing daily duties because they are the will of God.

He will discover how all of daily life is enriched when he says as Christ did, *"This command I have received from My Father"* (John 10:18). The Word will become the light and guide by which all his steps are ordered. His life will become the training school in which the power of the Word is proved and the mind is prepared to be taught and encouraged. The keeping of the commandments will be the key to every spiritual blessing.

Make a determined effort to understand what this life of full obedience means. Look at some of Christ's clearest commands: *"Love one another; as I have loved you"* (John 13:34); *"You also ought to wash one another's feet"* (v. 14); *"You should do as I have done to you"* (v. 15).

Then accept Christlike love and humility as the law of the supernatural life you are to live. Let this thought encourage you to put your hope entirely in Him. By His Spirit, He will work in you both to will and to do what pleases Him (Phil. 2:13).

Once again, our one aim must be perfect harmony between conscience and conduct. Every conviction must be carried into action. Christ's commands were meant to be obeyed. If this is not done, the accumulation of scriptural knowledge only hardens us and makes us unable to learn from the Spirit.

In your inner chamber each morning, you must decide whether you will keep the commandments of Christ throughout the day. This decision will also determine whether in future life you will be a person completely yielded to know and do the will of God.

chapter 12

# The Word Is Life

*And out of the ground made the LORD God to grow...the tree of life also in the midst of the garden, and the tree of knowledge of good and evil.*
—Genesis 2:9 KJV

There are two ways of knowing things. The one is in the mind by thought or idea—"I know about a thing." The other is by living—"I know by experience." An intelligent blind man may know all that science teaches about light by having books read to him. A child who has never thought about what light is knows more about light than the blind scholar. The scholar knows all about it by thinking. The child knows it in reality by seeing and enjoying it.

## THE HEART AND THE LIFE

This is also true in Christianity. The mind can form thoughts about God from the Bible and know all the doctrines of salvation, while the inner life does not know the power of God to save. This is why we read, *"He who does not love does not know God, for God is love"* (1 John 4:8). He may know all about God and love, and he may be able to express beautiful thoughts about it, but unless he loves, he does not know God. Only love can know God. The knowledge of God is life eternal.

God's Word is the Word of Life. *"Out of* [the heart] *spring the issues of life"* (Prov. 4:23). The life of a person can be strong, even when mental knowledge is limited. On the other hand, knowledge can be the object of diligent study and great delight, while the person's life is not affected by it.

An illustration may make this plain. Suppose we could give understanding to an apple tree, with eyes to see and hands to work. This might enable the apple tree to do for itself what the gardener does—to fertilize and water it. But the inner life of the apple tree would still be the same, quite different from the understanding given to it. Likewise, the inner, divine life of a person is something quite different from the intellect with which he knows about it. That intellect offers to the heart God's Word, which the Holy Spirit can quicken. Yet the intellect itself cannot impart or quicken the true life. It is only a servant that carries the food. It is the heart that must be nourished and live.

## KNOWLEDGE VERSUS LIFE

The two trees in the garden are God's revelation of the same truth. If Adam had eaten of the tree of life, he would have received and known all the good God had for him in living power as an experience. And he would have known evil only by being absolutely free from it. Eve was led astray by the desire for knowledge—*"a tree desirable to make one wise"* (Gen. 3:6). In this way, man got a knowledge of good without possessing it. He had a knowledge of good only from the evil that was its opposite. And since that day, man has searched for truth more in knowledge than in life.

It is only by experiencing God and His goodness that we can receive true knowledge. The knowledge of the intellect cannot quicken or revive. *"Though I...understand all mysteries and all knowledge,...but have not love, I am nothing"* (1 Cor. 13:2).

It is in our daily Bible reading that this danger must be met and conquered. We need the intellect to hear and understand God's Word in its human meaning. But we need to know that the possession of the truth by the intellect can only benefit us when the Holy Spirit makes it life and truth in the heart. We need to yield our hearts and wait on God in quiet submission and faith to work in us by that Spirit. As this becomes a holy habit, our intellects and hearts will work in perfect harmony. Each movement of the mind will be accompanied by the corresponding movement of the heart, waiting on and listening for the teaching of the Spirit.

chapter 13

# The Heart and the Intellect

*Trust in the LORD with all your heart, and lean not on*
*your own understanding.*
*—Proverbs 3:5*

The main purpose of the book of Proverbs is to teach knowledge and discretion and to guide in the path of wisdom and understanding. To understand righteousness, to understand the fear of the Lord, to find good understanding—it is to these that Proverbs guides us. The writer of Proverbs warned us to distinguish between trusting our own understanding and seeking the spiritual understanding that God gives.

*"Trust in the LORD with all your heart, and lean not on your own understanding."* In all our seeking after knowledge and wisdom, in all our plans for our lives or studying the Word, we have two powers at work: the understanding or intellect that knows things from the ideas we form, and the heart that knows them by experience as they become part of our wills and desires.

## DANGERS OF THE INTELLECT

One of the main reasons Bible teaching and Bible knowledge bear little fruit in the lives of Christians is because we trust in our own understanding.

Many people argue that God gave us our intellect, and without it there is no possibility of knowing God's Word. This is true, but in the Fall our whole human nature was disordered. The will became enslaved, our desires were perverted, and our understanding was darkened. Most people acknowledge that even the believer does not have in himself the power of a holy will and needs the daily renewing of the grace of Jesus Christ. They admit that the believer does not have the power to love God and his neighbor unless it is given to him by the Holy Spirit. But most people do not realize that the intellect is equally ruined spiritually and incapable of understanding spiritual truth.

It was especially this desire for knowledge that led Eve astray and was the outcome of the temptation. To think that we can take the knowledge of God's truth for ourselves out of His Word is still our greatest danger. We need a deep conviction of the inability of our understanding to really know the truth. We need to realize the terrible danger of self-confidence and self-deception and to see the need for this warning: *"Trust in the LORD with all your heart, and lean not on your own understanding."*

## Look to Your Heart

It is with the heart man believes (Rom. 10:10). It is with all the heart we are to seek (Deut. 4:29), serve (Deut. 10:12), and love (Deut. 6:5) God. It is only with the heart that we can know God or worship God in spirit and truth (John 4:23–24). It is in the heart, therefore, that the divine Word does the work. It is into our hearts that God has sent forth the Spirit of His Son. It is the heart, the inward life of desire and love and will, that the Holy Spirit guides into all truth (John 16:13).

The Bible says, *"Trust in the LORD with all your heart, and lean not on your own understanding."* Do not trust your own understanding. It can give you only thoughts and ideas about spiritual things without the reality of them. It will deceive you with the thought that the truth, if received into the mind, will somehow surely enter your heart. It will blind you to the terrible experience that is universal: the practice of daily Bible reading, listening to God's Word every Sunday, and yet becoming neither humble, nor holy, nor heavenly minded because of it.

Instead of trusting your understanding, come with your heart to the Bible and trust God. Let your whole heart be set upon the living God as the Teacher when you enter your prayer closet. Then you will find good understanding. God will give you an understanding heart, a spiritual understanding.

435

## TRUST IN THE LORD

You may ask, "But what am I to do? How am I to study my Bible? I see no way of doing so unless I use my understanding."

That is correct, but do not use it for what it cannot do. Remember two things. One is that your understanding can only give you a picture or thought of spiritual things. The moment it has done this, go with your heart to the Lord to make His Word life and truth in you. The other danger of leaning on your own understanding is that you will take pride in your own intellect. Nothing can save you from this except continual dependence of the heart on the Holy Spirit's teaching. When the Holy Spirit quickens the Word in the heart, then He can guide the intellect. *"The humble He guides in justice, and the humble He teaches His way"* (Ps. 25:9). *"The fear of the LORD is the beginning of wisdom"* (Prov. 9:10).

With every thought from the Word that your understanding grasps, bow before God in dependence and trust. Believe with your whole heart that God can and will make it true to you. Ask for the Holy Spirit to make it work in your heart until the Word becomes the strength of your life.

Persevere in this, and the time will come when the Holy Spirit, dwelling in the heart and life, will keep the understanding in subjection and let His holy light shine through it.

# God's Thoughts and Our Thoughts

*As the heavens are higher than the earth, so are...*
*My thoughts than your thoughts.*
—Isaiah 55:9

On earth the words of a wise man often mean something different from what the hearer understands them to mean. How natural, then, that the words of God, as He understands them, mean something infinitely higher than we understand at first. We must remember this, because it will cause us to search for the fuller meaning of God's Word as He meant it. It will give us confidence to hope that there is fulfillment in life beyond our highest thoughts.

## GOD'S THOUGHTS

God's Word has two meanings. The one is the meaning that originated in the mind of God, making human words the bearer of divine wisdom, power, and love. The other is our partial, distorted understanding of God's Word. Although such words as *the love of God, the grace of God,* and *the power of God* may seem very true and real to us, there is still an infinite fullness in the Word that we have not yet known. How strikingly this is put in our text from Isaiah: *"As the heavens are higher than the earth."* Our faith in this fact is so simple and clear that no one would dream of trying with his little arms to reach the sun or the stars. And now God says, *"My thoughts* [are higher] *than your thoughts."* Even when the Word has given us God's thoughts and our thoughts have tried to understand them, they still remain as high above our thoughts as the heavens are higher than the earth.

All the infinities of God and the eternal world dwell in the Word as the seeds of eternal life. And just as the full-grown oak tree is mysteriously greater than the acorn from which it sprang, so God's words are but seeds from which God's mighty wonders of grace and power can grow up.

## A CHILDLIKE SPIRIT

We should learn to come to the Word as little children. Jesus said, *"You have hidden these things from the wise and prudent and revealed them to babes"* (Luke 10:21). The prudent and the wise are not necessarily hypocrites or enemies. Many of God's own dear children, by neglecting to cultivate a childlike spirit, have spiritual truth hidden from them and never become spiritual men. *"What man knows the things of a man except the spirit of the man which is in him? Even so no one knows the things of God except the Spirit of God. Now we have received...the Spirit who is from God, that we might know"* (1 Cor. 2:11–12). Let a deep sense of our ignorance, a deep distrust of our own power to understand the things of God, influence our Bible study.

God wants to make His Word true in us. The Holy Spirit is already in us to reveal the things of God. In answer to our humble, believing prayer, God will give insight into the mystery of God—our wonderful union and likeness to Christ, His living in us, and our being as He was in this world.

If our hearts thirst, a time may come when, by a special communication of His Spirit, all our yearnings will be satisfied. Christ will take possession of the heart, and what was of faith will now become an experience. Then we will realize that, *"as the heavens are higher than the earth,"* His thoughts are higher than our thoughts.

chapter 15

# True Meditation

*Blessed is the man...[whose] delight is in the law of the LORD; and in His law he meditates day and night.*
—Psalm 1:1–2

*Let the words of my mouth and the meditation of my heart be acceptable in Your sight, O LORD, my strength and my Redeemer.*
—Psalm 19:14

T he true aim of education, study, and reading is not what is brought into us, but what is brought out of ourselves, when we actually put into practice what we have learned. This is as true of the study of the Bible as of any other study. God's Word only works when the truth it brings to us has stirred the inner life and reproduced itself in trust, love, or adoration. When the heart has received the Word through the mind and has had its spiritual powers exercised, the Word is no longer void, but has done what God intended it to do. It has become part of our lives and has strengthened us for new purpose and effort.

## THE ART OF MEDITATION

It is in meditation that the heart takes hold of the Word. Just as in reflection our understanding grasps all meaning of a truth, so in meditation the heart assimilates it and makes truth a part of its own life. We must remember that the heart is the will and the emotions. The meditation of the heart implies desire, acceptance, surrender, and love. *"Out of* [the heart] *spring the issues of life"* (Prov. 4:23). Whatever the heart truly believes, it receives and allows to master and rule the life. The intellect gathers and prepares the food on which we are to feed. In meditation the heart takes it in and feeds on it.

The art of meditation needs to be cultivated. Just as we need to be trained to concentrate our mental powers to think clearly, a Christian needs to meditate until he has formed the habit of yielding his whole heart to every word of God.

How can this power of meditation be cultivated? The very first thing we must do is present ourselves before God. It is His Word, and it has no power of blessing apart from Him. The Word is meant to bring us into His presence and fellowship. Practice His presence. Take the Word as from God Himself with the assurance that He will make it work in your heart. In Psalm 119, the word *meditate* is mentioned seven times, each time as part of a prayer addressed to God: *"I will meditate on Your precepts"* (v. 15); *"Your servant meditates on Your statutes"* (v. 23); *"Oh, how I love Your law! It is my meditation all the day"* (v. 97). Meditation is turning our hearts toward God and seeking to make His Word a part of our lives.

## PONDERING IN THE HEART

Another element of true meditation is quiet pondering. When we endeavor to master a teaching in Scripture, our intellects often need to put forth great effort. With meditation we must take a different approach. Instead of striving, we must hide the word we are studying in the depth of our hearts and believe that by the Holy Spirit its meaning and power will be revealed in our inner lives.

*"You desire truth in the inward parts, and in the hidden part You will make me to know wisdom"* (Ps. 51:6). Of our Lord's mother we are told, *"Mary kept all these things and pondered them in her heart"* (Luke 2:19). Here we have a believer who has come to know Christ and is on the sure way to knowing Him better.

In meditation, personal application takes a prominent place. This is not the case with our intellectual study of the Bible—its objective is to know and understand. In meditation the chief purpose is to take hold and experience. The true spirit of Bible study is a readiness to believe every promise implicitly and to obey every command unhesitatingly. It is in quiet meditation that faith is exercised, that full surrender to all God's will is made, and that the assurance of grace is received to perform our vows.

## MEDITATION AND PRAYER

Meditation must lead to prayer. It provides matter for prayer. It must lead on to prayer, to ask and receive definitely what it has seen in the Word or accepted in the Word. The value of meditation is that it prepares our hearts to pray about the needs the Word has revealed to us. The Word will open up and prove its power in the soul of the one who meekly and patiently waits for it.

There is reward in resting for a time from intellectual effort and in cultivating the habit of holy meditation. In time, the two will be brought into harmony, and our study will be enlightened by quiet waiting on God and a yielding of the heart and life to the Word.

We should have fellowship with God throughout the day. The habit of true meditation in the morning will bring us nearer the blessedness of the man of the first psalm: *"Blessed is the man...[whose] delight is in the law of the LORD; and in His law he meditates day and night."*

All Christian workers and leaders of God's people must remember that they need this time of meditation more than others. It will keep their own communication unbroken with their only source of strength and blessing. God says,

> *I will be with you. I will not leave you nor forsake you....Be strong and very courageous, that you may observe to do according to all the law...that you may prosper wherever you go. This Book of the Law shall not depart from your mouth, but you shall meditate in it day and night....Then you will have good success....Be strong and of good courage.* (Josh. 1:5, 7–9)

*"Let the words of my mouth and the meditation of my heart be acceptable in Your sight, O LORD, my strength and my Redeemer."* Let this be your aim, that your meditation may be acceptable in His sight—part of the spiritual sacrifice you offer. Let this be your prayer and expectation, that your meditation may be true worship—the living surrender of the heart to God's Word in His presence.

chapter 16

# Having a Childlike Spirit

*I thank You, Father, Lord of heaven and earth, that You have*
*hidden these things from the wise and prudent and have*
*revealed them to babes.*
*—Matthew 11:25*

The wise and prudent are those who have confidence in their reasoning ability to help them in their pursuit of spiritual knowledge. The babes are those whose chief work is not the mind and its power, but the heart and its emotions. Ignorance, helplessness, dependence, meekness, teachableness, trust, and love—these are the qualities God seeks in those whom He teaches. (See Psalm 25:9, 12, 14, 17, 20.)

One of the most important parts of our devotions is the study of God's Word. In order to receive the Word in the Spirit, we must wait for the Father to reveal its truth in us. We must have that childlike attitude to which the Father loves to impart the secrets of His love. With the wise and prudent, the most important thing is head knowledge. From them God hides the true spiritual meaning of the very thing they think they understand. With babes it is not the head and its knowledge, but the heart and its emotions that are important. Because they have a sense of humility, love, and trust, God reveals to them the very thing they know they cannot understand.

## A TEACHABLE SPIRIT

Education tells us that there are two styles of teaching. The ordinary teacher makes the communication of knowledge his main objective. He strives to cultivate the abilities of the child in order to help him attain this objective. On the other hand, the true teacher considers the amount of knowledge a secondary thing. His first aim is to develop the abilities of the child's mind and spirit. He helps the pupil, both mentally and morally, to use his abilities correctly in the pursuit and application of knowledge.

Along the same line, there are two classes of preachers. Some pour forth instruction, argument, and appeal and leave it to the hearers to make the best use they can of what is presented to them. The true preacher knows how much depends upon the condition of heart. He seeks, even as Jesus did, to make the teaching of objective truth or doctrine secondary to the cultivation of the attitudes that give value to teaching.

A hundred eloquent sermons can be preached to wise and prudent Christians who listen with the idea that they can understand, and that what they hear will somehow profit them. However, if one sermon is preached to hearers who are aware of their spiritual ignorance, they will receive the truth because of their childlike spirit. They will wait for and depend on the Father's teaching.

In the secret chamber, every man is his own teacher and preacher. He is to train himself to have a childlike simplicity and a teachable spirit. He must remember that there must be an individual revelation of divine truth to each person by the Holy Spirit. He must wait on the Father to reveal to him, and within him, the hidden mystery in its power in the inner life. With this attitude he exercises the childlike spirit and receives the kingdom as a little child.

All evangelical Christians believe in regeneration. However, few believe that when a man is born of God, his chief characteristic should be a childlike dependence on God for all teaching and strength. This was the one thing our Lord Jesus insisted on above all. He pronounced the poor in heart, the meek, the hungry, *"blessed"* (Matt. 5:3, 5–6). He called men to learn that He was *"meek and lowly in heart"* (Matt. 11:29 KJV). He spoke so often of humbling ourselves and becoming as little children. The first sign of being a child of God, of being like Jesus Christ, is an absolute dependence on God for any real knowledge of spiritual things.

## REVEALED TO BABES

Let each of us ask ourselves, "Have I considered the child-like spirit essential for my Bible study? What use is Bible study without the childlike spirit?" It is the only real key to God's school. We must set aside everything to attain this attitude. Only then will God reveal His hidden wisdom.

The new birth, being born of God, by which we become God's children, is intended to make us babes. It will give us the child-spirit as well as the child-teaching. It cannot do the second without the first. Let us yield ourselves to this new life in us, to the leading of the Spirit. He will breathe in us the spirit of little children. The first objective of Bible study is to learn the hidden wisdom of God. The first condition of obtaining this knowledge is to accept the fact that God Himself reveals it to us.

In order to receive a revelation of God, we must first have this childlike spirit. We all know the first thing a wise workman does is to see that he has the proper tools and that they are in proper order. He does not consider it lost time to stop his work and sharpen the tools. Similarly, it is not lost time to let the Bible study wait until you see whether you are in the right position—waiting for the Father's revelation with a meek and childlike spirit. If you feel that you have not read your Bible in this spirit, confess and forsake at once the self-confident spirit. Pray for the childlike spirit, and then believe you have it. Although it may be neglected and suppressed, it is in you. You can begin at once as a child of God to experience it.

This childlike spirit is in you as a seed in the new life, born of the Spirit. It must rise and grow in you as a birth of the indwelling Spirit. By faith you must pray for this grace of the Spirit and then exercise it. Live as a babe before God. As a newborn babe, *"desire the pure milk of the word"* (1 Pet. 2:2).

Beware of trying to assume this state of mind only when you want to study Scripture. It must be the permanent habit of your mind, the state of your heart. Only then can you enjoy the continual guidance of the Holy Spirit.

# Learning of Christ

*Take My yoke upon you and learn from Me, for I am gentle*
*[ "meek," KJV] and lowly in heart, and you will*
*find rest for your souls.*
*—Matthew 11:29*

A ll Bible study is learning. All Bible study, in order to be fruitful, should be learning of Christ. The Bible is the schoolbook, and Christ is the teacher. It is He who opens the understanding, the heart, and the seals. (See Luke 24:45; Acts 16:14; Revelation 5:9.) Christ is the living eternal Word of which the written words are the human expression. Christ's presence and teaching are the secret of all true Bible study. The written Word is powerless, except as it brings us to the living Word.

No one has ever thought of accusing our Lord of not honoring the Old Testament. In His own life He proved that He loved it because it came out of the mouth of God. He always pointed the Jews to it as the revelation of God and the witness to Himself. But with the disciples, it is remarkable how frequently He spoke of His own teaching as what they most needed and had to obey.

The Jews had their self-made interpretation of the Word, and made it the greatest barrier between themselves and Him of whom it spoke. Christians often do this, too. Our human understanding of Scripture, fortified by the authority of the church or our own denomination, becomes the greatest hindrance to Christ's teachings. Christ the living Word seeks first to find His place in our hearts and lives, to be our only Teacher. From Him we will learn to honor and understand Scripture.

## LEARN TO BE MEEK

*"Learn from Me, for I am gentle and lowly in heart."* Our Lord gives us the secret of His own inner life that He brought down to us from heaven. This secret that He has given and that He wants us to learn from Him is found in the words, *"I am gentle and lowly in heart."* It is the one virtue that makes Him the Lamb of God, our suffering Redeemer, our heavenly Teacher and Leader. It is the one attitude that He asks us to learn from Him—out of this all else will come.

For Bible study and our entire Christian lives, this is the one condition we need to truly learn of Christ. He, the Teacher, meek and lowly in heart, wants to make you what He is, because that is salvation. As a learner you must come and study and believe in Him, the meek and lowly One. You must seek to learn of Him how to be meek and lowly, too.

Why is this the first and all-important requirement? Because it lies at the root of the true relationship of the believer to God. God alone has life, goodness, and happiness. As the God of love, He delights to give these qualities and work them into us. Christ became the Son of Man to show us how to live in complete dependence on God. This is the meaning of His being lowly in heart.

Angels veil their faces and cast their crowns before God. God is everything to them. They delight to receive all and to give all. This is the root of the true Christian life: to be nothing before God and men; to wait on God alone; to delight in, to imitate, to learn of Christ, the meek and lowly One. This is the key to the teachings of Christ, the only key to the true knowledge of Scripture. It is in this character that Christ has come to teach; it is in this character alone that you can learn of Him.

## MEEKNESS AND BIBLE STUDY

In the Christian church there is a lack of humility and of the meek and lowly heart that was in the life of Christ and the teachings of God's Word. I am deeply persuaded that this lack lies at the root of ineffective and unfruitful work by the church. It is only as we are meek and lowly in heart that Christ can teach us by His Spirit what God has for us.

Let each of us begin with ourselves and consider this as the first condition of discipleship, the first lesson the Master will teach us. Let us make all our Bible study a time of learning about Christ, trusting Him who is meek, gentle, and kind to work His own spirit and likeness in us. In due time our morning watch will be the scene of daily fellowship and daily blessing.

I know how difficult it is to expect the meek and lowly heart to be the first consideration in Bible study. It is hard to make people realize that, in communion with God, our attitude and character mean everything. A meek and lowly heart is the very seed and root of all Christian character. It is hard to convince people that, without it, Bible study is of very little value. The meek and lowly heart is possible because it is the very thing Christ offers to give, teaching us how to find and receive it in Himself. I urge all Bible students, thoughtfully and prayerfully, to make this the very first question to be settled in the inner chamber: Is my heart in the condition that my Teacher desires it to be? And if not, my first work is to yield myself to Him to work it in me.

chapter 18

# Christ Your Teacher

*Take My yoke upon you and learn from Me, for I am gentle*
*["meek," KJV] and lowly in heart, and you will*
*find rest for your souls.*
—Matthew 11:29

The first virtue of a pupil is a willingness to be taught. What does this imply? He must have an awareness of his own ignorance, a readiness to give up his own way of thinking or doing. He must look at things from the teacher's standpoint. He must have a quiet confidence that the master knows and will show him how to learn to know, too. The meek and lowly spirit listens carefully to know what the teacher's will is and how to carry it out. If a pupil has this kind of spirit, it must be the teacher's fault if the student does not learn.

Why is it that, with Christ as our Teacher, there is so much failure and so little real growth in spiritual knowledge? Why is there so much hearing and reading of the Bible, so much profession of faith in it as our only rule of life, and yet such a lack of the manifestation of its spirit and its power? Why is there so much honest, earnest application in the prayer closet and in Bible study, but so little of the joy and strength God's Word can give?

These questions are ones of extreme importance. There must be some reason why there are so many disciples of Jesus who think they honestly desire to know and do His will, and yet, by their own confession, they are not holding forth the Word of Life as a light in the world. If the answer to this question could be found, their lives would be changed.

## LEARNING FROM CHRIST

*"Take My yoke upon you and learn from Me, for I am gentle*
*and lowly in heart, and you will find rest for your souls."* Many

448

people have taken Christ as Savior but not as Teacher. They have put their trust in Him as the Good Shepherd who gave His life for the sheep, but they know little of the reality of His daily shepherding His flock, calling everyone by name, hearing His voice, or following Him alone. They know little about following the Lamb or receiving from Him the lamb nature. They seldom seek to be like Him, meek and lowly in heart.

It was by their three year course in His school that Christ's disciples were equipped for the baptism of the Holy Spirit and the fulfillment of all the wonderful promises He had given them. As we daily wait for, receive, and follow Christ's teaching, we can truly find rest for our souls. All the weariness and burden of strain, failure, and disappointment give way to the divine peace that knows that all is being cared for by Christ Himself.

This teachable spirit that refuses to know or do anything in its own wisdom is to be the spirit of our entire lives, every day and all day long. In the morning hour this spirit is to be cultivated, and deliverance from self is to be achieved. It is there, while occupied with the words of God, that we need daily to realize that these words have value only as they are opened up by the personal teaching of Christ. We daily need this experience so that, as the living Lord Jesus comes near and takes charge of us, His teaching can be received. It is during this quiet time that we must definitely ask for and cultivate the teachable spirit that takes up His yoke and learns from Him.

It is said of the Holy Spirit who dwells in us, the Spirit of Christ Jesus, *"He will teach you all things"* (John 14:26). If His whole life and work in us is a divine teaching, then we must have this teachable spirit within us. This will make our communion with God's Word and our daily lives what our Lord Jesus can make them.

## UNLEARNING AND HUMILITY

### • UNLEARNING

Unlearning is often the most important part of learning; wrong impressions, prejudices, and beliefs are obstacles in the way of learning. Until these have been removed, the teacher labors in vain. The knowledge he communicates only touches the surface. Deep under the surface, the pupil is guided by what has become second nature to him. The first work of the teacher is to discover, to make the pupil see and remove these hindrances.

There can be no true and faithful learning about Christ when we are not ready to unlearn. By heredity, by education, by tradition, we have established our thoughts about religion and God's Word—thoughts that are often great hindrances to our learning the truth. To learn of Christ requires a willingness to subject every truth we hold to His inspection for criticism and correction.

### • HUMILITY

Humility is the root virtue of the Christian life. This law is absolute in God's kingdom: *"He who humbles himself will be exalted"* (Matt. 23:12). Our disappointment in striving after higher degrees of grace, faith, spiritual knowledge, and love depends on this law. We have not accepted the humility of Christ as the beginning and the perfection of His salvation. *"God... gives grace to the humble"* (James 4:6) has a far wider and deeper application than we think.

In the morning watch, we place ourselves as learners in Christ's school. Let humility be the distinguishing mark of the learner. Let us listen to the voice that says, *"Take My yoke upon you and learn from Me, for I am gentle and lowly in heart, and you will find rest for your souls."*

chapter 19

# The Life and the Light

*In the beginning was the Word, and the Word was with God,*
*and the Word was God....In Him was life, and the life*
*was the light of men.*
—John 1:1, 4

*He who follows Me shall not walk in darkness,*
*but have the light of life.*
—John 8:12

Because Christ was God, He could be the Word of God. Because He had the life of God in Himself, He could be the revealer of that life. And so, as the living Word, He is the life-giving Word. The written Word can be made void and of no effect when we trust human wisdom for an understanding of it. The written Word must be accepted as the seed in which the life of the living Word lies hidden. When it is quickened by the Holy Spirit, it can become to us the Word of Life. Our communion with God's written Word must be inspired and regulated by faith in the eternal Word, who is God.

## THE LIFE IS LIGHT

This same truth comes out in the expression that follows: the life is the light. When we see a light shining, we know that there is a source of that light in some form. This is also true in the spiritual world. There must be life before there can be light. There can be reflected light from a dead or dark object. There can be borrowed light without life. But true life alone can show true light. He who follows Christ will have the light of life.

These verses from John's gospel confirm what we know about the Spirit of God. Even as Christ knows the things of God

451

because He is the life of God, so Christ is the Word because He is God and has the life of God. The light of God shines only where the life of God is. When the written Word brings us the life of the eternal Word, its light within the heart shines into our lives. Only as the Holy Spirit, who knows the things of God because He is the life of God, makes them life and truth within us, can our study of Scripture really bless us.

The one great lesson the Spirit seeks to enforce in regard to God's Word is this: only as Scripture is received out of the life of God into our lives can there be any real knowledge of it. The Word is a seed that bears within it the divine life. When it is received in the good soil of a heart that hungers for that life, it will spring up and bring forth fruit like all seed, after its kind. It will reproduce in our lives the very life of God, the very likeness and character of the Father and the Son through the Holy Spirit.

## WAIT ON THE LORD

We need to apply these lessons in a practical way to our private Bible reading. The rules are very simple.

*"Be still, and know that I am God"* (Ps. 46:10). Take time to be quiet and to be aware of God. *"Be silent in the presence of the Lord GOD"* (Zeph. 1:7). *"Be silent...before the LORD"* (Zech. 2:13). *"The LORD is in His holy temple. Let all the earth keep silence before Him"* (Hab. 2:20). Worship and wait on Him so that He may speak to you. Remember that the Word comes out of the life, the heart of God carrying His life to impart it to yours. It is nothing less than the life of God, so nothing less than the power of God can make it live in you.

Believe in Christ the living Word. *"In Him was life, and the life was the light of men." "He who follows Me shall...have the light of life."* Follow Jesus in love and longing desire, in obedience and service, and His life will work in you—His life will be the light of your soul.

Ask the Father for the Holy Spirit to make the Word living and active in your heart. Hunger for the will of God as your daily food. Thirst for the living spring of the Spirit within you. Receive the Word into your will, your life, your joy—the life it brings will give the light with which it shines.

## UNDERSTANDING THE WORD

My own experience has taught me that it takes a long time before we clearly understand that the Word of God must be received into the life and not only into the mind. Even after we understand, it takes time before we fully believe and act on it. Study each lesson until you know it. The Word comes out of the life of God, carries that life in itself, and seeks to enter my life and fill it with the life of God. This life is the light of men and gives *"the light of the knowledge of the glory of God"* (2 Cor. 4:6).

You may find that this lesson takes more time than you think, that it hinders you more than it helps in your Bible study. Do not be afraid or impatient, but be assured that if you learn this lesson, you will realize that it has become a key you never had before to the hidden treasure of the Word, giving you true wisdom in *"the hidden part"* (Ps. 51:6).

So I repeat the simple words so blessed and true. The Spirit who lives in God alone knows the things of God. In the same way, it is only the Spirit living in me who can make me know the things of God by imparting them to my life.

Christ was the Word because He was God and had the life of God. In the same way, the written Word can bless me only as Christ, the living Word, brings the life of God to me. The life of Christ is the light of men. Therefore, only as I have the life of Christ through the Word do I have the light of the knowledge of God.

chapter 20

# Principles of Bible Study

*Blessed is the man...*[whose] *delight is in the law of the LORD, and in His law he meditates day and night.*
—Psalm 1:1–2

There is a desire in the church for more Bible study. Evangelists like D. L. Moody and many others have proved what power there is in preaching drawn directly from God's Word and inspired by the faith of its power. Earnest Christians have asked, "Why can't our ministers speak in the same way, giving the very Word of God more emphasis?" Many young ministers have come away from seminary confessing that they were taught everything except the knowledge of how to study the Word or how to help others study it. In some of our churches, the desire has been expressed to supply this need in the training of ministers. Yet it has been difficult for men with theological training to return to the simplicity and directness of God's Word. This simplicity is necessary in order to teach younger men the way to make Scripture the one source of their knowledge and teaching.

Bible study can bring a full blessing to individual lives by giving God's Word its true place in Christian work. Let us look at the principles underlying the demand for more Bible study and how they can be truly carried out.

## GOD'S WORD REVEALS GOD'S WILL

God's Word is the only authentic revelation of God's will. All human statements of divine truth, however correct, are defective and carry a measure of human authority. In the Word, the voice of God speaks to us directly. Every child of God is called to direct fellowship with the Father through the Word. God reveals His heart and grace in His Word. His child can receive from God all the life and power there is in the Word into his own heart and being.

We know how few secondhand reports of messages or events can be fully trusted. Very few men report accurately what they have heard. Every believer has the right and calling to stand in direct communication with God. God still reveals Himself to each individual in His Word.

This Word of God is a living Word (Heb. 4:12). It carries a divine quickening power in it. The human expression of the truth is often an idea or image of the truth, appealing to the mind and having little or no effect on the person. Because it is God's own Word, His presence and power in it make it effective. The words in which God has chosen to clothe His own divine thoughts are God-breathed, and the life of God dwells in them. *"God is not the God of the dead, but of the living"* (Matt. 22:32). The Word was inspired when first given, and the Spirit of God still breathes in it. God is still in and with His Word. Christians and teachers need to believe this. It will lead them to give the simple, divine Word a confidence that no human teaching can have.

## THE INTERPRETER OF THE WORD

Only God Himself can, and most surely will, be the Interpreter of His Word. Divine truth needs a divine Teacher. Spiritual understanding of spiritual things can only come from the Holy Spirit. The unique character of the Word is that it is essentially different from, and infinitely exalted above, all human understanding. The deeper our conviction of this fact, the more we will feel the need for supernatural, divine teaching. We will be brought to seek God Himself, and we will be led to find Him in the Holy Spirit who dwells in the heart. As we wait on and trust the Spirit, He will make us to know wisdom in *"the hidden part"* (Ps. 51:6), in our hearts and spirits. The Word, when prayerfully read and cherished in the heart by faith, will be both light and life within us through the Spirit.

## UNITY OF WILL AND LIFE

The Word brings us into the most intimate fellowship with God—unity of will and life. In the Word, God has revealed His whole heart and all His will. In His law and precepts, He tells us what He wants to do for us. As we accept that will in the Word as from God Himself and yield ourselves to its working, we learn to know God in His will. The Word works out His richest purpose as it fills us with the reverence and dependence that comes from the divine presence and nearness. Nothing less than this must be our aim and our experience in our study of the Bible.

In Holy Scripture we have the very words in which the holy God has spoken and in which He speaks to us. Today these words are full of the life of God. God is in them and makes His presence and power known to those who seek Him in them. To those who ask and wait for the teaching of the Holy Spirit who dwells within us, the Spirit will reveal the spiritual meaning and power of the Word. The Word is thus meant every day to be the means of the revelation of God Himself to the soul and of fellowship with Him.

Have we learned to apply these truths? The Word tells us to seek God, to listen for God, to wait for God. God will speak to you; let God teach you. All we hear about more Bible teaching and Bible study must lead to this one thing. We must be Christians in whom the Word is never separated from the living God Himself. We must live as Christians to whom God in heaven speaks every day and all day long.

chapter 21

# Your Position in Christ

*Set your mind on things above....For you died, and your life is
hidden with Christ in God.*
—Colossians 3:2–3

When entering God's presence in the morning hour, the
Christian must realize who he is himself and where he
stands in relation to God. Each person who claims access and an audience with the Most High must have a living
sense of the place he has in Christ before God.

## WHO YOU ARE

Who am I? Who is it that comes to ask God to meet me and
spend the whole day with me? I am one who knows, by the Word
and Spirit of God, that I am in Christ and that my life is *"hidden
with Christ in God."* In Christ I died to sin and the world. I am
now taken out of them, separated from them, and delivered
from their power. I have been raised together with Christ; and
in Him, I live unto God. My life is *"hidden with Christ in God."*
I can come to God to claim and obtain all the divine life that is
hidden away in Him for today's need and supply.

Yes, this is who I am. I say it to God in humble, holy reverence. I say it to myself to encourage others, as well as myself, to
seek and expect nothing less than grace to live the hidden life of
heaven here on earth. I am one who longs to say, who does say,
"Christ is my life." The longing of my soul is for Christ, revealed
by the Father Himself within the heart. Nothing less can satisfy
me. My life is *"hidden with Christ."* He can be my life in no
other way than as He is in my heart. I can be content with
nothing less than Christ in my heart. Christ is the Savior from

sin, the gift and instrument of God's love. Christ is my indwelling Friend and Lord.

If God should ask, "Who are you?" I would reply, "I live in Christ and Christ in me. Lord, You alone can make me know and be all that this truly means."

## LIVING HIS LIFE

I come as one who desires, who seeks, to be prepared to live the life of Christ today on earth, to translate His hidden, heavenly glory into the language of daily life. As Christ lived on earth only to do the will of God, it is my great desire to stand perfect and complete in all His will (Col. 4:12). My ignorance of that will is very great. My powerlessness to do His will is even greater. And yet I come to God as one who must not compromise, as one who in all honesty accepts the high calling of living out fully the will of God in all things.

This desire brings me to the prayer closet. As I think of all my failures in fulfilling God's will, as I look ahead to all the temptations and dangers that await me, I can say to God, "I come to claim the life hidden in Christ, so that I may live for Christ." I cannot be content without the quiet assurance that God will go with me and bless me. (See Genesis 32:26.)

Who am I, that I should ask these great and wonderful things of God? Can I expect to live the life *"hidden with Christ in God"* and manifest it in my mortal body? I can, because God Himself will work it in me by the Holy Spirit dwelling in me. The same God *"who raised Christ from the dead"* (Rom. 8:11) and then set Him at His right hand has raised me with Him and given me the Spirit of the glory of His Son in my heart. A life in Christ, given up to know and do all God's will, is the life God Himself will work and maintain increasingly in me by the Holy Spirit.

## PRESENTING MYSELF TO GOD

I come in the morning and present myself before Him to receive His hidden life, so that I can live it out in the flesh. I can wait confidently and quietly, as one in whom the Spirit dwells, for the Father to give the fresh anointing that teaches all things. I can wait for Him to take charge of the new day He has given me.

I am sure you realize how important the morning hour is to secure God's presence for the day. During that time, you take a firm stand on the foundation of full redemption. Believe what God says to you. Accept what God has bestowed on you in Christ. Be what God has made you to be. Take time before God to confess your position in Christ. In a battle, much depends upon an unshakable position. Take your place where God has placed you.

The very attempt to do this may at times interfere with your ordinary Bible study or prayer. This will be no loss. It will be fully recompensed later. Your life depends on knowing who your God is and who you are as His redeemed one in Christ. Your daily Christian walk depends on this knowledge. When you have learned the secret, it will, even when you do not think of it, be the strength of your heart, both in going in before God and going out with Him to the world.

# The Will of God

*Your will be done on earth as it is in heaven.*
—Matthew 6:10

T he will of God is the living power to which the world owes its existence. Through that will and according to that will, the world is what it is. The world is the manifestation or embodiment of that divine will in its wisdom, power, and goodness. The world has, in beauty and glory, only what God has willed it to have. As His will formed the world, so His will upholds it every day. Creation does what it was destined for; it shows forth the glory of God. *"You are worthy, O Lord, to receive glory...for You created all things, and by Your will they exist and were created"* (Rev. 4:11).

The divine will undertook the creation of a human will in His own image and likeness. This human will was created with the living power to know and cooperate with the will to which it owed its being. The unfallen angels consider it their highest honor and happiness to be able to will and do exactly what God wills and does. The glory of heaven is that God's will is done there. The sin and misery of fallen angels and men consists simply in their having turned away from and having refused to do the will of God.

## RESTORING GOD'S WILL

Redemption is the restoration of God's will to its place in the world. To this end, Christ came and showed, in a human life, how man has only one thing to live for: to do the will of God. Christ said, *"I have come to do Your will, O God"* (Heb. 10:9). He showed us how there was one way of conquering self-will— by a death to it, in obeying God's will even unto death. So He atoned for our self-will, conquered it for us, and opened a path through death and resurrection into a life entirely united to the will of God.

God's redeeming will is now able to do in fallen men what His creating will had done in nature. In Christ and His example, God has revealed the devotion to and the delight in His will that He asks and expects of us. In Christ and His Spirit, He renews and takes possession of our wills. He works our wills to make us able and willing to do all His will.

He Himself *"works all things according to the counsel of His will"* (Eph. 1:11), to *"make you complete in every good work to do His will, working in you what is well pleasing in His sight"* (Heb. 13:21). As this is revealed by the Holy Spirit, believed and received into the heart, we begin to acquire an insight into the prayer, *"Your will be done on earth as it is in heaven."* Then the true desire is awakened in us for the life it promises.

It is essential to the believer that he realize his relationship to God's will and its claim on him. Many believers have no idea of what their faith or their feelings ought to be in regard to the will of God. How few say, "My desire is to be in complete harmony with the will of God. I feel my one need is to maintain my surrender, to do what God wills me to do. By God's grace, every hour of my life can be lived in the will of God—doing His will as it is done in heaven."

## DOING GOD'S WILL

As the divine will works out its purposes in us and masters our hearts, we will have the courage to believe in the answer to the prayer our Lord taught us—*"Your will be done on earth as it is in heaven."* Through Jesus Christ, this working of God's will in us is carried out. It is close union to Him that gives the confidence that God will work everything in us. It is only this confidence in God, through Jesus Christ, that will assure us that we can do our part, and that our wills on earth can correspond and cooperate with the will of God. Let this be the one thing our hearts desire—that in everything the will of God be done in us and by us, as it is done in heaven.

The will of man cannot be disconnected from its living union with the Father here, nor from the living presence of the

Son. It is only by divine guidance, given through the Holy Spirit, that the will of God in its beauty and application to daily life can be truly known. This teaching will be given, not to *"the wise and prudent"* (Matt. 11:25), but to those with a childlike attitude who are willing to wait for and depend on what is given to them. Divine guidance will lead in the path of God's will.

Our secret communion with God is the place where we repeat and learn the great lessons concerning God's will.

The God whom I worship asks of me perfect union with His will. My worship means, *"I delight to do Your will, O my God"* (Ps. 40:8). The morning hour, the inner chamber, the secret fellowship with God—these bring the knowledge of God's will and the power to perform it. As we surrender to do all that God wills, our study of God's Word and our prayer time will bring true and full blessing.

chapter 23

# Feeding on the Word

*Your words were found, and I ate them, and Your word was to
me the joy and rejoicing of my heart.*
—Jeremiah 15:16

his verse teaches us three things. First, it teaches that the
finding of God's Word comes only to those who diligently
seek it. Second, the eating means personally taking hold
of the Word for our own sustenance, taking up the words of God
into our beings. *"Man shall not live by bread alone, but by every
word that proceeds from the mouth of God"* (Matt. 4:4). We also
learn about the rejoicing: *"The kingdom of heaven is like treasure hidden in a field, which a man found and hid; and for joy
over it he goes and sells all that he has and buys that field"*
(Matt. 13:44). In this verse we have the finding, the taking hold,
and the rejoicing. *"Your words were found, and I ate them, and
Your word was to me the joy and rejoicing of my heart."*

## FINDING AND EATING

Eating is here the central thought. It is preceded by the
searching and finding. It is accompanied and followed by the
rejoicing. It is the only aim and use of the one; it is the only
cause and life of the other. In the secrecy of the inner chamber,
much depends on this—*"I ate them!"*

To realize the difference between this and the finding of
God's words, compare the corn a man may have stored in his
granary with the bread he has on his table. All the diligent labor
he has put into sowing and harvesting his grain cannot profit
him unless he eats a daily portion of the bread his body requires.
Do you see the application of this to your Scripture study in the

463

morning quiet time? You need to find God's words and master them by careful thought, so as to have them stored in your mind and memory for your own use and that of others. In this work there may often be great joy, the joy of harvest or of victory—the joy of treasure secured or difficulties overcome. Yet we must remember that this finding and possessing the words of God is not the actual eating of them, which alone brings divine life and strength to the soul.

The fact that a farmer possesses good, wholesome corn will not nourish him. Similarly, the fact of being deeply interested in the knowledge of God's Word will not of itself nourish your soul. *"Your words were found"*—that happened first. *"And I ate them"*—that brought the joy and rejoicing.

## EATING EVERY DAY

What is this eating? The corn that the farmer had grown and rejoiced in as his very own could not nourish his life until he took it and ate it. He had to completely assimilate it, until it became part of himself, entering into his blood, forming his bones and flesh. This has to be done in a small quantity at a time, two or three times a day, every day of the year. This is the law of eating. Likewise, it is not the amount of truth I gather from God's Word. It is not the interest or success of my Bible study. It is not the increased insight or understanding I am obtaining that brings health and growth to my spiritual life. Rather, this often leaves me very unspiritual, with little of the holiness or humility of Christ Jesus. Something else is necessary in order for spiritual growth to take place.

Jesus said, *"My food is to do the will of Him who sent Me"* (John 4:34). We must take a small portion of God's Word, some definite command or duty of the new life, and quietly receive it into our wills and our hearts. We must yield our whole beings to its rule and vow to perform it in the power of the Lord Jesus. Then we must go and do it—this is eating the Word. We take it into our innermost beings until it becomes part of our very lives. The same process must take place with a truth or a promise. What you have eaten becomes part of yourself, and you carry it with you wherever you go as part of the life you live.

The two points of difference between the corn in the granary and the bread on the table can apply to your study of the Bible. The gathering of scriptural knowledge is one thing. The eating of God's Word, the receiving it into your very heart by the power of the life-giving Spirit, is something very different. The two laws of eating the food, in contrast to those of finding it, must always be obeyed. You can gather and store grain to last for years, but you cannot swallow a large enough quantity of bread to last for days. Day by day, and more than once a day, you take in your day's food. And so the eating of God's Word must be in small portions, only as much as the soul can receive and digest at one time. This must take place day by day, from one end of the year to the other.

It is such feeding on the Word that will enable you to say, *"And Your word was to me the joy and rejoicing of my heart."* George Müller said that he learned not to stop reading the Word each day until he felt happy in God. Then he felt prepared to go out and do his day's work.

chapter 24

# Holidays and Your Quiet Time

*If the master of the house had known what hour the thief*
*would come, he would have watched and not allowed*
*his house to be broken into.*
—Luke 12:39

How leisure time is spent is a very important question, since it greatly affects our characters. It has been said that "leisure hours are the hinge on which true education turns." It is true that developing a person's character is more important than training the mind and abilities. While a teacher can do much to stimulate and guide a student, every child has to work out his own character. It is in the leisure hours, when he is free from rules and observation, that a child shows what his true character is. This is the reason leisure time is considered all-important and all-powerful, the hinge on which true education turns. This statement can also be applied to Christianity.

## THE PROBLEM WITH VACATIONS

At Bible college or school, students will take time for their daily devotions as part of their regular routine. Their minds are geared for systematic work. They set aside time for devotions just as they do time for a class or private study.

When the time for vacation or a holiday comes and students are free to do exactly as they please, many find that the morning watch and fellowship with God interferes with their holiday pleasure. The holiday becomes the test of character, the proof of how one could say with Job, *"I have treasured the words of His mouth more than my necessary food"* (Job 23:12). The question of how we spend our leisure time is very important. It is then that we turn freely and naturally to what we love most.

A teacher in a large school in America is reported to have said, "The greatest difficulty with which we have to contend is the summer vacation. Just when we have brought a child to a good point of discipline, and he responds to the best ideals, we lose him. When he comes back in the autumn, we have to begin and do it all over. The summer holiday simply demoralizes him."

This statement, referring to ordinary study and duty, is strong. Within certain limits, it is applicable to the Christian life. The sudden relaxation of regular habits and the subtle thought that perfect freedom to do as one likes means perfect happiness cause many young students to backslide in their Christian walks. Older and more experienced Christians should help the younger ones to guard against this attitude. The attainment of months may be lost by the neglect of a week. We do not know what time the thief will come. The spirit of the morning watch means unceasing vigilance all day and every day.

## YOUR DAILY DUTY

During vacation time or holidays, the student is free from the rules under which he lives at school. But there are other laws—laws of morality and of health, from which there is no relaxation. The call to daily fellowship with God belongs not to the school rules but to the laws of duty. As much as we need every day during the holidays to eat and breathe, we need every day to eat the bread and breathe the air of heaven.

The morning watch, however, is not only a duty, but an unspeakable privilege and pleasure. Fellowship with God, abiding in Christ, loving the Word and meditating on it all day—these things are life and strength, health and gladness. Look upon them in this light. Believe in the power of the new nature within and act upon it. Although you do not feel the power, it will come true. Consider it a joy, and it will become a joy to you.

Above all, realize that the world needs you and depends on you to be its light. Christ is waiting for you as a member of His body, day by day, to do His saving work through you. Neither He, nor the world, nor you can afford to lose a single day. God has created and redeemed you so that through you He may, as through the sun He lightens the world, let His light, life, and love shine out upon men. You need every day anew to be in communication with the Fountain of all light.

Do not think of asking for a holiday from this communion with God. Cherish holidays for the special time they give you to study beyond your ordinary Bible study course. Cherish your holidays for the special opportunity of more fellowship with the Father and the Son. Instead of holidays becoming a snare, make them a blessed time for victory over self and the world, of increase in grace and strength, of being blessed and made a blessing.

chapter 25

# Your Inner Life

*Foolish ones! Did not He who made the outside*
*make the inside also?*
—Luke 11:40

E very spirit seeks to create for itself a form or shape in
which its life is embodied. The outward is the visible expression of the hidden, inward life. The outward is generally known before the inward. Through it the inward is devel-
oped and reaches its full perfection. The apostle Paul said,
*"However, the spiritual is not first, but the natural, and after-*
*ward the spiritual"* (1 Cor. 15:46). To understand and maintain
the right relationship between the inward and the outward is
one of the greatest secrets of the Christian life.

If Adam in the Garden had not listened to the Serpent, his
trial would have resulted in the perfecting of his inward life. The
cause of all his misery and sin came when he gave himself to the
power of the visible, outward world. Adam did not seek his happiness in the hidden, inward life of a heart in which God's command was honored. Instead, he fixed his desire on the world
around him, on the pleasure that the knowledge of good and evil
could give him.

## THE LIFE WITHIN

All false religion, from the most degrading idolatry to the
corruption of Judaism and Christianity, has its root in this desire. Deception takes place when the outward—that which
pleases the eye, interests the mind, or gratifies the taste—takes
the place of truth in the inward part, that hidden wisdom in the
heart that God gives.

The New Testament reveals the importance of the inner life. The promise of the new covenant is, *"I will put My law in their minds, and write it on their hearts"* (Jer. 31:33); *"I will give you a new heart and put a new spirit within you....I will put My Spirit within you"* (Ezek. 36:26–27). The promise of our Lord Jesus was, *"The Spirit of truth...will be in you....At that day you will know that I am...in you"* (John 14:17, 20).

Christianity is a matter of the heart—a heart into which God has sent forth the Spirit of His Son, a heart in which the love of God is poured out (Rom. 5:5) and true salvation is found. The inner chamber, with its secret communion with the Father *"who sees in secret"* (Matt. 6:4), is the symbol and the training school for the inner life. The faithful, daily use of the inner chamber will make the inner, hidden life strong.

In religion the great danger is giving more time and interest to outward experiences than to inward reality. It is not the intensity of your Bible study, or the frequency or the fervency of your prayers or good works that necessarily constitute a true spiritual life. What we need to realize is that God is a Spirit. There is also a spirit within us who can know and receive Him and become conformed to His likeness. We can be partakers of the very nature that characterizes Him as God in His goodness and love.

## YOUR HIDDEN TREASURE

Our salvation consists in the manifestation of the nature, life, and spirit of Christ Jesus in our outward and inward new man. This alone renews and regains the first life of God in the soul of man. Wherever you go, whatever you do, at home or at work, do all with a desire for union with Christ, in imitation of His character. Desire only what increases the spirit and life of Christ in your soul. Desire to have everything within you changed into the spirit of the holy Jesus.

Consider the treasure you have within you—the Savior of the world, the eternal Word of God. It is hidden in your heart as a seed of the divine nature, which overcomes sin and death within you and generates the life of heaven in your soul.

Look in your heart, and your heart will find its Savior, its God, within itself. If you see and feel nothing of God, it is because you seek Him in books, in the church, in outward religious exercises. You will not find Him there until you have first found Him in your heart. Seek Him in your heart, and you will never seek in vain, for He dwells there in His Holy Spirit!

# The Power for Daily Renewal

*Though our outward man is perishing, yet the inward man
is being renewed day by day.*
—2 Corinthians 4:16

*According to His mercy He saved us, through the washing of re-
generation and renewing of the Holy Spirit.*
—Titus 3:5

With every new day, the life of nature is renewed. As the
sun rises again with its light and warmth, the flowers
open, the birds sing, and life is everywhere stirred and
strengthened. As we rise from the rest of sleep and eat our
breakfast, we feel that we have gathered new strength for the
duties of the day.

Our inner life needs daily renewal, too. It is only by fresh
nourishment from God's Word and fresh communion with God
Himself in prayer, that the vigor of the spiritual life can be
maintained and grow. Our outward man may perish and the
strain of work may exhaust us, yet the inner man can be *"renewed day by day."*

## RENEWED BY THE SPIRIT

A quiet time and place with the Word and prayer are the
means for daily renewal. To be effective, these means must be
empowered by the Holy Spirit, the mighty power of God that
works in us. In the text verse from Titus, we are taught that we
have been *"saved...through the washing of regeneration and
renewing of the Holy Spirit."* These two expressions are not
meant to be a repetition. The regeneration is one great act, the

beginning of the Christian life. The renewing of the Holy Spirit is a work that is carried on continuously and never ends.

In Romans 12:2, we read that the progressive transformation of the Christian life comes by *"the renewing of your mind."* In Ephesians 4:22–23, while the words *"put off...the old man"* indicate an act done once for all, the words *"be renewed in the spirit of your mind"* are in the present tense and point to a progressive work. Even so in Colossians 3:10, we read, "[You] *have put on the new man who is renewed in knowledge according to the image of Him who created him."* We can count on the blessed Spirit for the daily renewal of the inner man in the inner chamber.

In our private devotions, everything depends upon our maintaining the true relationship to the adorable third person of the blessed Trinity. It is only through the Holy Spirit that the Father and the Son can do their work of saving love, and through whom the Christian can do his work. This relationship may be expressed in two very simple words, *faith* and *surrender*.

## FAITH AND SURRENDER

### • FAITH

Scripture says, *"God has sent forth the Spirit of His Son into your hearts, crying out, 'Abba, Father!'"* (Gal. 4:6). The child of God, who in his morning devotion offers up prayer pleasing to the Father, must remember that he has received the Holy Spirit as the spirit of prayer. The Spirit's help is necessary to enable us to pray effectively. (See Romans 8:26.)

This is also true with the Word of God. It is by the Holy Spirit alone that the truth in its divine meaning and power can be revealed to us and do its work in our hearts.

If the daily renewal of the inward man in the morning hour is to be a reality, take time to meditate, to worship, and to believe with your whole heart that the Holy Spirit has been given to you. Believe that He is within you and that through Him God will work the blessing that He gives through prayer and the Word.

473

### • SURRENDER

Do not forget that the Holy Spirit must have complete control. *"As many as are led by the Spirit of God, these are sons of God"* (Rom. 8:14). It is the ungrieved presence of the Spirit that can give the Word its light and keep us in the blessed life of childlike confidence and obedience that is pleasing to God. Let us praise God for this wonderful gift, the Holy Spirit in His renewing power. Let us look with new joy and hope to the inner chamber as the place where the inner man can indeed be renewed from day to day. Our lives will be kept fresh, and we will go on *"from strength to strength"* (Ps. 84:7) to bear much fruit, so that the Father may be glorified.

If all this is true, we need to know who the Holy Spirit is and what He does. As the third person of the Trinity, it is His work to bring the life of God to us, to hide Himself in the depth of our beings and make Himself one with us. He is to reveal the Father and the Son, to be the mighty power of God working in us, and to take control of our entire beings. He asks only one thing—simple obedience to His leading. The truly yielded soul will find in the daily renewing of the Holy Spirit the secret of growth, strength, and joy.

chapter 27

# Renewed in God's Image

*You...have put on the new man who is renewed in knowledge
according to the image of Him who created him.*
—Colossians 3:9–10

*If indeed you have heard Him and have been taught by Him,...
be renewed in the spirit of your mind, and...put on the new
man which was created according to God, in true
righteousness and holiness.*
—Ephesians 4:21, 23–24

In every pursuit it is essential to have the goal clearly defined.
It is not enough that there is movement and progress—we
need to know that the movement is headed in the right direction. When we are in partnership with another person, on whom
we are dependent, we need to know that our goals are the same.
If our daily renewal is to attain its objective, we need to know
clearly and hold firmly to what its purpose is.

*"You...have put on the new man who is renewed in knowl-
edge."* The divine life, the work of the Holy Spirit within us, is
no blind force. We are to be workers together with God (2 Cor.
6:1). Our cooperation is to be intelligent and voluntary. *"The
new man...is renewed in knowledge"* day by day. There is a
knowledge that the natural understanding can draw from the
Word, but it is without life and power. It has none of the real
truth and substance that spiritual knowledge brings. Only the
renewing power of the Holy Spirit gives true knowledge. This
involves an inward tasting, a living experience of the very things
of which the words are but the images. *"The new man...is renewed in knowledge."* However diligent our Bible study may be,
true knowledge is gained only as spiritual renewal is experienced. Renewal in the spirit of the mind, in its life and inward
being, can alone bring true divine knowledge.

## SPIRITUAL RENEWAL

What is the pattern that will be revealed to this spiritual knowledge that results from making renewal our only aim? *"The new man...is renewed in knowledge according to the image of Him who created him."* The image, the likeness of God, is the one aim of the Holy Spirit in His daily renewing. This must also be the aim of the believer who seeks that renewing.

This was God's purpose in creation, *"Let Us make man in Our image, according to Our likeness"* (Gen. 1:26). God breathed His own life into man in order to reproduce in man a perfect likeness to God. In Christ, that image of God has been revealed and seen in human form. We have been predestined and redeemed and called. We are being taught and equipped by the Holy Spirit to be *"conformed to the image of His Son"* (Rom. 8:29), to be *"imitators of God"* (Eph. 5:1), and to walk just as Christ walked (1 John 2:6). In order for daily renewal to take place and daily Bible study and prayer to be of value, we must set our hearts on what God has set His on. We must desire that the new man be renewed day by day *"according to the image of Him who created him."*

## RENEWED IN RIGHTEOUSNESS AND HOLINESS

In the passage from Ephesians, we have this same thought expressed somewhat differently: *"Be renewed in the spirit of your mind, and...put on the new man which was created according to God, in true righteousness and holiness."* Righteousness is God's hatred of sin and maintenance of what is right. Holiness is God's glory, in the perfect harmony of His righteousness and love, His infinite exaltation above the creature, His perfect union with him.

Righteousness in man includes all of God's will concerning our duty to Him and our fellowmen. Holiness involves our personal relationship to Him. Just as the new man has been created, so it has to be daily renewed *"according to God, in true righteousness and holiness."* The Holy Spirit is working in us to bring about this renewal. He waits for us day by day to yield ourselves to Him in His renewing grace and power.

The morning hour is the time for our daily renewing by the Holy Spirit into the image of God as righteousness and holiness. We need a time of meditation and prayer to get our hearts set upon God's purposes. We need a true vision of how the inward man can be renewed day by day into the very likeness of God, changed into the same image by the Spirit of the Lord. Let nothing less be your aim or satisfy your aspirations. The image of God, the life of God, is in you, and His likeness can be seen in you. Do not separate yourself from God and His likeness. Let all your trust in Him mean nothing less than finding His likeness formed in you by the renewing of the Holy Spirit.

Let this be your daily prayer—to be renewed according to the image of Him who created you.

# Renewed and Transformed

*Therefore we do not lose heart. Even though our outward man is perishing, yet the inward man is being renewed day by day.*
—2 Corinthians 4:16

*And do not be conformed to this world, but be transformed by the renewing of your mind.*
—Romans 12:2

It is not an easy thing to be a mature, strong Christian. It cost the Son of God His life. It is God's part to create a new man in every believer and to maintain that life with the unceasing daily care of the Holy Spirit.

When the new man is put on, it is our responsibility to see that the old man is put off. All the attitudes, habits, and pleasures of our own nature, which make up the life in which we have lived, are to be put away. All we have acquired by our natural birth from Adam is to be sold, if we are to possess the *"pearl of great price"* (Matt. 13:46). If a man is to come after Christ, he must deny himself and take up his cross (Matt. 16:24). He must forsake all and follow Christ in the path in which He walked. The Christian must cast away not only all sin, but everything, however legitimate and precious, that may cause him to sin. He is to hate his own life, to lose it, if he is to live in the power of eternal life. It is a serious thing, far more serious than most people think, to be a true Christian.

## RENEWING YOUR MIND

Paul spoke of the renewing of the inward man as being accompanied by the perishing of the outward man. The whole epistle of Second Corinthians shows us how the fellowship of the sufferings of Christ, even in conformity to His death (see Philippians 3:10), was the secret of Paul's life of power and blessing to the churches.

> *Always carrying about in the body the dying of the Lord Jesus, that the life of Jesus also may be manifested in our body. For we who live are always delivered to death for Jesus' sake, that the life of Jesus also may be manifested in our mortal flesh. So then death is working in us, but life in you.*
>
> (2 Cor. 4:10–12)

The full experience of the life of Christ in our persons, our bodies, and our work for others depends on our fellowship in His suffering and death. There can be no large measure of the renewal of the inward man without the sacrifice, the perishing of the outward man.

To be filled with heaven, the life must be emptied of earth. We have the same truth in our second text, *"Be transformed by the renewing of your mind."* An old house may be renewed and yet keep very much of its old appearance. Or the renewal may be so complete that people exclaim, "What a transformation!" The renewing of the mind by the Holy Spirit means an entire transformation, an entirely different way of thinking, judging, deciding. The fleshly mind gives place to a "spiritual understanding." (See Colossians 1:9 and 1 John 5:20.) This transformation is obtained only at the cost of giving up all that is of the old nature. *"Do not be conformed to this world, but be transformed."*

By nature we are of this world. When we are renewed by grace, we are still in the world, subject to its subtle influence from which we cannot escape. The world is still in us, as the leaven of the nature that nothing can purge except the mighty power of the Holy Spirit, who fills us with the life of heaven.

## BEING TRANSFORMED

Let us allow these truths to take hold of and master us. The divine transformation, by the daily renewing of our minds into His image, can proceed in us only as we seek to be freed from every conformity to this world. The negative, *"Do not be conformed to this world,"* needs to be emphasized as strongly as the positive, *"Be transformed."* The spirit of this world and the Spirit of God contend for the possession of our beings.

Only as the spirit of this world is recognized, renounced, and cast out can the heavenly Spirit enter in. Then the Holy Spirit can do His blessed work of renewing and transforming. The world and whatever is of the worldly spirit must be given up. Our lives and whatever is of self must be lost. This daily renewal of the inward man is very costly if we are trying to do it in our own strength. When we really learn that the Holy Spirit does everything, and by faith give up the struggle, the renewing becomes the simple, natural, healthy, joyful growth of the heavenly life in us.

The inner chamber then becomes the place we long for every day, in order to praise God for what He has done, is doing, and what we know He will do. Day by day, we yield ourselves afresh to the blessed Lord who has said, *"He who believes in Me,...out of his heart will flow rivers of living water"* (John 7:38). The renewing of ourselves by the Holy Spirit becomes one of the most blessed truths of the daily Christian life.

chapter 29

# To Be Made Holy

*Sanctify them by Your truth. Your word is truth.*
—John 17:17

I n His great intercessory prayer, our Lord spoke of the words that the Father had given Him, of giving them Himself to His disciples, and of their having received and believed them. It was this that made them disciples. It was their keeping these words that would really enable them to live the life and do the work of true disciples. Receiving the words of God from Christ and keeping them are the signs and power of true discipleship.

When praying to the Father, our Lord asked that He sanctify the disciples in the truth, as it dwells and works in His Word. Christ has said of Himself, *"I am...the truth"* (John 14:6). He is *"the only begotten of the Father, full of grace and truth"* (John 1:14). His teaching was not like that of the law that came by Moses. Jesus' words were more than a promise of good things to come. He proclaimed, *"The words that I speak to you are spirit, and they are life"* (John 6:63). Christ had spoken of the Spirit of truth who would lead the disciples into all the truth in Himself (John 16:13), not as a matter of knowledge or doctrine, but into the actual experience and enjoyment of truth.

He prayed that in this living truth the Father would sanctify them. He said, *"For their sakes I sanctify Myself, that they also may be sanctified by the truth"* (John 17:19). He asked the Father in His power and love to take charge of them, so that His objective—to sanctify them in the truth, through His Word that is truth—might be realized. His desire was that they, like Himself, might be sanctified in truth. Let us study the wonderful lessons given in this verse in regard to God's Word.

481

## THE WORD AS THE MEANS OF HOLINESS

*"Sanctify them by Your truth. Your word is truth."* The great objective of God's Word is to make us holy. No diligence or success in Bible study will really profit us unless it makes us humbler and holier. In our use of Holy Scripture, this must be our main objective. The reason there is often so much Bible reading with so little real result in a Christlike character is that *"salvation through sanctification by the Spirit and belief in the truth"* (2 Thess. 2:13) is not truly desired.

People imagine that if they study the Word and accept its truths, this will in some way benefit them. But experience teaches that it does not. The fruit of holy character, of a consecrated life, of power to bless others, does not come for the simple reason that we only get what we seek. Christ gave us God's Word to make us holy. When we make this our definite aim in all Bible study, the truth—not the doctrinal truth, but its divine quickening power—can impart the very life of God to us.

*"Sanctify them by Your truth. Your word is truth."* It is God Himself who alone can make us holy by His Word. The Word, apart from God and His direct operation, cannot accomplish anything in us. The Word is an instrument; God Himself must use it. God is the only Holy One. He alone can make holy. The unspeakable value of God's Word is that it is God's means of holiness. The terrible mistake of many people is that they forget that God alone can use it and make it effective.

It is not enough that I have access to the office of a physician. I need for him to prescribe a cure. Without him my use of his medicines could be fatal. This was true of the scribes and Pharisees of Jesus' day. They made their boast in God's law. They delighted in their study of Scripture and yet remained unsanctified. The Word did not sanctify them, because they did not seek this in the Word and did not yield to God to do it for them.

## GOD MAKES HOLY

*"Sanctify them by Your truth. Your word is truth."* This holiness through the Word must be sought and waited for from God in prayer. Our Lord taught His disciples that they must be

holy. He sanctified Himself for them, so that they might be sanctified in truth. He also brought His words and His work to the Father with the prayer that He would sanctify them. It is necessary to know God's Word and meditate on it. It is necessary to set our hearts upon being holy and to make this our primary objective in studying the Word. But all this is not enough. Everything depends upon our asking the Father to sanctify us through the Word. It is God, the holy Father, who makes us holy by the Spirit of holiness who dwells within us. He works in us the very mind and attitudes of Christ who is our sanctification.

*"No one is holy like the LORD"* (1 Sam. 2:2). All holiness is His, and He makes things holy by His holy presence. The tabernacle and temple were not holy by cleansing, separation, or consecration. They became holy by the incoming and indwelling God. His taking possession made them holy. God makes us holy through His Word bringing Christ and the Holy Spirit into us. The Father can do this only as we wait before Him and in deep dependence and full surrender give ourselves to Him. When we pray by faith, "Sanctify me through Your truth. Your Word is truth," our knowledge of God's Word will truly make us holy.

The morning watch is a sacred time. It is the time especially devoted to the yielding of ourselves to God's holiness, to be sanctified through the Word. Let us remember, the one aim of God's Word is to make us holy. Let this be our continual prayer, "Father, sanctify me through Your truth."

chapter 30

# Teachings from Psalm 119

*Oh, how I love Your law! It is my meditation all the day....*
*Consider how I love Your precepts....I love them exceedingly.*
—Psalm 119:97, 159, 167

There is one portion of Holy Scripture devoted to teaching us the place that God's Word should have in our lives. It is the longest chapter in the Bible, and in almost every one of its 176 verses the Word is mentioned, using different names. Anyone who really wants to know how to study his Bible according to God's will should make a careful study of this psalm.

There should come a time in your life when you resolve to study its teaching and practice it. It is no wonder that our Bible study does not bring us more spiritual profit and strength, if we neglect the divine directory given to us in this psalm. It is possible you have never read it once through as a whole. Take time to read it through and understand its main ideas. If you find it difficult to do this by reading it once, read it more than once. This approach will make you feel the need to give it more careful thought.

## STUDYING PSALM 119

The following hints may help you in studying this psalm.

Take note of all the different names that refer to God's Word. Then take note of all the different verbs expressing how we should feel and what we should do in regard to the Word. Let these observations lead you to consider carefully the place God's Word claims in your heart and life. Consider how every faculty of your being—desire, love, joy, trust, obedience, and action—is summoned by God's Word.

Count how many times the writer speaks in the past tense of his having kept, observed, and delighted in God's testimonies. Notice how many times he expresses in the present tense how he rejoices in, loves, and esteems God's law. Consider how, in the future tense, he promises and vows to observe God's precepts to the end. Put all these together and see how more than a hundred times he presents himself before God as one who honors and keeps His law. Study this, especially as these expressions are connected with his prayers to God, until you have a clear image of the *"righteous man"* whose *"effective, fervent prayer...avails much"* (James 5:17).

Study the prayers themselves, and note the different requests he makes with regard to the Word. The psalmist asks for understanding and the power to observe it. He prays to receive the blessing promised in the Word and to be found actually doing it. Note especially prayers like *"Teach me Your statutes"* (Ps. 119:12, for example) and *"Give me understanding"* (v. 33, for example). Also study those where the plea is *"according to Your word"* (v. 25, for example).

Count the verses in which there is any reference to affliction from his own sinful condition, from his enemies, or from the sins of the wicked. Note the times he believes God is delaying to help him. Learn how it is in the time of trouble that we need God's Word especially and that this alone can bring comfort to us.

## THE WORD AND FELLOWSHIP WITH GOD

Notice how the whole psalm is a prayer spoken to God. All the psalmist has to say about the Word of God, with regard to his own attachment to it and his need for God's teaching, is spoken to the face of God. He believes that it is pleasing to God and good for his own soul to connect his meditation on the Word by prayer with the living God Himself. Every thought of God's Word, instead of drawing him away from God, leads him to fellowship with God.

The Word of God becomes to him the rich and inexhaustible material for having communion with God. As we gradually gain insights into these truths, we will discover new meaning from

485

the individual verses. When we take a whole paragraph with its eight verses, we will find how they help to lift us into God's presence. We will be lifted into the life of obedience and joy that says, *"I have sworn and confirmed that I will keep Your righteous judgments"* (v. 106). *"Oh, how I love Your law! It is my meditation all the day."*

Let us seek by the grace of the Holy Spirit to have the kind of devotional life that this psalm reveals. Let God's Word every day, and before everything else, lead us to God. Let every blessing in it be a matter of prayer, especially regarding our need for divine teaching. Let our intense attachment to it be our childlike plea and confidence that the Father will help us. Let our prayers be followed by the vow that, as God revives and blesses us, we will obey His commandments. Let all that God's Word brings to us make us more earnest in longing to carry that Word to others.

# The Trinity and You

*For this reason I bow my knees to the Father of our Lord Jesus
Christ,...that He would grant you, according to the riches
of His glory, to be strengthened with might through His Spirit
in the inner man, that Christ may dwell in your hearts
through faith; that you, being rooted and grounded in love,
may be able...to know the love of Christ which passes knowledge;
that you may be filled with all the fullness of God.
Now to Him who is able to do exceedingly abundantly above all
that we ask or think, according to the power that works in us
[the Holy Spirit], to Him be glory in the church by Christ Jesus
to all generations, forever and ever. Amen.*
—Ephesians 3:14, 16–21

These words have often been regarded as one of the highest expressions of what the life of a believer may be on earth. Yet this view is not without its dangers, if it fosters the idea that the attainment of such an experience is something exceptional and distant. Rather, this truth is meant to be the certain and immediate inheritance of every child of God.

Every morning each believer has the right to say, "My Father will strengthen me today with power, is strengthening me even now in the inner man through His Spirit." Each day we are to be content with nothing less than the indwelling of Christ by faith, a life rooted in love, and made strong to know the love of Christ. Each day we must believe that the blessed work of being filled with all the fullness of God is being accomplished in us. Each day we must be strong in the faith of God's power and be giving Him glory in Christ. We must believe He is able to do above what we ask and think, according to the power of the Spirit working in us.

### THE TRINITY IN DAILY LIFE

The text from Ephesians presents the truth of the Holy Trinity in relation to practical life. Many Christians understand that it is necessary at different times in the Christian life to give special attention to the three persons of the blessed Trinity. They often feel it difficult to combine the various truths into one and to know how to worship the Three in one. Our text reveals this wonderful relationship and the perfect unity.

We have the Spirit within us as the power of God, and yet He does not work according to our wills or His own. It is the Father who grants us to be strengthened *"through His Spirit in the inner man."* It is the Father who does *"exceedingly abundantly above all that we ask or think, according to the power that works in us."* The Spirit within us makes us more dependent on the Father. The Spirit can only work as the Father works through Him. We need to combine trusting awareness of the Holy Spirit indwelling us with a dependent waiting on the Father to work through Him.

This combined work is also necessary in our relationship with Christ. We bow our knees to God as Father in the name of the Son. We ask Him to strengthen us through the Spirit so that Christ may dwell in our hearts. The Son leads to the Father, and the Father again reveals the Son in us. Then, as the Son dwells in the heart and we are *"rooted and grounded in love,"* we are led on to be *"filled with all the fullness of God."* Our hearts become the scene of the interchange of the operation of the Holy Three. As our hearts believe this, we give glory through Christ to Him who is able to do more than we can think by His Holy Spirit.

Our hearts become the scene of a wonderful performance: the Father breathing His Spirit into us and making our hearts the home of Christ; the Holy Spirit revealing and forming Christ within us, so that His very nature and character become ours; the Son imparting His life of love and leading us on to be filled with all the fullness of God.

Let us worship the three-in-one God in the fullness of faith every day. In whatever direction our Bible study and our prayer lead us, let this ever be the center from which we go out and to which we return. We were created in the image of the three-in-one God. The salvation by which God restores us is an inward salvation of our hearts. The God who saves us can do it in no other way than as the indwelling God, filling us with all His fullness. Let us worship and wait. Let us believe and give Him glory.

## THE TRINITY IN EPHESIANS

Have you ever noticed in Ephesians how the three persons of the Trinity are always mentioned together?

*Father...Jesus Christ...every spiritual* [Holy Spirit] *blessing* (Eph. 1:3).

*Our Lord Jesus...the Father...the spirit of wisdom* (v. 17).

*For through Him* [Christ] *we...have access by one Spirit to the Father* (Eph. 2:18).

*In whom* [Christ] *you also are being built together for a dwelling place of God in the Spirit* (v. 22).

*The mystery of Christ...revealed by the Spirit...*[preached by] *the grace of God...hidden in God* (Eph. 3:4–5, 7, 9).

*One Spirit...one Lord...one God and Father* (Eph. 4:4–6).

*Filled with the Spirit...giving thanks...to God...in the name of our Lord Jesus Christ* (Eph. 5:18, 20).

*Strong in the Lord...the whole armor of God...the sword of the Spirit...praying...in the Spirit* (Eph. 6:10–11, 17–18).

As you study and compare these passages, notice especially how practical this truth of the Holy Trinity is. Scripture teaches us little about its mystery in the divine nature, but refers only to God's work in us and our faith and experience of His salvation.

True faith in the Trinity will make us strong, alert, God-possessed Christians. The divine Spirit will make Himself one with our lives and inner beings. The blessed Son will dwell in us, as the way to perfect fellowship with God. The Father, through the Spirit and the Son, will work His purpose so that we are filled with all the fullness of God.

Let us bow our knees to the Father! Then the mystery of the Trinity will be known and experienced.

chapter 32

# Abiding in Christ

*Abide in Me, and I in you.*
*—John 15:4*

W hen some knowledge has been obtained in words or deeds, in nature or history, the mind is prepared to seek the inner meaning hidden in them. This is true with the teaching of Scripture concerning Jesus Christ. He is set before us as a man among us, before us, above us, doing a work for us here on earth and continuing that work for us in heaven. Many Christians never advance beyond an external exalted Lord, in whom they trust for what He has done and is doing for them and in them. They know and enjoy little of the power of the true mystery of Christ in us, of His inward presence, as an indwelling Savior.

The former and simpler view is that of the first three Gospels. The more advanced view is found in the Gospel of John. The former is the aspect of truth presented in the doctrine of justification. The latter is the teaching concerning the union of the believer with Christ and his continual abiding as taught in John and the epistles to the Ephesians and Colossians.

## A MATTER OF EXPERIENCE

This abiding in Christ and Christ in you must be more than a truth you hold in its right place in your scheme of gospel doctrine. It must be a matter of experience that inspires your faith in Christ and relationship with God. To be in a room means to have all that there is in it at your disposal—its furniture, its comforts, its light, its air, its shelter. To be in Christ, to abide in Christ, is not a matter of intellectual faith, but a spiritual reality.

Think who and what Christ is. Consider Him in the five stages that reveal His nature and work. First, He is the Incarnate One, in whom we see God's omnipotence united perfectly in the divine and human nature. Living in Him, we are partaking of the divine nature and of eternal life. Second, He is the Obedient One, living a life of entire surrender to God and perfect dependence on Him. Living in Him, our lives become ones of complete subjection to God's will and continual waiting upon His guidance. Third, He is the Crucified One, who died for sin and to sin so that He might take it away. Living in Him, we are free from its curse and dominion. We live, like Him, in death to the world and our own wills. Fourth, He is the Risen One, who lives forever. Living in Him, we share His resurrection power and *"walk in newness of life"* (Rom. 6:4), a life that has triumphed over sin and death. Finally, He is the Exalted One, sitting on the throne and carrying on His work for the salvation of men. Because we live in Him, His love possesses us, and we give ourselves to Him to be used in winning the world back to God.

Being in Christ, abiding in Him, means the soul is placed by God Himself in the midst of this wonderful environment of the life of Christ. We are given up to God in obedience and sacrifice, filled with God in resurrection life and glory. The nature and character of Jesus Christ—His attitudes and inclinations, His power and glory—these are the elements in which we live, the air we breathe, the life in which our lives exist and grow.

## THE INDWELLING CHRIST

The full manifestations of God and His saving love can come in no other way than by indwelling. In virtue of Christ's divinity and divine power, He can, as we abide in Him, dwell in us. To the degree our hearts are given to Him in faith and our wills are given in active obedience, He comes in and abides in us. We can say, because we know, *"Christ lives in me"* (Gal. 2:20).

If we are to actually live with Christ in us and we in Him, then we must be renewed and strengthened in our personal relationships with God in the morning watch. Our access to God, our sacrifice to God, our expectation from God must all be in Christ, in living fellowship with Him. If you feel that you want to get nearer to God, to realize His presence or power more fully, come to God in Christ. Think how Jesus, a man on earth, drew near to the Father in deep humility and dependence, in full surrender and entire obedience. We must come in His spirit and character, in union with Jesus.

Seek to take the very place before God that Christ has taken in heaven, that of an accomplished redemption, of a perfect victory, of full entrance to God's glory. Take the very place before God that Christ took on earth on His way to the victory and the glory. Do it by faith in His indwelling and enabling power in you here on earth. Expect your approach to God to be accepted, not according to your attainment, but according to your heart's surrender and your acceptance in Christ. Then you will be led on in the path in which Christ, living in you and speaking in you, will be truth and power.

chapter 33

# The Joy of Being Alone

*Therefore when Jesus perceived that they were about to come and take Him by force to make Him king, He departed again to the mountain by Himself alone.*
—John 6:15

T he Gospels frequently tell us of Christ's going into solitude for prayer. Luke mentioned Christ's praying eleven times. Mark told us in his very first chapter that, after a busy evening of healing many people, *"in the morning, having risen a long while before daylight, He went out and departed to a solitary place; and there He prayed"* (Mark 1:35). Before He chose His twelve apostles, *"He went out to the mountain to pray, and continued all night in prayer to God"* (Luke 6:12). This thought of complete retreat from others appears to have deeply impressed the disciples. John used the significant expression, *"He departed again to the mountain by Himself alone."* Matthew also wrote, *"He went up on the mountain by Himself to pray. Now when evening came, He was alone there"* (Matt. 14:23). The Man Christ Jesus felt the need for perfect solitude. Let us humbly seek to find out what this means.

## "BY HIMSELF ALONE"

Jesus went entirely by Himself. Relationships with people can draw us away from ourselves and exhaust our energies. The Man Christ Jesus knew this and felt the need to be apart by Himself. He needed to renew the consciousness of who He was and to realize His high destiny, His human weakness, His entire dependence on the Father.

How much more the child of God needs to be apart by himself! It may be for the maintenance of our own Christian lives, or the renewal of our power to influence men for God, but whatever the reason there is an urgent call to every believer to follow in the Master's steps. We must find the place and the time where we can indeed be alone with God.

## ALONE WITH SPIRITUAL REALITIES

When we withdraw completely from contact with temporal things, we are free to yield ourselves to the powers of the unseen world. Jesus needed quiet time to realize the power of the kingdom of darkness with which He had come to contend and to conquer. He needed a fresh awareness of the needs of this great world of mankind that He had come to save. He needed to be reminded of the presence and the power of the Father whose will He had come to do.

It is essential for a person in Christian service to set himself apart to think intensely on the spiritual realities with which he is so familiar, yet which often exercise so little power on his heart and life. The truths of eternity have an infinite power. They are often powerless because we do not give them time to reveal themselves. Taking time to be alone with God is the only remedy.

## ALONE WITH THE FATHER

It is sometimes said that work is worship, that service is fellowship. If ever there were a man who could dispense with special seasons for solitude and fellowship, it was our blessed Lord. But He could not do His work or maintain His fellowship in full power without His quiet time. As a man He felt the need to bring all His work, past and future, and present it before the Father. He needed to renew His sense of absolute dependence on the Father's power and His absolute confidence in the Father's love in seasons of special fellowship. When He said, *"The Son can do nothing of Himself"* (John 5:19), and *"As I hear, I judge"* (v. 30), He was only expressing the simple truth of His relationship to God. It was this relationship that made His going apart a necessity and an unspeakable joy.

Every servant of His should understand and practice this blessed art of being apart with God. The church should train its children to exercise this high and holy privilege. Every believer may and must have a time when he is alone with God. It is a blessed experience to have God all alone to myself and to know that God has me all alone to Himself.

## ALONE WITH THE WORD AND PRAYER

Jesus had to learn God's Word as a child. During the long years of His life in Nazareth, He fed on that Word and made it His own. In His solitude He conferred with the Father on all that the Word spoke about Him, on all the will of God it revealed for Him to do.

One of the deepest lessons a Christian has to learn is that the Word without the living God is of little value. The blessing of the Word comes when it brings us to the living God. The Word that we get from the mouth of God brings the power to know it and to do it. Let us learn this lesson: personal fellowship with God alone in secret can make the Word alive and powerful.

Prayer allows a person to lay open his whole life to God and to ask for His teaching and His strength. Just try for a moment to think what prayer meant to Jesus—what adoring worship, what humble love, what childlike pleading for all He needed. This must make us realize the joy that awaits the person who knows to follow in Christ's steps. God can do great things through the one who makes being alone with God his chief joy in life.

*"Himself alone"*—these words reveal to us the secret of the life of Christ on earth and of the life that He now lives in us. One of the most blessed elements of life in the Holy Spirit is that He reveals and imparts to us all that it means to be *"Himself alone."*

# The Power of Intercession

*Please tell me where your great strength lies.*
—Judges 16:6

This is the question we would like to ask the men who, as intercessors for others, have had power with God and have prevailed. More than one Christian who has desired to give himself to this ministry has wondered why he has found it so difficult to rejoice in it, to persevere, and to prevail. Let us study the lives of the leaders and heroes of the prayer world. Maybe some of the elements of their success will be revealed to us.

The true intercessor is a person who knows that his heart and life are wholly given up to God and His glory. This is the only condition on which an officer at the court of an earthly king could expect to exert much influence. Moses, Elijah, Daniel, and Paul proved that this is true in the spiritual world. Our blessed Lord is Himself the proof of it. He did not save us by intercession, but by self-sacrifice. His power of intercession has its roots in His sacrifice; it claims and receives what the sacrifice won.

*"He poured out His soul unto death, and He was numbered with the transgressors, and He bore the sin of many, and made intercession for the transgressors"* (Isa. 53:12). He first gave Himself up to the will of God. There He won the power to influence and guide that will. Because He gave Himself for sinners in all-consuming love, He won the power to intercede for them.

## YOU CAN INTERCEDE

The Christian who seeks to enter personally into death with Christ and gives himself for God and others will dare to be bold like Moses and Elijah, will persevere like Daniel or Paul. Whole hearted devotion and obedience to God are the characteristics o an intercessor.

You complain that you are not able to pray like a true intercessor and ask how you can be equipped to do so. You talk about the weakness of your faith in God, your lack of love for souls, and your lack of delight in prayer. The one who is to have power in intercession must stop these complaints. He must confess that he has a nature perfectly adapted to the work God has called him to do. The eye was created to see, and it is beautifully equipped for its work. An apple tree is only expected to bear apples, because it has the apple nature within it. You are *"His workmanship, created in Christ Jesus for good works"* (Eph. 2:10).

You are created in Christ to pray. It is your very nature as a child of God. Why do you think the Spirit has been sent into your heart? To cry *"Abba, Father"* (Gal. 4:6), to draw your heart up in childlike prayer. The Holy Spirit prays in us with *"groanings which cannot be uttered"* (Rom. 8:26), with a divine power that our minds and feelings cannot understand. If you want to be an intercessor, give the Holy Spirit much greater honor than He usually receives. Believe that He is praying within you, and then *"be strong and of good courage"* (Deut 31:6). As you pray, be still before God, and believe and yield to this wonderful power of prayer within you.

## POWER TO INTERCEDE

You have learned to pray in the name of Christ. This name means living power. You are in Christ, and He is in you. Your whole life is hidden and united with His, and His whole life is hidden and working in you. The Christian who is to intercede in power must clearly understand that he and Christ are one in the work of intercession. He appears before God clothed with the name and the nature, the righteousness and worthiness, the image, spirit, and life of Christ.

Do not spend your time in prayer repeating your petition, but humbly and confidently claim your place in Christ, your perfect union with Him, your access to God in Him. The believer

to God in Christ as his life and trust will have power
...

ession is primarily a work of faith. It requires faith
...ves that the prayer will be heard, as well as faith that
...table with heavenly realities. We must have faith that
... worry about our own unworthiness, because we are
... Christ. Intercession requires faith that does not depend
... feelings, but on the faithfulness of God. We need faith
...s overcome the world and sacrifices the visible so that the
...al may take possession of it. Our faith must know that it
...rd and receives what it asks, and therefore quietly perse-
... in its supplication until the answer comes. The true inter-
...r must be a person of faith.

## PRAYER AND WORK

The intercessor must be a messenger. He must be prepared
/ offer himself personally to receive the answer and to dispense
;. Praying and working go together. Think of Moses—his bold-
1ess in pleading with God for the people was no greater than his
pleading with the people for God. We see the same in Elijah—
the urgency of his prayer in secret is equaled by his jealousy for
God in public, as he witnessed against the sin of the nation. Let
intercession always be accompanied by humbly waiting on God
to receive His grace and to know more definitely what and how
He wants us to work. It is a great thing to begin the work of intercession—the drawing down to earth of the blessings that
heaven provides for every need. It is a greater thing as an intercessor to receive that blessing personally and go out from God's
face knowing that we have secured something that we can impart to someone else. May God make us all wholehearted, believing intercessors who are prepared to bless others.

chapter 35

# The True Intercessor

*The effective, fervent prayer of a righteous man avails much. Elijah was a man with a nature like ours.*
—James 5:16–17

We sometimes see the characters in the Bible as exceptional cases and think that what we see in them is not to be expected of us. The aim of God in Scripture is the very opposite. He gives us these men for our instruction and encouragement, as an example of what His grace can do. They are living testimonies to what His will and human nature at once demand and make possible.

To give confidence to all of us who aim at a life of effective prayer, James wrote, *"Elijah was a man with a nature like ours."* There was no difference between his nature and ours, or between the grace that worked in him and that works in us. There is no reason why we should not, like him, pray effectively. If our prayer is to have power, we must seek to have Elijah's spirit. The desire to pray like Elijah is perfectly legitimate and very necessary. If we honestly seek the secret of his power in prayer, we must study his life. We will find it in his life with God, his work for God, and his trust in God.

## ELIJAH'S PRAYERS

Prayer is the voice of our lives. As a man lives, so he prays. It is not the words or thoughts with which he is occupied at set times of prayer, but the condition of his heart as seen in his desires and actions, that is regarded by God as his real prayer. The life speaks louder and truer than the lips. To pray well I must live well. He who seeks to live with God will learn to know His mind and to please Him, so that he will be able to pray according to His will.

Elijah, in his first message to Ahab, spoke of *"the LORD God...before whom I stand"* (1 Kings 17:1). Think of his solitude at the brook Chrith, receiving his bread from God by the ravens, and then at Zarephath through the ministry to a poor widow. He walked with God; he learned to know God well. When the time came, he knew how to pray to a God whom he had proved to be faithful. It is only out of a life of true fellowship with God that the prayer of faith can be born. Let the link between life and prayer be clear and close. As we give ourselves to walk with God we will learn to pray.

Elijah went where God sent him. He did what God commanded him. He stood up for God and His service. He witnessed against the people and their sin. All who heard him could say, *"Now by this I know that you are a man of God, and that the word of the LORD in your mouth is the truth"* (1 Kings 17:24). His prayers were all in connection with his work for God. He was equally a man of action and a man of prayer. He prayed, and the drought came and then the rain. This was part of his prophetic work, so that the people, by judgment and mercy, might be brought back to God. When Elijah prayed down fire from heaven on the sacrifice, it was so that God might be known as the true God. All of his prayers were for the glory of God.

Believers often seek power in prayer so that they will be able to get good gifts for themselves. This secret selfishness robs them of the power and the answer. Only when self is lost in the desire for God's glory and our lives are devoted to work for God, can power to pray come. God lives to love, save, and bless men. The believer who gives himself up to God's service will find new life in prayer. Work for others proves the honesty of our prayer for them. Work for God reveals our need and our right to pray boldly. Say to God that you are completely given up to His service. This will strengthen your confidence in His hearing you.

## ELIJAH TRUSTED GOD

Elijah had learned to trust God for his personal needs during the famine, and he dared trust Him for greater things in answer to prayer for His people. Elijah had confidence that God would hear him when he made his appeal to the God who answers by fire. He had confidence that God would do what he would ask. He announced to Ahab that rain was coming and then, with his face to the earth, pleaded for it, while his servant, six times over, brought the message, *"There is nothing"* (1 Kings 18:43). Elijah's unwavering confidence in the promise and character of God, and God's personal friendship, gave him power for *"the effective, fervent prayer of a righteous man."*

The inner chamber is the place where this lesson has to be learned. The morning watch is the training school where we are to exercise the grace that can equip us to pray like Elijah. The God of Elijah still lives. The Spirit that was in him dwells in us. Let us cease our limited and selfish views of prayer, which only aim at enough grace to keep us standing. Let us cultivate the same awareness that Elijah had of living completely for God, and we will learn to pray as he did. Prayer will bring to us and to others the blessed experience that our prayers are effective and of great value.

In the power of our Savior, who ever lives to intercede (Heb. 7:25), let us have courage and not fear. We have given ourselves to God; we are working for Him. We are learning to know and trust Him. We can count on the life of God and the Holy Spirit dwelling in us to make us righteous men whose effective prayers avail much.

# Book Seven

## The Blessings of Obedience

# Preface

This book is presented with the fervent prayer that it will please our gracious Father to use it for the instruction and strengthening of the young men and women on whom the church and the world depend. May the God of all grace bless them abundantly!

It often happens after a conference, or even after writing a book, that it is as if one only then begins to realize the meaning and importance of the truth with which one has been occupied. I feel as if I had utterly failed in relating the spiritual character, indispensable necessity, divine and actual possibility, and the inconceivable blessings of entire obedience to our Father in heaven. Let me, therefore, summarize the main points that strike me with special power and ask every reader to note them as some of the chief lessons to be learned while growing in Christ's obedience.

Our Father in heaven expects every child of His to yield to Him wholehearted obedience. To enable His child to do this, He has made an abundant and sufficient provision in the promise of the new covenant and in the gift of His Son and Spirit. The Christian soul can enjoy God's provision and see promises fulfilled as His presence works daily in the believer.

The very entrance into this life demands the vow of absolute obedience. The new Christian agrees to surrender his whole being to be, think, speak, and do nothing but what is according to the will of God. Since these things are true, it is not enough that we agree with them. We need the Holy Spirit to give us such a vision of their glory and divine power that we will not rest until we accept everything God is willing to do for us.

Pray that God will, by the light of His Spirit, show us His loving and almighty will concerning us. Let us pray that it will be impossible for us to be disobedient to the heavenly vision.

ANDREW MURRAY

chapter 1

# Obedience: Its Place in Scripture

When studying the Bible or any Christian truth, it is always helpful to note how and when your topic occurs throughout Scripture. As you learn its place in God's pattern of Scripture, you will understand its significance in God's entire message. To prepare you to study obedience, let's look at various passages that reveal the mind of God concerning it.

*"And the LORD God commanded the man"* (Gen. 2:16). And later He said, *"Have you eaten from the tree of which I commanded you that you should not eat?"* (Gen. 3:11).

Obedience to God's command, which was the virtue of Paradise, included every good behavior God desires in His kingdom. It was the one condition of man's living there, the one thing his Creator asked of him.

Adam and Eve disobeyed God by eating fruit from the Tree of Knowledge. Immediately they understood the difference between good and evil.

They knew their sin would anger God, so they hid themselves. Yet God knew they had disobeyed Him. He could not tolerate disobedience in Paradise; *"the LORD God sent him out of the garden....He drove out the man"* (Gen. 3:23–24). God said nothing directly about faith, humility, or love because obedience includes all of these things. God's demand for obedience is as supreme as His authority. Obedience is the one thing necessary in man's life.

## RESTORING OUR OBEDIENCE

God carries the theme of obedience throughout His Word. In Revelation 22:14, He says, *"Blessed are those who do His commandments, that they may have the right to the tree of life."*

From beginning to end, from Paradise lost to paradise regained, God's law is unchangeable. Only obedience gives man access to the Tree of Life and God's favor.

You may ask how man gained access to the Tree of Life when his original disobedience closed the way. Romans 5:19 describes the work done through the Cross of Christ: *"For as by one man's disobedience many were made sinners, so also by one Man's obedience many will be made righteous."* (See also Philippians 2:8–9 and Hebrews 5:8–9.) The whole redemption of Christ consists of restoring obedience to its place. The beauty of His salvation is that He brings us back to the life of obedience, through which the creature can give the Creator the glory due Him. It is in this way that the creature can also receive the glory his Creator desires to give him.

Paradise, Calvary, and heaven all proclaim with one voice, "Child of God, the first and the last thing your God asks of you is simple, universal, unchanging obedience."

## OLD TESTAMENT OBEDIENCE

In the Old Testament, obedience always came into special prominence with any new beginning in the history of God's kingdom. Noah, the new father of the human race, acted *"according to all that God commanded him"* (Gen. 6:22). The Bible mentions Noah's obedience four times. God entrusts His work to the man who does what He commands. God will use the obedient man to save His people.

*"By faith Abraham obeyed"* (Heb. 11:8). God chose Abraham to be the father of the chosen race because He knew Abraham had an obedient heart. After Abraham had spent forty years learning faith and obedience, God came to perfect Abraham's faith and crown it with His fullest blessing. Nothing could prepare him for this but a supreme act of obedience. When Abraham had tied his son on the altar, God said, *"By Myself I have sworn,...blessing I will bless you, and multiplying I will multiply your descendants....In your seed all the nations...shall be blessed, because you have obeyed My voice"* (Gen. 22:16–18).

This blessing continued for Isaac: *"I will perform the oath which I swore to Abraham...because Abraham obeyed My voice"*

(Gen. 26:3, 5). When will we learn how unspeakably pleasing obedience is in God's sight? When will we understand how great the reward is that He bestows because of obedience? To be a blessing to the world, be obedient. Let God and the world know you by this one characteristic—a will completely given up to God's will.

On Mount Sinai, God gave Moses this message: *"If you will indeed obey My voice...you shall be a special treasure to Me above all people"* (Exod. 19:5).

In the very nature of things, it cannot be otherwise. God's holy will is His glory and perfection. Only by entering His will through obedience is it possible to be His people. The Bible says nineteen times that Moses, while building the sanctuary where God was to dwell, acted *"according to all that the LORD had commanded"* (Exod. 40:16, for example). Because Moses obeyed God, *"the glory of the LORD filled the tabernacle"* (v. 34). *"The glory of the LORD appeared to all the people, and fire came out from before the LORD and consumed the burnt offering"* (Lev. 9:23–24).

God delights to dwell in the midst of His people's obedience. He crowns the obedient with His favor and presence.

After the forty years of wandering in the wilderness and its terrible revelation of the fruit of disobedience, the Hebrews were ready for a new beginning. They were about to enter Canaan. In describing the Hebrew nation at this time, the book of Deuteronomy uses the word *obey* more frequently and speaks of the blessing obedience brings more than any other book. The whole idea is summed up in the words, *"I set before you...the blessing, if you obey...and the curse, if you do not obey"* (Deut. 11:26–28).

Yes, a *"blessing, if you obey"*! This is the keynote of the Christian life. Our Canaan, just like Paradise and heaven, is the place of blessing as well as the place of obedience. It would be wonderful if we could take it in! But beware of praying only for a blessing. Let us be concerned with obedience; God will take care of the blessing. Let your one thought as a Christian be how you can obey and please your God perfectly.

## OBEDIENCE AND THE KINGS OF ISRAEL

Obedience was crucial again in the appointment of kings in Israel. In the story of Saul, we have the solemn warning about the need for exact and entire obedience in a man whom God is to trust as ruler of His people. Samuel commanded Saul, *"Seven days you shall wait, till I come to you and show you what you should do"* (1 Sam. 10:8). When Samuel delayed, Saul took it upon himself to offer the sacrifice.

When Samuel finally came, he said, *"You have not kept the commandment of the LORD your God, which He commanded you....Now your kingdom shall not continue...because you have not kept what the LORD commanded you"* (1 Sam. 13:13–14). God will not honor the man who is not obedient.

Saul had a second opportunity to show God what was in his heart. God sent him to execute judgment against Amalek. Saul obeyed. He gathered an army of 200,000 men, started the journey into the wilderness, and destroyed Amalek. But while God commanded him to *"utterly destroy all...and do not spare them"* (1 Sam. 15:3), Saul spared the best of the cattle and Agag.

God spoke to Samuel, saying, *"I greatly regret that I have set up Saul as king, for he...has not performed My commandments"* (v. 11).

When Samuel came, Saul said to him, *"I have performed the commandment of the LORD"* (v. 13); *"I have obeyed the voice of the LORD"* (v. 20).

He had obeyed, as many would think. But his obedience had not been entire. God claims exact, full obedience. God had said, *"Utterly destroy all...and do not spare them"* (v. 3). Saul had not done this. He had spared the best sheep for a sacrifice to the Lord. And Samuel said, *"To obey is better than* [any] *sacrifice....Because you have rejected the word of the LORD, He also has rejected you"* (vv. 22–23). There is no substitute for obedience.

Saul's partial obedience is sadly typical of contemporary obedience that performs God's commandment in part, yet is not the obedience God desires! God says of all sin and disobedience, *"Utterly destroy all...and do not spare* [it]*"* (v. 3). May God reveal to us whether we are indeed going all lengths with Him, seeking to destroy all sin, and sparing nothing within us that is not in perfect harmony with His will. It is only a wholehearted obedience, down to the smallest detail, that can satisfy God. Let nothing less satisfy you so that you will not say, "I have obeyed," while God says, *"You have rejected the word of the LORD"* (1 Sam. 15:26).

## BENEFITS OF OBEDIENCE

Jeremiah is also a book full of the word *obey*, though it usually complains that the people had not obeyed God. God sums up all His dealings with the fathers in this passage: *"I did not speak to your fathers...concerning...sacrifices. But this is what I commanded them, saying, 'Obey My voice, and I will be your God'"* (Jer. 7:22–23).

We need to learn that sacrifices, even the sacrifice of God's beloved Son, are subordinate to one thing—restoring His creature to full obedience. You cannot enter God's blessing when He says, *"I will be your God,"* unless you first *"obey* [His] *voice."*

In the New Testament, we immediately think of our blessed Lord Jesus Christ and the importance He placed on obedience as the one reason He came into the world. Jesus entered the world saying, *"Behold, I have come to do Your will, O God"* (Heb. 10:9). He always confessed to men, *"I do not seek My own will but the will of the Father who sent Me"* (John 5:30). Of all He did and suffered, even to death, He said, *"This command I have received from My Father"* (John 10:18). In Christ's teaching, we find everywhere that He claims the same obedience He rendered to the Father from everyone who desires to be His disciple.

During His entire ministry, from beginning to end, He said obedience was the very essence of salvation. In the Sermon on the Mount, He began with this subject. No one could enter the kingdom *"but he who does the will of My Father in heaven"* (Matt. 7:21). In His farewell discourse, He wonderfully revealed the spiritual character of true obedience. It is born of love, is inspired by it, and opens the way into the love of God.

Take into your heart these wonderful words:

*If you love Me, keep My commandments. And...the Father...will give you another Helper....He who has My commandments and keeps them, it is he who loves Me. And he...will be loved by My Father, and I will love him and manifest Myself to him....If anyone loves Me, he will keep My*

*word; and My Father will love him, and We will come to him*
*and make Our home with him.*          (John 14:15–16, 21, 23)

No words could express more simply or more powerfully the
glorious place Christ gives to obedience. It is only possible with a
loving heart. Obedience opens the door to all that God has to
give of His Holy Spirit, His wonderful love, and His indwelling
in Christ Jesus. No Scripture passage gives a higher revelation
of the spiritual life or the power of loving obedience than John
14. Let us pray and earnestly ask God that, by His Holy Spirit,
light may transfigure our daily obedience with its heavenly
glory.

## LIVING DAILY IN HIS COMMANDMENTS

The next chapter of John's gospel, the Parable of the Vine,
confirms this idea. How often and earnestly we have asked to be
able to live continually like Christ! We think that studying the
Word, having more faith, offering more prayer, or attaining more
communion with God will make us Christlike. Yet we have over-
looked one simple truth. Jesus clearly teaches, *"If you keep My*
*commandments, you will abide in My love, just as I have kept My*
*Father's commandments and abide in His love"* (John 15:10).

For Him, as for us, the only way under heaven to live in divine love is to keep the commandments. Have you known obedience? Have you heard it preached? Have you believed it and
proved it true in your experience that obedience on earth is the
key to a place in God's love in heaven? Unless there is some cor-
respondence between God's wholehearted love in heaven and
our wholehearted, loving obedience on earth, Christ cannot
manifest Himself to us. God cannot abide in us. We cannot live
in His love.

In the book of Acts, Peter showed how our Lord's teaching
entered into him. He said it was by *"the Holy Spirit whom God*
*has given to those who obey Him"* (Acts 5:32). He showed that
the preparation for Pentecost was surrender to Christ. He also
said, *"We* [must] *obey God rather than men"* (v. 29). We are to be
obedient, even unto death. Nothing on earth can dare to hinder
obedience in the man who has given himself to God.

In Paul's epistle to the Romans, he asserted, in the opening and closing verses, that *"obedience to the faith among all nations"* (Rom. 1:5; 16:26) was the reason he had been made an apostle. He spoke of what God made happen *"to make the Gentiles obedient"* (Rom. 15:18). He taught that as the obedience of Christ makes us righteous, we become the servants of obedience. As disobedience in Adam and in us was what brought death, so obedience in Christ and in us is the one thing that the Gospel makes known as the way of restoration to God and His favor.

## LISTENING TO AND OBEYING THE WORD

James warned us, *"Be doers of the word, and not hearers only"* (James 1:22). He then described how Abraham was justified and his faith was perfected by his works.

In Peter's first epistle, obedience has an important place in his system. In 1 Peter 1:2, he spoke to the *"elect...in sanctification of the Spirit, for obedience and sprinkling of the blood of Jesus Christ."* He showed us that obedience is the eternal purpose of the Father. It is the great objective of the work of the Spirit and a chief part of the salvation of Christ. He wrote, *"As obedient children* [born of it, marked by it, subject to it]*...be holy in all your conduct"* (vv. 14–15).

Obedience is the starting point of true holiness. In verse twenty-two we read, *"Since you have purified your souls in obeying the truth."* Complete acceptance of God's truth is not merely a matter of intellectual assent or strong emotion. It is subjecting one's life to the dominion of the truth of God. The Christian life is, first and foremost, characterized by obedience.

We know how strong John's statements are. *"He who says, 'I know Him,' and does not keep His commandments, is a liar, and the truth is not in him"* (1 John 2:4). Obedience is the certificate of Christian character.

> *Let us...love...in deed and in truth....By this we...shall assure our hearts before Him....And whatever we ask we receive from Him, because we keep His commandments and do those things that are pleasing in His sight.* (1 John 3:18–19, 22)

## Is God Listening to You?

Obedience is the secret of a good conscience and the confidence that God hears us. *"This is the love of God, that we keep His commandments"* (1 John 5:3). We reveal our love for God, to Him as well as to the world, through our cheerful obedience.

Obedience holds this high place in Scripture, in the mind of God, and in the hearts of His servants. We should ask ourselves if it takes that place in our hearts and lives. Have we given obedience the supreme place of authority over ourselves that God intends it to have? Is it the inspiration of every action and every approach to Him?

If we yield ourselves to the searching of God's Spirit, we may find that we never gave obedience its proper proportion in our scheme of life and that this lack is the cause of all our failure in prayer and in work. We may see that the deeper blessings of God's grace, and the full enjoyment of God's love and nearness, have been beyond our reach simply because we never made obedience what God intended it to be. It is the starting point and the goal of our Christian lives.

Let this, our first study, awaken in us an earnest desire to fully know God's will concerning this truth. Let us unite in prayer that the Holy Spirit will show us how defective the Christian's life is when obedience does not rule everything. Let Him show us how that life can be exchanged for one of full surrender and absolute obedience. We can then be sure that God in Christ will enable us to live this life successfully.

chapter 2

# Christ's Obedience

*So also by one Man's obedience many will be made righteous.*
—Romans 5:19

*Do you not know that...you are...slaves...of obedience
leading to righteousness?*
—Romans 6:16

Through the obedience of One, many will be made righteous. These words tell us what we owe Christ. In Adam,
we were made sinners; in Christ, we are made righteous.

The words also tell us that we owe our righteousness to the
obedience of Christ. Among the treasures of our inheritance in
Christ, this is one of the richest. Many people have never studied the blessing of obedience so as to love it, delight in it, and
receive the full blessing of it. May God by His Holy Spirit reveal
the glory of obedience and make us partakers of its power.

You are most likely familiar with the blessed truth of justification by faith. From Romans 3:21 to 5:11, Paul taught that
the foundation of our justification was the atonement of the
blood of Christ. He taught that the way to receive it is by faith
in the free grace of God, *"who justifies the ungodly"* (Rom. 4:5).
The blessed fruit of justification is the bestowment of Christ's
righteousness, immediate access into God's favor, and the hope
of future glory.

In Romans 5:19, where we read, *"So also by one Man's obedience many will be made righteous,"* Paul discussed our union
with Adam and all the consequences that flow from that union.
He proved how reasonable it is that those who receive Christ by
faith, and are then united with Him, share His life and His
righteousness in God's eyes. In this argument, Paul emphasized
the contrast between Adam's disobedience, with the condemnation and death it brought, and Christ's obedience, with the
goodness and life it brought.

## THE TWOFOLD CONNECTION

*"By one man's disobedience many were made sinners"* (Rom. 5:19). How was this?

There was a twofold connection between Adam and his descendants: the judicial and the inherited. Through the judicial, the whole race, though unborn, was immediately under the sentence of death. *"Death reigned from Adam to Moses, even over those who had not sinned according to the likeness of the transgression of Adam"* (v. 14). This even included little children.

This judicial relationship was rooted in the inherited connection. The sentence could not have come upon them if they had not been descendants of Adam. Each child of Adam enters life under the power of sin and death. Through the disobedience of one, *"many were made sinners"* (v. 19). We were all subject to the curse of sin; and by nature, we were subject to sin's power.

*"Adam...is a type of Him who was to come"* (v. 14). Jesus, who is called the Second Adam, is the second Father of the race. The effects of Adam's disobedience are exactly parallel to those of Christ's obedience. When a sinner believes in Jesus Christ, he is united to Him. Immediately by a judicial sentence, the believer is accepted as conforming to God's will—in God's sight. The judicial relationship is rooted in the physical.

Man has Christ's righteousness only by believing his sins are forgiven because of Christ's sacrifice. Before a saved person understands any of the fine points about living for Jesus, he can rest assured that he is acquitted and accepted. The believer is then led on to know that, as real and complete as was his participation in Adam's disobedience, so his participation in Christ's obedience is also real. He now enjoys both the righteousness and the obedient life and nature that comes from it.

## A DEEPER LOOK

Through Adam's disobedience, we were made sinners. The one thing God asked of Adam in Paradise was obedience. The one thing by which a creature can glorify God or enjoy His favor and blessing is obedience.

Sin has power in the world because of disobedience. The entire curse of sin is due to disobedience imputed to us. The power of sin working in us is nothing but Adam's nature. We have inherited his disobedience. We are born *"the sons of disobedience"* (Eph. 2:2).

It is evident that Christ needed to remove this disobedience—its curse, its dominion, its evil nature and workings. Disobedience is the root of all sin and misery. The first goal of His salvation was to cut away the evil root and restore man to his original destiny: a life of obedience to his God.

How did Christ do this?

First, He did this by coming as the Second Adam to undo what the First Adam had done. Sin made us believe it was humiliating to continually be seeking to know and do God's will. Christ came to show us the nobility, the blessedness, and the delight of obedience. When God gave us the robe of creaturehood to wear, we did not know that its beauty and unspotted purity was from obedience to God. Christ came, put on that robe, and showed us how to wear it. He showed us how we could enter into the presence and glory of God. Christ came to overcome, take away our disobedience, and replace it with His own obedience. As universal, as mighty, as all-pervading as was the disobedience of Adam, far more pervasive was the power of Christ's obedience.

## CHRIST'S THREE-PART GOAL

The purpose of Christ's life of obedience was threefold. First, He came to be an example of true obedience. Second, He came to be our Surety, to fulfill all righteousness for us by His obedience. Finally, He came to be our Head, to prepare a new and obedient nature in us.

He also died to show us that His obedience meant a readiness to obey to the uttermost, to die for God. Obedience is the vicarious endurance and atonement of the guilt of our disobedience. It means a death to sin as an entrance to the life of God for Him and for us.

The disobedience of Adam and all of its repercussions were to be put away and replaced by the obedience of Christ. Judicially, by that obedience, we are made righteous. Just as we were made sinners by Adam's disobedience, we are immediately and completely justified and delivered from the power of sin and death. We stand before God as righteous men and women in Christ. The life we receive in Him is a life of obedience.

Everyone who desires to understand obedience should consider this well. Obeying Christ is the secret of conforming to God's will and the salvation one finds in Him. Obedience is the very essence of that righteousness. Obedience is salvation. The obedience of Jesus should be accepted, trusted, and rejoiced in as covering, swallowing up, and ending disobedience. Jesus Christ's obedience to God is the one unchanging, never-to-be-forsaken basis of my acceptance. And then, His obedience becomes the life power of the new nature in me, just as Adam's disobedience was the power of death that ruled my life. *"If by the one man's offense death reigned through the one, much more those who receive abundance of grace and of the gift of righteousness will reign in life through the One, Jesus Christ....The free gift came to all men, resulting in justification of life"* (Rom. 5:17–18).

As we examine the significance of the first and Second Adam, we see the parallel between death and disobedience, and life and obedience. We cannot escape being inheritors of Adam's death through his disobedience. In the same way, when we believe in Jesus Christ, we are equally inseparable from His obedience and life. We have His obedience by association as well as for our personal possession. By accepting the atoning work of Christ's blood, we exchange our death inheritance for His life inheritance.

## DISCUSSION IN ROMANS

Paul drew this connection in Romans 6:12–13 for the first time in his letter. Paul directed the Roman church, *"Do not let sin reign....Present yourselves to God."* Then he immediately proceeded to teach how this means nothing but obedience: *"Do you not know that...you are...slaves...of sin leading to death, or of obedience leading to righteousness?"* (v. 16).

Our relationship to obedience is a practical one. we have been delivered from disobedience (Adam's and our own), and now we are servants of obedience *"to righteousness."* Christ's obedience was righteousness—God's gift to us. Our subjection to obedience is the only way we can maintain our relationship to God and righteousness. Christ's obedience, which gained us righteousness, is only the beginning of life for us. Our conforming to God's will is the only way to continue life.

## ONE LAW

There is only one law for the head and the members. As surely as it was disobedience and death for Adam and his seed, it is obedience and life for Christ and His seed. The one bond of union, the one likeness between Adam and his seed, was disobedience. The resemblance between Christ and His seed is obedience.

Obedience alone made Christ the object of the Father's love and, as a result, our Redeemer.

> *Therefore My Father loves Me, because I lay down My life that I may take it again. No one takes it from Me, but I lay it down of Myself. I have power to lay it down, and I have power to take it again. This command I have received from My Father.*
> (John 10:17–18)

Only obedience can lead us to dwell in that love and enjoy that redemption.

> *He who has My commandments and keeps them, it is he who loves Me. And he who loves Me will be loved by My Father, and I will love him and manifest Myself to him....If anyone loves Me, he will keep My word; and My Father will love him, and We will come to him and make Our home with him.*
> (John 14:21, 23)

Everything depends on our knowledge of and participation in obedience. Obedience is the gateway and path to the full enjoyment of a right relationship to God. At conversion, righteousness is given because of faith—once, completely, and forever. We receive righteousness even though we have little or no knowledge of obedience. But as the Christian believes he is in God's favor, submits to God's will, and seeks to be a servant of righteousness, this sanctification in God's eyes will pour blessing on him and lead back to its divine origin. The stronger our hold of the righteousness of Christ in the power of the Spirit, the more intense our desire will be to share in the obedience out of which it came.

## PRINCIPLES OF CHRIST'S OBEDIENCE

Studying the following principles of Christ's obedience will help us to live as servants of obedience who desire a right relationship with God. In Christ, this obedience was a life principle. Obedience with Him did not mean a single act of obedience now and then or even a series of acts, but the spirit of His whole life. *"I have come...not to do My own will"* (John 6:38). *"Behold, I have come to do Your will, O God"* (Heb. 10:9). Jesus came into the world for one purpose. He lived only to carry out God's will. The single, supreme, all-controlling power of His life was obedience.

Jesus is willing to make us able to do the same. This was what He promised when He said, *"Whoever does the will of My Father in heaven is My brother and sister and mother"* (Matt. 12:50).

The link in a family is a common life shared by all and a family likeness. The bond between Christ and us is that together we do the will of God.

For Christ this obedience was a joy. *"I delight to do Your will, O my God"* (Ps. 40:8). *"My food is to do the will of Him who sent Me"* (John 4:34).

Our food is refreshment and invigoration. The healthy man eats his bread with pleasure. But food is more than enjoyment; it is a necessity of life. Likewise, doing the will of God was the food that Christ hungered after; without this, He could not live. Obedience was the one thing that satisfied His hunger, the one thing that refreshed Him, strengthened Him, and made Him happy.

This was David's idea when he spoke of God's Word being *"sweeter...than honey and the honeycomb"* (Ps. 19:10). As this is understood and accepted, obedience will become more natural and necessary to us. It will become more refreshing than our daily food.

For Christ this obedience led to His waiting for God to reveal His will.

God did not reveal all His will to Christ at once, but day by day, according to the circumstances of the hour. In His life of obedience, there was growth and progress; the most difficult lesson was the last. Each act of obedience equipped Him for the new discovery of the Father's next command. He spoke, *"My ears You have opened....I delight to do Your will, O my God"* (Ps. 40:6, 8).

As obedience becomes the fervor of our lives, God's Spirit will open our ears to wait for His teaching. We will be content with nothing less than divine guidance into God's perfect will for us.

In Christ this obedience was unto death.

When He spoke, *"I have come...not to do My own will, but the will of Him who sent Me"* (John 6:38), He was ready to go to all lengths in denying His own will and doing the Father's will. He may have said to Himself, "In nothing My will; at all costs God's will."

This is the obedience to which He invites us and for which He empowers us. This wholehearted surrender to obedience in everything is the only true obedience. It is the only power that will survive to carry us through life. If only Christians could understand that nothing less than obedience brings the soul joy and strength!

As long as there is a doubt about universal obedience, and with that a lurking sense of the possibility of failure, we lose the confidence that secures the victory. But when we recognize that God is asking for full obedience, we must then decide to work at it and offer Him nothing less. If we give ourselves up to the working of the divine power, the Holy Spirit can master our entire lives.

In Christ this obedience sprang from the deepest humility. *"Let this mind be in you which was also in Christ Jesus, who...made Himself of no reputation, taking the form of a bond-servant, and...humbled Himself and became obedient to the point of death"* (Phil. 2:5–8).

It is the man who is willing to entirely empty himself, to be and to live as a servant of obedience, to be humbled very low before God and man, to whom the obedience of Jesus will unfold its heavenly beauty and power. He may have a strong will that secretly trusts in self, that strives for obedience and fails. Only as we approach God in humility, meekness, patience, and entire resignation to His will does He reveal to us the blessings in obedience. To see this blessing in our duty, we must bow in absolute helplessness and dependence on Him, turning away wholly from self.

In Christ, this obedience was faith in entire dependence upon God's strength. *"I can of Myself do nothing"* (John 5:30). *"The Father who dwells in Me does the works"* (John 14:10).

The Son's unreserved surrender to the Father's will was met by the Father's unceasing and unreserved bestowment of His power working in Him.

## GOD'S POWER—OUR OBEDIENCE

It will be even so with us. If we learn that giving up our wills to God is always the measure of His giving His power to us, we will see that a surrender to full obedience is nothing but a full faith that God will work all in us.

God's promises of the new covenant all rest on this Scripture: *"And the LORD your God will circumcise your heart...to love the LORD your God with all your heart....And you will again obey the...LORD your God"* (Deut. 30:6, 8–9). *"I will put My Spirit within you and cause you to walk in My statutes, and you will keep My judgments"* (Ezek. 36:27).

Let us, like the Son, believe that God works everything in us, and we will have the courage to yield ourselves to an unreserved obedience, an obedience unto death. This yielding ourselves up to God will become the entrance into the blessed experience of conformity to the Son of God in His doing the Father's will because He counted on the Father's power. Let us give ourselves completely to God. He will work His entire work in us.

Do you know that because you were made righteous by the obedience of Jesus, you are like Him? In Him you are servants of obedience, growing more and more consistent with God's nature. It is in the obedience of the One that the obedience of the many has its root, its life, and its security. Make it a point to study Christ and believe in Him as the Obedient One. Seek, receive, and love Him as the One to conform yourself to. As His righteousness is our one hope, let His obedience be our one desire.

Let us prove our sincerity and confidence in God's supernatural power by accepting Jesus Christ as the Obedient One, the Christ who dwells in us.

chapter 3

# Christ's School of Obedience

*He learned obedience.*
—Hebrews 5:8

The secret of true obedience is a close and unmistakable personal relationship with God. All our attempts to be fully obedient will be failures until we gain access to His abiding fellowship. It is God's holy presence consciously abiding with us that keeps us from disobeying Him.

Defective obedience is always the result of a defective life. To rouse and spur on that defective life by arguments and motives has its use. The chief blessing of the arguments must be that they make us feel the need for a different life, a life so entirely under the power of God that obedience will be natural.

The defective life, the life of broken and irregular fellowship with God, must be healed to make way for a full and healthy life. Then, full obedience will become possible. The secret of true obedience is the return to close and continual fellowship with God.

## THE NECESSITY OF OBEDIENCE

*"He learned obedience."* Why was this necessary for Christ? What is the blessing He brings us? *"He learned obedience by the things which He suffered. And...He became the author of eternal salvation to all who obey Him"* (Heb. 5:8–9).

Suffering is unnatural to us and therefore calls for the surrender of our wills.

Christ needed to suffer so that He could learn to obey and give up His will to the Father at any cost. He needed to learn obedience so that as our great High Priest, He would be made perfect. *"He learned obedience."* He became obedient even to

523

death so that He could become the Author of our salvation. As the Author of salvation through obedience, He now saves those who obey Him.

The very essence of salvation is obedience to God. Christ as the Obedient One saves us as His obedient ones. Whether in His suffering on earth or in His glory in heaven, Christ's heart is set on obedience.

On earth Christ learned in the school of obedience. From heaven He teaches obedience to His disciples here on earth. In a world where disobedience reigns for death, the restoration of obedience is in Christ's hands. As in His own life, so in us, He has made a contract to maintain obedience in us. He teaches us and works it in us.

Think about what and how He teaches. When we think of an ordinary school, we usually ask about the teacher, the textbooks, and the students. Let us examine these things regarding Christ's school of obedience. It may be we will see how little we have devoted ourselves to learning obedience and only obedience.

## THE TEACHER

*"He learned obedience."* Now Jesus teaches us by unfolding the secret of His own obedience to the Father.

I have said that we find the power of true obedience in our personal relationship with God. It was the same with our Lord Jesus. Of all His teaching, He said,

> For I have not spoken on My own authority; but the Father who sent Me gave Me a command, what I should say and what I should speak. And I know that His command is everlasting life. Therefore, whatever I speak, just as the Father has told Me, so I speak. (John 12:49–50)

This does not mean that Christ received God's commandment in eternity as part of the Father's commission to Him on entering the world. No. Day by day, as He taught and worked, He lived in continual communication with the Father. He received the Father's instructions as He needed them.

He even said,

> *The Son can do nothing of Himself, but what He sees the Father do....For the Father...shows Him all things that He Himself does; and He will show Him greater works....As I hear, I judge....I am not alone, but I am with the Father who sent me....I do not speak on My own authority; but the Father who dwells in Me.*          (John 5:19–20, 30; 8:16; 14:10)

Obedience is constant dependence on a moment-by-moment fellowship and operation of God, a hearing and seeing of what God speaks, does, and shows.

Our Lord always spoke of His relationship with the Father as parallel to our relationship with Him and with the Father through Him. This parallel relationship carried the same promise, as well. With us as with Jesus, the life of continual obedience is impossible without continual fellowship and teaching. We must believe in God's power and receive Him into our lives. We must believe His presence is eternal the same way Jesus believed. Only then will we have any hope of bringing every thought into captivity—into Christlike obedience (2 Cor. 10:5).

The absolute necessity of continually receiving our orders and instructions from God Himself is what the Bible implies when it says, *"Obey My voice, and I will be your God"* (Jer. 7:23).

The expression "obeying the commandments" is seldom used in Scripture. God usually says, "Obeying Me" or "Obeying (or hearkening to) My voice." The army commander, the school teacher, and the head of a family do not win obedience through a code of laws, rewards, or threats. Their personal living influence awakens love and enthusiasm. It is the joy of hearing the Father's voice that will provide the joy and strength of true obedience. God's voice gives power to obey the Word; the Word without His living voice brings no profit.

The Bible contrasts this principle with what we see in Israel. The people had heard the voice of God on Mount Sinai and were afraid. They asked Moses to ask God not to speak to them. They wanted Moses to receive the Word of God and bring it to them. The Israelites thought only of the command. They did not know that the only power to obey is in the presence of God and

His voice speaking to us. With only Moses and the tablets of stone to speak to them, their whole history is one of disobedience because they were afraid of direct contact with God.

Christians are often the same way today. Many Christians find it much easier to take their teaching from godly men than to serve God and receive it directly from Him. Their faith stands in the wisdom of men and not in the power of God. (See 1 Corinthians 2:5.)

Learn the great lesson from our Lord, who learned obedience by waiting, moment by moment, to see and hear what the Father had to teach. It is only when, like Jesus and through Him, we always walk with God and hear His voice, that we can possibly attempt to offer God the obedience He asks for and promises to work in us.

Out of the depths of His own life and experience, Christ can give and teach us obedience. Pray earnestly that God will show you the foolishness of attempting to obey without the same strength Christ needed. Pray that He will make you willing to give up everything for the Christlike joy of the Father's constant presence.

## THE TEXTBOOK

Christ's direct communication with the Father did not make Him independent of Scripture. In the divine school of obedience, there is only one textbook, whether for our Older Brother, Jesus, or the younger children. While He learned obedience, He used the same textbook we have. He needed the Word and used it for His own special life and guidance as well as when He had to teach or convince others.

From the beginning of His public life to its close, He lived by the Word of God. *"It is written"* was the sword of the Spirit with which He conquered Satan (Matt. 4:4, 7, 10). *"The Spirit of the LORD is upon Me"* (Luke 4:18). This word of Scripture was the frame of reference with which He opened His gospel preaching.

*"That the Scripture might be fulfilled"* (John 17:12) was the light in which He accepted all suffering and even gave Himself to the death. After the Resurrection, He expounded to the disciples

*"in all the Scriptures the things concerning Himself"* (Luke 24:27).

In Scripture He found God's plan and path marked out for Him. He gave Himself to fulfill it. It was in and with the use of God's Word that He received the Father's continual, direct teaching.

In God's school of obedience, the Bible is the only textbook. This fact shows us the attitude in which we are to come to the Bible. We are to come with the simple desire to find God's will concerning us, and then we are to do it.

Scripture was not written to increase our knowledge. It was written to guide our conduct, *"that the man of God may be complete, thoroughly equipped for every good work"* (2 Tim. 3:17). *"If anyone wants to do His will, he shall know concerning the doctrine, whether it is from God"* (John 7:17).

Learn from Christ's example that God's goal is for man to be prepared to do His will as it is done in heaven. He desires man to be restored to perfect obedience and its blessings. The scriptural revelation of God, His love, and His counsel are secondary to His main goal.

In God's school of obedience, His Word is the only textbook. To apply that Word in His own life and conduct, to know when each portion was to be taken up and carried out, Christ needed and received divine instruction. Jesus Christ spoke in Isaiah, *"The Lord GOD...awakens Me morning by morning, He awakens My ear to hear as the learned. The Lord GOD has opened My ear"* (Isa. 50:4–5).

Jesus teaches us in this same way by giving us the Holy Spirit as the divine Interpreter of the Word. This is the great work of the indwelling Holy Spirit. The Word we read, He plants in our hearts. He coaches us to think about it. It then works effectively in our wills, our love, and our whole beings. When we do not understand this, the Word has no power to help us in obedience.

Speaking plainly about this, we rejoice in the increased attention given to Bible study, and in testimonies about the benefit received. But let's not deceive ourselves. We may delight in studying the Bible. We may admire and be charmed with the views we see of God's truth. The thoughts suggested may make a deep impression and awaken the most pleasing religious emotions. Yet the practical influence in making us holy, humble, loving, patient, and ready, either for service or suffering, may be very small. The one reason for this is that we do not receive the Word as the Word of a living God who must speak to us Himself in order for its divine power to be exerted.

The letter of the Word, however we study and delight in it, has no saving or sanctifying power. Human wisdom and human will, however strenuous their effort, cannot give or command that power. The Holy Spirit is the mighty power of God. It is only as the Holy Spirit teaches you, only as the Gospel is preached to you by man or book, *"by the Holy Spirit sent from heaven"* (1 Pet. 1:12), that it will really give you the strength to obey the very thing commanded.

With man, knowing, doing, willing, and performing are, for lack of power, often separate and even at opposite poles. This is never so in the Holy Spirit. He is at once the light and the might of God. All He is, does, and gives has in it equally the truth and the power of God. When He shows you God's command, He always shows it to you as a possible and a certain thing. He shows it to you as a divine life, a gift prepared for you, which He is able to give.

Beloved, learn to believe that it is only when Christ, through the Holy Spirit, teaches you to understand and take the Word into your hearts that He can really teach you to obey the Father as He did. Believe, every time you open your Bible, that just as sure as you listen to the divine, Spirit-breathed Word, your Father will, in answer to the prayer of faith, give the Holy Spirit's living operation in your hearts.

Let all your Bible study be done in faith. Do not simply try to believe the truths or promises you read. Your faith may then be in your own power. Believe in the Holy Spirit, in His being in you, and in God's working in you through Him. Take the Word into your hearts in the quiet faith that He will enable you to love it, yield to it, and keep it. Believe that our blessed Lord Jesus will make the Bible mean to you what it meant to Him when He spoke of *"the things* [that are written] *concerning Himself"* (Luke 24:27). Scripture will become the simple revelation of what God is going to do for you, in you, and through you.

## THE STUDENT

We have seen how our Lord teaches us obedience by unfolding the secret of His learning it. He shows us His unceasing dependence on the Father. We have seen how He teaches us to use the sacred Book as He used it, as a divine revelation of what God has ordained for us.

He has given us the Holy Spirit to expound and enforce the Word in us. If we now consider the place the believer takes in the school of obedience as a student, we will better understand what Christ the Son requires in order for us to do His work in us effectively.

In a faithful student, there are several things that make up his feelings toward a trusted teacher. He submits himself entirely to his leading. He has perfect trust in him. He gives the teacher just as much time and attention as he asks.

When we see and consent that Jesus Christ has a right to all this, we can hope to experience how wonderfully He can teach us an obedience like His own. The good student, great musicians and painters say, yields his master a wholehearted and unhesitating submission. In practicing scales or mixing colors, in the slow and patient study of the elements of art, the student knows that it is wise to simply and fully obey his teacher.

It is this wholehearted surrender to His guidance, this implicit submission to His authority, that Christ asks. We come to Him asking Him to teach us the lost art of obeying God as He did. He asks us if we are ready to pay the price. The price is to entirely deny self! It is to give up our wills and our lives to the death! It is to be ready to do whatever He says!

The only way to learn to do something is to do it. The only way to learn obedience from Christ is to give up our wills to Him and make doing His will the one desire and delight of our hearts.

Unless you take the vow of absolute obedience as you enter this class of Christ's school, it will be impossible for you to make any progress.

The true scholar of a great master finds it easy to render him this implicit obedience, simply because he trusts his teacher. He gladly sacrifices his own wisdom and will to be guided by a higher authority.

We need this confidence in our Lord Jesus. He came from heaven to learn obedience and be able to teach it well. His obedience is the treasury out of which the debt of our past is paid and the grace for our present obedience is supplied. In His divine love and perfect human sympathy, in His divine power over our hearts and lives, He invites, He deserves, and He wins our trust.

Jesus touches us through our attachment to and admiration of Him. Through the power of His divine love, His Holy Spirit awakens within us a responsive love. Jesus then awakens our confidence and communicates to us the secret of true success.

As absolutely as we have trusted Him as our Savior who atoned for our disobedience, we can trust Him as a teacher to lead us out of it. Christ is our prophet and teacher. A heart that enthusiastically believes in His power and success as a teacher will, in the joy of that faith, find it easy to obey God. It is Christ's presence with us all day that will be our key to true obedience.

A scholar gives his master just as much of his attendance and attention as he asks. The master determines how much time must be devoted to personal fellowship and instruction.

Obedience to God is a heavenly art. Our human nature is so utterly unfamiliar with it. We must not doubt if obedience does not come all at once, since the path in which the Son Himself learned it was slow and long. Nor must we wonder if we need to spend more time than most believers are ready to give waiting in prayer, meditation, and dependent self-sacrifice. Simply give it.

In Christ Jesus, heavenly obedience has become human again. Obedience has become our birthright and our life breath. Let us cling to our Lord; let us believe and claim His abiding presence. With Jesus Christ who learned obedience as our Savior, and who teaches obedience as our Master, we can live lives of obedience. We cannot study His lesson too seriously. His obedience is our salvation. In Him, the living Christ, we find obedience and partake of it moment by moment.

We must pray to God, asking Him to show us how Christ and His obedience are to be part of our daily lives. We must ask that He will then make us pupils who give Him all of our hearts and all of our time. He will teach us to keep His commandments and live in His love, even as He kept His Father's commandments and lives in His love.

chapter 4

# Morning Prayer

*For if the firstfruit is holy, the lump is also holy; and if the*
*root is holy, so are the branches.*
—Romans 11:16

The first day of the week, the holy day of rest, is a wonderful blessing from God. It is not that we have one day of rest and spiritual refreshment in the weariness of life; but this holy day, at the beginning of the week, can sanctify the whole. It will help us and prepare us to carry God's holy presence into the entire week and its work. With the first fruit holy, the entire lump is holy. With the root holy, all the branches are holy, too.

The Old Testament gives many types and examples of God providing power over temptation throughout the day as a result of a morning hour of prayer. The unspeakably gracious bond formed in that morning hour unites us with God and can be so firmly tied that when we have to live in the rush of men and duties, and we can scarcely think of God, our souls are kept safe and pure. The soul can so completely give itself into God's keeping during the time of secret worship that temptation only unites it closer with God. What cause for praise and joy, that the morning prayer can renew and strengthen our surrender to Jesus and faith in Him! The life of obedience can be maintained in fresh vigor and continue *"from strength to strength"* (Ps. 84:7).

The connection between obedience and morning prayer is intimate and vital. The desire for a life of entire obedience will give new meaning and value to our morning prayer, because this alone gives the strength and courage we need daily.

If we see prayer simply as a duty and a necessary part of our religious life, it will soon become a burden. Or if we pray thinking of our own happiness and safety, prayer will not be truly attractive. Only one thing will do—the desire for fellowship with God.

This is the reason we were created in God's likeness. Only living in His likeness can prepare us for a true and blessed life, either here or in heaven. He invites us to enter His inner chambers to know Him better, to receive His communication of love and strength, and to have our lives filled with His. It is in private, in morning prayer, that our spiritual lives are both tested and strengthened. That is the battlefield where it is decided whether we will give God absolute obedience. If we truly conquer there, giving ourselves into the hands of our almighty Lord, the victory during the day is certain. It is in the inner chamber where we prove whether we really delight in God and aim to love Him with our whole hearts.

Our first lesson is that the presence of God must be the chief thing in our devotions. When we learn that the purpose behind our morning prayer is to find His blessing, we will learn to long for it and delight in it. We will cherish meeting God, giving ourselves into His holy will, knowing we are pleasing Him, having Him lay His hands upon us, blessing us, and giving us our instructions. He then says, *"Go in this might of yours"* (Judg. 6:14).

## READING THE BIBLE

Reading God's Word is part of our morning prayer time. I have several things I wish to say about this. Unless we are careful, the Word that is meant to point us to God may actually intervene and hide Him from us.

The mind may be occupied, interested, and delighted at what it finds. Yet because this is more head knowledge than anything else, it may bring us little good. If it does not lead us to wait on God, glorify Him, receive His grace and power for sweetening and sanctifying our lives, our reading becomes a hindrance instead of a help.

Another lesson that I cannot repeat too often is that it is only by the Holy Spirit's teaching that we can get at the real meaning of God's Word, and that the Word will really reach into our inner lives and work in us.

Our Father in heaven, who gave us His Word from heaven with its divine mysteries and message, also put His Holy Spirit in us to explain that Word and to allow us to take hold of it. The Father wants us to ask His Holy Spirit for teaching each time. He wants us to bow in a meek, teachable frame of mind and believe that the Spirit will, in the hidden depths of our hearts, make His Word live and work. He wants us to remember that He gave us the Spirit so that we would be led by Him, walk after Him, and have our whole lives under His rule. Therefore, He cannot teach us in the morning unless we honestly give ourselves up to His leading. But if we do this, wait patiently for Him, and serve Him, not to receive new thoughts, but to receive the power of the Word in our hearts, we can count on His teaching.

Let your closet be the classroom. Let your morning prayer be the study hour when you prove your relationship of entire dependence on and submission to the Holy Spirit's teaching.

Third, I want to confirm what was said above. Always study God's Word in the spirit of an unreserved surrender to obey. You know how often Christ and His apostles, in their epistles, spoke of hearing God's Word and not doing it. If you accustom yourself to studying the Bible without an earnest and very definite purpose to obey, you will harden yourself in disobedience.

Never read God's will concerning you without honestly giving yourself up to do it immediately.

Ask for grace to do it. God gave us His Word to tell us what He wants us to do and how He provides His grace to enable us to do it. How sad to think it a pious thing just to read the Bible without any sincere effort to obey it! May God keep us from this terrible sin!

Let us make it a sacred habit to tell God, "Lord, whatever I know to be Your will, I will immediately obey." Always read with a heart yielded in willing obedience.

Finally, I have spoken of the commands we already know, and those that are easily understood. But remember, there are many commands that you may never have noticed, and others whose application is so wide and unceasing that you have not taken them in. Read God's Word with a deep desire to know all of His will. If there are things that appear difficult, commands that seem too high, commands for which you need divine guidance to carry out, let them drive you to seek a divine teaching. It is not the text that is easiest and most encouraging that brings the most blessing. It is the text, whether easy or difficult, that throws you most upon God that brings the greatest blessing. God wants you to be *"filled with the knowledge of His will in all wisdom and spiritual understanding"* (Col. 1:9). It is in the prayer closet where this wonderful work is to be done. Remember, it is only when you *know* God is telling you to do something that you feel sure He gives the strength to do it. It is only as we are willing to know all of God's will that He, from time to time, will reveal more of it to us, and that we will be able to do it all.

What a power the morning prayer time may be in the life of one who is determined to meet God daily! The person who renews his surrender to absolute obedience, and humbly and patiently waits on the Holy Spirit to teach God's will, is certain to find that every assurance and promise given in the Word is true.

## COMMUNION WITH GOD

In the light of these thoughts, I would like to say a few words about what prayer should be in the morning prayer time.

First, secure the presence of God. Do not be content with anything less than having the assurance that God is looking at you in love, listening to you, and working in you.

If our daily lives are to be full of God, we need our morning prayer time where the life of the day can have God's seal stamped on it. In our religion we need more of God—His love, His will, His holiness, His Spirit living in us, and His power working in us for our fellowmen. Under heaven there is no way of getting this except by close personal communion with Him. There is no better time for securing and practicing our communion with God than our morning prayer time.

The superficiality and feebleness of our religion and religious work all come from having little real contact with God. Since it is true that God alone is the foundation of all love and good and happiness, then our trust and highest happiness must be in Him. We desire to have in Him, as much as possible, His presence, His fellowship, His will, and the opportunity to serve

Him. All of this being true, meeting God in morning prayer ought to be our first priority.

To have God appear to them and speak was the secret behind the obedience of the Old Testament believers. Give God time in secret to reveal Himself so that your soul may call the name of the place *Peniel,* which means, *"for I have seen God face to face"* (Gen. 32:30).

## COMPLETE SURRENDER IN PRAYER

My next thought is this: let the renewal of your surrender to absolute obedience for that day be a main part of your morning prayer.

Let any confession of sin be very definite, a plucking out and cutting off of everything that has been grieving God. (See Matthew 5:29–30.) Let any prayer for grace or for a holy walk be definite also. In your prayer, ask for and accept in faith the very grace and strength you are particularly in need of. Steadfastly resolve, as you start each day, that you will keep obedience to God as your controlling principle.

There is no other possible way of entering into God's love and blessing in prayer than by getting into His will. In prayer, give yourself up completely to the blessed will of God. This will bring you more than numerous requests. Ask God to show you great mercy enabling you to enter into His will and live there. His enabling power will make the doing of His will a blessed certainty. Let your prayer indeed be a morning sacrifice, a figurative placing of yourself as a whole burnt offering on the altar of the Lord. (See Leviticus 9:17.)

The measure of your surrender to full obedience will be the measure of your confidence toward God.

## ASSURANCE AND CONFIDENCE

Then remember that true prayer and fellowship with God cannot be one-sided.

We need to be still, wait, and hear God's response. This is the Holy Spirit's duty, to be the voice of God to us. In the hidden depths of the heart, He can give a secret yet certain assurance that we are heard, that we are well-pleasing, and that the Father plans to do for us what we have asked. To receive this assurance, we need to quietly and humbly wait on God. We need to wait in the quiet faith that trusts God.

When we serve God and take His side in our prayers, He gives us the confidence that we receive what we ask. He gives us the confidence that our sacrifice of self in obedience is accepted. We can then count on the Holy Spirit to guide us into all the will of God as He plans for us to know and do it.

What glory would come to us in morning prayer, and through it into our daily lives, if we make it an hour spent with the triune God. The Father, through the Son and the Spirit, will take conscious possession of us for the day.

## CONSECRATED INTERCESSION

Last and best, let your prayer be intercessional on behalf of others.

In the obedience of our Lord Jesus, as in all His fellowship with the Father, the essential element was that it was all done for others. This Spirit flows through every member of the body of Christ's church. The more we know it and yield to it, the more our lives will be what God desires to make them. The highest form of prayer is intercession. God chose Abraham, Israel, and us to make us a blessing to the world. We are *"a royal priesthood"* (1 Pet. 2:9), a priestly people. As long as we only use prayer as a means of personal improvement and happiness, we cannot know its full power. Let intercession be a real longing for the souls of those around us, a real bearing of the burden of their sin and need, a real pleading for the extension of God's kingdom. Let such intercession be what our morning prayer time is consecrated to, and see what new interest and attraction it will have.

Intercession! Oh, to realize what it means! To take the name and the righteousness and the worthiness of Christ, put them on, and appear in them before God! *"On Christ's behalf"* (2 Cor. 5:20) we must pray, now that He is no longer bodily in the world, to ask God by name for the individual men and women, and for the needs where His grace can do its work! In the faith of our own acceptance and of the anointing with the Spirit to prepare us for the work, we know that our prayer can *"save a soul from death"* (James 5:20) and bring the blessing of heaven upon earth. To think that in the morning prayer hour this work can be renewed and carried on day by day!

It is in intercession, more than zeal (which works in its own strength), that true Christlikeness is cultivated. It is in intercession that a believer rises to his true nobility in the power of imparting life and blessing. We must look to intercession for any large increase of the power of God in the church and its work for men.

## MAINTAINING HIS PRESENCE

In conclusion, think again about the vital connection between obedience and morning prayer.

Without obedience there cannot be the spiritual power to enter into the knowledge of God's Word and will. Without obedience there cannot be the confidence, boldness, and liberty that knows the prayer is heard. Obedience is fellowship with God in His will. Without it there is no capacity for seeing, claiming, and holding the blessing He has for us.

On the other hand, without solid, living communication with God in morning prayer, you cannot possibly maintain the life of obedience. It is there that the vow of obedience can be renewed every morning in power and be confirmed from above. It is there that the presence and fellowship can be secured that make obedience possible. In morning fellowship with Him, in the obedience of the One, we receive the strength to do all that God can ask. It is there that we receive the spiritual understanding of God's will.

God has called His children to live a wonderful, heavenly, supernatural life. Let daily, morning prayer open the gate of heaven through which its light and power stream in on your waiting heart. Walk away from your morning prayer ready to walk with God all day.

# chapter 5

# Entering the Life of Full Obedience

*He...became obedient to the point of death.*
—Philippians 2:8

After all that has been said on the life of obedience, let us consider what it is to enter this life. You might think it a mistake to take this text, in which you have obedience in its very highest perfection, as our subject in speaking of starting the obedient life. But it is no mistake. The secret of success in a race is to aim at a clearly defined goal from the start.

*"He...became obedient to the point of death."* There is no other Christ for any of us, no other obedience that pleases God, no other example for us to follow, no other teacher from whom to learn to obey. Christians suffer inconceivably because they do not immediately and heartily accept His obedience as the only obedience they are to aim at.

To determine to be obedient unto death is a strength in the young Christian. It is at once the beauty and the glory of Christ. A share in His obedience is the highest blessing He has to give. The desire for and the surrender to it are possible to even the youngest believer.

An ancient story illustrates the kind of obedience Jesus desires from His people. A proud king, with a great army following him, demanded the submission of the king of a small but brave nation. When the ambassadors had delivered their message, the second king called one of his soldiers to stab himself. He did it at once. A second was called; he too obeyed at once. A third was summoned; and he too was obedient to death.

"Go and tell your master that I have three thousand such men; let him come."

The king dared to count on men who would give up their life when the king's word called for it.

It is this type of loyal obedience that God wants. It is this obedience Christ gave. It is this obedience He teaches. We must seek to learn obedience and nothing less. From the very outset of the Christian life, let this be our aim: to avoid the fatal mistake of calling Christ Master yet not doing what He says.

Let all who have been convicted of the sin of disobedience, in any degree, pay close attention as we study from God's Word. He shows the way to escape from that sin and how to gain access to the life Christ can give—the entrance to the life of full obedience.

## CONFESSION AND CLEANSING

It is easy to see that this must be the first step. In the book of Jeremiah, the prophet who spoke of the disobedience of God's people most, God says, *"Return, backsliding Israel,...for I am merciful....Only acknowledge your iniquity, that...you have not obeyed My voice,' says the LORD. 'Return, O backsliding children,' says the LORD"* (Jer. 3:12–14).

At conversion, we cannot receive pardon without confession. After conversion, there cannot be deliverance from the overcoming power of sin and its disobedience without a new and deeper conviction and confession.

The thought of our disobedience must not be a vague generality. We must confess our sins, naming them specifically. We then give them up and place them in the hands of Christ. By Him, they are cleansed away. Only then can we hope to enter the way of true obedience.

Let us search our lives by the light of our Lord's teaching.

He did not come to destroy the law, but to secure its fulfillment. To the young ruler, He said, *"You know the commandments"* (Mark 10:19). Let the law be our first test.

Let us take a single sin such as that of lying. I had a note from a young lady once, saying that she wished to obey fully and that she felt urged to confess an untruth she had told me. It was not a matter of importance, yet she was right in thinking that the confession would help cast it from her.

There is much in ordinary society that will not stand the test of strict truthfulness! We must be careful to obey every commandment—even the last that forbids covetousness. Too frequently the Christian gives way to disobedience, and he covets and lusts after what is not his.

All this must come to a complete end. We must confess it and, in God's strength, put it away forever if we are to have any thought of entering a life of full obedience.

## THE NEW LAW OF LOVE

To be merciful as the Father in heaven, to forgive just as He does, to love enemies, to do good to those who hate us, and to live lives of self-sacrifice and beneficence—this is what Jesus taught.

Let us look on an unforgiving spirit when we are provoked or ill-used, unloving thoughts and sharp or unkind words, the neglect of the call to show mercy, do good, and bless, as sheer disobedience. It must be felt, mourned over, and plucked out like a right eye before the power of full obedience can be ours. (See Matthew 5:29.)

Self is the root of all lack of love and all disobedience. Our Lord calls each of His disciples to deny himself, take up his cross, forsake everything, lose his own life, humble himself, and become the servant of all. He asks all this because self—self-will, self-pleasing, self-seeking—is simply the source of all sin.

When we give in to the flesh by overindulgence in eating and drinking; when we gratify self by seeking, accepting, or rejoicing in that which indulges our pride; when self-will is allowed to assert itself and we make provision for the fulfillment of its desire, we are guilty of disobedience to His command. This gradually clouds the soul and makes the full enjoyment of His light and peace impossible.

## THE LOVE OF THE WHOLE HEART

The Christian who has not definitely aimed to sacrifice everything, who has not determined to seek grace in order to live, is guilty of disobedience. There may be much in his religion that appears good and earnest, but he cannot possibly have the joyful consciousness of knowing he is doing the will of his Lord and keeping His commandments.

When the call is heard to come and begin a true life of obedience again, many try to slip quietly into it. They think that by more prayer and Bible study they will grow into obedience and that it will come gradually. They are greatly mistaken. The word God uses in Jeremiah might teach them their mistake: *"'Return, O backsliding children,' says the LORD"* (Jer. 3:14).

A soul that is in full earnest and has taken the vow of full obedience may grow out of a feeble obedience into a fuller one. But there is no growing out of disobedience into obedience. A turning back, a turning away, a decision, a crisis is needed. That only comes by very definite insight into what has been wrong and confession of the sin with shame and penitence.

Only in penance will the soul seek divine and mighty cleansing from its filthiness. Repentance prepares the consciousness for the gift of a new heart. God's Spirit will cause us to walk in His statutes.

If you hope to lead a different life, to become a man or a woman who exhibits Christlike obedience, begin by asking God for the Holy Spirit of conviction to show you all your disobedience. He will lead you, in humble confession, to the cleansing God has provided. Do not rest until you have received it.

## POSSIBILITY OF OBEDIENCE

The second step is to understand clearly what obedience is. To this end we must pay careful attention to the difference between *voluntary* and *involuntary* sin. Obedience deals only with voluntary sin.

We know that the new heart that God gives His child is placed in the midst of the flesh with its sinfulness. Out of this fleshly sinfulness, even in one who is walking in true obedience, evil suggestions of pride, unlovingness, and impurities arise. They are, by nature, sinful and vile. But they are not blamed on a man as acts of transgression. They are not acts of disobedience that he can break off and cast out as he can the disobedience of which we have spoken.

The deliverance from them comes in another way, not through the will of the reborn man, by which obedience always comes, but through the cleansing power of the blood and the indwelling Spirit of Christ. As the sinful nature rises, all man can do is abhor it and trust in Christ's blood that immediately cleanses him and keeps him clean.

It is of great consequence to note the distinction. It keeps the Christian from thinking that obedience is impossible. It encourages him to seek and offer his obedience in the sphere where it can be effective. In proportion to the power of the will, the power of the Spirit can be trusted and obtained to do the cleansing work that is beyond the reach of the will.

When this difficulty has been removed, often a second one arises to make us doubt whether obedience is possible.

Men connect obedience with absolute perfection. They put together all the commands of the Bible and think of all the graces these commands point to in their highest possible measure. They think of a man who displays all of the graces in full perfection as an obedient man.

How different is the demand of our Father in heaven! He takes account of each of His children's different abilities and achievements. He asks only obedience for each day—each hour—at a time. He sees whether I have, in fact, given myself up to the wholehearted performance of every known command. He sees whether I am really longing to know and do His will completely. And when His child does this in simple faith and love, the obedience is acceptable. The Spirit gives us the sweet assurance that we are well-pleasing to Him and enables us to *"have confidence toward God...because* [we know that] *we keep His commandments and do those things that are pleasing in His sight"* (1 John 3:21–22).

We can attain this degree of grace for obedience. Having faith to obtain grace for obedience is indispensable in the Christian walk. If you ask for the basis of that faith in God's Word, you can find it in God's new covenant promise, *"I will...write...* [My law] *on their hearts....I will put My fear in their hearts so that they will not depart from Me"* (Jer. 31:33; 32:40).

The problem for man with the old covenant was that it demanded but did not provide the power for obedience. The new covenant does. The heart means the love, the life. Having the law written on the heart means that it has taken possession of the innermost life of the renewed man. The new heart delights in God's law. The heart is willing and able to obey it.

You may doubt this because your experience does not confirm it. No wonder! A promise of God is a thing of faith. Because you do not believe it, you cannot experience it.

Do you know what invisible ink is? It is fluid that you write with but nothing shows on paper. A man who is not aware of the secret can see nothing. Tell him of the secret, and, by faith, he knows it is true. Hold the writing up to the sun or put some chemical on it, and out comes the secret writing. God's law is written in your heart. If you believe this firmly and say to God that His law is there in your innermost part, you can hold up that heart to the light and heat of the Holy Spirit, and you will find that His law is there. When the law is written on your heart, you will have the fervent love of God's commands, with the power to obey them. How plain, how certain, how all-sufficient the provision is that has been made in the new covenant, the covenant of grace, for securing our obedience!

Napoleon's doctor was trying to extract a bullet lodged in the heart region of one of his soldiers, when the soldier cried, "Cut deeper, you will find *Napoleon* carved there."

Christian, believe that God's law lives in your innermost being. Speak in faith the words of David and of Christ: *"I delight to do Your will, O my God, and Your law is within* [written on] *my heart"* (Ps. 40:8).

Faith in this psalm will assure you that obedience is possible. Such faith will help you in the life of true obedience.

## OBEDIENCE BY SURRENDER

*"Return* [to Me], *you backsliding children, and I will heal your backslidings"* (Jer. 3:22), God said to Israel. They were His people but had turned from Him. Their return had to be immediate and entire. To turn our backs on the divided life of disobedience and say, in the faith of God's grace, "I will obey," may only last for a moment.

The power for obedience, to take the vow and keep it, comes from the loving Christ. I have said before that the power of obedience lies in the mighty influence of Jesus Christ's living, personal presence. As long as we take our knowledge of God's will from a book or from men, we can only fail. If we think of Jesus as our Lord and strength, we can obey Him.

The voice that commands us is the voice that inspires. The eye that guides us is the eye that encourages. Christ becomes everything to us—the Master who commands, the Example who teaches, the Helper who strengthens. Turn from your life of disobedience to Christ. Give yourself up to Him in faith.

Let Him have everything. Give up your life to be as full of Him, His presence, His will, and His service as He can make it. Give yourself to Him so that He may have you wholly for Himself as a vessel, a channel, that He can fill with Himself, with His life and love for men, in His blessed service.

When a soul sees this new thing in Christ, the power for continual obedience, it needs a new faith to take in the special blessing of His great redemption. The faith that only understood that *"He...became obedient to the point of death"* of His atonement, as a motive to love and obedience, now learns to take the word as Scripture speaks it: *"Let this mind be in you which was also in Christ Jesus, who...humbled Himself and became obedient to the point of death"* (Phil. 2:5–6, 8). It believes that Christ put His own mind and Spirit into us, and in the faith of this, His Spirit prepares us to live and act in obedience.

God sent Christ into the world to restore obedience to its place in our hearts and lives. His purpose is to restore man to his place in the obedience to God. Christ came and, becoming obedient unto death, proved what the only true obedience is. He brought it about and perfected it in Himself as a life that He won through death. He now communicates this obedience to us. The Christ who loves us, lives in us, who leads, teaches, and strengthens us, is the Christ who was obedient unto death. *"Obedient to the point of death"* is the essence of the life He gives. Will we not accept it and trust Him to create it in us?

Would you like to enter into the blessed life of obedience? See, here is the open gate. Christ says, *"I am the door"* (John 10:7). Christ says, *"I am the way"* (John 14:6). He is the *"new and living way"* (Heb. 10:20).

We begin to see it. Our disobedience comes from our not knowing Christ correctly. Obedience is only possible in a life of unceasing fellowship with Him. The inspiration of His voice, the light of His eyes, the grasp of His hand make it possible, make it certain.

Come, let us bow down and yield ourselves to this Christ, obedient to death in the faith that He makes us partakers, with Himself, of all He is and has.

# chapter 6

# The Obedience of Faith

*By faith Abraham obeyed when he was called to go out to the
place which he would receive as an inheritance. And he went out,
not knowing where he was going.*
—Hebrews 11:8

Abraham believed there was a land of Canaan of which God had spoken. He believed it was a *"land of promise"* (Heb. 11:9) secured to him as an inheritance. He believed that God would bring him there, show it to him, and give it to him. In that faith, he dared go out, *"not knowing where he was going."* In the blessed ignorance of faith, he trusted God, obeyed Him, and received the inheritance.

The land of promise that is set before us is the blessed life of obedience. We have heard God's call to go out and dwell there; about this there can be no mistake. We have heard the promise of Christ to bring us there and to give us possession of the land. This, too, is clear and sure.

We have surrendered ourselves to our Lord and asked our Father to make all this true in us. Our desire now is that all our life and work will be lifted up to the level of a holy and joyful obedience, and that through us God may make obedience the keynote of the Christian life we aim at promoting in others. Our aim is high. We can only reach it by a new inflow of the power that comes from above. Only by a faith that springs from new vision and clasps the power of heaven, as secured by Jesus Christ, can we obey and obtain the promise.

As we think of all this, of cultivating in ourselves and others the conviction that we live only to please Him, some are ready to say, "This is not a land of promise we are called to enter, but a life of burden, difficulty, and certain failure."

Do not say this, my friend! God calls you to a land of promise. Come and prove what He can work in you. Come and experience the nobility of a Christlike obedience that is unto death. Come and see what a blessing God will give the person who, with Christ, gives himself completely to the holy will of God. Trust in the glory of this good land of wholehearted obedience, in God who calls you to it, in Christ who will bring you into it, and in the Holy Spirit who dwells and works there. He who believes will enter.

Five simple words express the disposition of a believing heart that enters that life in the good land: I see it, desire it, expect it, accept it, and trust Christ for it.

## FAITHFUL VISION

I have been trying to show you the map of the land and to indicate the most important places in the land, the points where God meets and blesses the soul. What we need now is to settle the question quietly and definitely in faith. Is there really such a land of promise where continuous obedience is completely possible?

As long as there is any doubt on this point, it is out of the question to go up and possess the land. Think of Abraham's faith. It rested in God's omnipotence and His faithfulness. I have put before you the promises of God. Look at another of them: *"I will give you a new heart and...I will put My Spirit within you and cause you to walk in My statutes, and you will keep My judgments and do them"* (Ezek. 36:26–27). Here is God's covenant promise. He adds, *"I, the LORD, have spoken it, and I will do it"* (v. 36). He endeavors to cause and enable you to obey. In Christ and the Holy Spirit, He has made the most wonderful provision for fulfilling His promise.

Do what Abraham did. Fix your heart on God. *"He...was strengthened in faith, giving glory to God, and being fully convinced that what He had promised He was also able to perform"* (Rom. 4:20–21). God's omnipotence was Abraham's pillar. Let it be yours.

God gives us many promises in the Bible, promises that require His power in order to come to pass. He promises us a blameless heart and a life that keeps His commandments. His working in us, and our trust that He is working in us, will make this life of full obedience possible. Let the assurance that a life of full obedience is possible permeate your thoughts. Faith can see the invisible and the impossible. Gaze on the vision until your heart says, "It must be true. It is true. There is a life promised that I have never yet known."

## FAITH'S DESIRE

When I read the gospel story and see how ready the sick, the blind, and the needy were to believe Christ's word, I often ask myself what it was that made them so much more ready to believe than we are. The answer I find in the Word is this: the one great difference lies in the honesty and intensity of the desire. They desired deliverance with their whole hearts. Jesus did not need to plead with them to make them willing to take His blessing.

It should be the same with us. Everyone wishes, in some way, to be better than they are. But how few people truly *"hunger and thirst for righteousness"* (Matt. 5:6). How few people intensely long and cry after a life of close obedience and the continual consciousness of being pleasing to God.

There can be no strong faith without strong desire. Desire is the great motivating power in the universe. It was God's desire to save us that moved Him to send His Son. It is desire that moves men to study and work and suffer. It is only the desire for salvation that brings a sinner to Christ. It is the desire for God and the closest possible fellowship with Him—the desire to be exactly what He would have us be and to have as much of His will as possible—that will make the promised land attractive to us. It is this desire that will inspire us to forsake everything to get our full share in the obedience of Christ.

And how can the desire be awakened? Shame on us that we need to ask the question, that the most desirable of all things— likeness to God in union with His will—has so little attraction for us! Let us take it as a sign of our blindness and beg God to give us, by His Spirit, enlightened eyes of the heart. Then we may know *"the riches of the glory of His inheritance"* (Eph.

1:18), waiting upon the life of true obedience. Let us turn and gaze, in this light of God's Spirit, on the obedient life as a thing that is possible, certain, divinely secured, and divinely blessed. Let us look until our faith begins to burn with desire and we say, "I long to have it. With my whole heart I will seek it."

## EXPECTANT FAITH

The difference between desire and expectation is great. It is a great step forward when desire grows into expectation, and the soul begins to say, "I am sure spiritual blessing is for me, and, though I do not see how, I confidently expect to obtain it."

The life of obedience is no longer an unattainable ideal held out by God to make us strive to at least get a little nearer to it. It is now a reality meant for flesh and blood here on earth. Expect it. It is meant for you. Expect God to make it true.

Many things may hinder this expectation. Your past failures, disagreeable temperament, unfavorable circumstances, feeble faith, your difficulty as to what such a devotion—obedience to the point of death—may demand, and a conscious lack of power for it can make you say, "It may be for others, but it is not for me."

Do not speak this way. You are leaving God out of the picture. Expect your blessing! Look up to His power and His love, and say, "It is for me!"

From his youth, Gerhard Tersteegen sought to serve the Lord. After a time, he lost the sense of God's grace. For five long years, he was far away on the great sea of spiritual isolation, where neither sun nor stars appear. "But," he said, "my hope was in Jesus."

All at once a light broke on him that never went out. He wrote his famous letter to the Lord Jesus. "From this evening to all eternity, Thy will, not mine be done. Command and rule and reign in me. I yield up myself without reserve, and I promise, with Thy help and power, rather to give up the last drop of my blood than knowingly or willingly be untrue or disobedient to Thee."

This was his obedience to the point of death.

Set your heart on it and expect it. The same God still lives. Set your hope on Him, and He will do it.

## ACCEPTING IN FAITH

To accept is more than to expect. Many wait and hope yet never possess because they do not accept.

To all who have not accepted and feel as if they are not ready to accept—start by expecting. If the expectation is from the heart and is truly set on God Himself, it will lead the soul to accept. To those who say they do expect, it is time for the next step—accept. Faith has that wonderful, God-given power of saying, "I accept, I take, I have."

It is the lack of definite faith—faith that claims and takes hold of the spiritual blessing we desire—that makes so many prayers appear fruitless. Not every believer is ready for such an act of faith. Another reason a believer's prayers appear to be fruitless is that the believer simply does not have the capacity to accept a blessing. Often there is no true conviction of the sin of disobedience or any sorrow for the lack of conviction.

In addition, believers may not have a strong longing or resolution to obey God in everything.

Many do not even have the necessary deep interest in the Scripture message that shows how God wants to perfect us. In short, the Christian is content to remain a baby. He only wants to drink the milk of consolation. He is not able to tolerate the strong meat that Jesus ate—doing the will of His Father.

Despite our human frailty, God asks us to accept the grace for this wondrous new life of obedience. Accept it now. Without this, your act of consecration will amount to little. Without this, your goal of trying to be more obedient will fail. Has God not shown you that there is an entirely new position for you to take, a position of simple, childlike obedience? His grace makes it possible for you to daily obey every command He gives you through the Holy Spirit. Christians can live in simple, childlike dependence on God's grace for obedience.

I beg you, even now, to take that position, to make that surrender, to take that grace. Accept and enter the true life of faith and the unceasing obedience of faith. May your faith be as unlimited and solid as God's promise and power. Your simple, childlike obedience will be as unlimited as your faith. Ask God for His aid, and accept everything that He has offered you.

## TRUSTING JESUS CHRIST FOR EVERYTHING

*"All the promises of God in Him* [Christ Jesus] *are Yes, and in Him Amen, to the glory of God through us"* (2 Cor. 1:20). It is possible that as I have spoken of the life of obedience there have been questions and difficulties arising for which you cannot find answers.

You may feel as if you cannot take it in all at once or reconcile it with all of your old habits of thought and speech and action. You fear you will not be able to bring everything immediately into subjection to this supreme principle. Do everything as the will of God. Do everything as obedience to Him.

There is one answer, one deliverance from all these fears. It is Jesus Christ. He is the living Savior, who knows all. He asks you to trust yourself to Him for the wisdom and the power to always walk in the obedience of faith.

We have seen, more than once, how His whole redemption, as He made it come to be, is nothing but obedience. As He communicates redemption, the message is still the same. He gives us the spirit of obedience as the spirit of life. This spirit comes to us each moment through Him.

Jesus Himself keeps charge of our obedience. He offers Himself to us as our Surety for its maintenance and asks us to trust Him for it. It is in Jesus Himself that all our fears are removed, all our needs supplied, all our desires met. *"Delight yourself also in the LORD, and He shall give you the desires of your heart"* (Ps. 37:4). Just as He, the Righteous One, is your righteousness, He, the Obedient One, is also your obedience.

Will you not trust Him for it? What faith sees, desires, expects, and accepts, surely it can trust Christ to give and work.

Will you not take the opportunity today of giving glory to God and His Son by trusting Jesus now to lead you into the promised land? Look up to your glorified Lord in heaven. In His strength, renew your vow of allegiance, your vow to never willingly do anything that would offend Him.

Trust Him for the faith to make the vow, the heart to keep it, and the strength to carry it out. Trust Him—dare to join in an act of communion—and be assured that He promises and devotes Himself to honor your act. He does this to bring honor to God through us.

chapter 7

# More about Obedience

*Gather up the fragments that remain, so that nothing is lost.*
—John 6:12

In this chapter I wish to mention some points not yet touched on or expressed with sufficient clarity. I hope that they will help someone who truly desires to grow in obedience to Jesus Christ.

First, let me warn against a misunderstanding of the expression "learning obedience."

We are likely to think that absolute obedience—obedience unto death—is something we can only learn gradually. This is a great mistake with harmful potential. What we have to learn, and do learn gradually, is to practice new and more difficult commands. But as to the principle, Christ wants us to make the vow of entire obedience from the very beginning of our Christian walk.

A little child of five can be as implicitly obedient as a youth of eighteen. The difference between the two lies not in the principle but in the nature of the work demanded.

Though Christ's obedience to the point of death came literally at the end of His life, the spirit of His obedience was the same from the beginning. Wholehearted obedience is not the end but the beginning of our learning in Christ. The goal is qualification for God's service when obedience has placed us fully at God's disposal. A heart yielded to God in unreserved obedience is the one condition of growth in the spiritual knowledge of God's will.

Young Christian, get this matter settled at once. Remember God's rule—all for all. Give Him all, and He will give you all. Consecration avails nothing unless it means presenting yourself as a living sacrifice to do nothing but the will of God. The vow of entire obedience is the seed that must be planted by anyone who wants to grow in obedience and be closer to Christ.

## LEARNING TO KNOW GOD'S WILL

This unreserved surrender to obey is the first condition of entering Christ's school of obedience. It is the only frame of mind for receiving instruction on God's will for us.

God has a general will for all of His children. We can learn it, in some measure, from the Bible. But there is also a special, individual application of these commands—God's will concerning us personally—that only the Holy Spirit can teach. He will only teach God's will to those who have taken the vow of obedience.

This is why there are so many unanswered prayers for God to make known His will. Jesus said, *"If anyone wants to do His will, he shall know concerning the doctrine, whether it is from God"* (John 7:17). If a man's will is determined to do God's will, and he does it to the extent that he knows it, he will know more about what God has to teach him.

It is simply what is true of every scholar with the art he studies, of every apprentice with his trade, of every man in business—doing is the one condition of truly knowing. Likewise, our capacity for receiving the true knowledge of God's will for us rests in our vowing to do, then our obeying God's will, as far as we know it, and as He reveals it to us. In connection with this, let me focus on three things.

First, seek to have a deep sense of your great ignorance of God's will and your inability through your own effort to know it correctly. Being conscious of your ignorance will make you teachable. *"The humble He guides in...His way"* (Ps. 25:9). Those who humbly confess their need of teaching are meek and humble. Head knowledge only gives human thoughts without power. God, by His Spirit, gives a living knowledge that enters the love of the heart and works effectively.

Second, cultivate a strong faith that God will make you know wisdom in the hidden part—your heart. (See Psalm 51:6.) This thought may appear strange. Learn that God's working, the place where He gives His life and light, is in the heart. He works at a deeper level than all our thoughts. Any uncertainty about God's will makes a joyful obedience impossible. Believe confidently that the Father is willing to make known what He wants you to do. Count on Him for this. Expect it with certainty.

Third, remembering the dark and deceitful nature of the flesh and fleshy mind, ask God earnestly for the searching and convincing light of the Holy Spirit. There may be many things that you have been accustomed to think are lawful or allowable that your Father wants to change. Assuming that these things are the will of God because you and others think so may effectively shut you out from knowing God's will in other things. Bring everything, without reserve, to the judgment of the Word as explained and applied by the Holy Spirit. Serve God and wait for Him to lead you to know that everything you are and do is pleasing in His sight.

## OBEDIENCE EVEN TO DEATH

A deeper aspect of complete obedience even to death does not usually come up in the early stages of the Christian life. Yet every believer should be aware of the privilege that awaits him. Wholehearted obedience can bring the believer into an experience where obedience to God will lead to his death.

Let us see what this means. During our Lord's life, His resistance to sin and the world was perfect and complete. Yet His final deliverance from their temptations and His victory over their power—achieved by His obedience—was not complete until He had died to the earthly life and to sin. In that death He gave up His life, in perfect helplessness, to the Father's hands, waiting for the Father to raise Him up. It was through death that He received the fullness of His new life and glory. Only through death, by giving up His life, could obedience lead Him into the glory of God.

The believer shares with Christ in this death to sin. In regeneration, he is baptized by the Holy Spirit into obedience. Due to ignorance and unbelief, he may know little by experience of this entire death to sin. When the Holy Spirit reveals to the believer what he possesses in Christ, and the believer takes hold of it in faith, the Spirit works in him the very same disposition that animated Christ in His death.

Christ completely surrendered control of His life to God. He offered a helpless committal of His Spirit into the Father's hands. This was the complete fulfillment of the Father's command. Out of the perfect self-oblivion of the grave, He entered the glory of the Father.

It is into this fellowship that a believer is brought. He finds, even in the most unreserved obedience for which God's Spirit prepares him, there is still a secret element of self and self-will. He longs to be delivered from it. He is taught in God's Word that this can only be through death.

The Spirit helps him to claim more fully that he is indeed dead to sin in Christ. The Spirit also shows him that the power of this death can work mightily in him. He is made willing to be obedient unto death. This entire death to self makes him truly nothing. In this he gains full entrance into the life of Christ.

To see the need of this entire death to self, to be made willing to do it, to be led into the entire self-emptying and humility of our Lord Jesus—this is the highest lesson our obedience has to learn. This is, indeed, the Christlike obedience, even to death.

In due time, God Himself will teach more on this particular subject to those who are entirely faithful.

## THE VOICE OF CONSCIENCE

In regard to the knowledge of God's will, we must give conscience its place and submit to its authority.

There are a thousand little things in which the law of nature or education teaches us what is right and good. But even earnest Christians do not hold themselves bound to obey these things. Remember Jesus said, *"He who is faithful in what is least is faithful also in much"* (Luke 16:10). If you are unfaithful with small things, who will trust you with larger things? Not God.

If the voice of conscience tells you that one course of action is nobler or better, and you choose another because it is easier or pleasing to self, you block yourself from the teaching of the Spirit by disobeying the voice of God in nature. A strong desire to always do the right thing is a desire to do God's will. Paul wrote, *"I am not lying, my conscience also bearing me witness in the Holy Spirit"* (Rom. 9:1). The Holy Spirit speaks through conscience. If you disobey and hurt your conscience, you make it impossible for God to speak to you.

One who obeys God's will also respects the voice of his conscience. This holds true with regard to eating and drinking, sleeping and resting, spending money and seeking pleasure. Everything should be brought into subjection to the will of God.

If you desire to live the life of true obedience, make sure you maintain a good conscience before God and never knowingly indulge in anything that is contrary to His mind. George Müller attributed all of his happiness, during seventy years, to obedience and his love of God's Word. He maintained a good conscience in everything, not continuing in any action he knew was contrary to God's will. Conscience is the guardian God gives you to warn you when anything is going wrong.

According to the light you have, listen to your conscience. Ask God, by the teaching of His will, to give it more light. Seek the witness of conscience that you are acting according to that light.

Your conscience will become your encouragement and your helper. It will give you the confidence, both that your obedience is accepted and that your prayer for increasing knowledge of God's will is heard.

## LEGAL AND EVANGELICAL OBEDIENCE

Even when a Christian has taken the vow of unreserved obedience, there may still be two sorts of obedience. One is the obedience of the law, and the other is that of the Gospel. Just as there are two testaments (an old and a new), there are also two styles of religion, two ways of serving God. This is what Paul spoke about in Romans when he said, *"Sin shall not have dominion over you, for you are not under law but under grace"* (Rom. 6:14). He spoke more about our being *"free from that law"* (Rom. 7:3), *"so that we should serve in the newness of the Spirit and not in the oldness of the letter"* (v. 6). Again he reminded us,

*"For you did not receive the spirit of bondage again to fear, but you received the Spirit of adoption"* (Rom. 8:15).

These verses clearly point to the danger of a Christian acting as if he was under the law—serving in the oldness of the letter and in the spirit of bondage. One great cause of the feebleness of so much Christian living is that it is under law more than under grace. Let us see what the difference is.

What the law demands from us, grace promises and performs for us. The law deals with what we should do, whether we can do it or not. The law, motivating us out of fear and love, stirs us up to do our best. But it gives no real strength and thus only leads to failure and condemnation. Grace points to what we cannot do and offers to do it for us and in us.

The law comes with commands on stone or in a book. Grace comes in a living, gracious Person who gives His presence and His power.

The law promises life if we obey. Grace gives life, even the Holy Spirit, with the assurance that we can obey.

Human nature is always prone to slip back out of grace into law and secretly trust in its own ability to do its best. The promises of grace are so divine, the gift of the Holy Spirit to complete everything in us is so wonderful, that few believe it. This is why they never dare to take the vow of obedience. Or, having taken it, they turn away again.

I beg you, study well what gospel obedience is. The Gospel is good news. Its obedience is part of the good news—that grace, by the Holy Spirit, will do everything in you. Believe and let every undertaking to obey God be in the joyous hope that comes from faith in Christ's abundance of grace, in the mighty indwelling of the Holy Spirit, in the blessed love of Jesus whose abiding presence makes obedience possible and certain.

## THE OBEDIENCE OF LOVE

Obedience out of love is one of the special and most beautiful aspects of gospel obedience. The grace that promises to complete everything through the Holy Spirit is the gift of eternal love. The Lord Jesus (who takes charge of our obedience, teaches it, and by His presence secures it to us) is He who loved us to the death, who loves us with a love that surpasses our understanding.

Nothing can receive or know love but a loving heart. It is this loving heart that enables us to obey. Obedience is the loving response to the divine love resting on us. It is the only access to a fuller enjoyment of that love.

How our Lord insisted on this in His farewell discourse! He repeated it three times in John 14: *"If you love Me, keep My commandments....He who has My commandments and keeps them, it is he who loves Me....If anyone loves Me, he will keep My word"* (John 14:15, 21, 23).

Is it not clear that love alone can give the obedience Jesus asks, and that love alone can receive the blessing Jesus gives to obedience? Loving obedience gives the believer a cycle of blessings. The desire to obey the Lord and accept Jesus brings God's gift of the Holy Spirit living within us, access to the Father's love, and Christ's own love. These three, in turn, assure success in the obedient life.

In the next chapter of John's gospel, he looked at another side of obedience and showed how it leads to the enjoyment of God's love. Jesus kept His Father's commandments and now lives in His love. If we keep His commandments, we will also live in His love. Jesus proved His love by giving His life for us. We are His friends, and we will enjoy His love if we do what He commands us. Obedience is the one indispensable link between His loving us first and our love in response, as well as between our love and His fuller love in response to ours. True, full obedience is impossible unless we live and love. *"This is the love of God, that we keep His commandments. And His commandments are not burdensome"* (1 John 5:3).

Beware of falling into the legal obedience trap, which is struggling to live a life of true obedience out of a sense of duty. Ask God to show you the *"newness of life"* (Rom. 6:4) that will bring you the life of vibrant obedience, one full of blessings. Claim the promise, "[I] *will circumcise your heart...to love the* LORD *your God with all your heart and...you will again obey the voice of the* LORD" (Deut. 30:6, 8).

Believe in the love of God and the grace of our Lord Jesus. Believe that the Holy Spirit whom Jesus gave you enables you to love and walk in God's statutes. Only the continual, loving presence of Jesus can keep you in continual obedience.

## IS OBEDIENCE POSSIBLE?

The question of the possibility of obedience lies at the very root of life. The secret, half-unconscious thought that always living a pleasing life before God is beyond our reach eats away the very root of our strength. I urge you to give a definite answer to this question.

If in the light of God's provision for obedience—His promise of working all His good pleasure in you, His giving you a new heart, the indwelling of His Son and Spirit—you still believe obedience is not possible, ask God to open your eyes to truly know His will. If you agree to the truth theoretically, yet fear to give yourself up to this life, ask God to open your eyes. Ask Him to let you know His will for you. Beware, lest the secret fear of having to give up too much, having to become too odd and entirely devoted to God, keeps you back. Beware of seeking just enough religion to ease your conscience, then not desiring to do and be and give God everything He is worthy of. Beware, above all, of limiting God, of making Him a liar by refusing to believe what He has said He can and will do for you.

If our learning obedience is to bring us any blessing, do not rest until you have written this down: "Daily obedience, doing everything God desires, is possible for me. With His strength, I yield myself to Him, trusting Him to accomplish my obedience."

Remember this one condition. It is not the strength of your own resolve or effort, but the unceasing presence of Christ and the continuous teaching, grace, and power of the Holy Spirit, that brings the blessing of obedience. Christ the Obedient One, living in you, will secure your obedience. Obedience will be to you a life of love and joy in His fellowship.

# chapter 8

# Obeying His Final Command

*Go therefore and make disciples of all the nations.*
—Matthew 28:19

*Go into all the world and preach the gospel to every creature.*
—Mark 16:15

*As You sent Me into the world, I also have
sent them into the world.*
—John 17:18

*You shall receive power when the Holy Spirit has come upon you;
and you shall be witnesses...to the end of the earth.*
—Acts 1:8

All these words speak of nothing less than the spirit of world conversion: *"all the nations," "all the world," "every creature," "the end of the earth."* Each expression indicates that the heart of Christ was set on claiming His rightful dominion over the world He had redeemed and won for Himself. He counted on His disciples to carry out this work. As He stood at the foot of the throne, ready to ascend and reign, He told them, *"All authority has been given to Me in heaven and on earth"* (Matt. 28:18). He immediately pointed them to *"the end of the earth"* as the object of His and their desire and efforts. As the King on the throne, He Himself would be their Helper. *"I am with you always"* (Matt. 28:20).

Christians are to be the advance guard of His conquering hosts, even to the far corners of the world. Jesus Himself will carry on the war. He seeks to inspire His people with His own assurance of victory. It is His own purpose to make winning the world back to God the only thing worth living or dying for.

Christ does not teach or argue, ask or plead. He simply commands. He had trained His disciples to obedience. He had attached them to Himself in a love that can obey. He had already breathed His own resurrection Spirit into them. He could count on them. He dared to say to them, *"Go into all the world."*

Formerly, during His life on earth, they had more than once expressed their doubts about the possibility of fulfilling His commands. But here, as quietly and simply as He spoke these divine words, His disciples accepted them. No sooner had He ascended than they went to the appointed place to wait for the heavenly power from their Lord in heaven. This heavenly power would equip them for the heavenly work of making all the nations His disciples. They accepted the command and passed it on to those who through them believed on His name.

Within a generation, simple men, whose names we do not even know, had preached the Gospel in Antioch, Rome, and the regions beyond. The command was passed on and taken up into the heart and life, as meant for all ages, as meant for every disciple.

The command is for each of us, too. In the church, there is no single, privileged clan to which the honor belongs or any servile clan on which the duty of carrying the Gospel to every creature rests. The life Christ imparts is His own life; the Spirit He breathes is His very own Spirit; the one disposition He works is His own self-sacrificing love. It lies in the very nature of His salvation that every member of His body, in full and healthy access with Him, feels urged to give what he has received.

The command is no arbitrary law from the outside. By consenting to and obeying His final command, we acknowledge that we live to glorify the Father. As part of His church body, we are His representatives on earth. We confirm that His love and His will now carry us through the work of winning lost souls back to Christ.

How terribly the church has failed in obeying the command! How many Christians there are who never knew there was such a command! Many hear of it but do not earnestly desire to obey it. Many seek to obey it, but only in a way that is convenient.

We have been studying what obedience is. We have said that we give ourselves up to wholehearted obedience. Surely we are prepared to gladly listen to anything that can help us understand and carry out our Lord's last and greatest command to give the Gospel to every creature.

Let me tell you what I have to say by giving you three simple points—accept His command, place yourself entirely at His disposal, and begin immediately to live for His kingdom.

## ACCEPTING HIS COMMAND

There are several things that weaken the force of this command. We have the impression that a command given to everyone and so general in its nature is not as binding as one that is personal and specific. We tend to believe that if others do not do their part, our share of the blame is comparatively small. We feel that where the difficulties are extreme, obedience cannot be an absolute demand. Finally, we think if we are willing to do our best, this is all anyone can ask of us.

Brothers and sisters, this is not obedience! This is not the spirit in which the first disciples accepted the Great Commission. This is not the spirit in which we wish to live with our beloved Lord. We need to say, each one of us, "Even if there is no one else, by His grace, I will give myself and my life to live for His kingdom. Let me, for a moment, separate myself from all others and think of my personal relationship to Jesus."

I am a member of Christ's body. He expects every member to be at His disposal, to be animated by His Spirit, to live for what He is and does. It is the same with my body. I carry every healthy member with me day by day in the assurance that I can count on it to do its part. Our Lord has taken me so completely up into His body that He can ask and expect nothing else from me. I have so completely yielded myself to Him that there is no thought of my wanting anything except to know and do His will.

Let me use the illustration of the vine and the branches. The branch has the same single purpose for its existence as the vine—bearing fruit. If I really am a branch of Christ's vine, my purpose, as much as His, is to bring forth fruit—to live and work for the salvation of men. Look at another illustration. Christ bought me with His blood. No slave conquered by force or purchased by money was ever so entirely the property of his master as my soul, which is redeemed and won by Christ's blood. My soul is given up and bound to Him by love. My soul is His property, for Him alone to do with it what He pleases. He claims my soul by divine right, working through the Holy Spirit in an infinite power, and I have given my full consent to live only for His kingdom and service. This is my joy and my glory.

There was a time when it was different. To illustrate this, notice that there are two ways in which a man can bestow his money or service on another. There was once a slave, who by his trade earned large sums of money. All the money went to the master. The master was kind and treated the slave well. Finally, by saving the money his master had allowed him, the slave was able to purchase his liberty. In time the master became impoverished and had to come to his former slave for help. The slave was not only able but willing to give it. He gave liberally, in gratitude for the master's former kindness.

You can immediately see the difference between the giving of his money and service when he was a slave and when he was free. In the former case, he gave everything because he and his earnings belonged to the master. In the latter, he gave only what he chose.

In which way should we give to Christ Jesus? I am afraid many give as if they were free to give what they chose, what they think they can afford. The believer who is now purchased by Christ's blood delights in knowing that he is the bondservant of redeeming love. He lays everything he has at his Master's feet.

Have you ever wondered why the disciples accepted the great command so easily and so heartily? They came fresh from Calvary, where they had seen Christ's blood. They had met the Risen One, and He had breathed His Spirit into them. During the forty days, *"He through the Holy Spirit had given commandments to the apostles"* (Acts 1:2). Jesus was their Savior, Master, Friend, and Lord. His Word was divine power. They could do nothing but obey. Oh, let us bow at His feet and yield to the Holy Spirit. Let Him reveal and assert His mighty claim, and without hesitation let us wholeheartedly accept this command as our one life purpose. Give the Gospel to every creature!

## PLACE YOURSELF AT HIS DISPOSAL

The last great command has been so prominently urged in connection with foreign missions that many are inclined to confine it to that. This is a serious mistake. Our Lord's words, *"Make disciples of all the nations,...teaching them to observe all things that I have commanded you"* (Matt. 28:19–20), tell us what our aim is to be. Our aim is nothing less than to make every man a true disciple, living in holy obedience to all Christ's will.

What a work there is to be done in our churches and so-called Christian communities before we can say that the command has been carried out! And what a need for every believer in the church to realize that this work is the only purpose of its existence! The complete Gospel brought to every creature—this is the mission. This should be the passion of every redeemed soul. For this alone is the Spirit, likeness, and life of Christ formed in you.

If there is one thing the church needs to preach in the power of the Holy Spirit, it is the absolute and immediate duty of every child of God not only to take part in this work, but also to give himself to Christ the Master to be guided and used. Therefore, I say to every reader who has taken the vow of full obedience, can we dare to consider ourselves true Christians if we have not done so? Immediately place yourself at Christ's disposal.

This last command, to take the Gospel to every creature, is as binding as God's first great command, *"You shall love the LORD your God with all your heart"* (Luke 10:27). Before you know what your work may be, and before you feel any special desire, call, or ability for a particular work, if you are willing to accept the command, place yourself at His disposal.

It is His promise as Master to train, guide, and use you. Do not be afraid. Come out of the selfish religion that puts your own will and comfort first. Come out of the religion that lets you give Christ only what you deem necessary. Let the Master know He can have you completely. Enroll yourself with Him now as a volunteer for His service.

Obey Christ's call, even if it is to give yourself to foreign missionary work. These simple words, "It is my desire, if it is

God's will, to become a foreign missionary," have brought countless blessings into thousands of lives! Meanwhile, some who cannot travel abroad have missed countless blessings because they did not simply resolve, "By the grace of God I devote my life completely to the service of Christ's kingdom."

The foreign volunteer may struggle less with this resolution because he has broken the ties to those things that could hinder him. The devoted Christian who stays at home may not need this separation from home. Yet he needs all the help that a pledge to loyalty, given in secret or in union with others, can bring. The Holy Spirit can use this commitment to lead lives to be entirely devoted to God.

Accept the Great Commission with your whole heart. Place yourselves entirely at His disposal.

## ACTING ON YOUR VOW OF OBEDIENCE

Whatever your circumstances, it is your privilege to have within reach souls that can be won for God. All around you there are countless Christian ministries that invite your help and offer you theirs. Look on yourself as bought by Christ for His service and as blessed with His Spirit to give you His disposition. Take up humbly, but boldly, your life calling to participate in the great work of winning the world back to God. Whether you are led by God to join one of the many agencies already at work or to walk in a more solitary path, remember not to view the work as your church's, society's, or as your own, but as the Lord's.

Always remember Paul's instructions, *"Whatever you do, do it heartily, as to the Lord"* (Col. 3:23). You are a servant who is under orders and simply carrying them out. Then your work will not come between you and your fellowship with Christ, but it will link you inseparably to Him, His strength, and His approval.

It is easy to become so engrossed in the human part of our work that we lose sight of its spiritual character and the need for God's supernatural power. When Jesus is our focus, His work fills us with heavenly joy and hope. Keep your eyes on your Master, on your King, on His throne.

Before He gave the command and pointed His servants to the great field of the world, He first drew their eyes to Himself on the throne. *"All authority has been given to Me in heaven and on earth"* (Matt. 28:18). It is the vision, the faith of Christ on the throne, that assures us of His sufficient, divine power. Do not obey as you would a command, but think of yourself as obeying the living, almighty Lord of glory. Faith in Him will give you heavenly strength.

These words followed: *"Lo, I am with you always"* (v. 20). We not only need Christ on the throne, but we also need His abiding presence working for us and through us. Christ's power in heaven, Christ's presence on earth—between these two pillar promises lies the gate through which the church enters the conquest of the world. Each of us must follow Jesus, receive from Him our orders as to our share in the work, and never falter in our vow of obedience that has given itself to live only for His will and work.

Such a beginning will be a training time, preparing us fully to know and follow His leading. If His pleading call for the millions of dying heathens comes to us, we will be ready to go. If His providence does not permit our going, our devotion at home will be as complete and intense as if we had gone. Whether it is at home or abroad, if the ranks of the obedient are filled up, Christ will have His heart's desire. The Gospel will find its way to every creature.

Blessed Son of God! Here I am. By Your grace, I give my life to the carrying out of Your last great command. Let my heart be as Your heart. Let my weakness be as Your strength. In Your name I take the vow of entire and everlasting obedience. Amen.